ENGLISH ARISTOCRATIC WOMEN
1450–1550

Mabel Clifford Fitzwilliam, countess of Southampton. By courtesy of the National Portrait Gallery, London.

English Aristocratic Women, 1450–1550

MARRIAGE AND FAMILY, PROPERTY AND CAREERS

Barbara J. Harris

OXFORD

UNIVERSITY PRESS

2002

OXFORD
UNIVERSITY PRESS

Oxford New York

Auckland Bangkok Buenos Aires Cape Town Chennai
Dar es Salaam Delhi Hong Kong Istanbul Karachi Kolkata
Kuala Lumpur Madrid Melbourne Mexico City Mumbai Nairobi
São Paulo Shanghai Singapore Taipei Tokyo Toronto

and an associated company in Berlin

Copyright © 2002 by Oxford University Press, Inc.

Published by Oxford University Press, Inc.
198 Madison Avenue, New York, New York 10016

www.oup.com

Oxford is a registered trademark of Oxford University Press.

Library of Congress Cataloging-in-Publication Data
Harris, Barbara J. (Barbara Jean), 1942–
English aristocratic women, 1450–1550: marriage and family, property and careers /
Barbara J. Harris.
p. cm.
Includes bibliographical references and index.
ISBN 0-19-505620-5; ISBN 0-19-515128-3 (pbk.)
1. Women—England—History—Renaissance, 1450–1600.
2. Upper-class women—England—History. 3. Aristocracy
(Social class)—England—History. I. Title.
HQ1599.E5 H37   2002
305.42′0942—dc21   2001036534

Cover art: This portrait celebrates Lady Dacre's success in securing for her sons
the restoration of the Dacre title and property, which had forfeited to the crown
in 1540 when her husband was hanged for murder. It contains one of
the earliest portraits of an English woman writing.

1 3 5 7 9 8 6 4 2

Printed in the United States of America
on acid-free paper

To Stan

PREFACE

ATES APPEAR in the Old Style, but the year is assumed to have begun on 1 January rather than on 25 March. Money appears in the predecimal form in effect until 1971: 20s. equaled £1; 12 p. equaled 1s. Spelling and punctuation in quotations have been modernized.

At a time when a laborer in the building trades earned less than £4 a year and a master mason less than £8, the minumum landed income of a nobleman was £1,000 a year and of an average knight £200–£400 a year. These figures give some idea of the aristocracy's relative wealth.

The wives and widows of noblemen were referred to as *Lady* or by their specific rank within the peerage. Knights' wives were called *Lady* during their husbands' lives but *Dame* after they were widowed since knighthood was a status that ended when the men died.

Legal terms, items of clothing, musical instruments, and other obscure terms are explained in the glossary.

References in the notes are in shortened form. Full information appears in the bibliography. In printed works, the numerical reference is to the page number except for collections of primary sources that use item numbers. In the latter case, page and subdivision numbers, in parentheses, follow the item number for clarification; page numbers indicated by "p." refer to editorial material. In multivolume works, the volume is indicated by a number followed by a colon and the page or item number (e.g., 4:479).

Chapel Hill, North Carolina   B. J. H.
September 2001

ACKNOWLEDGMENTS

S I LOOK back on the seventeen years during which I worked on this book, I am overwhelmed at the number of people and institutions who have assisted me. It is a pleasure to thank them now in print. My thanks go first to Joseph Pastore, then provost of Pace University, who permanently reduced my course load from eight to six courses a year when I first began working on this project. I am equally grateful to the University of North Carolina at Chapel Hill (UNC-CH), which has supported my research and writing generously since I joined the faculty in 1989. The College of Arts and Sciences, the Department of History, the W. N. Reynolds Foundation, and the Institute for the Arts and Humanities have all funded leaves that permitted me to work on this book full time. In addition, grants from the University Research Council supported my archival research in England and paid for the illustrations in this volume.

I also owe a tremendous debt to the public and private organizations that have supported this project. The American Council of Learned Societies, the American Philosophical Society, and two awards from the National Endowment for the Humanities (NEH) Travel to Collections Program helped to finance my research trips to England. In 1987–1988 NEH assisted me further with a Research Fellowship for College Teachers. In the latter year, a grant from the Huntington Library in San Marino, California, also enabled me to work in its collections for two glorious months. In 1994–1995 I was a fellow at the National Humanities Center, once again with funding from NEH, which gave me the opportunity to begin writing in an environment I can only describe as a scholar's paradise.

I also want to thank the many librarians and archivists whose collections I have used all over England and at the Folger and Huntington libraries in the United States for their assistance. This book could not have been written without them. I owe a particular debt to the National Register of Archives, whose centralized indexes and lists enabled me to locate documents in archives throughout Great Britain from a search room in London. The Institute for Historical Research within the University of London is another of the extraordinary institutions that has facilitated my work. I am particularly grateful for its open-stack library and, more uniquely, for its tearoom, which serves as a gathering point for historians working in London. In the United States, I have a special relationship with the Folger Shakespeare Library in Washington, D.C., whose librarians I want to thank for their perennial welcome and assistance. Directing a seminar, Women, Politics and Political Thought in Early Modern England, for the Folger Institute Center for British Political Thought in 1993 proved to be a turning point in the evolution of my ideas about my subject. I am grateful to Lena Orlin and Lois Schwoerer for their part in giving me this opportunity. More recently, Adam Grumitt of the Heinz Library at the National Portrait Gallery, London, Dr. Barbara Thompson and Melanie Blake of the Witt Library and Geoffrey Fisher of the Conway Library, both at the Courteauld Institute, London, and Raven Amiro of the National Gallery of Canada graciously helped me to select and obtain permission to use the illustrations in this volume.

Throughout the years I have worked on this project, I have benefited from the insights and suggestions of many colleagues and friends. Judith Bennett, Stan Chojnacki, Cynthia Herrup, Martha Howell, Linda Levy Peck, Joe Slavin, and Judy Walkowitz have regularly taken time from their busy schedules to read and critique my work. I am especially grateful to Bob Webb, who recommended my project to Oxford University Press on the basis of a paper he heard me give in 1987, and to Nancy Lane, then a senior editor at the press, for offering me a contract on the basis of my prospectus. Joe Biancolano, Jane Burns, Elizabeth A. Clark, Anne Dewindt, Edwin Dewindt, Barbara Donegan, Laura Engelstein, Ted Evergates, Ian Gentles, Henry Horowitz, Alison Isenberg, Norma Landau, Janet Loengard, Megan Matchinske, Mavis Mate, JoAnn McNamara, Katherine McGinnis, Linda Pollock, Jan Radway, Don Raleigh, Mary Robertson, Lois Schwoerer, Joe Slavin, David Starkey, Susan Sheridan Walker, Diane Willen, Margery Wolf, and Steve Zwicker have all shared their knowledge and ideas with me. Susan Ferber of Oxford University Press is a model editor—enthusiatic, responsive to her author's concerns, and a constructive critic. I am delighted to have the opportunity to thank them here.

Thanks go also to the members of the Family History Group, to which I belonged in New York City; the members of the Vann Seminar at Emory University in 1995; and my colleages at the Institute of the Arts and Humanities at UNC-CH in the spring of 2001, all of whom read and responded to parts of this book. Members of the North Carolina Research Group on Medieval and Early Modern Women, which I joined when I arrived in Chapel Hill, have read and commented on more than half of it. I have found their cumulative advice to be invaluable. I also had the help of three superb research assistants, Anastasia Crosswhite, Melissa Franklin-Harkrider, and Miranda Wilson, all graduate students at UNC-CH. Melissa also completed the enormous task of checking the notes to printed sources. Finally, Judith Bennett, Stan Chojnacki, Felicity Heal, Cynthia Herrup, Martha Howell, Linda Peck, Jan Radway, and Susan Ferber read and commented on the entire manuscript with extraordinary thoughtfulness. It is impossible to thank them enough for their labor and intelligent criticism. If any errors remain, it is no fault of theirs.

I am also grateful to friends and colleagues who helped me in more unusual ways. David Starkey put his marvelous library and incomparable notes on members of Henry VIII's Privy Chamber at my disposal in the summers I house-sat for him in Highbury, London. During one of those summers, when the tube and buses were both on strike, Gail Savage came to my rescue by offering me a place to sleep in her apartment near the Public Record Office on Chancery Lane.

In the end, I would never have finished this long project without the encouragement of an extraordinary group of friends: Judith Bennett, Jane Brown, Cynthia Herrup, Martha Howell, Linda Peck, Jan Radway, Lois Schwoerer, Joe Slavin, and Judy Walkowitz. At moments when I was discouraged by my slow progress and doubted whether I could do justice to the material I had accumulated, they insisted on the importance of the conclusions I was reaching and that I was nearer to finishing than I thought. I am especially grateful to Jane Brown and Jan Radway for listening to me during our monthly lunches and dinners and to Linda Peck for her enthusiasm and common sense during our long telephone calls and visits to each other's homes. Tragically, one of my oldest and dearest friends, Marilyn T. Williams, a New York City historian and colleague at Pace University, died last November and cannot join me in celebrating the publication of the book we talked about for so many years. There is no way to compensate for her absence.

Since we met in 1989, this book has been an integral part of my relationship with Stanley Chojnacki. We have talked and argued about every idea in it, and he has read more versions of each chapter than either of us can now remember. Whatever flaws remain, the final version is immeasurably better for our ongoing dialogue. Even more important, our work together has taught me that a feminist woman and feminist man can create a partnership that equally nurtures their respective personal and professional lives. It is with love and deep appreciation of his role in helping me to realize this elusive dream that I dedicate this book to him.

CONTENTS

ENGLISH ARISTOCRATIC WOMEN
1450–1550

INTRODUCTION

*W*HEN LADY LETTICE TRESHAM wrote her will in June 1557, she could look back with satisfaction on a life during which she had married three times; borne eight children; launched her eldest son's, Francis's, political career; and triumphantly defended her property against her stepson. Her ambitions and the basic course of her life resembled those of hundreds of other aristocratic women who lived between 1450 and 1550. Like Lady Tresham, they married more than once, bore large numbers of children, became rich through consecutive marriages, arranged their children's careers and marriages, litigated successfully against their stepsons or in-laws, exploited their connections at court, and carefully distributed their property when they died.

Because Lady Tresham's activities and achievements are so characteristic of the women of her class, examining them in greater detail highlights the ways in which aristocratic women accumulated property and political capital, gained authority in their families, and secured some independence as they performed their roles as wives, mothers, and widows. Her two greatest assets were her connections at court and the wealth and practical knowledge she acquired during her successive marriages. Her ties to the court depended on her close relationship to Sir Thomas and Lady Margaret Bryan, who raised her with their son, Francis. Both Lady Margaret and Sir Thomas held offices in the royal household. Francis Bryan, who described himself as Lady Tresham's "great friend," became a member of Henry VIII's Privy Chamber and one of his closest companions.[1]

Lady Tresham's links to the court almost certainly accounted for her successive marriages to members of the king's household. Her first husband, Robert Knollys, an usher in the Privy Chamber, died in 1521 and left her a rich woman. In addition to lifelong use of his chief manor at Rotherfield, Oxford-

3

shire, he gave her outright possession of most of his movable goods and, as long as she remained single, the income and management of his other real property.[2] Knollys expected her to use this wealth to raise and promote their four children.

Despite her maternal responsibilites and the threat of losing all Knollys's land except Rotherfield, Lady Tresham married another courtier, Sir Robert Lee, within a few years, with the assistance of her friend Sir Francis Bryan.[3] During her second marriage, she gave birth to four more children. She also became the stepmother of Lee's children by his first wife. When Sir Robert died in 1539, Lady Tresham and his heir, Sir Anthony, quarreled bitterly over his will. Lee had anticipated their feud and tried to forestall it by leaving his wife a generous bequest and her jointure (land assigned to her in their marriage contract) if she renounced her legal right to her common-law dower (one-third of her husband's real estate), a condition designed to limit her claim on her stepson's inheritance.[4] Anthony resented his father's provision for his widow and their four children (i.e., Anthony's half-siblings) nonetheless and sued her in Chancery for wrongfully retaining his father's ready money (i.e., cash), plate, jewels, beasts, chattels, and household stuff.[5]

Although Lady Tresham described herself "as a poor and desolate widow" at this juncture, she was quite the opposite and successfully enlisted her friends in the royal household on her side. Sir Francis Bryan immediately wrote to Thomas Cromwell, the king's leading minister, on her behalf.[6] Lady Tresham also petitioned Cromwell directly, emphasizing her helplessness: "And whereas before, by the provision of my husband I need not to care for anything, now I am subject to all trouble, care, and heaviness and am left here a sorrowful widow." She was knowledgeable enough about the ways of the court to accompany her request with a gift of £10 and a promise to renew Cromwell's office as Master of the Game on an estate she held.[7] These appeals achieved their goal: Cromwell not only agreed to arbitrate the dispute but also sent Lady Tresham a draft of his award before issuing it as a formal decree. She responded with a detailed critique and set of requests that revealed her practical acumen and determination to secure every possible advantage against her stepson.[8] Although neither the draft nor final settlement has survived, Cromwell's notes record his conclusion that if Lady Tresham agreed to renounce her dower, she should receive 100 marks in cash, all of her jewelry, 1,000 sheep and all the corn (i.e., grain) and cattle at Rotherfield (property she held from her first marriage), half the household stuff at Rotherfield and Quarrendon (the Lees' chief mansion), 400 more sheep from the estate she held as her jointure from Lee, and half his gold and silver plate.[9]

Surprisingly perhaps, the suit with her stepson did not discourage Lady Tresham from marrying a third time. Once again she chose a royal servant, Thomas Tresham, an esquire of the king's body, who was knighted by 1524. Like Lee, Tresham was a widower with children.[10] Before they married, Lady

Tresham, worried about the legal inability of wives to write wills and, perhaps feeling her age, apparently insisted that he sign a prenuptial agreement that gave her testamentary power over the goods she brought into their marriage. Without this agreement, she could not have written a will, as she did, when she predeceased Tresham in 1558.[11]

Lady Tresham's effectiveness in protecting her property was evident in both her precaution about securing this premarital contract and the success of her legal battle against her stepson. She was equally astute about promoting the interests of the next generation of her family. Despite their quarrel, she helped to launch the career of her stepson Sir Anthony Lee at court.[12] She also arranged marriages for her two daughters by Lee.[13] But her greatest success was promoting the career of her eldest son, Francis Knollys, who became Edward VI's Master of the Horse in 1547. She arranged a brilliant match for him with Catherine Carey, daughter of Sir William and Mary Boleyn. The Boleyn connection and Francis's staunch Protestantism—he and his wife went into exile during Mary's reign—ensured his fortune when Elizabeth became queen in 1558. She appointed him to the Privy Council soon after her accession. He ranked high at court and in the government until his death in 1596.[14]

When Lady Tresham wrote her will in 1557, during the Marian persecution, she completely ignored her two sons by Robert Knollys, Francis and Henry. They may have been legally incapable of inheriting from her since they were both devout Protestants and had gone into exile after Mary ascended the throne.[15] Whatever her reasons, Lady Tresham divided her cash, jewelery, clothes, and other goods among her surviving children by Sir Robert Lee, a son named Benet and two married daughters, Margaret Lane and Elizabeth Fachell. Her choice of Sir Henry Lee, heir to her stepson Sir Anthony, as supervisor of her estate indicates that she and the Lees had long since forgotten their quarrel over her second husband's estate, a reconciliation that benefited both families and was typical of the advantages women gained by accumulating kin through their successive marriages.[16]

Cumulatively, the responsibilities Lady Tresham and other aristocratic women assumed and carried out as wives, mothers, and widows constituted female careers that had as much political and economic as domestic importance and were as crucial to the survival and prosperity of their families and class as the careers of their male kin. The term *career* is used here to mean a person's course or progress through life, especially a vocation that is publicly conspicuous and significant.[17] The Yorkist and early Tudor word that comes closest to capturing this meaning is *preferment*, which referred to a person's advancement or promotion in condition, status, or position. Parents often used the word as a verb and spoke about preferring their daughters to marriage as a way of securing their futures.[18] Careers defined in this way were not professions in the modern sense of vocations that require advanced training, especially in the liberal arts or sciences, although, as we shall see in chapter 2, aristocratic daughters were trained for their future roles.[19]

As in all careers, aristocratic women gained prestige, power, and financial rewards by performing their duties successfully. They possessed and disposed of considerable resources, both in cash and kind; acquired substantial de facto authority over large numbers of people—kin, neighbors, clients, and servants—who resided in their households; and gained considerable freedom of action in their everyday lives. For women from court families, appointments to the queen's household enhanced their familial careers by situating them in the most advantageous position to secure royal patronage. Positions at court dramatically increased the political importance of their activities.

Understanding aristocratic women's activities as careers underscores the full extent and political significance of their contribution to their families, class, and society. But it also directs our attention to one of the most perplexing features of Yorkist and early Tudor society—the contradiction between aristocratic women's actual lives and the deeply rooted patriarchal structures that defined their legal rights and material situation. These interlocking structures, examined in detail in chapter 1, included the common-law doctrine of coverture, a primogenital inheritance system, arranged patrilocal marriages, a marital property regime that gave widows only limited rights to their husbands' land, and a pervasive ideology of female inferiority and subordination. In concert, these institutions ought to have restricted aristocratic women to a narrow sphere of activity, limited their access to and control of wealth, and deprived them of authority and power. Nonetheless, overwhelming evidence points in the opposite direction and demonstrates that aristocratic women gained wealth, authority, and power as they managed their husbands' property and households, arranged the marriages and careers of their children, maintained and exploited the kin and client networks essential to their families' political power, and supervised the transmission and distribution of property to the next generation.

The central purpose of this project is to explore both sides of this contradiction and to show how they interacted to create a life course that simultaneously surbordinated and empowered aristocratic wives and widows. The women whose careers form the subject of this investigation were the wives and daughters of noblemen and knights.[20] Although knights are usually categorized as the top stratum of the gentry, in crucial ways their resources and positions were much more akin to those of the nobility. They jointly ruled England in partnership with the crown, organized and maintained the patronage networks that enabled its formal political and legal institutions to function effectively, intermarried regularly, and shared a common outlook. Their position rested on their ownership of a huge amount of land, the basis for wealth, power, and status throughout the Yorkist and early Tudor periods. Although they constituted less than 1 percent of the total population, they controlled 15 percent to 20 percent of the cultivated land in England. The richest nobles owned much more land than most knights, but there was considerable overlap between the poorest nobles and the wealthiest knights.[21] Even more important in blurring the distinction between noble and knightly families was the practice of primogeniture, which restricted the descent of titles and most real property to first sons. The younger sons of peers, almost all of whom were knighted, never inherited titles and were more likely to marry the daughters of other knights than of peers. In addition, the small size of the nobility meant that peers often married their daughters to knights rather than to other noblemen or their heirs. Joint political activities reinforced the social integration that resulted from these marriage practices. Noblemen and knights served together on the commissions of the peace that played an ever larger role in ruling the countryside, while the younger sons of peers often sat in the House of Commons with men from knightly families. Within the aristocracy, a small number of knights—courtiers and kin or friends of the king—were promoted into the peerage.[22]

The aristocracy was not, of course, a closed caste. Some families moved into it throughout the Yorkist and Tudor periods, although the amount of upward mobility was relatively small.[23] The heiresses of esquires and mere gentlemen were often able to use their property to marry into knightly families. Anne, heir of John Pimpe and wife of Sir Richard Guildford; Elizabeth, heir of John Winter and wife of Sir William Gascoigne of Cardington; and Elizabeth, coheir of John Clervaux and wife of Sir Thomas Hilton, are three of many examples of this pattern.[24] The younger sons of knights—Sir Peter Carew, Sir Anthony Denny, and Sir Henry Guildford, for instance—who did not inherit sufficient property to support knighthoods, sometimes earned them through service at court or legal careers.[25] Men from more modest gentry families and even occasionally the sons of yeomen, such as Sir Reginald Bray, Sir William Paget, and Sir William Petre, also rose through service to the crown. Paget's and Bray's heirs actually acquired titles.[26] Still other men converted fortunes made in wool or trade into landed estates, knighthoods, and, some generations later, titles. Three families who appear frequently in this book, the Kitsons, Greshams, and Spencers, did so.

One of the primary functions of aristocratic families was, of course, to reproduce the next generation. But their large-scale landownership and control of local and regional patronage networks meant that Yorkist and early Tudor noble and knightly families were also political and economic enterprises. Far more than residential units, aristocratic households were stages for the display of their owners' status and wealth, headquarters for estate management, regional centers of consumption and social life, and the focal points for local and county government. Although historians have long recognized the public and political character of aristocratic households, they have not applied that insight systematically to their account of women's experience.[27] Rather, they

have continued to discuss their lives in predominantly reproductive and domestic terms organized around the female life cycle. In contrast, this study
demonstrates that because aristocratic women's lives were constructed by the
same forces that shaped their families and households, their activities also
combined domestic, economic, and political functions, conflating duties historians inaccurately dichotomize as either public or private. Neither the conception of the public and the private nor the actuality of public and private
spheres played a significant role in shaping their lives.[28]

Whatever noblemen and knights felt in the abstract about women's abilities and the necessity of asserting male authority, in practice they had few
alternatives to relying on their wives. Their large families, huge households,
far-flung estates, and numerous servants demanded an enormous amount of
supervision and attention to detail. Although they employed an army of professional and semiprofessional servants to assist them, there was no substitute
for the informed, energetic attention of the male head of the household and
his wife or, after his death, his widow. Noblemen and knights spent long periods away from home visiting their estates, pursuing legal business in London,
attending Parliament and the local assizes, and serving the crown. Their absences provided them with compelling reasons for treating their mates as de
facto, if junior, partners in the family enterprise and entrusting them with the
resources and power necessary to succeed in this role. The demographic
reality—69 percent of 755 knights and noblemen who married at least once
predeceased their spouses—provided an additional incentive for men to enable their wives to act as their substitutes. Collectively, therefore, aristocratic
women played a crucial part in ensuring the survival of their families and
class and, therefore, in preserving social stability in a period marked by numerous political disruptions and a major religious revolution. Aristocratic
men's dependence on their wives and widows limited the degree to which
they could subordinate them in practice, whatever their individual inclinations. Indeed, as we shall see, when it suited their interests, husbands permitted and even directed their wives to perform tasks forbidden to them by the
common law. Similarly, many noblemen and knights bequeathed their widows more movable and real property than they were required to by the common law or their marriage contracts. Aristocratic women could and did exploit these realities to set their own agendas and gain considerable freedom in
their daily lives.

In spite of these practicalities, patriarchal institutions and expectations remained securely intact throughout the Yorkist and early Tudor periods. The
failure of aristocratic women's careers to produce substantial change in the
male dominant structure of society was rooted in the convergence of a number of factors. In the most general sense, members of the aristocracy of both
sexes had every reason, as a well-established elite, to resist fundamental
change of any kind. On a more specific level, aristocratic men relied on key

patriarchal institutions—most obviously, patrilocal arranged marriages and primogeniture—to preserve their position.

Aristocratic women actively assisted their male kin to support the status quo in gender relations and to sustain the patriarchal legal and material structures that subordinated them. Their attitude and behavior were partly due to the success of their upbringing and education, which taught them to accept male dominance as god-given and natural. In addition, from an early age, aristocratic women were almost certainly aware of the advantages they gained from their fathers' and husbands' wealth, status, and power. Thus, although individual aristocratic women might criticize or quarrel with their male relatives, there is no evidence that as a group they imagined an essential difference between their interests and those of their male kin or that they articulated ambitions for themselves that were incompatible with their duties in the family.[29] Instead, they contributed to the social reproduction of their families and class by executing a wide range of tasks that perpetuated the existing patriarchal regime. In return, they accumulated considerable power, resources, and personal prestige. The exchange is an example of the "patriarchal bargain" that Denise Kandiyoti has identified as the conscious and unconscious strategy that women adopt for dealing with the structures of male dominance that define their lives. These bargains give women, particularly those from the propertied classes, a vested interest in maintaining the system that oppresses them and exert a powerful influence on shaping female subjectivity.[30] Both these consequences are apparent in the behavior and attitudes of the women who appear in this book.

Nonetheless, the contradiction between aristocratic women's interests as members of the ruling elite and a subordinated gender did create a space that permitted and encouraged them to develop a distinct female perspective. Although it was always a minor note in the totality of their lives, this point of view was evident in the care with which they developed networks centered on their mothers, daughters, sisters, aunts, and nieces. These ties encouraged them to assist one another emotionally and materially throughout their lives and influenced the way in which widows distributed their property. Childless aristocratic women often had particularly strong bonds with their sisters and nieces and chose them as major beneficiaries of their estates. There are even traces of evidence suggesting that aristocratic mothers were less punitive toward daughters who married without parental permission than were the girls' fathers, an implicit critique of the system of arranged marriages that treated daughters as assets to be exchanged in the interests of their families.

Aristocratic women's large households gave them the spaces and opportunities to form and cultivate these female networks. Most obvious were the exclusive female rituals surrounding childbirth, but the custom of placing adolescent girls in the care of women other than their mothers was also significant. It created a pattern in which young women circulated through the households of their grandmothers, aunts, and more distant female kin, a process that strengthened the cross-generational ties between female relatives and forged bonds between young noblewomen and gentlewomen who lived together before they married. Architectural developments in late medieval castles and great houses facilitated these female relationships because more and more of them included separate chambers or suites for the mistress of the household.[31] Although the time they spent together in these spaces or participating in exclusively female rituals was relatively short, aristocratic women valued the friendships and emotional support they received from these networks and customs.

Aristocratic women also gained space in which to pursue their own definitions of their interests by taking advantage of their membership in multiple familes. Although land and noble titles descended according to the rules of primogeniture, in virtually every other area kinship among the English aristocracy was bilateral. In contrast to the situation Christiane Klapisch-Zuber has described so compellingly in Renaissance Florence, aristocratic women were far more than "passing guests" in their natal and marital families.[32] Rather, as massive evidence demonstrates, they received support and retained resources from each of their families as they moved from one to another. Although wives could never become blood members of their spouses' patrilineages, they occupied central places in them as mothers of the next generation and as widows responsible for the transmission of much of their husbands' property to their heirs and other children. If they married more than once, as at least 45 percent of them did, they accumulated multiple marital families. Consequently, from women's point of view, patriarchal power was dispersed among their fathers, brothers, sons, husbands, and male in-laws, enabling them to avoid some of the worst consequences of their subordinate position by maneuvering among them. As in the case of male-headed households, therefore, the impact of aristocratic women's families on them was far more complex than their patriarchal structure might suggest and contributes to the contradiction that forms the center of this study—the apparent disjunction between aristocratic women's power, authority, and control of resources and the patriarchal institutions that framed their lives.

As it examines this paradox, this book contributes to our understanding of two theoretical issues central to the writing of women's history: historicizing patriarchy and exploring the way in which women's gender and class positions interact to construct their social identity and roles. In conceptualizing my approach to the first of these issues, I have adopted Theodore Koditschek's definition of patriarchy as a "loosely connected constellation of related social systems" that ensures "the systematic subordination and social inferiority of women and their relative exclusion from access to wealth, status, and power."[33] His definition captures the situation reflected in my evidence—that patriarchy in late fifteenth- and early sixteenth-century England consisted of a series of social structures and practices that converged to produce and sustain male dominance rather than an integrated, unified system. These multiple structures did not fit together to create an internally consistent whole; instead they often worked at cross-purposes and created disjunctures in the structure of male dominance. The spaces and internal contradictions that resulted gave both women and men the opportunity to negotiate their relationships and interaction, although these negotiations always took place between unequals and were limited by the structural framework in which they occurred.[34] The focus of this study on a very specific time, period, and place demonstrates in detail the historical, contingent, and evolving nature of patriarchy.[35] Within this framework, it explores how class and gender jointly constructed aristocratic women's identity, social position, and roles and, reciprocally, how their identity, social position, and roles constructed the meaning of class and gender in their society. Because they constituted a small, homogeneous, and well-documented group, they provide an ideal case study for addressing these issues.[36]

The chronological boundaries of this project, 1450 and 1550, reflect both the availability of sufficient primary sources to carry out broad archival research on aristocratic women as they are defined in this book and the continuity in fundamental areas of their lives. Wills, both male and female, and Chancery cases, two sources that have proved essential to this project, first became plentiful in the mid-fifteenth century. In addition, few family archives including accounts and letters about aristocratic women's role in the family, marriage, or household and estate management survive from before 1450, and these are almost entirely about noblewomen.[37] Even the Stonor, Paston, and Plumpton letters—three major printed collections that have proved a treasure trove for fifteenth-century historians—were almost all written after 1450. From a structural point of view, the two institutions that played the most important part in defining aristocratic women's lives, family and household, remained fundamentally unchanged throughout the period.[38]

Treating the period 1450–1550 as a unit also fits evidence about aristocratic women's religious views. As their own wills and as their behavior as executors of their husbands' wills indicate, they remained devoted to traditional religious practices and were generous about supporting the church in the decades before the break with Rome. Afterward, their views changed at a slow pace, although a small group, mostly connected to the court, actively supported reform. Furthermore, the dissolution of the monasteries had relatively little effect on aristocratic women since only 2 percent of them became nuns. An even tinier percentage—2 of 132 female testators who indicated where they wanted to be buried in pre-1535 wills—asked to be buried in convents. In addition, their legacies to religious houses were modest compared to their bequests to their parish churches, for prayers for their souls, and for alms.[39]

The chronological limits of this book align it with the growing historical literature that has rejected the traditional notion that 1485, the year the Tudors ascended the throne, or 1500, the year conventionally cited as the end of the Middle Ages and beginning of the early modern period, are meaningful in English political history.[40] They also support the revisionist interpretation of the origins of the Reformation and slow pace of religious change articulated by historians such as Christopher Haigh, J. J. Scarisbrick, and Eamon Duffy.[41] In the field of women's history specifically, they strengthen Judith Bennett's persuasive argument for continuity across the "great divide" of the medieval and modern periods.[42]

On the other hand, the recognition of continuity in aristocratic women's religious beliefs and practices and the political and patriarchal structures that shaped their roles and activities does not mean that their lives remained completely unchanged from 1450 to 1550. They profited, for example, from the invention of legal mechanisms to break entails that restricted inheritance to men, a subject discussed in greater detail in chapter 1. Women also benefited from the cessation of the Wars of the Roses, the last battle of which occurred at Stoke in 1487. For the better part of the previous forty years, the deaths and attainders of a disproportionate number of nobles and knights had a considerable impact on their female kin. In addition to their personal loss, the wives and widows of attainted men were often treated punitively by the crown, as we shall see in chapter 7.[43]

Equally important, aristocratic women profited from the fitful growth of the Yorkist and early Tudor monarchy, particularly the expansion of the court, where their presence and access to royal patronage increased notably, a subject explored in detail in chapter 9. Their success in exploiting their offices in the queen's household and contact with the king and his favorites enhanced their political significance in a period when royal patronage played a larger and larger role in shaping the fortunes of the aristocracy. In addition, the slowly shifting balance of political and financial resources in favor of the central government improved its efficacy as a counterweight to the noblemen and knights who controlled the countryside. This development encouraged the crown to respond postively to women's petitions when they accused their male relatives and neighbors of breaking the law and causing local violence. Rather than intensifying patriarchal power, therefore, the growth of the monarchy shifted it from periphery to center.

The responsiveness of the crown to their petitions encouraged the wives and widows of noblemen and knights to flood the king, his ministers, and favorites with petitions for patronage or the redress of grievances on behalf of themselves, their kin, and their clients and rewarded their active participation in their families' networks. They sought and received grants of land, annuities, crown offices, wardships, and places at court; assistance defending their inheritances and dowers or jointures; protection against brutal or neglectful

spouses; and exemption from the penalties of forfeiture imposed on their husbands. What is surprising is the time and energy the king's leading servants
spent in responding to them, even in periods when the government was dealing with major dynastic, political, and religious issues.[44] The crown's attention to their petitions highlights one of the less dramatic ways in which the
monarchy rewarded aristocratic families for their unpaid service to the
crown. This attention associated the interests of king and aristocracy and
tempered the impact of royal policies such as regulating retaining and exploiting bonds and wardships that created antagonism between the expanding
monarchy and its most powerful subjects. To a considerable extent, the stability of the state depended on the crown's success in maintaining the equilibrium between these two divergent dimensions of its relations with the
aristocracy.

These political gains were not embodied in permanent institutional
change, nor did they affect the misogynist ideology that justified female subordination and exclusion from formal political power. Rather, women benefited from the evolution of the late medieval, early modern English monarchy
during the limited period when the growth of the crown occurred in a context in which the king lacked the financial resources to create a royal army or
bureaucracy. Instead, he depended on the unpaid service of the aristocracy,
whom he rewarded with the limited patronage at his disposal, and developed
the court as the political and symbolic center of the monarchy. By the late
Stuart period, however, the growth of Parliament, new bureaucratic institutions, and nascent political parties drained power and resources from
king, court, and patronage networks, the institutions that facilitated aristocratic women's political activity.[45] The circumstances that expanded their opportunities to participate significantly in politics were, therefore, relatively
short-lived.[46]

The impact of the Yorkist and early Tudor monarchy on aristocratic
women raises questions about two related ideas that have had considerable
influence on historians of medieval and early modern women. The first, an
interpretation associated with medievalists such as David Herlihy, JoAnn Mc-
Namara, and Suzanne Wemple, suggests that women gain power, control of
resources, and autonomy in periods of relative disorder and weak political
and religious institutions.[47] Evidence marshalled in chapter 7 shows that this
correlation was not true for aristocratic women during the Wars of the Roses.
Although the period was a low point in the history of the medieval English
monarchy, the intermittent battles, executions, and changes of dynasty had
relatively little effect on the functioning of political and legal institutions except for short, discontinuous periods of time, and the breakdown of law enforcement was often very localized. In addition, the short, sporadic nature of
the battles did not remove men from home for long periods, which women
could exploit to increase their power and authority, as historians have con-

tended their predecessors did during the Crusades.[48] At the same time, the contrast between the impact of the Wars of the Roses on English aristocratic women and the positive impact of the religious wars on the power of noblewomen in late sixteenth-century France underscore the historical specificity of the English situation.[49]

The second, related idea connects the growth of the early modern state with the reinforcement of patriarchy, a view articulated by historians who focus on city-states, such as Joan Kelly, Martha Howell, Merry Weisner, and Lyndal Roper, and on monarchies, such as Lawrence Stone and Sarah Hanley.[50] The argument is intuitively persuasive because formal political institutions were fundamentally male, whatever their form, even when they were headed by queens. Yet, for reasons explained above, this was not the case in England during the century covered in this study. The contrast between the impact of the monarchy on Yorkist and early Tudor England and the societies studied by the historians cited here underscores the historicity and variability of patriarchal regimes.[51]

This book explores still another issue central to women's history, the interplay of female agency and subordination. In the field of early modern Englishwomen's history, two recent works, Tim Stretton's *Women Waging Law in Elizabethan England* and Amy Erickson's *Women and Property in Early Modern England*, explore these issues in the lives of women from the middling ranks in the late sixteenth and early seventeenth centuries.[52] Like this book, they grapple with women's paradoxical position as subjects in a double sense—that is, as subjects of their own lives and as subjects of male domination.[53] But this study is unique in its focus on women from knightly and noble families, whose activities had political, as well as familial, significance.[54]

The rich literature on elite medieval and early modern English and European women published in the last thirty years provides the broader historiographical context for this study. On one end of the interpretative spectrum are scholars—Nancy Roelker, Retha Warnicke, John King, Caroline Hibbard, Jennifer Ward, and Magdalena Sanchez, to name only a few—whose work focuses on aristocratic women's contributions to their families and involvement in politics, religion, and every aspect of social life in a wide variety of contexts and implicitly or explicitly emphasizes their agency.[55] Biographies and biographical essays on individual women, such as Margaret, Lady Hungerford; Lady Margaret Beaufort; and Anne Boleyn, also contribute to this interpretation.[56]

On the other end of the spectrum are historians who emphasize the intensity of female subordination and the narrow scope of women's experience, such as Sarah Hanley and Christiane Klapisch-Zuber. Klapisch-Zuber's work on Renaissance Florence, which has been particularly influential in its analysis of the patriarchal, patrilineal family, underscores its role in subordinating its female members and exploiting them for its own purposes. She maintains that bilateral filiation was obliterated among this class in law and practice in late medieval Europe and that the dowry system effectively excluded women from their natal families by depriving them of inheritance rights to their property.[57] Hanley's analysis of what she calls the "family state compact" argues that the late sixteenth- and early seventeenth-century French monarchy grew at the expense of women from the propertied classes, who were confined ever more rigorously within their patriarchal families.

My analysis falls between these two interpretative poles in its thesis that the stages of aristocratic women's life cycle constituted careers and its emphasis on their contribution to their families and class. It also demontrates that kinship among the English aristocracy was bilateral, that aristocratic women were concurrently members and recipients of tangible and intangible resources from their natal and successive marital families, that they functioned effectively in the patronage networks undergirding politics and social life, and that they benefited substantially from the relative reestablishment of law and order in the Yorkist and early Tudor periods. But it balances this postive assessment with continual attention to the patriarchal structures that restricted and exploited them. As a group, aristocratic women were never equal to the men of their class and were at a particular disadvantage when they disagreed or quarreled with their husbands. They could often only gain their objectives by enlisting other male kin to right the balance. In the historiographical context, this perspective aligns my study with Joel Rosenthal's work on the fifteenth-century English nobility, Stanley Chojnacki's on patrician women in Renaissance Venice, and Sharon Kettering's and Kristin Neuschel's on noblewomen in sixteenth-century France. These scholars all elucidate the persistent tension among women's activities, their legal disabilities, and their exclusion from official governmental bodies.[58]

In designing the research program for this project, my goal was to amass sufficient material on a large enough group of aristocratic women to write a persuasive collective biography of them as a class. I was particularly anxious not to depend on the handful of women who have been studied repeatedly. I began, therefore, by reading systematically through categories of documents, such as wills probated in the Prerogative Court of Canterbury, Chancery cases, State Papers, and the Cotton and Harleian Collections at the British Library, and included any woman who fit my definition of the aristocracy in my data. From there I moved on to family archives and local record offices. Altogether I collected far more evidence than I had ever expected to find. It included hundreds, perhaps even thousands, of letters by, to, or about aristocratic women; 763 male and 266 female wills; and 551 cases in Chancery, Star Chamber, or the Court of Requests. In addition, but in smaller numbers, there were marriage contracts, household and estate accounts, crown grants, private bills, and inventories. I also compiled genealogical files on all the women whose names appeared in the archival and printed sources I used.

Ultimately, I had information on about 1,200 aristocratic couples and their children. This information is the basis of the statistics that appear throughout this study.

This rich material inspired me to conceive of aristocratic women's lives as careers, to grasp fully the bilateral character of their families, to recognize that they accumulated families instead of passing from one to another as they married and remarried, and to appreciate the complicated, even erratic, ways that everyday realities and individual relationships muted and shaped the impact of patriarchal institutions on them. The activities of hundreds of aristocratic women like Lady Tresham emerged, in greater or less detail, from these documents. Their careers form the central subject of this book. To set the stage for reconstructing and analyzing them, it begins with a detailed analysis of the patriarchal institutions and practices—ideological, legal, and economic—that shaped their lives.

CHAPTER I. STRUCTURES

OF PATRIARCHY

*T*HE SUBORDINATION of Yorkist and early Tudor aristocratic women to their male kin rested on an interlocking series of economic, legal, and political institutions, the most fundamental of which were the common law, with its doctrine of coverture; a primogenital inheritance system reinforced by male entail; and a system of arranged marriages based on the dowry and jointure. Their contemporaries justified these institutions by appealing to divine and natural laws that decreed women's inferiority and subjection. Together these material and ideological constructs created a regime in which the exclusion of aristocratic women from formal political power and office appeared to be completely natural and was virtually unquestioned.[1]

Although this patriarchal regime served the interests of aristocratic men, strictly observing the common law posed serious problems to them as they struggled to manage their families, households, and estates on a day-to-day basis. The limitations the doctrine of coverture imposed on wives frequently made it difficult, if not impossible, for women to carry out their responsibilities. In other cases, men's strategies for transmitting their inheritances to the next generation conflicted with the rules of primogeniture or the entails on their estates. In still other cases, arranging desirable marriages for themselves or their sons required them to establish separate property rights for the prospective brides, even though neither common-law nor equity courts recognized such arrangements. In practice, therefore, aristocratic men collaborated with their lawyers to modify or circumvent the law so that they could achieve their goals for themselves and their families. The result was that there was considerable flexibility in the impact of patriarchal institutions on particular aristocratic women. A delicate, ever-changing equilibrium developed between these structures and everyday practice. The purpose of this chapter is to explain the central institutions of patriarchy in Yorkist and early Tudor

England and the devices invented to adapt them to the actual needs of the men and famlies they were meant to protect.

The legal doctrine of coverture defined and enforced women's subordination to their husbands. It held that marriage obliterated, literally "covered," women's legal existence. Coverture was crucial in establishing the parameters of aristocratic women's lives because they almost all married. Of 2,209 Yorkist and early Tudor aristocratic women whom I have traced, 94 percent married, almost always before they were 21 and often in their mid- to late teens.[2] Their marriage pattern was a major exception to the northern European model, characterized by high rates of celibacy and a relatively late age at first marriage, which historians routinely ascribe to England in the later Middle Ages and early modern periods.[3]

Because of coverture, wives had seriously attenuated property rights and could not sign a binding contract, initiate or defend a lawsuit, or write a will.[4] If they were heiresses, their husbands administered and received the profits from their estates, although they could not sell or mortgage them.[5] Husbands also acquired absolute legal rights to any personal property their wives brought into or inherited during their marriages. Because married women could not hold goods and chattels (the comprehensive contemporary term for personal property) in their own right, they could not write testaments without their husbands' consent. The common-law courts did not uphold even these wills until 1426.[6] In practice, few Yorkist and early Tudor aristocratic wives exercised this privilege: they wrote only 6 of the 266 female wills used in this project.[7] In addition, 9 of 763 male testators recorded that they had granted this right to their deceased spouses. Of this total of 15 wives who wrote wills, 13 were either heiresses or widows, both situations in which women were more likely to be protected by prenuptial agreements than noninheriting wives in first marriages. The Statute of Wills (1540), which first established a common-law right to will land, excluded married women.[8]

Wives had no reciprocal rights in their husbands' personal property. In London, Wales, and the archdiocese of York, widows retained their customary right to one-third of their husbands' goods and chattels until the late seventeenth century. But in the archdiocese of Canterbury, men acquired complete testamentary power over their personal property during the fourteenth century. If they died intestate, their widows could claim one-third of their goods and chattels when they had surviving children, one-half when they did not. But if the men wrote wills, their wives could claim only the legacies left them and their *paraphernalia*, the necessities and personal ornaments appropriate to their degree.[9] Despite their entitlement to their *paraphernalia*, some aristocratic men explicitly bequeathed the clothes and jewels their wives "used to wear" to them, perhaps to protect them from quarrels with their heirs or executors about specific items. The testaments of 59 of 523 men who predeceased their wives contained legacies of this type. Since payment of a testator's debts took precedence over his widow's claim to her ornaments, she might well lose her jewels regardless of such provisions.[10]

In addition to extensive control over their spouses' property, husbands had almost unlimited physical power over their wives. The law permitted them to control their wives' movement, place of residence, and contact with other people; to punish them physically; and to confine them to their castles and great houses. In 1528 or 1529, for example, the sixth earl of Northumberland wrote to the duke of Norfolk that he had put three of his servants in charge of his wife, whom he accused of "malicious acts" against him. Her father, the earl of Shrewsbury, sent some of his servants to see the countess, but Northumberland denied them access to her.[11] Men's power over their mates was consonant with a legal system that defined the husband as his wife's baron or lord and her murder of him as petty treason.[12]

During the late sixteenth and seventeenth centuries, Chancery remedied some of the disabilities of coverture by enforcing prenuptial contracts or trusts that created married women's separate property.[13] But these devices did not exist in the Yorkist and early Tudor periods. Although single women who owned property could negotiate prenuptial contracts, giving them control of their goods during their upcoming marriages, after their weddings they had no way to enforce them because they were under coverture.[14] Wives were equally powerless over any land they brought into their marriages. In 1467 and 1479, Chancery specifically rejected a wife's capacity to dispose of or otherwise exercise rights over land settled to her use before her marriage.[15] It did not uphold married women's separate estate in property held in trust for them until a full century later.[16] Thus, in 1485, when Henry VII wanted to ensure that his mother, Margaret Beaufort, countess of Richmond, then married to the earl of Derby, retained control over the vast estates granted to her, he resorted to a special act of Parliament, giving her the status of *feme sole*, a married woman who was as independent of her husband with respect to her property as if she were unmarried.[17]

Despite the common law, members of the Yorkist and early Tudor aristocracy negotiated marriage settlements and created *uses* (early forms of the trust) to establish married women's separate property. Virtually all these agreements involved heiresses or widows bringing land and goods from their first marriages into their second.[18] These contracts protected women against some of the disabilities of coverture vis-à-vis their new husbands. Men agreed to them because they benefited from their wives' wealth even if they had limited control over it. Prenuptial agreements of this kind illustrate the way in which aristocratic couples collaborated to mitigate the impact of coverture. When William, marquess Berkeley, married Joan, widow of Sir William Willoughby, in 1468, for example, he agreed to allow her to use an annuity she had inherited from her first husband "at her pleasure, for the maintenance of herself and her children, and of her women servants."[19] The marriage settlement of Lady Margaret Long and her third husband, the second earl of Bath, gave her complete control over the extensive personal property she brought into their marriage, including the right to devise it by will should she predecease him. The settlement was actually worded and signed as if it were a contract between the earl and two of Lady Margaret's sons-in-law, John Spencer and Thomas Pakington. This arrangement protected Margaret from the disabilities of coverture should the earl break the agreement since Spencer and Pakington could sue him on her behalf.[20] Using male kin and friends to sign their marriage settlements may have been the conventional way widows circumvented their inability to enforce contracts themselves after their weddings.[21] Although these arrangements perpetuated aristocratic women's dependence on men, they are an example of the way in which women could protect themselves by moving between different groups of their male relatives, a phenomenon mentioned in the introduction.

Men's wills contain additional evidence of prenuptial agreements that gave their wives sole control of their property *during* their marriages. Sir John Say's will noted that he had entered a bond that required his heirs and executors to return all the goods his widow had brought into their marriage.[22] Sir Edward Boughton referred explicitly to the agreement he had signed with his wife and her friends before their marriage; Sir John Clerk, to "a pair of indentures of our marriage." Sir John noted carefully that he had paid his wife for twelve of her silver spoons that he was bequeathing to his heir.[23] Some of the wills indicate that women conducted business on their own during their marriages. Sir Thomas Barnardiston left his wife "all her own money with all her bargains with whomsoever she made them,"[24] and Sir Edward Green gave his widow all the goods that were hers "before marriage between us withal and at the time of my decease not sold nor given away afore by her will and counsel."[25]

While coverture deprived wives of their legal identity, primogeniture and male entails severely restricted women's right to inherit land. Under the common law, land descended to males rather than to females who stood in the same relationship to the deceased. In other words, sons of the deceased inherited before daughters, but daughters inherited before any of their fathers' other male kin. When land descended to men, it was impartible and passed to one son at a time in birth order; when it descended to daughters, it was divided equally among them.[26]

Statistically, in a relatively stationary population (the situation prevailing in Yorkist and early Tudor England), about 20 percent of the men who married would have daughters but no sons. Another 20 percent would have no children at all.[27] In fact, the percentage of land that descended to the daughters of noblemen or knights was considerably less than 20 percent. One of the reasons is that the statistical probability is based on the number of children born to a single couple. In practice, many members of the aristocracy married more than once, thus reducing the likelihood that daughters would inherit their land. In 179 cases in which the sons of noblemen inherited their land, 26 of the heirs were the offspring of second, third, or fourth marriages. The same was true of 37 of 328 sons who inherited land from parliamentary knights.

Moreover, from the late fourteenth century, many landowners restricted female inheritance further by means of the male entail. An entail was a gift of land that limited the estate to the recipient and the heirs of his or her body or certain classes of those heirs. The most popular form of entail, male tail, restricted the descent of land to men. Unlike primogeniture, it put collateral males—most often the deceased's brothers or nephews—ahead of daughters.[28] Although the entail was invented to exclude more women from land ownership than did the rules of common-law primogeniture, over the long run it had serious disadvantages.[29] At some point, depending on how much of a patriline's real estate was held in male tail, one of the heirs would have no land with which to provide for his younger sons and daughters. In addition, some men without sons preferred to leave their property to their daughters rather than their brothers or nephews. By the fifteenth century, therefore, some landowners wanted to bar (i.e., break) entails on their inheritances. In response, lawyers, undoubtedly at the behest of their clients, invented the common recovery, a collusive lawsuit allowing landowners to void entails and bequeath their estates freely.[30] By 1500 the common recovery had transformed the entail into a "freely convertible" estate and permitted fathers to leave their land to their daughters if they had no sons.[31] To secure his daughter Agnes's advantageous marriage to Sir Edmund Brudenell, for example, John Bussey, an ordinary gentleman, broke the entail on his inheritance in her favor. Sir John Shelton, who had only one son, wanted to break the entail on his estates so that if the boy died his three daughters would inherit rather than his (i.e., Sir John's) brother.[32] The common recovery left the initiative in determining the descent of land in men's hands and permitted fathers to bend the rules in favor of their daughters at the expense of their collateral male relatives. Predictably, few excluded male heirs acquiesced quietly in the loss of their inheritances. Lady Shelton and her husband's brother Thomas had such a violent quarrel that she feared he would kill her husband and son before the anticipated common recovery was completed. The Busseys fought the loss of their family estates to Agnes for decades.[33]

The spread of enfeoffments or uses during the late fifteenth century provided another mechanism for landowners to determine the descent of their land. Most of the land in England was enfeoffed by the end of the fifteenth century.[34] The use conveyed the legal title to their land to persons known as feoffees for specific purposes stated in the deed of enfeoffment. The effect was to separate common-law ownership, now vested in feoffees, from the beneficiary, the person who received the income and profits from the land.

The beneficiary was often the original owner, at least in the first instance. The advantage of the use was that enfeoffed land could be devised by will, which permitted landowners to alter the rules of common-law primogeniture.[35] Chancery enforced uses and wills as a matter of equity since common-law courts would not. Uses also shielded land from the burdens of feudal tenure, which affected almost all of the aristocracy's land and gave the king guardianship of minor heirs, possession of the minors' land, and control of the marriages of heirs and widows.[36]

Despite the availability of the will and common recovery, aristocratic men usually allowed their land to descend according to the traditional rules of primogeniture, which clearly reflected their preference as a class. Some of them also continued to respect male tails established by their ancestors. In addition, men without sons who survived their wives often remarried and had male heirs on the second try. Consequently, much less than 20 percent of the land that belonged to the aristocracy descended to female heirs. The estates of only 12 percent of 249 noblemen who died in the Yorkist and early Tudor period descended to women. Barely 7 percent of the knights who sat in Parliament between 1509 and 1558 had female heirs.[37] As a result, heiresses were extremely valuable commodities on the marriage market and tended to marry earlier than noninheriting daughters. They are also disproportionately visible in contemporary documents. Even as wives under coverture, they seemed to have had more leverage than noninheriting wives, as this book clearly demonstrates.

Marriage settlements complemented this inheritance system. Their primary purpose was to ensure that women, particularly those entering their first marriages, were supported adequately if they were widowed. The widow's income was almost always the subject of the first and most important substantive provisions in aristocratic marriage contracts. These clauses guaranteed the bride's financial security without enabling her to alter the descent of her husband's land to his heirs. Widows could receive their income in one of two ways, as common-law dowers or jointures. Both arrangements assigned them life rights in their husbands' land rather than title to or inheritance rights in it. Dower gave widows one-third of the land their late husband held in fee, that is, with the fullest rights possible under the common law.[38] No action at the time of women's marriages was necessary to entitle them to their dowers, which were an automatic share of their husband's estates. Alternatively, widows could receive a jointure, income from land conveyed to them and their husbands by the grooms' family to hold jointly during their marriage and solely during the life of the survivor.[39] The marriage contract created the jointure, which did not exist without it; normally it assigned the land to be used for this purpose and often (though not always) indicated its annual value. To safeguard the settlement, jointure land was usually conveyed to feoffees to hold for the use of the couple; the survivor of the marriage; and, after the survivor's death, the lawful heir(s) of the couple's bodies. During the marriage the husband received the income from the jointure.[40]

Contemporary sources indicate that establishing jointures was the norm among the aristocracy in the late fifteenth and early sixteenth centuries. Increasing reliance on the jointure instead of the dower was directly connected to the spread of the use because enfeoffments barred the common-law dower.[41] In 1519, for example, Thomas, Lord Dacre, petitioned the crown for permission to put his entire inheritance into feoffment so that if he remarried his wife "shall not be endowable."[42] Sir Edward Tame bequeathed a life estate in some of his property to his wife because "the most part of my lands hath been in feoffees' hands before my marriage and since, so that my wife can claim no dower by the common law."[43] Fathers negotiated jointures for their daughters because they knew that most aristocratic estates would not support adequate common-law dowers for them. With a single exception, the eighty-one marriage contracts used in this study created jointures for the support of the new couple and "the longer liver of them."[44] Jointures were at issue in 52 percent of 189 Chancery suits about marriage settlements in this period,[45] while just over half of 299 men's wills that assigned incomes to their widows or daughters-in-law established jointures for them.[46]

Provisions about the size and payment of the bride's dowry, known in Tudor idiom as her marriage money or portion, followed those establishing her jointure. Despite its name, the bride neither received nor controlled her dowry. The money was paid by her father (or his substitute) to her father-in-law or groom, usually in installments, with the first payment on the day the marriage contract was signed or on the day of the wedding.[47] The groom and his father were not required to use the dowry for the bride's benefit or to put it at her disposal during or after the marriage. Indeed, men who were short of cash frequently viewed their sons' marriages as the best way of raising money. In 1523, Thomas, Lord Dacre, wrote quite bluntly to Lady Maud Parr, in connection with a proposed marriage between her daughter and his grandson, "undoubtedly my said lord [the boy's father] must needs have some money, and he has nothing to make it of, but only of the marriage of his said son."[48]

The ubiquity of the jointure is evident in contemporary understanding of the meaning and function of the bride's dowry. Many marriage contracts stated explicitly that the bride's father was paying her marriage money "in consideration" of the promise to create her jointure or "for this cause."[49] Thus, Thomas, first marquis of Dorset, agreed to pay his daughter Cecily's father-in-law £1,000, in return for a jointure of £100.[50] The nature of the exchange was so clear that in 1523 Thomas, Lord Dacre, described "the common course of marriage" in the following terms: "to give 100 marks jointure for the payment of 1100 marks."[51] This interpretation of the financial exchange that accompanied marriage meant that failure to pay a woman's dowry was often construed as nullifying her right to her jointure.

Women could claim dower in any land their deceased husbands held in fee in addition to their jointures until passage of the Statute of Uses in 1536. The statute eliminated the possibility of this kind of double dipping by prohibiting widows from claiming dower if jointures were settled on them before their marriages. If jointures were created for them after their marriages, they could choose between them and their dower rights.[52] This change probably had little effect on most aristocratic women because so much of the land owned by members of their class was already enfeoffed. In addition, marriage settlements and wills often stated explicitly that the jointures they created barred or fully satisfied the widows' dower.[53]

Many historians regard the Statute of Uses as a landmark in the long decline of women's claim to land in the transition from the medieval to modern periods because it marked the moment when their claim to a substantial, fixed share of their husbands' estates, the common-law dower, gave way to negotiable shares, the jointure.[54] Among the aristocracy, however, the jointure was the conventional way of providing for widows for at least three-quarters of a century before passage of this bill. Furthermore, in the short run, the act had little effect on the legal form of marriage settlements.[55] Some scholars also contend that the change affected women negatively because the jointure was a much smaller share of their husband's estate than the widow's traditional third.[56] As yet, however, there is no systematic or large-scale study either supporting or disproving this assertion.

In addition to its material and legal foundations, the patriarchal regime that framed aristocratic women's lives rested on an ideology rooted in Christianity, the classics, and contemporary science. At its center were the linked assumptions that women were morally and intellectually inferior to men and that male dominance accorded with divine and natural law.[57] These ideas were not the property of men alone. Indeed, in conjunction with the class interests discussed in the introduction, they help to explain aristocratic women's willingness to participate in perpetuating the institutions that subordinated them to their fathers and husbands. One of the most popular prescriptive works based on these assumptions, Juan Vives's *De Institutione Christianae Feminae*, was actually written at Henry VIII's court. Both the original Latin version (1523) and the English translation (1528) were dedicated to Katherine of Aragon; the first printed version probably appeared before her death.[58] Despite his reputation as a humanist and the title of his tract, Vives was far more concerned with women's "honesty and chastity" than in education as we understand it. His work was shaped by a pervasive suspicion of women and the necessity of preventing them from sinning. Although many of his ideas seem more compatible with Spanish than English practice, *Institutione Christianae Feminae* remained popular throughout the Tudor period, suggesting that it resonated with contemporary ideas about female nature and the conviction that men needed to control women. Although individual religious and secular writers challenged the reigning patriarchal ideology, their work did not seriously affect everyday assumptions about female nature or the appropriate relations between the sexes.[59]

On the rare occasions when members of the aristocracy commented about women in general in extant sources, they almost always described them in negative terms. In 1537, Thomas Cromwell called women's views about religion "fond flickerings"; a few years later William Paget referred to their "imbecilities."[60] When women displayed admirable qualities such as bravery or constancy, men invariably described them as virile, a formula that constructed virtue and femininity as incompatible.[61] In 1537, for example, Sir Thomas Tempest, who reported that the countess of Westmorland had prevented a second outbreak of the Pilgrimage of Grace in her region of the North, commented that she "rather playeth the part of a knight than a lady."[62] The next year, when the countess of Salisbury refused to admit any guilt after she was accused of committing treason, the earl of Southampton, who was questioning her, commented, "We may call her rather a strong constant man than a woman. For in all behavior, however we have used her, she hath showed herself so earnest, vehement and precise that more could not be."[63]

Whether most aristocratic women internalized negative ideas about their sex is impossible to say. They certainly repeated them when it was to their advantage to do so, although there is no way of knowing whether they were cynically employing a useful rhetorical strategy or expressing views they shared. In 1535, Gertrude, marchioness of Exeter, excused herself for her involvement with the Nun of Kent by reminding Henry VIII that she was "first and chiefly" a woman "whose fragility and brittleness is such as most facilely, easily, and lightly is seduced and brought into abuse and light belief."[64] Widows who were petitioning the crown regularly referred to themselves as "poor widows" and complained about their isolation, no matter how inappropriate the label might seem to us. Three women who were prominent at court in the 1530s, Lady Jane Guildford; her daughter-in-law Lady Mary Guildford; and Lady Mary's sister, Margaret, marchioness of Dorset, all referred to themselves in these terms.[65]

Such broadly accepted ideas about female nature were believed to justify the subordination of women. Indeed, male domination functioned as a primary metaphor for the proper distribution of power. In his 1548 treatise on government, William Thomas argued, "Wherefore I determine, it is impossible any estate should long prosper, where the power is in the commonalty. For like as it becometh neither the man to be governed of the woman, nor the master of the servant, even so in all other regiments it is not convenient the inferior should have power to direct the superior."[66]

Nowhere was the insistence on female subordination more evident than in the marital relationship. Vives insisted that women ought to obey their husbands' commandments as if they were divine law because "the husband beareth the room of God here in earth unto his wife."[67] William Harrington emphasized wives' obligation to obey their husbands and defended their husbands' right to punish them even though he generally advocated a more mutual relationship between spouses than Vives.[68] Members of the aristocracy who articulated their views about marriage invariably treated obedience as wives' primary virtue. Sir Philip Champernon praised his mate for "the most obedient duty and gentleness" she always showed him, and Dame Alice Belknapp referred to the "love, gentleness and obedience . . . [that] a wife ought to [show] her husband."[69]

The patriarchal regime described in this chapter imposed harsh restrictions on aristocratic women. Nonetheless, most of them exercised considerable power and authority within their households, participated in politics, and contributed in vital ways to the prosperity of their families and class. The gateway to these possibilities was marriage, which constituted their career throughout the Yorkist and early Tudor period. Sir John Baker's unusually discursive will clearly equated marriage, the normative female vocation, with men's service to the crown. He charged his three single daughters "above all things to serve God and to be faithful, assured, true, humble, loving and obedient wives unto your husbands" and his sons to "serve God and thy sovereign lord and lady the king and queen; apply thy learning; be gentle and courteous to everybody . . . [and] avoid bribery, extortion, corruption and dissumulation."[70] The next chapter examines how this marital destiny shaped aristocratic daughters' experience of daughterhood and the education they received for their future roles.

CHAPTER 2. DAUGHTERS—

WIVES IN THE MAKING

*I*N YORKIST and early Tudor England, the expectation that aristocratic women would marry shaped their lives from the moment of their birth. From their earliest years they were socialized to view themselves as future wives. The goal of their educations was to teach them the manners and religious values of their class and the skills they would need to manage their great households and serve their families. Parents also fostered their daughters' relationships with their kin and patrons in the hope they would promote the girls' marriages and careers as they approached adolesence.

Contemporary prescriptive literature was unanimous that parents' first duty was to raise their daughters to become chaste and obedient women. In his popular manual, *The Instruction of a Christian Woman*, Juan Vives exalted chastity, synonymous in this period with honesty, as the primary female virtue. Contrary to the situation of men, who required a range of virtues and talents, "in a woman . . . honesty is instead of all." To achieve it, daughters should be raised to be shamefaced, sober, devout, and meek.[1] Vives's contemporary, Sir Robert Lee, who had three unmarried daughters when he wrote his will, carefully instructed his executors to bring them up "in virtue and honesty til they be married as maidens."[2] John Husee's advice to his employer, Honor, Lady Lisle, before she sent her daughters to court provides one of the clearest statements outside prescriptive literature about the conduct expected of young unmarried women: "Exhort them to be sober, sad, wise and discrete and lowly above all things, and to be obedient, and governed and ruled by . . . your ladyship's friends . . . to serve God well and to be sober of tongue."[3] Henry VIII also connected piety and female virtue when he instructed his daughter Mary's governess, the countess of Salisbury, to give the highest priority to "her honorable education, and training in all virtuous demeanor. That is to say, at due times to serve God."[4] The emphasis remained much the same after the break with Rome, although advocates of reform were more explicit about connecting religion to reading the Bible. In 1551, for example, Henry, duke of Suffolk, thanked the Swiss reformer Heinrich Bullinger for exhorting his daughter "to a true faith in Christ, the study of scriptures, purity of manners and innocence of life."[5]

On a practical level, aristocratic girls had to be taught to perform all the roles expected of successful wives. They needed to be literate in English, have some knowledge of arithmetic, receive hands-on training in household and estate management, and understand something about property law. Over and above specific skills, they had to learn to exercise authority over large numbers of people and take considerable initiative as mistresses of their households without violating their subordinate position. Aristocratic women were expected to be obedient to their fathers, husbands, and eldest brothers, but they were not expected to be passive. Learning to exercise this kind of "subordinate agency," a phrase that captures the contradictions built into their position, was probably the most important lesson daughters learned by observing and imitating their mothers and the adult women in other households in which they resided.[6]

Fathers expressed great confidence in their wives' devotion to their daughters and their capacity to supervise their upbringing and prepare them for the duties of wifehood. The wills of men who died while their noninheriting daughters were still single show that most of them gave the girls' mothers the power to arrange their marriages. Of 187 fathers in this situation who left widows, 139 (74 percent) granted this power to them alone or in concert with others. Three additional men assigned this power to the girls' stepmothers. Although a much smaller number, 52 (27 percent), gave them sole or joint custody of the girls, overwhelming evidence indicates that fathers assumed that their noninheriting, unmarried daughters would live with their mothers, even if they remarried.

On a qualitative level, fathers were eloquent about the strength of their wives' attachment to their daughters and their ability to oversee their educations and launch them into adulthood—as long as they remained single and free from the disabilities of coverture. Sir Edmund Bedingfield gave "the rule and governance" of all their children to his wife, whom he trusted "afore all creatures, as long as she remained single."[7] Sir George Giffard stated firmly that unless she remarried, "I know no creature will be so faithful, natural and kind to her and my children as she will be. Wherefore I have left no creature to interrupt her the while she liveth sole and hath power over herself."[8] Women's wills are much less forthcoming about their relationships with their unmarried daughters because they could only write them as widows. Consequently, they were usually older than aristocratic men who wrote wills and less likely to have young children.

Natural and kind motherhood did not mean that aristocratic women performed the routine, physical tasks necessary to care for their daughters themselves. Instead, they placed them in the hands of nurses and other household
servants immediately after they were born, an arrangement consonant with
the aristocracy's customary practice of hiring servants to perform all their
routine and menial tasks. Although they would not have seen it that way,
there was a conflict between the demands of motherhood and women's responsibilities as wives, household managers, and ladies of the court. Furthermore, infants and children occupied exceedingly marginal positions in their
parents' households, which were organized to display their owners' wealth
and power and to function as local centers of employment, consumption, patronage, and social life. High mortality and remarriage rates accentuated the
tendency to give child rearing a low priority because many girls spent much
of their childhoods and adolesence in the households of stepparents. In the
late 1460s, to give a particularly vivid example, Sir John Howard's household
contained the offspring of five marriages: his children by both his wives; his
second wife's children by her two previous husbands; and his second wife's
youngest stepdaughter, the child of her second husband by his first wife.[9]

The absence of aristocratic parents from home for considerable periods of
time increased their dependence on servants for child care. Fathers were often
away for days, weeks, and even months at a time for a wide variety of public
and personal reasons. Sir John Howard's movements provide a good example
from the second half of the fifteenth century.[10] Although aristocratic mothers
remained at home much more than their husbands, they certainly did not always do so. Both Howard's wives often accompanied him when he departed
for more than a few days.[11] The third duke of Buckingham and his wife provide another example. In June 1502, they left their household at Bletchingley
for an unspecified amount of time. Before he departed, Buckingham signed
an indenture with a gentlewoman named Margaret Hexstall to care for his
children, the oldest of whom was 5.[12] The next year the duchess accompanied
her husband on his annual Easter progress to his favorite religious shrines and
monasteries, again leaving their children at home.[13]

In addition, a small group of aristocratic mothers had their own offices or
duties at court during their childbearing years. For these women, attendance
on the queen and participation in royal celebrations and ceremonies took
precedence over their responsibilities to their families and required them to
leave home for lengthy periods on a regular basis. In 1502–1503, Elizabeth of
York's sister, Katherine Courteney, lived at court while Margaret Cotton cared
for her children in Essex. At the time, her son was 4 or 5 and her daughter no
more than 7.[14] In 1538, the countess of Sussex had a son in March, miscarried
the following August, and was back at court in November.[15] Joan Denny, who
gave birth to nine children between 1538 and 1549, was a member of the
queen's household throughout the 1540s.[16]

Eleanor, countess of Rutland, is one of the best-documented aristocratic women active at court despite her frequent pregnancies and numerous children. The countess gave birth to her eldest son in 1526.[17] She had ten other children, the youngest of whom was probably the daughter born in July 1539.[18] Yet, in September 1532, Lady Rutland participated in the ceremony that created Anne Boleyn marchioness of Pembroke.[19] The next month she and her husband accompanied the king when he took Anne to Calais to meet Francis I.[20] In 1536, the countess was at court in June and rode with the king on his summer progress in July.[21] Although she had a child in January 1537, she returned to court by spring and remained for much of the summer and fall. In November, she was one of the chief mourners at Jane Seymour's funeral and burial.[22] April 1539 found her at Halliwell, the Rutlands' London residence, for her daughter Gertrude's marriage to George, Lord Talbot.[23] Only a week after the wedding, she wrote Lady Lisle that she was "so big with child" that she would soon depart for Belvoir Castle. In the event, she did not leave until mid-June, about a month before she gave birth.[24]

In these circumstances the gap between the model of motherhood presented in prescriptive literature and the reality in aristocratic families was a large one. Vives told women unequivocally, for example, to regard their children as "all their treasure" and to devote themselves to their upbringing. He thought mothers should nurse their infants themselves in accord with the "commandment of nature" and personally instruct their daughters in book learning, "women's crafts" such as sewing and weaving, and housewifery.[25] Bullinger also believed that women should breastfeed their babies and teach their daughters household management.[26]

In practice, the duties of the nurses aristocratic women hired to care for their infants almost certainly included breastfeeding, although most of the evidence from the Yorkist and early Tudor period is indirect. Part of the problem is one of language since the specific term *wet nurse* was not used until the seventeenth century. Before that, the general term *nurse* described women who cared for infants and children whatever their duties.[27] One of the few unambiguous references to wet nurses appears in Sir William Petre's household account for the winter of 1549–1550; he not only hired Alice Humphry to breastfeed his son but also paid another woman (at a lower rate) to nurse Alice's baby.[28]

The high fertility of elite women provides circumstantial evidence of wet nursing since mothers who breastfeed their infants usually experience a temporary period of infertility that lengthens the time between their pregnancies and reduces the total number of their children.[29] Fertile aristocratic women were pregnant often and bore large numbers of children. Forty percent of 2,333 women had five or more children; 29 percent, 6 or more. Of 2,310 couples, 39 percent had five or more children; 26 percent, 6 or more. The most fertile 10 percent of women and couples had 9 or more offspring.[30] Many of them gave birth almost every year. Cecily, duchess of York, had eleven children in fourteen years.[31] Her daughter-in-law, Queen Elizabeth Woodville, gave birth to ten in the same length of time.[32] Lady Mary Denny had sixteen children (including two sets of twins) in sixteen years.[33] Sir William Cavendish's first wife had five children in five years; his second, who died giving birth to her third child, two in eighteen months; his third wife, seven in nine years.[34] The fact that women with positions in the queen's household returned to court within weeks of giving birth makes it virtually certain that they used wet nurses to feed their infants since they never took their infants with them.

Although they employed wet nurses, aristocratic Yorkist and early Tudor parents usually did not send infants of either sex away from home to be nursed for extended periods. Instead, their households included nurseries headed by women of gentle status who supervised their offsprings' upbringing in infancy and early childhood. In the early sixteenth century, the third duke of Buckingham employed a staff of five, including three gentlewomen and a laundress, to care for his four children.[35] In 1539, the earl of Rutland's infant daughter Katherine, her nurse, and five of his older children and their companions lived in his household.[36] At midcentury, a single gentlewoman cared for Sir William Petre's five children.[37] At best, given their other responsibilities and frequent absences from home, aristocratic mothers supervised the care and education of their daughters in a general, if distant, fashion. That so many men praised their wives in this area is probably a reflection of their own experience as children and the meager expectations it created.

Although most aristocratic daughters remained at home until they were adolescents, a tiny number lived at court or in the households of the king's relatives and favorites. What parents thought about the effect of these moves on their daughters is unclear, but they apparently could not resist the opportunity of securing royal patronage for them, especially assistance in arranging their marriages. Thus, Henry VII's mother, Margaret Beaufort, raised two of her grandnieces, Elizabeth and Eleanor Zouche, at Collyweston, which functioned as an extension of the court throughout her son's reign.[38] The king and his mother eventually arranged and financed the marriage of one of the girls.[39] After the birth of Edward VI, the chance of a royal marriage inevitably sparked the imaginations of ambitious families with good connections at court. Sir William Sidney, the prince's tutor and chamberlain, placed his granddaughter in Princess Mary's household and arranged for her to visit the future king frequently.[40] Similarly, Lady Jane Grey's father sent her to live with the dowager queen, Katherine Parr, as part of a scheme hatched by Parr's new husband to marry Jane to Edward.[41]

The crown's right to the wardships of minor heiresses also led to their removal from their mothers' households. Wardship resulted from the fact that members of the aristocracy held virtually all their land as feudal tenants of the crown. Wardship gave the king custody of minor heirs and the right to arrange their marriages and collect the income from their estates until they came of age. Given the shortage and high value of female heirs on the marriage market, members of the aristocracy competed fiercely for the privilege of purchasing their wardships from the crown, which reaped huge profits from selling them. Parents often purchased these wardships to secure brides for their own sons and immediately betrothed their female wards to them; others resold the wardships at a profit to someone else who intended to do so. The resulting couples, often no more than children, usually lived with the groom's parents until they came of age. Edward IV's favorite, William, Lord Hastings, purchased the wardship of Mary, heir of Sir Thomas Hungerford and of her great-grandmother, Margaret, Lady Botreaux, and married her to his heir, Edward.[42] Sir Edward Grevill of Milcote purchased the wardship of the three daughters and coheirs of Sir Edward Willoughby. His younger son Foulke married one of them.[43] Likewise, Grevill's contemporary, Sir Richard Gresham, married his son to his ward, Frances Thwaites, heir of Sir Henry.[44] Although wardship removed minor heiresses from their mothers' care even more completely than the general pattern of aristocratic life, it affected only a small number of girls because so few women inherited their fathers' estates.

Contemporary sources reveal very little about the rearing and daily lives of infants and very young children. The large number of primers and psalters in aristocratic libraries and wills suggests that their religious education began at an early age. In 1463, Brian Roucliffe reported proudly, for example, that his 4-year-old daughter-in-law, Margaret, "hath near hand learned her psalter."[45] Aside from expenses incurred when they were born or died, children appear most frequently in household accounts and letters when clothes were purchased for them or they required medical care. If the fifteenth-century Howard family accounts are typical, they needed shoes frequently.[46] On the other hand, the accounts contain only one reference to a toy.[47] Lady Lisle's correspondence about her stepdaughter Bridget, living at St. Mary's convent in Winchester while the Lisles were in Calais, focuses almost entirely on her clothes and the details of her care.[48]

When girls were old enough to be instructed formally, parents and servants taught them the practical skills they needed to carry out the duties of wifehood and introduced them to the accomplishments associated with gentility that would increase their attractiveness as potential brides. This part of their education, almost certainly informal, was based on observation and assisting their mothers, the gentlewomen who supervised them in their mothers' absence, and the mistresses of the households in which they lived as adolescents.[49] In his 1552 will, Sir Edmund Molyneux outlined the practical skills and accomplishments he wanted his daughters to have. He asked his executors to bring them up "in virtue, good manners, and learning to play the gentlewomen; and good housewives to dress meat and oversee their households."[50] Outside of educational tracts, his is a unique statement about the necessity of teaching housewifery to aristocratic girls. Although it is hard to imagine the wife of a nobleman or knight cooking regularly in the great kitchens of their manor houses and castles, they certainly needed to know enough to supervise the servants who did so. In addition, many women had specialties that they prepared personally to serve at their own tables or give as gifts. Lady Lisle's quince marmalade was among her most successful presents to Henry VIII, who liked it "wondrous well."[51] Although in many ways learning how to manage a household was the most important aspect of women's education, given their marital destinies, the process is virtually invisible in surviving records.

Daughters also often learned something about the practice of nonacademic, herbal medicine. As adults, their medical knowledge and skill were highly valued. The inventory of Elizabeth Lewkenor's goods taken in 1465 listed "a book of medicines."[52] Some years later, Elizabeth Stonor, who often acted as her husband's doctor, sent him a recipe for a concoction that would give him "great ease" after his "falling." She seemed shocked that he had not written for a remedy sooner.[53] Agnes, duchess of Norfolk, administered herbal medicines to members of her household and parish during an epidemic of the sweating sickness. When she offered her services to Cardinal Wolsey, she claimed that no one whom she had assisted had died of the often fatal disease.[54] The duchess's son Edmund once thanked Lady Lisle for sending him a medicine that broke up his kidney stone.[55] Some women acquired their medical knowledge from their mothers; two such mothers, Lady Jane Dynham and Dame Elizabeth Spelman, bequeathed books of "physic" or "medicines" to their daughters.[56]

Of all aristocratic women's practical abilities, the most evidence exists about their needlework and weaving. Their expertise ranged from sewing fine shirts as New Year's gifts to embroidering bed hangings and carpets.[57] The expensive fabrics and thread they used to produce luxury goods reflected their wealth and status at the same time that it involved them in quintessential female activities, sewing and textile production. Although their efforts were not needed to contribute to their families' necessities or income, as they were for the great majority of women, needlework provided them with a respectable, useful, and creative way to spend their time. After her first husband, Sir Edward Burgh, died, Katherine Parr went to live with her stepdaughter at Sizergh Castle in Westmorland, where she passed at least some of the time in embroidering a white silk counterpane and toilette cover that still survive.[58] When Margery Waldegrave bequeathed all her samplers, damask and Venetian gold cloth, unwrought silk, and weaving stools to her two daughters, she did so with the express intention "that their young folk may therewith be well occupied."[59] Nine years later, when one of her daughters, Bridget, Lady Marney, died, she continued the tradition, leaving her samplers, unworked silk and gold, weaving stools, and everything else belonging to her "silk works" to her two goddaughter-nieces "so that they may well occupy themselves."[60] The women's emphasis on occupying the girls' time may well have been a reflection of their underlying concern about protecting their chastity. Their comments certainly echo Vives's remark that all women should learn "to handle wool and flax . . . two crafts yet left of the old innocent world, both profitable and keepers of temperance." He pointedly praised Ferdinand and Isabella of Spain for insisting that their daughters, all destined for royal marriages, learn to spin and sew.[61]

Even more than their training in producing and sewing luxury fabrics, however, the musical education of aristocratic daughters was an accomplishment that marked their high status. Although music was closely associated with the culture of the early Tudor court, playing musical instruments and patronizing musicians spread far beyond the royal family. Wills and inventories reveal that many aristocratic women learned to play the lute and virginals. When John, Lord Marney, died in 1525, he left one of his daughters a great lute and two pairs of virginals, and her sister a third pair of virginals and portable organ.[62] Lady Lisle's daughter, Mary Bassett, studied the spinet, virginals, and lute.[63] Lady Joan Bray owned an early sixteenth-century book of madrigals.[64]

In addition to education in domestic skills and genteel accomplishments, aristocratic daughters routinely learned to read and write English.[65] It is not clear who taught them, but many aristocratic households included resident chaplains and/or schoolmasters, who could have done so.[66] In a society in which illiteracy was widespread, particularly among women, they clearly benefited from their position as members of a privileged elite. Reading English gave them access to the expanding world of printed books, which included a growing number of translations from other languages, and writing enhanced their skills as household managers. The archives are filled with letters, mostly about practical and domestic matters, written by women or containing postscripts in their hands. The best-known published collections—those of the Pastons, Stonors, Plumptons, Cliffords, and Lisles—all contain holograph letters from women, as do the multiauthored collections compiled by Henry Ellis and M. A. E. Wood Green.[67] Even when they used scribes, a practice common among female and male members of this class, women often signed their wills and letters. Thirty-one (12 percent) of the 266 women who wrote wills used in this project signed them or wrote the entire document themselves.

Historians sometimes cite women's poor handwriting and erratic spelling as evidence of their poor educations and near illiteracy.[68] Their frequent apologies for their "scribbling" and "rude hands" could be interpreted as an indication that they were aware of their deprivation.[69] But many aristocratic men also exhibited—and asked to be excused for—these failings, which suggests that they were not gender specific.[70] J. S. Brewer, editor of the *Letters and Papers of Henry VIII*, remarked contemptuously, "Of the three greatest noblemen of the time, the duke of Suffolk, the duke of Buckingham, and the marquess of Dorset, it would be hard to say which was the most illiterate. Perhaps the spelling of the duke of Suffolk is the most tortuous and ingeniously perverse."[71]

In fact, some of the most literate and best-educated aristocratic women and men wrote poorly, spelled irregularly, and apologized for their handwriting. Among highly educated women, Mary Howard, duchess of Richmond, who referred to her "evil hand" and "travail in writing," is a perfect example.[72] Mary Boleyn, who probably received as fine an education as her sister Anne, described a long letter she wrote as "scribbled with her ill hand."[73] Katherine Parr, who had an exceptionally good handwriting, commented that one of her letters to Henry VIII was "scribbled."[74] Like these women, John Paston III mentioned his "lewd hand" in one of his letters, although he wrote well enough to act as his mother's secretary from 1459 to 1462.[75] The signature of Edward Stafford, third duke of Buckingham, one of the noblemen Brewer called illiterate, certainly looks like that of a man uncomfortable while holding a pen.[76] Yet, however scrawling his handwriting, he was not only able to read and write well enough to keep a personal eye on his financial affairs, but he also purchased books for himself and his children and patronized the publication of a chivalric tale.[77] The signatures of Sir William Sidney and Sir Anthony Wingfield also appear to be those of men with little practice in writing, but both men undoubtedly had far more than a minimal English education: Sir William was appointed Edward VI's tutor in 1538; Sir Anthony was a member of the Privy Council, an executor of Henry VIII's will, and comptroller of Edward VI's household.[78]

A much more plausible explanation for poor handwriting and spelling is that aristocratic women and men routinely used scribes or secretaries, most often clerics resident in their households or attached to their parish churches, to do their writing for them, just as they employed servants to perform their other manual tasks. The earl of Rutland's accounts show, for example, that a secretary resided in his household in addition to his chaplain.[79] In this context, "scribbling" was not so much a sign of illiteracy as the product of traditional ideas about the kind of work compatible with gentility.[80] As for their knowledge of spelling, "correct" spelling was not a part or a mark of education in late fifteenth- and early sixteenth-century England. The idea of a standardized, "correct" English spelling did not emerge until the second half of the sixteenth century, and authoritative dictionaries did not appear until the eighteenth.[81]

The evidence for women's ability to read English is more episodic than that for their ability to write, but no less convincing. It is certainly the most obvious and sensible explanation for their ownership of books and the frequency with which women received bequests of English books from testators of both sexes.[82] Of fifty aristocratic wills containing such legacies, thirty-seven (74 percent) of the testators left at least one English book to a woman.[83] Twenty-five of these testators were themselves female. Although the vast majority of English books that belonged to women were religious, women also owned copies of Chaucer, Froissart, Lydgate's *Seige of Troy*, Gower, a prose Merlin, and Boccaccio.[84]

A smaller (but indeterminable) number of aristocratic women also learned French, the language of diplomacy and the court.[85] In 1498, the Spanish ambassador to Henry VII asked Ferdinand and Isabella to prepare their daughter for her marriage to Prince Arthur by ensuring that she was fluent in French before she arrived because neither the queen nor the king's mother knew Latin or Spanish.[86] French-speaking parents or servants probably gave young girls their first lessons in the language since it is hard to believe that Sir William Plumpton's 4-year-old granddaughter, Margaret, was already studying with a tutor when her father-in-law reported proudly that she "speaketh prettily and French."[87] In the 1460s, Sir John Howard's household included a Frenchwoman who may have introduced his children to the language.[88] Beyond the elementary level, parents hired professionals to instruct their children or placed them in households where such instruction was available, although a sixteenth-century Frenchman's observation that every English noble family employed a French tutor was undoubtedly an exaggeration.[89] In 1523, Thomas, Lord Dacre, recommended that if his young grandson married Katherine Parr, he should be sent to live with her widowed mother because "he might learn with her as well as in any place that I know . . . French and other languages."[90] Although Dacre did not give any details about the Parr household, contemporary sources indicate that popular tutors like John Palsgrave, Alexander Barclay, Pierre Valence, Nicholas Denisot, and Nicolas Bourbon taught French to aristocratic children throughout Henry VIII's reign.[91] After 1483, when Caxton published his *Dialogues in French and English*, printed teaching manuals and French grammar books were also available.[92]

In addition, some of the most ambitious parents sent their daughters abroad to learn or perfect their French. Both Sir Thomas Boleyn and Charles Brandon, duke of Suffolk, did so in the 1510s.[93] When Henry VIII's sister married Louis XII in 1514, the parents of the maids-in-waiting who accompanied her undoubtedly anticipated that becoming fluent in French would be one of the advantages of their appointments.[94] In the 1530s, Lady Lisle, anxious to place her daughters at court, sent two of them, Anne and Mary, to live with members of the French nobility.[95]

Book ownership provides the best indication of fifteenth-century women who knew French, if one assumes that those who owned French books or received them as legacies could indeed read the language. Sir Richard Roos bequeathed a volume of the French grail romances to his niece, Eleanor, who later married Sir Richard Hawte; it contains both their autographs. She subsequently gave the book to her first cousin, Elizabeth Woodville.[96] The duchess of Buckingham left her daughter-in-law, Margaret Beaufort, two French books.[97] Beaufort subsequently purchased a French edition of a contemporary romance.[98] She was skillful enough in the language to translate devotional works from French into English as a regular religious exercise.[99] William Pynson published her translation of *The Mirror of Gold for the Sinful Soul* in 1507.[100] When Lady Margaret died, her bequests included two French volumes.[101]

Many of the women at Henry VIII's court were proficient French speakers. George Cavendish recorded with pride that when the king entertained the French ambassadors at Greenwich in 1518, all the women present could converse in good French and that the visitors were "delighted . . . to hear these Ladies speak to them in their own tongue."[102] Although Anne Boleyn's fluency in the language is well known, Katherine Parr's is less so. Edward VI wrote to her in French at least once, she composed a devotional poem in the language, and Princess Elizabeth asked her to correct her English translation of the French *Glasse of the Sinful Soul.*[103] Circumstantial evidence strongly suggests that Henry VIII's daughter-in-law, the duchess of Richmond, and his nieces, Frances and Eleanor Brandon, daughters of the duke and duchess of Suffolk, also knew French.[104] In the next generation, Margaret Willoughby, Lady Jane Grey's first cousin, purchased two French books when she was only 9 years old.[105]

While knowledge of French was widespread among Yorkist and early Tudor aristocratic women and was almost essential for those who sought positions at court, I have not found evidence of a single laywoman of this class who learned Latin before the reign of Henry VIII. The king's grandmother, Lady Margaret Beaufort, one of the best educated and most intellectual women of her generation, openly regretted that "in her youth she had not given her to the understanding of latin."[106] In a society where education was almost entirely directed to vocational ends, men studied Latin, the language of the church and the law, to prepare for careers closed to women. There was also a widespread fear, ultimately rooted in the story of original sin, that knowledge would lead women to commit evil deeds.[107] The exclusion, therefore, also functioned as a marker of their presumed moral and intellectual inferiority. The effect was to restrict academic and learned culture to men. Women's ignorance of Latin also meant that no matter how pious they were, they could not fully understand the service books they used in church. There is something poignant about Bishop Fisher's remark that Margaret Beaufort, known for her piety and love of learning, had only "a little perceiving" of the "rubric of the ordinal for the saying of her service."[108]

On a practical level, ignorance of Latin increased women's dependence on their male relatives and servants because it was the language used in legal and official documents, land transactions, manorial accounts, and court rolls. In an interesting adjustment to this situation, when Eleanor Townshend's husband died and she assumed complete authority over his estates in 1491, the accounts were kept in English for her benefit; when she died in 1499 and her heir took over, they were kept in Latin once again.[109] Ignorance of Latin also increased women's vulnerability to fraud. In an English will she wrote entirely by herself, Jane Huddleston accused her son John (the offspring of her second marriage) of tricking her into signing a "fair deed of release of my title [to her inheritance] . . . after my decease to him and to his heirs forever, neither reading nor declaring thereof to me . . . [he] caused me to seal the said deed . . . saying, 'now by this writing I stand as officer unto you in the offices of bailiff and receiver' . . . and therein utterly and untruly he hath distrained me."[110] The fraudulent document was almost certainly written in Latin, the language normally used for deeds and grants. Lady Huddleston would have been able to read it if it were in English.

In estimating the significance of women's exclusion from education in Latin, it is important to remember that many aristocratic men did not know the language either, although Nicholas Orme thinks that most of them understood enough to oversee their affairs.[111] In the second half of the fifteenth century, knights and noblemen closely connected to the court were probably those least likely to know Latin, while those educated at the Inns of Court were most likely to do so. During the sixteenth century, members of the court aristocracy increasingly recognized that a Latin education enhanced their chances of rising in the king's service; as the century progressed, therefore, they sent their sons to grammar schools and the universities more frequently, even if the sons did not stay long enough to earn degrees.[112] Thus, in his 1513 will, Nicholas, Lord Vaux, directed his executors to keep his younger son, William, in school until he was 24, "as may be most best for his preferment, that is to say in Latin and French."[113] The continued—indeed growing—educational disparity between women and men is evident in wills like that of Sir Henry Heydon, who left his wife any of his English books that she wanted, and Sir Richard Elyot, who bequeathed his English books to his daughters, his Latin and French books to his sons.[114]

In this context, the education of some two dozen aristocratic women in the classics during Henry VIII's reign was a remarkable departure from the norm. It is best understood as a consequence of the successful introduction of humanism to the early Tudor court.[115] Humanists such as Thomas More, Richard Hyrde, Juan Vives, and Sir Thomas Elyot argued systematically and persuasively against the deep-rooted belief in the intellectual inferiority of women and in favor of their studying the classics to increase their virtue and prepare them for their duties as wives, mothers, and in exceptional cases, queens. The fathers who provided classical instruction for their daughters were either themselves humanists, like Sir Thomas More or Sir Anthony Cook, or courtiers who followed the precedent Henry VIII set in the education of his own daughters. The success of this tiny group at learning Latin and Greek proved that women were as capable as men of mastering the humanist curriculum, but because they were—and were always recognized by their contemporaries to be—extraordinary exceptions, their example had little effect on the education of the great majority of their peers. Aristocratic fathers who were neither courtiers nor humanists had no reason to follow their lead since the classics did not prepare their daughters for their careers as wives. What is impossible to know, given the silence of the surviving sources, is whether this development affected aristocratic women's estimate of their own intellectual capacities, or that of women in general, or encouraged them to think critically about the educations they had received.

Shortly before and after they entered adolesence, daughters who were still single were usually sent from their parents' households to live elsewhere to complete their educations, expand their social circles, and secure the assistance of another well-connected family in arranging their marriages. Sir Edward Knyvett underscored the last function of "putting girls out," as the custom was called, when he bequeathed 100 marks to his niece Elizabeth for her marriage "if she be married by the advice of my especially good lady the duchess of Norfolk, with whom the said Elizabeth is in service."[116] Given these objectives, aristocratic parents made enormous efforts to place their daughters with the highest ranking, wealthiest families possible. Women played a key role in the networks activated for this purpose because they were the ones who accepted responsibility for the girls who resided in their homes. When Lady Lisle asked Edward Seymour, then earl of Hertford, to take her daughter into his household, for example, he reported that he "not only pondered the same with myself, but also declared it unto my wife," before responding in the affirmative.[117] Women were far more likely to take on this role for the daughters of their natal kin than for girls from their husbands' families. In the 1460s, the countess of Oxford helped her cousin, John Howard, place two of his daughters, one in her household and the other in her own daughter's residence.[118] In her will of 1496, Dame Margery Salvin remarked on her "niece Langton, being with me."[119] Decades later, two of the duchess of Norfolk's nieces lived with her.[120]

Women's position in the households they joined varied considerably. Some assumed the role of surrogate daughters. Madame de Bours repeatedly told Honor Lisle that she loved Mary Basset like a daughter and clearly treated her as such.[121] Others served as maids-in-waiting to the mistresses of their households, performing duties much like those of the queen's maids-in-waiting at court. Lady Elizabeth Cavendish's sister must have been "in service" in this sense while she lived in the Cavendish household since she received quarterly wages.[122] Katherine Basset revealed her sensitivity to the status differences implicit in these alternatives in her response to the suggestion that she move from the countess of Rutland's household to the earl of Hertford's in 1539. John Husee, her mother's business agent in England, told Lady Lisle, who was then in Calais, that Katherine "reckoneth it better to be with my Lady Rutland, in case she being with my Lady Hertford should be taken but as her woman; for my Lady Rutland doth not so take her nor use her."[123] A position in the queen's household was the most prestigious form of service available. Above all, it held out the prospect of a splendid marriage since the court gave young women an unparallelled opportunity to meet eligible men from the most powerful, wealthiest families; to obtain assistance from the king and queen in arranging and financing their matches; and to secure royal patronage for their families and friends.

Aristocratic households, with their huge numbers of servants and traditions of open hospitality, were poor enviroments for insulating adolescent girls from threats to their honor. The households were too large and filled with too many single men of all ages, ranks, and ambitions to cloister the girls in any meaningful sense of the word. To make matters worse, during their frequent absences from home, aristocratic women left their daughers and other girls living in their households in the charge of servants, who had far less reason than they to interrupt flirtations that might develop into imprudent, clandestine marriages. These conditions made it difficult to guard the girls' chastity and prevent them from marrying unwisely. The aristocracy's custom of sending their adolescent daughters to live at court or with higher ranking noble or knightly families increased these problems since young people tended to congregate in the largest, and therefore potentially least supervised, establishments. The conflict between this practice and ensuring their daughters' honor was one of the contradictions that resulted from the incompatibility between the aristocracy's moral and religious values and a pattern of child rearing rooted in feudal relationships and their dependence on the networks that linked them to the crown and their peers. The description of life in the household of Agnes, dowager duchess of Norfolk, that emerged during the trial of her granddaughter, Catherine Howard, may have been exaggerated, but it provides a unique glimpse of a situation that undoubtedly existed elsewhere in less dramatic forms. Catherine had lived with her grandmother at Horsham and Lambeth in the years before her marriage to Henry VIII. The duchess had apparently paid scant attention to the activities of the young people who were living under her roof. If the deponents are to be believed, young men had virtually free access to the chamber where Catherine and her female companions slept.[124]

Shakespeare set Romeo and Juliet in Italy, but similar situations arose with the aid of complicitous nurses and other servants in Yorkist and early Tudor castles and manor houses.[125] An incident in the household of Henry VIII's sister Mary and her husband, the duke of Suffolk, in 1517 might have been the beginning of a remarkably similar story had not the duke heard about the affair at an early stage. A friend of the duchess, a Mistress Jerningham, secretly betrothed her daughter-in-law, Lady Anne Grey, to one of the king's wards, who was living in the Suffolk household. The duke was horrified at this breach of the trust the king had shown in him by placing the ward, "young Berkeley," in his care. He reported the episode to the king's chief minister, Cardinal Wolsey, immediately because he was terrified that misinformation about it would reach the king and arouse his anger. He also asked Wolsey "so to order this matter that it may be an example to all others . . . how they move any such matters within any noble man's or woman's house hereafter and in especial with any of the king's wards."[126] Two decades later, Sir Richard Weston and his wife Lady Anne dismissed a "young man [who] had nothing" from their household because he was courting one of Sir Christopher More's daughters, who was also in their service. Sir Richard, who was reluctant to risk any further misbehavior on the young people's part, insisted that his wife find another place for the young woman, whom she recommended to Lady Lisle, living safely on the other side of the English Channel.[127] Suffolk's and Weston's resolute reaction when faced with the prospect of young people for whom they were responsible contracting their own marriages indicates how seriously they and their contemporaries took such behavior. But the incidents also illustrate the danger inherent in the practice of placing adolescents in the largest, most prestigious households of members of their class.

Whatever arrangements they made for their daughters, aristocratic parents invested considerable amounts of money in supporting them in a manner befitting their rank, educating them in the appropriate accomplishments, and seeking opportunities to marry them off advantageously. Despite men's stated preference for sons and the fact that they often received more formal schooling than their sisters, parents of both sexes bequeathed very similar sums to maintain or "find" their unmarried daughters and younger sons. Most families allotted between £6 13s. 4d. and £20 a year for each dependent child. Some fathers, Sir Alexander Unton, for example, provided larger allowances for their daughters than for their sons; others, like Sir Giles Strangeways, did the reverse.[128] The will of Beatrice, Lady Greystock, illustrates how individualized these legacies often were. She bequeathed the same amount— £7 per annum—to two daughters and a son, but she gave a second son £6 13s. 4d. per annum for three years while he was at Cambridge and £10 per annum for five years after he turned 16 "towards his finding and exhibition in the court and chancery."[129]

Whatever their relative resources and specific arrangements, the money aristocratic parents spent in supporting and educating their daughters was always intended to prepare the girls for their destiny as wives and to place them in optimal positions for securing desirable husbands. The next chapter will explore the culminination of their efforts—the complicated process of finding appropriate mates for them and then negotiating their marriage contracts.

CHAPTER 3. THE

ARRANGEMENT

OF MARRIAGE

*A*RISTOCRATIC women's first marriages played a crucial part in determining the character and quality of their entire adult lives. On a personal level, their happiness and emotional well-being rested in large measure on their relationships with their husbands and their success in performing their duties as wives. On the material level, their position within the aristocracy, their standard of living, and their access to patronage and the court depended almost entirely on their spouses' rank, wealth, and political power. Their reliance on their parents or other kin for the resources to marry well in these terms reinforced their status as dependents without economic resources of their own.

When they married, aristocratic daughters carried significant resources from their natal to their marital families. In most cases these assets were economic—large amounts of cash or, in the case of heiresses, land. But occasionally their crucial capital was their fathers' political influence or high rank. Aristocratic women's role in transferring resources from one family to another encouraged men—their fathers, brothers, or the king himself—to exploit them for their own purposes. The pressure to treat them instrumentally was even stronger because the matches their fathers (or their substitutes) arranged for them were sensitive, public signifiers of their own position within the aristocracy. Paradoxically, therefore, the very importance of aristocratic women's marriages contributed to their subjection as daughters.

In this context, aristocratic parents who were contemplating their daughters' futures had two related goals. First and foremost was ensuring their daughters' financial security and social position by marrying them to men of their class, since, as we saw in chapter 1, women acquired what they and their contemporaries called their livelihoods or livings through marriage. Second, within the limits set by their own economic, political, and social resources, they sought to marry their daughters into the wealthiest, highest ranking, most powerful families possible. The ultimate goal was to secure sons-in-law from families with more of these assets than their own. If they succeeded, their daughters' marriages enhanced their natal families' status, connected them to more influential kin and patronage networks, and improved their position at court.

This chapter will analyze how the process of arranging daughters' marriages incorporated and advanced these goals. It will begin by examining the financial exchange, embodied in the marriage contract, through which aristocratic parents purchased livings for their daughters and matched them with desirable mates. It will then look more closely at their specific priorities as they weighed the attractiveness of potential sons-in-law. Finally, it will focus on the material, legal, and ideological factors that ensured that most daughters would agree to the matches their parents negotiated for them. With few exceptions, parents were the actors and daughters the objects in the transactions that turned single women into wives. Some daughters did, of course, fall in love and desire to marry men of their own choosing. This chapter will conclude by looking at the exceptional circumstances in which love matches occurred and the price women paid when they defied their families to marry men they loved.

Members of the Yorkist and early Tudor aristocracy used the language of the marketplace to describe the negotiations and exchanges involved in finding husbands for their children.[1] Mabel Parr and Elizabeth Lucy both referred to the terms of marriage contracts as "a bargain,"[2] while parents regularly spoke about "selling" their sons' marriages to secure the dowries of their daughters-in-law. When Lord Lisle needed money to pay the debt he owed Edward Seymour, for example, his servant, John Husee, commented, "I cannot see which way it may be made, unless your lordship and my lady would depart with the wardship [in effect, the marriage] of Mr. Basset [Lady Lisle's son by her first marriage]."[3] In the 1550s, the countess of Bath's servant reported to her, "I do understand . . . that Sir John Horsey is now driven to make shift for money and supposeth that he goeth about to sell the marriage of his son, which is a very proper child. And thought good by Mr. Colles and me to move your ladyship of it for one of your young ladies."[4]

The key issue in these negotiations was setting the size of the bride's dowry and jointure. On the woman's side, her father or other guardian agreed to pay a dowry—almost always a specific amount of money, usually in installments at stated times and places—to her husband or, if he were a minor, to his father or guardian. Once the dowry was paid, it belonged completely to the groom or his father or guardian. The bride herself had no control over its use or any further claim on it. The dowry constituted a woman's share of her father's estate and was therefore also called her portion.[5] On rare

occasions, noninheriting daughters received land instead of cash as their marriage portion. Sir John Howard gave his daughter Margaret the manor of
Colby when she married his ward, Sir John Wyndham, and Sir Thomas Fenys
gave his daughter Jane life rights in the manor of Pechard.[6] The records of
these transactions do not indicate why these fathers departed from the usual
custom of giving cash dowries.

In return for the bride's dowry, the groom and his family promised to convey specific estates or pieces of land to the couple to hold jointly during their
marriage and solely during the life of the survivor. The income from these estates constituted the wife's jointure or living, and was supposed to support
her if she survived her husband. Both families regarded the dowry as payment for the jointure. Marriage contracts often stated explicitly that her portion was being paid "in consideration" of the promise to create her jointure.[7]
In 1536, for example, when his daughter Dorothy married Lord Ferrers's heir,
George, first earl of Huntingdon, agreed to give her a dowry of 2,000 marks
in return for a jointure of 200 marks.[8] Thomas, Lord Dacre, believed that
there was a prevailing custom that the income from the jointure should be 10
percent of the total cash dowry: "From the highest degree into the lowest, it
is custom and so used always for every 100 marks of [marriage] money, ten
marks of jointure."[9]

Many settlements required repayment of the dowry if the marriage was
not completed according to the requirements of ecclesiastical law. Problems
arose because, whatever the age of the couple, the father of the bride usually
paid the first installment of her dowry when the contract was signed or the
marriage solemnized. Under ecclesiastical law, however, girls under the age of
12 and boys under the age of 14 could not make binding matches and could renounce their marriages when they reached these ages. Marriage contracts,
therefore, often required repayment of the dowry if the bride or groom rejected the marriage on reaching the age of consent or if either of them died
before they had sexual relations. Many contracts also stipulated that the
dowry should be returned if either the bride or groom died before the age of
16, which suggests that marriages were not consummated until couples
reached that age even if they had been solemnized and the couple had consented to them.[10]

The main exception to this pattern of exchange—jointure for dowry—
occurred when the bride was herself an heiress. In the great majority of these
cases, the groom's family paid what was in effect a reverse dowry.[11] The
groom's family almost always also established a jointure for the bride.[12] The
primary obligation of the heiress's family was to guarantee the size of her inheritance. The contract might require return of the payment by the groom's
family and payment of the customary dowry if the bride's father had a male
heir after the marriage occurred.[13]

The negotiations about proposed marriages and the financial transactions accompanying them were often contentious. In 1524, Mabel Parr ended talks about a marriage between her daughter Katherine and Henry, Lord Scrope's heir, after eight months of discussion. She wrote in exasperation that his offer "concerning the jointure . . . is so little and so far from the custom of the country and his demands is so great" that she had decided not to "meddle with the said bargain" any longer.[14] In the face of similar difficulties, Margaret Paston acted resolutely to prevent the failure of discussions, then five months old, about the marriage of her son to Margery Brews. Noting that she was as happy about the proposed marriage "as ever I was for any marriage in mine life," she offered to meet Margery's mother in Norwich to "take some way that it shall not break." To end the deadlock, she gave her son a manor she had inherited to use for Margery's jointure.[15] Dame Anne Rede drove such a hard bargain in her negotiations for a marriage between her daughter and Sir Giles Grevill that he told her business agent that "the cause standeth so, the conclusion not had, obloquy and diverse speeches will follow, to little praise and no worship to the gentlewoman neither to me"; and he wished that "it had never been spoken of." Despite Grevill's anger, the marriage eventually took place.[16]

Aristocratic fathers were well aware that their daughters could not marry within their class without sizable dowries, which represented their natal families' major financial investment in them. Men facing death took great care to ensure that their unmarried daughters would receive adequate portions. Of 268 male testators with unmarried daughters, 257 (96 percent) left them dowries. Fathers who had neglected or were unable to fulfill this responsibility expressed distress at their failure. John Tyrrell noted regretfully in his 1540 will that he had not been able to provide adequately for his daughter Katherine "for that my time hath been but short and thereby not of such substance in goods to advance and set forth my said daughter according to my mind." He reminded his brother and heir that he "might have done [so] if I would have hindered my said inheritance or sold away my said great woods" and begged him, "considering the premises . . . [to] give her some honest sum of money for her better advancement."[17] Some men also financed the matches of their granddaughters, nieces, sisters, and stepdaughters. Sixteen percent of the 763 men's wills used in this project contained bequests of this kind.[18]

Although aristocratic women's dowries varied considerably—from the low of 30 marks that Sir Robert Fenys left his two daughters in 1509 to the 4,000 marks that Edward, Lord Hastings, gave his daughter in the same decade[19]— most portions clustered around two figures far from these extremes, one for the daughters of knights, the other for the daughters of noblemen. The markedly different size of dowries in the two groups reflected one of the major differences between most peers and most knights: the vastly greater wealth of the former. In the 105 years from 1450 to 1555, the median portion for knights' daughters was 200 to 300 marks; for peers' daughters, 750 to 1,000 marks.[20] Dowry size was remarkably stable throughout the period.[21]

A woman's dowry constituted her inheritance and forestalled her making any further claim on the family estate, although fathers could, and often did, leave their daughters additional legacies in their wills.[22] In 1478, for example, Sir Ralph Verney divided his goods, chattels, and debts into three parts and gave relatively small legacies out of the second part to his two married daughters and three granddaughters. He left the remainder in equal portions to his two younger sons "for as much as my daughters . . . have had their preferment at their marriages of their portions . . . and my sons . . . have not had their such preferment."[23] Sir Edmund Denny bequeathed dowries to two of his daughters "in name of their full and whole portion of all my goods moveable,"[24] and Sir John Fulford stated that his daughters' marriage money constituted "full recompence and satisfaction of their child's parts of all the residue of my goods and cattle."[25] Correspondence after an award of 4,000 marks for breach of promise to Katherine Fitzalan, daughter of William, earl of Arundel, indicates that women shared this understanding. In explaining why she could not agree to a reduction of the award, she told Cromwell, "for more than that only I shall never have . . . of my lord my father nor of other of my kin."[26]

Fathers with more than one daughter exhibited a strong impulse to give them equal dowries. In a group of ninety men in this situation, sixty-seven (74 percent) made this choice. In the sources that recorded sisters' marriage portions, equal size was most evident in their fathers' wills. In those cases, the men depended on their widows and executors to arrange their daughters' matches. They may have worried about favoritism if their executors had the power to allocate their money to their daughters, but most likely they were thinking about the girls' dowries as their inheritance and wanted to give them equal shares of the paternal estate. Differences in the size of sisters' marriage portions were more likely when fathers arranged their daughters' marriages themselves and could weigh the relative advantages of specific matches. They could also compensate the daughters who received smaller dowries when they died. Therefore, only a minority of fathers—Thomas, Lord Hoo, and Sir Thomas Fairfax are examples—empowered their executors to allocate a single dowry fund among their daughters.[27]

Since women's dowries constituted their share of their fathers' estates, comparing the size of their dowries to the provisions for their noninheriting brothers is a useful way of investigating aristocratic families' relative investment in their daughters and sons.[28] Unlike their sisters, who almost always received their inheritance as dowries, younger sons might receive land or annuities as well as cash. Of thirty-nine fathers whose wills provided for younger sons and unmarried daughters, meaningful comparison is possible in twenty-nine cases; in the others, the men did not treat children of the same sex equally so that it is difficult to compare their provisions for sons and daughters as distinct groups.[29]

In the remaining twenty-nine cases, ten men gave their sons annuities; eight, land; nine, cash; and two, cash plus another source of income.[30] The small number of these wills make the results of analyzing them tentative, but they strongly suggest that fathers treated their noninheriting children similarly regardless of sex. The real gulf in aristocratic families was between the heir and all his sisters and younger brothers. The issue was primogeniture, not distinction on the ground of sex. Of the sons who received cash, five received the same amount of money as their sisters, two received more, and two received less. Sir Andrew Lutterell even specified that both his daughters and younger sons should use their equal portions "for their preferment in marriage."[31] The value of men's annuities depended to a large extent on their longevity, but a comparison with their sisters' dowries at the end of ten and fifteen years yields similar results. At the end of a decade, three of the younger sons in my sample would have received more money from the family estate than their sisters; three, the same amount; and four, less. At the end of fifteen years, five of the younger sons would have received more money than their sisters; three, the same amount; and two, less. There was also little difference between the provision for sisters and brothers when fathers left their younger sons land for life with no rights of inheritance. At the end of ten years, one of the sons would have received more money from the family estates than his sisters; one, the same; and four less. Five years later, the numbers in each category would have remained the same. Only four younger sons clearly did better than their sisters: in two cases they received an annuity or a manor in addition to an equal cash portion; in a third, a cash portion almost as large as their sisters' dowries plus land of unspecified value with unrestricted inheritance rights; and in the fourth, land worth £10 per annum with full inheritance rights.[32]

The combination of near universal female marriage and large families meant that fathers devoted significant portions of the income from their estates to paying their daughters' dowries over long periods of time.[33] The strength of their preference is particularly clear if we look at the wills of fifty-three fathers who had four or more unmarried daughters and died before 1534.[34] These were the men most likely to face economic difficulties raising the large dowries necessary to marry all their daughters within the aristocracy and who might, therefore, be most tempted to provide for some of them with the smaller sums required to place them in convents.[35] Twenty-seven of these men, just over half, arranged marriages for four or more daughters; the fate of the daughters of fourteen of them is unknown; and eight of the remaining twelve testators found husbands for three of their female offspring. To put these figures another way, in thirty-six of the thirty-nine cases in which we know what happened to all the testators' daughters, 92 percent of those with four or more daughters arranged marriages for at least three of them. And even these figures do not fully reveal the strength of men's preference for marrying their daughters to placing them in convents because they hide the cases of men like Sir William Brandon, who married seven of his seven daughters; Sir John Danvers, who found husbands for six of six; Thomas, first marquess of Dorset, who did so for six of eight; and Sir Giles Bridges, who married five of five.[36]

English noblemen and knights could finance so many marriages because they used the income from their estates to pay their daughters' dowries, usually over a period of years. In 1495, for example, Thomas, first marquess of Dorset, agreed to pay a dowry of 1,000 marks in three installments when his daughter Elizabeth married Sir John Arundell—200 marks before the wedding, 200 marks at the Christmas after Arundell completed the legal arrangements to assure Elizabeth's jointure, and the balance the following May.[37] In 1518, Margaret, countess of Salisbury, agreed to a dowry of 3,000 marks for the marriage of her daughter Ursula to Henry Stafford, heir of the third duke of Buckingham, over a five-year period.[38] When members of the aristocracy finished making these payments, they still possessed their land, the basic form their capital took, and the annual income it yielded. They were not, therefore, permanently impoverished as a result of their daughters' marriages. Paying in installments also meant that parents did not have to save their daughters' dowries in advance.[39] In this context, it is not surprising that they opted to find husbands for as many of them as possible, given the emphasis on marriage as women's vocation and the value of marriage ties in reinforcing and extending their kin and patronage networks.

While women's dowries represented a major, albeit bearable, expense to their natal families, they constituted a large, welcome infusion of cash into the coffers of their husbands and fathers-in-law, some of whom used the money to provide their own daughters' dowries. In his 1492 will, for example, Edward, Viscount Lisle, explained that he had intended to use the money he received for the marriage of his heir for the dowries of his two unmarried daughters, "which resteth yet undone, to his great discomfort."[40] John Fettiplace bequeathed his daughter Elizabeth 100 marks for her dowry from the money Sir John Mordaunt owed him for the marriage of his heir.[41] Thomas, Lord Berkeley, financed his daughter Muriel's marriage with his daughter-in-law's portion.[42] As Lord Dacre rightly told Mabel Parr, the dowries of their daughters-in-law were one of the few ways in which men could raise large sums of money without borrowing.[43]

The size of a woman's jointure was related to a number of factors in addition to the size of her marriage portion, the most important of which were the relative rank, wealth, and political influence of her and her husband's families. In practice, therefore, there was far more variety in the ratio between the size of the jointure and that of the dowry than Lord Dacre's comment suggested—that the customary jointure was 10 percent of the dowry.[44] In a sample of forty-eight marriage settlements, the jointure varied from a high of 66 percent of the dowry to a low of 4 percent, although 10 percent was most common.[45] All but five of the contracts gave the wife a jointure equal to 10 percent or more of her portion.[46] The contrast between the contracts Thomas Wriotheseley, earl of Southampton, negotiated for two of his daughters demonstrates how relative rank, wealth, and political influence might affect the ratio between women's dowries and jointures. When Anne was contracted to Henry Wallop, whose father was not even a knight, her dowry was relatively small, only 450 marks, but her jointure was eventually going to rise to 66 percent of her marriage portion. In effect, the Wallops were paying heavily to secure the daughter of an earl and privy councillor for their son.[47] In contrast, her sister Elizabeth received a much larger portion, 1,600 marks, because her husband, Thomas, was the earl of Sussex's heir. The high status of both families required a large dowry. Elizabeth also received a large jointure, 500 marks, which would allow her to live in a manner befitting her status. Nonetheless, her jointure was a smaller percentage of her dowry than in her sister Anne's case because of the relative equality of her and her husband's families.[48] This comparison underscores the way in which the relative social and political status of the bride's and groom's families affected the relative size of a woman's dowry and jointure. It also demonstrates that the absolute sums invested in aristocratic marriages increased as one moved upward through its ranks.

In the small number of cases when noninheriting women brought land into their marriages, they received relatively large jointures in return because real estate was the most valuable asset among the aristocracy. This was especially true when the king or queen sponsored the matches and paid all or part of the bride's dowry with crown land. In 1516, for example, Henry VIII and Katherine of Aragon financed the marriage of her maid-in-waiting, Maria Salinas, to William, Lord Willoughby. The queen promised Maria a dowry of 1,100 marks, and the king gave her the reversion of four manors in Lincolnshire.[49] In return, Lord Willoughby assigned her a jointure of 500 marks. Two years later, the king promised land worth 100 marks *per annum* to Sir Thomas Fettiplace and Elizabeth Carew, the daughter and sister of two of Henry's favorites. In return, Sir Thomas agreed to give a jointure of 100 marks, the full annual value of the land, to his intended wife. These terms make it clear that the king's generosity was a gift to the Carews, not to Fettiplace; Sir Nicholas was one of his favorites at this time.[50]

However carefully they were drawn up, marriage contracts were, of course, statements of intent, which inevitably raises questions about the frequency and scrupulousness with which they were carried out. Not surprisingly, given how much preliminary discussion and negotiation occured before they were signed and sealed, most contracts did result in legally binding, consummated marriages. This occurred in 70, or 86 percent, of the eighty-two agreements used in this project. Implementation of the financial provisions was much more uncertain, particularly whether or not wives would be assigned their agreed-upon jointures.

The prevailing understanding of the financial exchange that accompanied marriage—jointure for dowry—meant that failure to pay a woman's dowry was interpreted as nullifying her right to her jointure. When the widowed Elizabeth Clere sued her father-in-law for her jointure, he replied that she could not claim it legally because "the money [i.e., her dowry] for the which her jointure is to her made is not paid."[51] In one of the best known examples in the period, Mary, countess of Northumberland, petitioned Henry VIII for her jointure because her deceased husband—estranged from his wife and childless—had bequeathed all his land to the crown. The king replied she had no right to it because her father had never paid her dowry.[52]

Arguing from the same point of view, some men refused to complete payment of their daughters' portions when the groom or his family failed to assure her jointure. In 1517, Sir Richard Elyot; his widowed stepdaughter, Dorothy; and his wife, Dorothy's mother, explained in Chancery that they had paid only half her dowry because her father-in-law had never secured her jointure. Sir Richard affirmed his readiness to pay the remaining £40 as soon as he did so.[53] Sir John St. John stopped paying his daughter Margaret's dowry for the same reason.[54]

Because their jointures depended on payment of their dowries, women, their husbands, and their fathers-in-law shared a strong interest in their portions being paid promptly. Although married daughters had little leverage over their fathers besides appeals to their affection, they could count on support, even legal action, from their marital families should the money not be forthcoming. In 1536, for example, Parliament assigned income from estates belonging to George, earl of Huntingdon, for his daughter Dorothy's dowry because he had fallen behind in his payments.[55] Nonetheless, the records of litigation in Chancery, Star Chamber, and Requests suggest that most fathers were conscientious about paying their daughters' dowries. Only twenty-seven of 189 cases about aristocratic marriage settlements revolved around women's unpaid portions. Of these, only three involved fathers who were living at the time of the complaint. The combination of paternal affection and self-interest probably accounted for their reliability; most men cared about their daughters' economic security and expected to benefit from the matches they had negotiated for them. It made little sense for them to antagonize their daughters' husbands and in-laws. Indeed, fathers who were facing death before they had completed paying their daughters' dowries carefully ordered their executors to do so. Edward, Lord Hastings; Sir John Gresham; and Sir John Horsey left bequests of this sort to their married daughters.[56] Most litigation about the payment of dowries arose—in seventeen of the twenty-seven cases—when fathers died before they had arranged their daughters' marriages or paid their portions.[57] The defendants were most frequently their executors or feoffees (six cases) or the bride's mother or brother (three cases each).[58]

More difficulty arose about the groom's family legally establishing the bride's jointure and respecting her rights after her husband died because of their strong identification with their land. Here, more than in any other area, wives and widows remained outsiders in their marital families, which often resented their lifelong claim to their estates. Aristocratic men and their families forgot all too easily that their wives' families had paid huge sums of money for their jointures, while many heirs regarded their mothers' and stepmothers' jointures as drains on their rightful income rather than as payments on investments the women's families had made years before. Not surprisingly, therefore, challenges to women's jointure rights began the moment their marriage contracts were signed and continued throughout their lives. They came from a wide variety of people—their fathers-in-law, husbands, sons, stepsons, brothers-in-law, and husbands' executors and/or feoffees—but the underlying issue was always the same: the unwillingness of someone in the woman's marital family to accept her life interest in their estates. Ninety-nine, or 52 percent, of the 189 court cases about marriage settlements involved women's jointures.[59] There were 19 similar cases about their dower lands.

Wills contain additional evidence about the failure of women's marital families to establish or respect their jointures. In 1467, for example, Sir William Vernon left one of his lordships to his widow in "recompense of her jointure that she departed with unto her son and his wife."[60] Sir Richard Grenville bequeathed considerable property to his wife because she had consented to the sale of part of her jointure to finance his service to the king.[61] A number of men who had failed to secure the jointures of their daughters-in-law directed their sons or executors to do so.[62]

The precariousness of women's rights in their jointures and dowers perpetuated their dependence on their natal male kin. Since wives were under coverture, they could not take legal action against their fathers-in-law and husbands unless their fathers or brothers acted for them. As a result, all but two of the fourteen Chancery suits about the failure of the groom or his family to establish women's jointures were initiated by widows rather than their natal kin. This pattern may indicate that women could not count on their fathers and brothers for help of this kind.[63] But is also possible that at least some women chose not to act until they were widowed because they were reluctant to disrupt their relationships with their husbands over financial matters or feared their husbands would retaliate if they did.[64]

Some men did, of course, intervene to protect their daughters', sisters', and nieces' jointures. Sir James Tyrrell sued his daughter's father-in-law in

Chancery and withheld the last 100 marks of her dowry because he had not established the jointure promised in her marriage contract.[65] Sir John Mordaunt initiated a suit against his son-in-law to stop him from executing a fine that would destroy his daughter's title and interest in property enfeoffed for her jointure. He claimed that her husband had employed "importunate means" to gain her agreement.[66] In 1537 Sir William Gascoigne petitioned Cromwell to protect his daughter Dorothy's jointure because her husband's family had forfeited its land to the crown after the Pilgrimmage of Grace. Cromwell gave Sir William custody of the jointure lands until Dorothy's husband reached the age of 16; after that the original marriage agreement would take effect.[67]

Another strategy appears in the wills of fathers who made bequests to their sons-in-law conditional on their securing their daughters' jointures. Sir Edward Ferrers left his son-in-law and daughter £20, which was to be paid within three months of his legally establishing her jointure.[68] Sir Edmund Denny withheld half of his daughter Martha's dowry because her husband had not established the second half of her jointure.[69] Sir Thomas Markenfield was worried enough about his widowed daughter to leave her an income for as long as she remained single and unable to enjoy all her jointure lands.[70] All of these cases demonstrate the important role men played in protecting their married daughters and sisters and provide evidence of married women's continued membership in their natal families.

Within the framework set by the size of the dowries they could afford and the jointures they wanted for their daughters, fathers (or their substitutes) had to decide what characteristics they considered most important in their sons-in-law. Their wills and letters make clear that most of them considered the extent of a man's land his primary qualification as a husband. Although Thomas, Lord de la Warre, and Sir William Holles spoke in general terms about "men of substance,"[71] many fathers specified the amount of income from land they required of their sons-in-law. In 1496, Sir Robert Radcliffe said that his daughters should marry men with land worth 200 marks a year or more.[72] Half a century later, Sir John Shelton made his daughter Mary's dowry conditional on her marriage to a man with an income of £200 or £300.[73] Charles Somerset, earl of Worcester, required his daughter's husband to be worth 300 marks if his income came from inherited land, 400 marks if it did not.[74]

The other crucial financial consideration was the amount of jointure the groom or his father promised the bride. Fathers were concerned about the absolute size of their daughters' jointures and the standard of living it would provide, as well as the ratio between their jointures and their dowries. Many men required that their daughters be given a specific sum. Sir Robert Radcliffe not only indicated the minimal income his daughter's husband should have but also insisted that she be given a jointure of £40 or more.[75] Sir Edward Montague stipulated that his daughter should have a legally secure estate of £20 or more on the day of her marriage.[76]

Fathers were also keenly interested in the social status and rank of their prospective sons-in-law. John Shirley's will revoked his daughters' dowries entirely if they married men of lesser rank, and Sir Robert Lee directed his executors "to prefer every of my said daughters to convenable marriage without disparagement."[77] Some members of the nobility specified precisely the rank and status they had in mind. In 1556, Henry, earl of Sussex, directed that his daughter should lose her dowry if she married a man below the degree of knight or his heir apparent.[78] William, Lord Lovel, left his granddaughter a dowry on the condition that she marry a peer or a peer's heir.[79] Henry, first earl of Cumberland, actually calibrated the size of his daughter's portion to the rank of her husband: if the groom were an earl or his heir apparent, she would receive £1,000; if a baron or his heir apparent, 1,000 marks; if a knight, only 800 marks.[80]

Less explicit evidence exists of fathers who selected their daughters' husbands for strategic political reasons rather than for social status and wealth. The contrast may be at least partly a result of the nature of the extant sources since most of our information comes from marriage contracts, wills, and court cases, which were more likely to focus on financial than political issues. The most obvious and dramatic exceptions to this generalization occur in the tiny group of families who were closely linked to the crown and had hopes of marrying their offspring to the king's children or dominating the government. The Nevills and Plantagenets in the fifteenth century and the Howards, Greys, Dudleys, and Seymours in the sixteenth fall into this category. The political feuds and conspiracies of Edward VI's reign, to give one example, led to a number of matches of this kind.[81] In 1550, the duke of Northumberland's eldest son married the duke of Somerset's daughter Anne to effect a reconciliation between them.[82] Northumberland's plot to put Lady Jane Grey on the throne led to two other marriages. His son Guildford married Lady Jane herself; his ally, the earl of Pembroke, betrothed his heir to her younger sister Katherine. When it became clear that the conspiracy would fail, Pembroke broke off the match and had it declared invalid.[83]

Strategic political marriages outside these exalted circles are much less evident in extant sources. In the mid-1530s, the third duke of Norfolk suggested such a marriage to Sir William Musgrave, who had sacrificed his position in the North by accusing William, Lord Dacre, of treason. Norfolk told him the only way he could regain his reputation was by marrying his heir to Dacre's daughter and warned that if he refused, Dacre would ruin him and his family.[84] Three decades later, in another case, the sixth earl of Shrewsbury supported his sister's marriage to Thomas, Lord Wharton, as part of a general reconciliation between Wharton, the earl of Cumberland, and Lord Dacre.[85] In addition, the tight marital connections over many generations between neighboring families were almost certainly conscious attempts to per-petuate their control of county and local affairs, although such motives do not appear in marriage contracts and related documents.

Fathers were even less explicit in surviving sources about the moral charac-ter or personal qualities they desired in their sons-in-law than about their po-litical assets. In this respect, Sir Anthony Denny and Sir William Holles were unusual among the testators of male wills used in this project. Holles stated specifically that he wanted his granddaughter to wed "an honest man, of good name and fame," as well as one "of substance."[86] Denny expressed the hope that his daughters would marry his wards, "who being the heirs of my friends, for the good qualities and virtues of their parents . . . I . . . obtained to be coupled in matrimony with mine." He added that his "greatest care was that my posterity and those that should be coupled in matrimony with them might rightly be taught the love and fear of God, their obedience to their sovereign lord, and duty to their country." Denny was a known reformer, and his will is unique in its extensive attention to the religious education of his children and the character of their mates. But he also required his sons-in-law to possess or be heirs to 400 marks a year.[87] Even in the most dramatic and exceptional case on record, therefore, character was an addition to, not a substitute for, wealth, which reinforces the argument that material issues were the primary consider-ation when parents negotiated their daughters' marriages.

The ubiquity of marriages arranged by parents for economic and political rea-sons does not mean that they were indifferent to their daughters' happiness or always unresponsive to their wishes. In 1477, Richard Fowler, chancellor of the Duchy of Lancaster, willed that his son Richard should marry Anne Stradling if she became an heir "in case he and she can find in their hearts to love either other by way of marriage and else not."[88] Sir Anthony Denny explained at length that when he bought the wardships of potential mates for his children, he intended that "they being brought up with my children, and my children with them, [and] their conditions and qualities being known one to the other, they may . . . one liking the other to be joined in matrimony." He wanted his wife and executors to look for "tokens and agreement of faithful love" before they allowed the couples to wed.[89] In a similar spirit, Sir William Drury bought a ward to marry to his daughter Elizabeth but ordered his executors to sell the wardship and use the proceeds as Elizabeth's dowry if either of them objected to the match.[90] Occasionally, a father made a single daughter one of his coex-ecutors, which gave her some legal power over the dowry he bequeathed her and a greater voice in the arrangement of her marriage.[91]

Many parents were willing to provide the necessary dowries and negotiate appropriate jointures for daughters who fell in love with men of appropriate status and wealth. Elizabeth Brews's and Margaret Paston's support of the mar-riage between their offspring, Margery Brews and John Paston III, is one of the best-known examples.[92] Sir Edward Willoughby of Wollaton supported his daughter's love match despite the objections of the prospective groom's father. At one point, Sir Edward even suggested that the couple marry secretly.[93] Sir Edward Grevill allowed his ward, Elizabeth Willoughby, coheir of Robert, first Lord Willoughby de Broke, to marry his younger son Foulke instead of his heir, as he had originally planned, because she preferred him.[94]

What neither parents nor guardians would accept or support were love matches that disparaged their daughters. Margaret Paston's complete break with her daughter Margery after her clandestine marriage to the family bailiff is well known.[95] Less so is the Pastons' successful intervention in the relationship of Margery's sister Anne with another family servant, whom they fired.[96] After twelve years, Thomas, Lord Wentworth had still not forgiven his sister Thomasine for eloping with a man of lower status, and continued to withhold the dowry their father had bequeathed her on the condition that she marry with his consent.[97] Sir Richard Grenville did pardon his daughter for marrying Richard Lee without his permission, but only because he was under considerable pressure to do so from Lee's patron, Thomas Cromwell, then Henry VIII's most powerful minister, and Lord Lisle, his uncle by marriage.[98]

Margery Paston and Thomasine Wentworth were exceptional in risking their financial security, class position, and relationship with their families by defiantly marrying downward. In the overwhelming number of cases, the material and ideological structures that defined aristocratic culture collaborated to secure women's compliance with the system of arranged marriages. On the prescriptive level, girls were raised from their earliest years to regard marriage as the most desirable goal for their adult lives, while religious and educational writers insisted that the fifth commandment, with its absolute injunction on children to obey their fathers and mothers, included parental control over their marriages.[99] On the practical level, aristocratic women tried to prevent their daughters and nieces from becoming attached to or eloping with unsuitable men by keeping them busy with needlework and other activities. As we saw in the last chapter, they spoke explicitly about occupying them when they left them their samplers and patterns.

Parents and guardians also took the precaution of arranging appropriate matches for their charges when they were relatively young. Early first marriages inevitably reflected parental decisions rather than those of the girls. Forty-one Yorkist or early Tudor aristocratic brides in a sample of fifty-three were 16 or under at their first marriages; twelve of the forty were 12 or less, and only three were 21 or more. A majority—twenty-nine of the fifty-three—were between the ages of 13 and 16. This age distribution is probably weighted in favor of early marriages since a disproportionate number of the fifty-three women—sixteen, or almost 30 percent—were heiresses at a time when only 12 percent of the land of the aristocracy descended to women.[100]

The incentives for families to marry heiresses very young was particularly strong. Most important, married heiresses did not become royal wards no matter how young they were when their fathers died, and their families avoided the crown's collecting the income from their land during their minorities and arranging the girls' marriages to serve the king's interests. In addition, their families often needed the reverse dowry they received from the groom or his father. Since heiresses were especially desirable brides, families were tempted to exploit their marriages as soon as possible. Sir William Plumpton married Margaret, his granddaughter and coheir, to John Roucliffe and sent her to live with Roucliffe's family before she was 5.[101] Sir Thomas Cheyney's 9-year-old daughter and heir was already married when he died in 1514.[102] Not one of the fifty-three women who married at 17 or older was an heiress. On the other hand, the most common marriage age of the thirty-six noninheriting women was 13 to 16; five of the the girls were 12 or less. In other words, early marriage was the norm among the aristocracy, although most child marriages involved heiresses. The contrast is another indication of the fact that inheritance rather than gender was the critical divide in aristocratic families, as we saw in the case of their provision for their daughters and younger sons.

Parents also had no compunctions about using their control over their daughters' dowries to compel them to agree to matches they or their executors advocated. Of 257 fathers who left portions to their daughters, 77 (30 percent) made their bequests conditional on their marrying men selected or approved by people they appointed for that purpose. In 1455, Thomas, Lord Hoo and Hastings, provided that his daughters' portions were contingent on their being "ruled, governed, and married" by his wife and brother.[103] Sir John Danvers stated emphatically that his daughters should have their dowries only "if they be of good rule and disposition, and to be ordered by mine executors. And else not [to] have a penny worth of my goods."[104] Sir Richard Grenville ordered his executors to reduce his daughter's dowry by half if she married without her mother's consent.[105] Grandfathers and uncles attached similar conditions to their gifts. Sir William Essex stipulated that his executors should withhold his granddaughters' portions if "upon lightness" they married "any unmeet or light person without the assent of her father and mother and my executors."[106] Even if testators omitted such provisions, in practice their executors had as much control over the girls' marriages as their fathers would have had, given the girls' young ages and the fact that the executors had physical possession of the girls' portions or were empowered to raise them from their deceased fathers' estates.

For their part, aristocratic daughters were well aware that they needed their parents' assistance and large dowries to marry within their class. Their petitions to the courts of Chancery and Requests indicate that they had no illusions about their dependence on their dowries. Sometime, in the 1460s, for example, Katherine and Anne Drury, whose father had died in 1450, sued their mother, stepfather, and his feoffees for withholding their portions "to their great hurt and to the hinderance of their marriage."[107] Dorothy Grey, daughter of the first marquess of Dorset, sued his executors to give her her dowry, whereby she was "like to lose her preferment," although her mother and stepfather had arranged a match for her.[108]

In some cases, aristocratic mothers may have been more sympathetic to daughters who married without consent than fathers, brothers, and other male kin. Although women usually conformed to the dominant values and practices of their class, their response to this situation was one of the occasions when their distinct experience as females and their lesser identification with the interests of the patrilineage came into play. Their lack of voice in their own first marriages seems to have made them more sensitive to the feelings of daughters who faced the prospect of unattractive matches or were being forced to give up men they loved. Katherine Willoughby, duchess of Suffolk, married at the age of 14 to her 49-year-old guardian, wrote the only explicit contemporary condemnation of the arranged marriage by a member of the aristocracy uncovered in the course of my research: "I cannot tell what more unkindness one of us might work more wickedly than to bring our children into so miserable a state [as] not to choose by their own liking such as they must profess so strait a bond and so great a love to forever."[109]

As women who had faced widowhood themselves and experienced their dependence on their jointures, aristocratic mothers also worried about the economic security of daughters who married without the legal protection of marriage contracts. In her 1527 will, Dame Elizabeth Baynham stated that her deceased husband had left their daughter Jane a dowry of 200 marks "so that she were married by mine assent and advice." Instead, Jane had married "hastily and unknown to me." Dame Elizabeth expressed concern, not about her daughter's disobedience, but that because of her precipitous action "I had never communication with her husband for a jointure of land that conveniently I ought to have required of him for her." To make sure her daughter was protected financially, she left 200 marks in trust with her (i.e., the testator's) brother and instructed him to give it to Jane's husband after he had assured a jointure of £20 to her. If he refused, her executors were to keep the money for Jane in case she was widowed.[110] In the same year, Cecily, marchioness of Dorset, left a dowry of £1,000 to her daughter Elizabeth, countess of Kildare, although she married "without the assent of her friends, contrary to the will of the lord marquess her father, by reason whereof the said £1,000 . . . ought not to be paid." Cecily explained that she was giving Elizabeth the money nonetheless "forasmuch as the said marriage is honorable and I and all her friends have cause to be content with the same."[111] The "honorable" character of the marriage almost certainly lay in the high rank of Elizabeth's husband. More surprisingly, perhaps, the countess of Bath forgave her widowed daughter Frances, Lady Fitzwarren, when she eloped with William Barnaby, the countess's steward, to her mother's "grief and disquietness."[112]

But these cases were clearly exceptional. The combination of their dependence on their dowries, their young age at first marriage, the obvious advantages of marrying socially and politically prominent, wealthy men, and the force of a culture that insisted that disobedience to one's parents was a mortal sin meant that the great majority of Yorkist and early Tudor women married men chosen for them by their fathers. When men died before their daughters were betrothed, they usually delegated their authority in this area to the girls' mothers. Of 257 fathers who bequeathed dowries to their daughters in their wills, 168 (65 percent) did so.[113] When they designated other relatives to perform this function, they turned most frequently to their daughters' brothers—in 82, or 32 percent, of the cases. They named other male kin, their daughters' paternal and maternal uncles and brothers-in-law, much less often.[114] Very few fathers—only 5—nominated women other than their widows for this role.

Although their marriages vitally affected their emotional lives, financial security, and social and political status, women's youth and legal and economic dependence at the time of their first marriages made them the objects of other people's decisions and agendas rather than active participants in the choice of their husbands. Taken as a whole, the arrangement of women's marriages was probably the moment when the combined force of the patriarchal structures under which they lived subjugated them most effectively and with the most enduring results. The vast majority married men chosen for them by their parents or their substitutes and gave little more than formal consent to the matches at their weddings. Nonetheless, even this disempowered situation allowed a few daughters room to maneuver if they were determined enough and had receptive parents. Many mothers and fathers cautioned their executors against forcing their daughters into matches to which they objected, and a small number even forgave them for eloping. Overall, parents controlled the process of arranging their daughters' marriages, but they could not—and perhaps did not want to—exclude them from the process completely.

Fortunately, the way in which marriages were arranged did not determine the character of the unions that resulted. Although most matches were contracted for worldly and practical reasons, many couples developed loving relationships or, failing that, mutually satisfying partnerships. However passive they were before they married, young brides could and did mature into confident, competent women who succeeded in the complex careers of wives. The next chapter focuses on these careers.

Sir John Donne and Lady Elizabeth Donne. By courtesy of the National Portrait Gallery, London.

CHAPTER 4. WIVES—

PARTNERSHIP AND PATRIARCHY

*W*IVES WHO were living in households headed by their husbands occupied the most powerful, socially desirable position open to aristocratic women in Yorkist and early Tudor England, with the exception of the tiny number who combined marriage with appointments at court. Wifehood constituted a career that incorporated reproductive, managerial, political, and social functions essential to the survival and prosperity of their husbands' patrilineages. With few exceptions, wives devoted their energy and attention to their marital families and the households in which they resided from the time they married. But these responsibilities required them to look beyond their residences and to maintain ties with their natal kin, more distant marital relatives, and friends at court since they needed these networks to advance their husbands' and sons' careers and arrange their daughters' marriages. Wives also remained important to their families of birth by serving as intermediaries for them with their husbands and in-laws. Wives who carried out these duties successfully were rewarded materially for their accomplishments and earned the love and respect of their husbands and the admiration of their wider circle of family and friends.

Paradoxically, given wives' practical importance to their husbands and marital relatives, they had far fewer legal rights than single women and widows. The doctrine of coverture merged their identity with that of their husbands, whom the common law literally defined as their barons or lords. Indeed, it subordinated them to their spouses far more completely than feudal law ever subordinated vassals to their lords. Describing their husbands as their barons captured the essential nature of the spousal relationship as a political one, involving an unequal distribution of power and the subjection of wives. This feudal metaphor spread far beyond legal circles. *The Book of the Knight of the Tower* described a woman's husband as her lord in the fourteenth century

as did the humanist Vives in the sixteenth.[1] The clergy also articulated and defended this construction of the husband/wife relationship. Sermons and di-
dactic literature based on religious precepts traced the subjection of wives to
divine law and lectured women endlessly about their duty to submit to their
spouses.[2] Thomas Becon, an early English reformer, compared disobedient
wives to beasts.[3]

Women's legal subjection and economic dependence on their husbands
and parental arrangement of their marriages might be expected to produce
passive wives and hierarchical, emotionally distant marital relationships. But
most of the extant evidence points in the opposite direction. Many aristocratic couples developed affectionate, even loving ties to each other as they
cooperated to manage their households and estates, care for their children,
and promote the fortunes of their families. The frequent absence of the male
head of household meant that wives were often required to take initiative, act
energetically, and make decisions about specific matters on their own. In this
context, married women praised for obedience were neither passive nor dependent on specific instructions about how to handle everyday business.
Rather, they identified with, and were therefore committed to advancing,
their husbands' ambitions and those of their marital families as their mates
defined them. They accepted the patriarchal authority and power that shaped
their relationships with their spouses, obeyed directions when they were
forthcoming, and avoided opposing their own wills or desires to their husbands'. As long as they remained obedient in this sense, competent wives
were able to claim a considerable degree of agency, shape their lives in satisfying directions, and exercise substantial authority and power within their
households. This chapter examines how the tension between the practicalities
of everyday life, the legal reality of coverture, and the culture's persistent de-
mand for female submission shaped the experience of aristocratic wives and
how individual couples and women modified the dominant model of wifehood to fit their own relationships and needs.[4]

Aristocratic women's careers evolved gradually as they moved through a uxorial cycle that transformed them from inexperienced brides into mature, capable wives.[5] Because they married young and their husbands were usually of a
similar age, most of them lived in their parents' or in-laws' households after
their weddings and remained under their tutelage. In the late fifteenth century, three of Sir John Howard's daughters, Anne, Margaret, and Catherine,
wed before they were 16 and remained in their father's household. In two
cases, their husbands were their father's wards and were also in residence. In
the third, the 14-year-old groom continued to reside with his mother and
stepfather. The family accounts indicate that as long as they lived at home, the
Howards treated the girls like any dependent daughters.[6]

Arrangements of this sort continued well into the sixteenth century. Jane

Paget and Thomas Kitson, who married in their mid- to late teens in 1557 or 1558, lived with his mother, the countess of Bath.[7] In June 1558, Jane visited her parents while one of her sisters was lying-in at their London residence. Her father, Sir William, asked the countess for permission to extend Jane's stay with them. He claimed she was suffering from a conditon he called green sickness, which he hoped doctors in the city would be able to cure.[8] A year and a half later, Jane visited her parents once again. On this occasion Lady Paget thought her daughter was ill with consumption. She wanted her to remain at home indefinitely and asked the countess to allow Jane's husband to join her. The countess's servant doubted Lady Paget's diagnosis—he remarked that her father thought Jane had never looked better—and suggested her mother was inventing an excuse to keep her in London.[9]

As the Pagets' situation demonstrates, parents, rather than the young couple, decided where they would live. The decision often rested upon who had agreed to support them until the groom was old enough to receive the income from his wife's jointure or, if his father were dead, until he came of age and took possession of his inheritance. In 1458, the first duke of Buckingham assumed custody of Constance Green, the heiress marrying his younger son, and promised to support them.[10] When Sir Thomas Lestrange's 17-year-old heir Nicholas married Ellen Fitzwilliam, daughter of Sir William, in 1528, he agreed to "govern" and support them and any children they had until Nicholas was 21. Nicholas, his wife, and his children continued to live in his parents' household even after he came of age, remaining in a semi-dependent position until his father died thirteen years later.[11]

The pattern of young marriage and residence with the brides' parents or in-laws meant that many women gave birth to some or all of their children before they had households of their own. Isabel Babthorpe Plumpton, wife of William, esq., married in 1496 and spent her entire married life at Plumpton, her husband's family's chief manor, where she gave birth to her two sons. Her father-in-law, Sir Robert, headed the household until 1515 and died in 1523; her mother-in-law survived him and continued to live with them.[12] Ursula Pole Stafford gave birth to her first child in the household of her father-in-law, the third duke of Buckingham.[13] Her contemporary, Ellen Fitzwilliam Lestrange, gave birth to all five of her children in her in-laws' household.[14] The presence of their mothers or mothers-in-law, who could supply practical assistance and emotional support during their confinements and deliveries, was one of the obvious benefits of these living arrangements for young wives.

Wives entered the next phase of the uxorial cycle when they and their husbands became heads of their own households. If their fathers-in-law were dead, this stage began when their mates turned 21. Sir Robert Plumpton's daughter Anne and her husband, Germain Pole, lived with him during Pole's minority but moved to his estate in Derbyshire soon after he came of age in

1504.[15] Henry Grey, marquess of Dorset, and his wife took control of the Greys' family seat shortly after his twenty-first birthday.[16] This transition was delayed, often for years, if women's fathers-in-law were alive when their husbands came of age because only the wealthiest families could establish their heirs in sufficiently grand, separate households. The future second earl of Cumberland and his wife were unusual, even in a privileged class, in having their own establishment at Brougham Castle while his parents resided at Skipton.[17] Ellen Lestrange had a more typical experience. She was married for seventeen years before her father-in-law died and she became mistress of her own household. Even then, she may have felt some doubt about her authority since her mother-in-law remained in residence.[18] As we have just seen, Isabel Plumpton waited even longer to assume the full duties of aristocratic wifehood.[19]

When wives assumed control of their households, they often felt insecure about their position and anxious about proving their value as partners in managing the family enterprise. The first countess of Rutland asked her father, one of Sir Thomas Lovell's executors, to use his position to do as much as possible for her husband, one of Lovell's beneficiaries. "I beseech you," she wrote, "as ever you loved me, that there may be no fault found in you."[20] Another noblewoman, Elizabeth, countess of Kildare, wife of the ninth earl, petitioned Cardinal Wolsey, then Henry VIII's chief minister, "to be good and gracious . . . unto my lord my husband. . . . That it may appear unto [his servants] . . . that your grace is so much all the better unto them at this my humble petition." She explained that she was especially anxious to assist her husband because her mother had not yet paid her dowry.[21]

Young wives did not always find growing into their role easy. Even Margaret Paston, who is legendary among historians for her forcefulness, had difficulty in asserting herself as long as her mother-in-law, Agnes, remained involved in Paston affairs. In 1448, four years after her husband inherited his estates, Margaret's account of her efforts to persuade Lady Morley not to sue him reflects her fear about appearing to be ineffective. Margaret was humiliated when Lady Morley refused her request and then yielded to Agnes.[22] Another young wife, Anne, countess of Oxford, failed to influence her spendthrift husband, the fourteenth earl, or cooperate with him in managing their affairs. In desperation she appealed to Cardinal Wolsey to pressure him into reforming.[23]

As they gained experience, most wives emerged as their husbands' de facto, if junior, partners in supervising their families and managing their assets. Once women had proved their competence, the majority of men delegated considerable power and control over their resources to them, whatever they thought in the abstract about female abilities and male authority. Their huge establishments demanded an enormous amount of supervision. The head of the household, his wife, and his children formed the core of the household, but it included scores of others—widowed parents, unmarried siblings, married children and their spouses, adolescent offspring of their friends and kin who were "in service" with them, and household and estate servants of every description and status. Although aristocratic men employed professional and semiprofessional household and estate officials to assist them, no substitute existed for competent wives who shared their husbands' interests and on whose loyalty they could count. Wives' supervision was particularly important because their husbands were frequently away, visiting their scattered estates, pursuing legal business in London, and attending the king or otherwise serving the crown. In their absence, men needed someone who shared, even identified with, their interests to take charge of their households and estates and to keep them informed of local news that ought to be passed on to the crown. In times of crisis, they depended on their wives to protect their families and property until they could return or the central government could act.[24] William Harleston's warning to his nephew, Sir William Stonor, after his first wife died, recognizes this reality: "And moreover, sir, for God's sake beware now, for now ye may break your household with honor and worship, now after the decease of my good lady your wife."[25]

As a result, virtually all the substantial archives on Yorkist and early Tudor aristocratic families document wives who were actively engaged in managing their households and families. The women who cut such large figures in the published Paston, Plumpton, Stonor, and Lisle letters are well known in this respect; but material about scores of other wives demonstrates that they were not exceptional in the initiative, energy, and competence with which they carried out the practical duties of aristocratic wifehood.[26] Indeed, the fragile nature of many of the extant documents—those from the Tyrell and Townshend families, for example—strongly suggest that only a tiny fraction of this kind of evidence has survived.[27] Anne Petre, wife of Sir William, and Elizabeth, wife of William, Lord Dacre, are among the less well-known women who performed these functions. Lady Petre kept a detailed record of income and expenses during the final illness of her first husband, John Tyrrell of Heron. Fifteen years later, during her second marriage, she managed considerable amounts of money for herself and her children. Petre's steward recorded that she gave him the hefty sum of £327 12s. 9½d. between December 1554 and November 1555 alone.[28]

Lady Dacre, who lived in the far north, near the troubled borders with Scotland, acted on her husband's behalf in a wide variety of domestic and public matters in his absence. After announcing the birth and christening of their daughter, Elizabeth, in March 1534, for example, she passed on news she had received from spies in Scotland.[29] In his reply from London, Lord Dacre addressed her as his "most entirely well beloved bedfellow" and expressed his pleasure and that of her father, the earl of Shrewsbury, at the "most comfortable news of your good expedience and deliverance." He also asked her to

collect some revenue from his estates to pay the fee he owed Sir Thomas Clifford, to install one of his servants as bailiff of Horseley Forest after pulling
down some enclosures there, and to assist a clergyman he was sending to collect his income in Yorkshire and Durham.[30] Later that month Lady Elizabeth
sent him a lengthy report on the state of the borders and the ongoing difficulties with Sir William Musgrave, who accused her husband of treason in
May.[31] She went to London shortly after his arrest to petition the king on his
behalf, although her father, the earl of Shrewsbury, told Thomas Cromwell,
"She hath not been accustomed or brought up in any affairs or uncomfortable
business, but after the homely fashion of the country."[32]

Despite Shrewsbury's demurrer, many women had a working knowledge
of the law and legal procedure.[33] Lady Agnes Plumpton was fully conversant
with the legal technicalities involved when, in 1502, she and her son William
evicted tenants who would not pay their rent from some of her husband's
property in Yorkshire and distrained their cattle for the money they owed.[34]
Two decades later, the wife of Thomas, Lord Darcy, went to London to assist
a widowed cousin, Katherine Mirfield, in responding to a subpeona about her
deceased husband's inheritance. Lord Darcy clearly thought she was fully
competent to deal with the complicated legal issues involved and asked his
lawyer to give her full credence.[35] Lady Margaret Shelton wrote a long letter
to Sir John Gates in 1544 about the necessity of breaking the entail on her husband's lands, which showed she fully understood such intricacies of property
law as the entail, fine, recovery, and enfeoffment.[36]

This expertise served wives well throughout their marriages as they participated in the land transactions that were a constant concern to the aristocracy.
Heiresses and women in second and third marriages, who held dower or jointure lands from their previous husbands, were especially active in managing
real estate. Many of the land transfers in which they participated were, of
course, quite routine. In 1468, Rose Merston, wife of Sir John, sold the reversion of the manor of Tixhale in Staffordshire; in 1490, Edward, Lord Hastings,
and his wife, Mary, made a joint grant of various ecclesiastical benefices to
his brother and three other men; in 1547, Sir Fulke Grevill and his wife sold
Wardour Castle, manor, and park, part of Lady Grevill's inheritance, to Sir
Thomas Arundell.[37] Katherine Willoughby, duchess of Suffolk, one of the
greatest heiresses of her generation, probably executed dozens of grants and
leases during her long life; twenty-nine survive in the Lincolnshire Archives
Office. Of these, she executed fourteen alone, five with her first husband,
Charles, duke of Suffolk, and ten with her second, Richard Bertie.[38] Many
wives also had enough expertise to promote or block contentious transfers of
land. In 1510, for example, Lady Elizabeth Lucy recounted the convoluted history of her ultimately unsuccessful efforts to secure title to Stratford upon
Fosse, which her first husband's uncle had promised to sell him, in the face of
determined opposition by Sir Richard Clement, who married the uncle's

widow. Her account exhibited an easy familiarity with the technicalities of the fine and recovery and the way in which they might be used to thwart her.[39]

Looking in detail at two exemplary women—Lady Anne Lestrange and Eleanor, countess of Rutland—will provide a fuller, more concrete picture of the model of aristocratic wifehood outlined above. For both women, wifehood constituted a career—a set of activities that formed the center of their lives and defined their place in society. Their families' appreciation of their competence and the importance of their activities was evident in the respect and power they gained as they performed their roles successfully. Lady Anne Lestrange was the daughter of Nicholas, Lord Vaux, a successful courtier under Henry VII and Henry VIII, and wife of Sir Thomas Lestrange, head of a well-established Norfolk family.[40] The Lestranges married in 1501 when Anne was 7 and Thomas 10. Anne gave birth to Nicholas, her oldest son, between 1511 and 1513. He was probably the first of her thirteen or more children since aristocratic parents rarely allowed their offspring to consummate their marriages before they were 16.[41] In 1515, at the age of 24, Thomas inherited Hunstanton and the other Lestrange estates from a first cousin.[42]

Lady Anne's activities are documented in household accounts that list all the Lestrange's cash outlays, no matter how small, and name all the visitors who dined at Hunstanton. For historians interested in the uxorial cycle, the Lestrange accounts track the development of a woman who married as a child and gradually grew into her role as a wife. The earliest annual accounts used here began in September 1519. They show Anne, then 25 and pregnant, playing a relatively marginal role in the Lestrange household. She occasionally ordered clothes for her children and once received a small lump sum for their expenses and hers.[43] The accounts for the early and mid-1520s create a similar impression.[44] By 1530, however, Lady Anne was supervising both the Lestrange household and estates and keeping detailed accounts of her cash transactions.[45] This striking change coincided with two major developments: Lady Anne had stopped having children, and her husband had become prominent at court because he was related to the Boleyns and supported Henry VIII's divorce from Katherine of Aragon. In 1532, Sir Thomas was among the royal servants who accompanied the king to introduce Anne Boleyn to Francis I at Calais. In 1533, he attended their wedding and Anne's coronation.[46] In his absence, Lady Lestrange managed their affairs in Norfolk.

The accounts for 1533–1534 provide a fair representation of Lady Anne's activities during this period. She received rent and tithes from the Lestranges' tenants, profits from the sale of wood and malt, her husband's fee from the Abbot of Ramsey, and money Sir Thomas collected and sent to her.[47] She used the money to pay their servants and rents they owed, to buy supplies for the household, to purchase clothes and other necessities for the children, to make repairs, and to reward or reimburse the scores of people who ran their errands and delivered goods and letters.[48] Lady Anne also sent her husband cash when he needed it.[49] In addition to such routine expenses, Lady Anne paid her mother-in-law's annuity; installments on her daughter Alice's dowry; and the bequest of Sir Roger Lestrange, her husband's uncle, to Gonville Hall, Cambridge.[50] She also supplied funds for a number of land transactions, including the lease of a manor that cost the substantial sum of £116 13s. 4d.[51]

The accounts indicate that Lady Anne rarely left Hunstanton. The only recorded time she traveled outside of Norfolk was in 1520, when she journeyed to Northamptonshire, perhaps to visit her father, whose main residence was in that county. Two years later, she made a much shorter journey to Walsingham, the most important English pilgrimage site after Canterbury, which was about 15 miles from Hunstanton.[52] Otherwise Lady Anne remained very close to home. With a single exception, when she and her husband visited his distant kinsman, Sir Roger Woodhouse, she does not even seem to have reciprocated the endless visits reflected in the Lestranges' accounts.[53] Since the Lestranges' guests included many wives, Lady Anne appears to have been unusual in this respect. Frequent pregnancies or health problems may explain her immobility.

In any case, Lady Anne was not isolated at Hunstanton, where she received a steady flow of aristocratic female visitors. In 1519–1520, they included Lady Elizabeth Woodhouse, Sir Roger's wife, who assisted her during her month-long confinement; Margaret Lestrange, another aunt; Lady Elizabeth Robsart; and Anne Boleyn's first cousin, Anne Shelton.[54] The guests in 1526 again included Lady Robsart and Anne Shelton—now married and identified as Mistress Knyvett—suggesting their ongoing friendship with the Lestranges. The Knyvetts actually visited Hunstanton more than once that year. The first time, Elizabeth Boleyn, the future queen's mother, accompanied them. On another occasion, the Knyvetts stayed for a week and a half.[55] The most frequent guests were Sir Thomas's sister Catherine Hastings and her husband. Sometimes they came together; sometimes Catherine came alone.[56] The Lestranges also entertained Lady Catherine Lovell, Anne Lovell, Lady Bedingfield, and Mary Mordaunt that year.[57] All these women lived within 40 miles of Hunstanton, suggesting a pattern of sociability concentrated in relatively small local areas. These women journeyed outside their neighborhoods infrequently, with two exceptions, Elizabeth Boleyn and Anne Shelton Knyvett. They both belonged to important court families and traveled regularly between Norfolk, London, and the royal palaces along the Thames where Henry VIII usually resided.

Offices in the queen's household, the major reason aristocratic women left their households for extended periods, modified the pattern of wifehood evident in the life of Lady Anne Lestrange. Eleanor, countess of Rutland, lady-in-waiting to four of Henry VIII's queens, exemplies this somewhat different type of aristocratic wifehood. The countess married Thomas, first earl of

Rutland, by 1523 and gave birth to the first of her eleven or more children, a daughter named Anne, that year or soon thereafter.[58] Her last child, Katherine, was born in 1539.[59] The countess's career at court flourished during the same years she was bearing children. Her first recorded appearance there occurred when she attended Anne Boleyn at the ceremony that created her marchioness of Pembroke in 1532.[60] She probably served as one of Anne's ladies-in-waiting after she became queen and certainly held that position under Jane Seymour, Anne of Cleves, and Catherine Howard.[61] During this period, she traveled regularly between the court; the Rutlands' main residence at Belvoir Castle, Lincolnshire; their London mansion at Holywell; and their manor at Endfield, Middlesex, just outside the city.[62] Her mobile lifestyle differs dramatically from Lady Lestrange's.

Residence at court and in London or its vicinity opened a rich social life to Lady Rutland. She developed friendships with other members of the queen's Privy Chamber, particularly Lady Coffin; the countess of Sussex; Lady Beauchamp; and the duchess of Suffolk. In 1539 she named her last daughter Katherine for the duchess, who visited Belvoir Castle at least once.[63] Lady Coffin sent a gift after the child's birth. Some years later, Lady Coffin married the countess's brother-in-law, Sir Richard Manners, as her third husband.[64] Lady Rutland also became friends with such women as Honor, Lady Lisle, who came to court occasionally but did not hold offices there.[65]

Since members of the court were unlikely to travel as far north as Belvoir Castle, the Rutlands entertained at Holywell, their London mansion. In July 1536, they used Holywell for the triple wedding of their eldest son and the heirs of the earls of Westmorland and Oxford, the major social event of the year outside the court itself. All the highest ranking members of the peerage attended, while the king himself appeared after dinner to dance and feast at a late-night banquet.[66] Three years later, the Rutlands used their London home to celebrate their daughter Gertrude's marriage to the earl of Shrewsbury's heir.[67]

The countess's peripatetic existence prevented her from supervising the Rutlands' numerous households or recording their daily expenses, as Lady Lestrange did at Hunstanton. Instead, the earl employed a treasurer who kept records of their expenditures. The records sometimes noted they were making payments "by my Lady's commandment."[68] In addition, Lady Rutland occasionally paid for extraordinary or nonrecurring items on her own, keeping separate accounts of her expenditures. During the year beginning December 1530, for example, she purchased satin for a nightgown for her husband, paid a glazier to make a window for the parish church at Endfield, rewarded servants who delivered gifts and other goods to her, paid for New Year's gifts for the king, and rewarded itinerant entertainers such as minstrels. The countess also paid some of her children's expenses, although, once again, she was far less likely to make routine purchases for them than Lady Lestrange. Her disbursements included unusual items such as her eldest son's dancing lessons, a "physic" to cure the children's worms, and a bow and arrows for Anne.[69] In addition, she assumed responsibility for payments to her husband's brothers and married sisters. Although these occasionally involved large sums, such as the final installments on the dowries of two of her sisters-in-law, they were more likely to be one-time gifts or the modest allowances the earl gave his sisters.[70] The countess explicitly noted when she spent money "by my lord's commandment," which suggests that she usually acted independently.[71]

Lady Rutland's duties at court, high rank, and multiple households therefore created a variation on Lady Lestrange's model of mature wifehood. Because of her frequent absences from home and itinerant lifestyle, she could not assume day-to-day responsibilities for her children or domestic arrangements. Nonetheless, like her husband, who was also often away from Belvoir, she played an essential part in supervising their joint affairs. When it came to crucial issues, such as finding husbands for her daughters and negotiating the terms of their matches, she was very much involved. In a letter to her father, written from Holywell, for example, she reported the apparent failure of her negotiations for a match between one of her daughters and an unnamed gentleman. "Howsoever it goeth," she wrote, "I trust by your good help, and with the help of my lord, to provide her of another as good as he." The countess's wording and use of the first-person singular indicate that she had taken, and expected to continue to take, initiative in this area.[72] Likewise, in 1539, she, not the earl, paid the first installment of their daughter Gertrude's dowry.[73] Her husband's confidence in her was evident in the will he wrote in 1542 before departing to fight in the wars in Scotland.[74] In addition to naming her one of his executors and leaving her all his jewels, plate, and household goods, he assigned her land worth almost £700 a year for her jointure and dower—far more than the traditional third—because he trusted her "to be loving, benevolent, and favorable to our children."[75]

Remarriage, a relatively common experience since a majority of aristocratic women married more than once, created still another type of wifehood because women in second and third marriages almost always had heavy additional obligations as executors of their deceased husbands' estates and guardians of their noninheriting children. Their households were also more complex because they usually brought these children with them to their new residences. Their new husbands also often had children from previous marriages. Margaret, countess of Bath (d. 1561), who outlived three husbands, provides a well-documented example of this variety of aristocratic wifehood.[76] The countess, sole heir of an ordinary Middlesex gentleman, first married a successful London merchant, Thomas Kitson. They had five children, including one son. Before Kitson died in 1540, he had acquired a knighthood and a manor at Hengrave, Suffolk. In accordance with his deathbed wishes, his widow received use of the Suffolk estate for life and was appointed adminstrator of his movable goods.[77] She purchased their son's wardship from the king and continued to live at Hengrave.[78]

The countess, now a wealthy widow, as well as an heiress, remarried within the year, making a brilliant match that carried her into the inner circle of the early Tudor political and social elite and brought her to court.[79] Her new husband, Sir Richard Long, belonged to Henry VIII's Privy Chamber. During this marriage, Margaret gave birth to another son and three more daughters. When Sir Richard died in 1546, he left her two-thirds of his land as her jointure and named her sole executor of his estate.[80]

Two year later, Margaret used her still greater wealth and enhanced status to secure a title by marrying John Bourchier, second earl of Bath. Her social ambition was evident in their marriage contract, which arranged a match between her daughter Frances Kitson and the earl's heir.[81] During this, the longest lasting of her three marriages, Margaret had two more daughters. Her husband also had nine children by two former wives. The countess continued to live at Hengrave, which became the couple's main residence, although she wanted her husband's daughters to live elsewhere.[82]

Lady Bath's previous marriages had taught her enough about coverture to insist on limiting her husband's rights to the movable property she brought into their joint household. Before their wedding, he signed a prenuptial contract that included an inventory of all her possessions and gave her the right to dispose of them as freely as if she were single. The earl promised to compensate her if he diminished her goods in any way or if they were lost or stolen. He also agreed to leave her all the movable property she brought into the marriage when he died and to permit her to bequeath it by will if she predeceased him.[83] Because the countess could not enforce the agreement herself while she was married, the husbands of two of her Kitson daughters signed the document for her, which gave them standing to sue on her behalf should the necessity arise. The countess's foresight proved to be wise since her husband, who was deeply in debt, sold some of her goods to pay his creditors, although the evidence does not indicate if she agreed to the sales beforehand or not. In either case, Bath agreed to compensate her for her loss. In a bond for £1,000 signed in 1551, he promised to bequeath her all his household goods and a large proportion of his horses, livestock, corn, and farm equipment when he died.[84] The episode not only shows how prudent the countess had been to protect herself so carefully but also explains her perennial concern about her husband's extravagance.[85]

The letters among the countess of Bath, her husband, and their servants show that she was actively involved in managing their property and finances. Both the earl and his servants reported to her regularly about his estates. In her responses, the countess had no reservations about expressing her opinions.[86] Lady Bath was especially concerned about the earl's expenses and frequently cautioned him about his imprudence.[87] She reported to him angrily when she thought her husband's heir was trying to prevent his father from raising cash to pay his debts by selling some of his land and woods. She also pressured Bath to save money by spending as little time as possible in attending the queen or serving the crown.

Bath displayed the greatest confidence in his wife. In 1552, he asked her to conduct legal and other business for him in London. Five years later, he wanted her to petition the Privy Council on his behalf.[88] That same year, Bath sent her a memorandum that illustrates the wide variety of matters she handled for him: he directed her to speak to his lawyer about leasing a house to his daughter-in-law; to consider the multiple possibilities of raising money by selling one of his wards, leasing pasture, increasing the income from his fishing rights, and selling wood; and generally to advise him on how to increase his income.[89] Two days before his death, in 1561, the earl wrote an indignant letter to a nephew who had seized deeds and other evidence about his estates when he heard incorrectly that his uncle had died. Bath told him angrily that he had no intention of trusting him with any business related to his heir or inheritance. Rather, for their "greater trust and surety," everything "were to be committed to my said wife," whom he appointed sole executor of his estate.[90]

Aristocratic women's wide-ranging activities and heavy responsibilities provide the key to understanding what they and their husbands meant by obedience and love, terms and subjects that appear repeatedly in their letters and wills. Men regularly praised their wives and rewarded them materially for being obedient. In explaining his decision to appoint his wife as his sole executor in 1545, for example, Sir Philip Champernon recalled "the most obedient duty and gentleness that my said wife hath always . . . ministered and shewed unto me."[91] A decade later, Sir John Baker told his daughters that God would reward them if they were "faithful, assured, true, humble and obedient wives."[92] In a general sense, the model of the obedient wife prominent in contemporary prescriptive literature resonated positively with the aristocratic emphasis on hierarchical, patriarchal relationships. But at the same time, the prescriptive model suggested a degree of passivity and submissiveness at odds with the kind of initiative and energy at the heart of successful aristocratic wifehood. In his popular manual, *Institutione Christianae Feminae,* for example, Vives asserted that a wife should obey her husband "none otherwise than as though she had been bought into the house as a bond and handmaid."[93]

What Yorkist and early Tudor men had in mind, however, were not passive or overly submissive bondmaids but helpmates, fully capable of managing their families, households, and estates and taking initiative when necessary. When they extolled obedient wives, they had a far more capacious view of obedience in mind, the meaning of which is clarified by the frequency with which they linked it to gentleness. This linkage suggests that what was at issue was not passivity or unthinking submissiveness but willfullness. Good wives accepted their husbands' definition of their collective interests and priorities, dedicated themselves to advancing their husbands' goals, adapted to their husbands' habits and ways of life, and identified with their interests. In a revealing letter to Thomas Cromwell, asking him to be a "good lord" to her husband, Elizabeth Musgrave, wife of Sir William, explicitly connected the obligations that the marriage vows imposed on her—her identification with her husband's interests and her dependence on his moods. She told Cromwell that if her spouse had been rewarded properly for his service during the Pilgrimage of Grace, she would have had "thereby the more joy of his company." Instead, he was "pensive and discomfited . . . whose heaviness must needs be mine by God's law that hath joined us together in marriage." She asked Cromwell and the king to show him some sign of favor so that "he and I should have as merry and quiet a life as any poor couple."[94]

What is more difficult to ascertain is what fifteenth- and sixteenth-century English aristocratic women and men felt and meant when they spoke or wrote about loving their mates. They certainly did not think of marital love in romantic, erotic terms or consider "falling in love" essential to a good marriage. Rather, they belonged to a class and culture deeply suspicious of sexual passion because it led to sin and threatened the system of arranged marriages. What they seemed to mean instead was a combination of affection, fidelity, trust, and kindness, emotions that could develop between a couple after their wedding and that would facilitate their cooperation as partners in the family enterprise. Some prescriptive writers suggested that marital love should also involve a unique intensity and exclusiveness. William Harrington, a doctor of canon law, wrote, for example, that "love in marriage should exceed all other love under the love of God," while Juan Vives considered "great love for her husband" one of the two essential virtues in married women.[95]

In this context, women who married defiantly for love and defended their behavior in romantic terms were in a weak position in contemporary eyes. After her secret marriage to Charles Brandon, duke of Suffolk, for example, Mary Tudor explained to her brother, Henry VIII, that the marriage was "the thing which I desired most in the world" and spoke of her "good mind" and "affection" toward her husband. But she also carefully assured him that she had not acted "simply, carnally, or of any sensual appetite."[96] To underscore the strength and duration of her feelings and deflect charges of frivolity and light-mindedness, she reminded Henry that he had known about her feelings even before she married Louis XII of France to further his diplomatic goals and that he had promised to let her choose her next husband freely if she were widowed. Henry should not, therefore, be angry at her for marrying Brandon soon after Louis's death.[97]

That Vives, who advocated an extremely rigorous form of wifely obedience, should also champion marital love, at least on the woman's side, highlights the contemporary assumption that obedience and this kind of love were compatible, even mutually constitutive, elements of a good marriage. Similarly, Vives's contemporary, Roger Le Grande, maintained that wives should love their husbands and have a "dread of disobeying" them.[98] Members of the aristocracy would have agreed. Women's wedding vows, in which they promised to obey, serve, love, honor, and keep their spouses, set the standard for both their and their husbands' behavior.[99] Sir Thomas Wyatt advised his newly married son accordingly: "Frame well yourself to love, and rule well and honestly your wife as your fellow, and she shall love and reverence you as her head."[100]

Whatever they meant by love, many, though certainly not all, aristocratic couples believed that they experienced it in their marriages and affirmed their affection for each other in their letters. Elizabeth Stonor regularly told her husband how much she missed him and, on one occasion, referred with pleasure to the fact that he shared her feelings: "Sir, I thank you heartily that it pleased you to wish me with you with all my heart."[101] On another, she begged him to come to London because smallpox had broken out at Stonor, "wherefore I am right heavy and sorry of your being there, for the ire of pox is full contagious." If he couldn't or wouldn't come, she would go to him "for in good faith I can find it in my heart to put myself in jeopardy there as ye be . . . I thought never so long since I see you, for in truth I had well hoped that your horses should have been here at this night."[102] The earl and countess of Bath expressed similar sentiments. On one occasion, the countess thanked her husband for his "gentle letter" and remarked with obvious pleasure, "I do perceive, though your self being absent, your heart is present, the which of my part shall not be forgotten."[103] On another occasion, she thanked him for a ring he had sent her, but added, "I would have been very glad that you had brought it yourself."[104] During his absence in March 1554, she commented, "And where you write that you shall think [it] long to be there from me, not so long, my lord, as I think it until I may have you here again with me."[105] The earl was still away in May when he wrote, "praying to God shortly to send us to meet. I assure you I never thought so long. For I am weary of this life."[106]

The most extravagant expression of marital love by an aristocratic husband during the period occurred in two letters from William Paget to his friend William Petre. Paget, in Brussels on a mission for the crown, had heard, falsely as it turned out, that his wife had died. "If she be dead," he exclaimed, "I am the most unhappy man in the world and desire no longer to live, for it is the plague of God that is fallen unto me. Ah, Mr. Petre, what a loss have I."[107] Three days later, he lamented that the memory of "my most obedient, wise, gentle and chaste wife sitteth so deep in my heart that it maketh the same well near to burst for pain and anguish." He concluded that if it were not for the goodness of the king and his desire to serve him and the commonwealth, he "would desire no longer to live, for the world is but a vanity, which, as I have always thought in opinion, so now the experience of my great grief and regret doth confirm it in me."[108]

While no wives were as effusive about their feelings as Paget, recently widowed women often expressed their sense of bereavement and loss. In 1537, Lady Elizabeth Englefield said that her recently deceased husband was her "only joy and worldly comfort."[109] Lettice Lee (Tresham) regretted losing her "loving husband, whose goodness I shall ever lack."[110] The countess of Rutland wrote a distraught letter to her father, Sir William Paston, shortly before her husband's death in September 1543. In response, he cautioned her, "For God's love remember, if you should fully cast away yourself, you should not only displease God, but also hinder my lord and your children and many others." He told her to pray for "good comfort and counsel" and promised that he and her mother would come to her "so fast as we may."[111]

Although letters like these are relatively rare, men often stated in their wills how much they loved their wives. Of 523 testators who predeceased their mates, 99 described them with such phrases as "well beloved" and "entirely beloved." Others recorded their feelings in more individualized language. William Herbert, earl of Pembroke, closed his testament by reminding his spouse, "ye had in my life my heart and love."[112] Sir Richard Morison declared his "great love and affection" for his wife, and Sir Edmund Bedingfield, John, Lord Welles, and Sir Thomas Willoughby all said that they trusted their mates "before all other creatures."[113]

Aristocratic women's wills are far less revealing about their marital relationships than men's because they were almost always widows when they wrote them. Much more indicative of their feelings is the large percentage of them who wanted to be buried with their deceased spouses. Of 207 female testators who stated their preferences in their testaments, 131, or 66 percent, asked to be buried beside their late husbands. In a group of 134 noble couples, 80 were buried together; in all but 5 of these cases, the women had survived their husbands and chosen this arrangement. Five women preferred to be buried with other husbands.[114]

However successful aristocratic couples were in developing affectionate, even loving working partnerships, the material conditions of their lives meant that their relationships were not companionate or intimate in the modern sense. They lived apart much of the time, mostly because of men's absences but also because women had their own appointments at court and practical affairs to attend to. These separations limited the amount of their lives that they shared. As a result, they had somewhat different social lives and engaged in separate leisure activities. The household accounts of the earl and countess of

Rutland show, for example, that the earl visited the duchess of Norfolk and the duke of Richmond and attended the earl of Surrey's wedding without his wife, and the countess attended Lord Bray's wedding on her own. The countess of Westmorland, the duchess of Suffolk, and Lady Byron all visited Belvoir without their husbands.[115] The Lestrange accounts reveal a similar pattern. Lady Lestrange went to Northamptonshire and Walsingham without her husband in the early 1520s, and he hunted and visited his mother and the French Queen on his own.[116] Sir Roger Woodhouse and his wife, Elizabeth, frequent guests in the Lestrange household, often came alone or left separately.[117]

Women's reproductive lives also separated aristocratic husbands and wives. The reticence of contemporary sources makes it easy to overlook the impact of women's fertility patterns on their marriages. Many of them spent weeks every year or two secluded from their husbands in their lying-in chambers, where they lived entirely in the company of women. The expecting women's friends gathered to participate in their lyings-in, and many mothers traveled considerable distances to be with their daughters when they gave birth. Noblemen and knights, on the other hand, were just as likely to be away as at home when their wives delivered their babies.

Even when they were together, conditions in aristocratic households provided little of the privacy that encourages intimacy. It is unlikely, for example, that couples ever ate meals alone together. Although some families withdrew from the great halls characteristic of medieval castles and manors to more private chambers and dining rooms, they still shared their tables with any members of the nobility and gentry who were eating in their households. Whether visitors were present or not, there were servants everywhere. They waited on their masters and mistresses at meals, assisted them in dressing, accompanied them wherever they went, and ran errands for them throughout the day. One of the most striking features of court depositions in the period is how ubiquitous servants were and how little went on that they did not observe or hear about.[118]

Finally, the legal subordination and economic dependence of wives meant that however much aristocratic couples loved each other and however successfully they cooperated in promoting their common concerns, they always related as unequal parties. The fiction inscribed in the Christian view of marriage and the doctrine of coverture, that couples were one, mystified the coercive element in their relationship, which rested firmly on wives' legal incapacities, economic dependence, and the cultural ideal of the obedient wife. But this fiction could not and did not completely mask reality. Whatever they thought in the abstract about their culture's prescriptive and legal model of marriage, both women and men knew that husbands and wives were not one; that they often had different perspectives and interests, even in generally happy relationships; that many women, especially heiresses and widows, turned their property over to their spouses reluctantly and protested when their husbands sold or wasted it; and that couples interacted not as equals but as subordinates and superordinates. From an emotional point of view, this hierarchical distance and power differential reinforced those aspects of their lives—the lack of privacy and frequent separations—that discouraged marital intimacy and companionship.

In this context, conforming to the model of the obedient wife put considerable pressure on women to accept and internalize their husbands' definition of their common interests and to forge and maintain the delicate equilibrium between capably performing their duties and cheerfully complying with their husbands' directives and priorities. Needless to say, the role scripted for them assumed that they had loving and competent mates. In real life, of course, some husbands disliked their wives and mistreated or neglected them, and others were unable or unwilling to fulfill their obligations as patriarchs. The reverse was also true. Not all wives were loving, obedient, and competent. In other cases, couples disagreed about how to manage their resources or provide for their children in the context of relatively good relationships. All these situations exposed the premise of spousal unity for what it was—a social myth, masking the subordination of wives and the way in which patriarchal legal and economic structures constructed the aristocratic marriage. In these circumstances, many wives found it difficult, if not impossible, to remain respectful and compliant or to refrain from trying to protect themselves, their children, or their property by acting independently. Men, on the other hand, could ignore or coerce their wives. The common law placed no limits on their rights over their spouses' movable goods. In addition, although they needed the women's consent to sell their jointures and inheritances, they were often able to force them to comply. If all else failed, vengeful husbands could punish their wives physically or financially. The most brutal exercises of men's power over their mates occurred in marriages that had failed completely. The examples these husbands set—the third duke of Norfolk, who physically abused his wife, stripped her of her clothes and jewels, and incarcerated her for over a decade in a manor he rented from the crown, created an open scandal in the 1530s—must have influenced the strategies women adopted when they disagreed with their husbands or were disappointed in them.[119] Even in less extreme situations, hostile or incompetent spouses made it difficult, if not impossible, for aristocratic wives to succeed at the careers that represented fulfillment for women of their class.

Fiscal irresponsibility, incompetent management of their households and estates, and aristocratic men's estrangement from their wives often went together, although there is rarely enough evidence to speculate about which came first. Women in such positions had little hope of relief unless they could enlist men as powerful as their husbands, usually their natal kin, to assist them. A number of fathers responded to such situations by providing for their daughters in their wills. Sir William Knyvett lamented, for example, that his daughter Anne lived "a poor life" because his son-in-law "by his negligence and misordered living is brought into great danger and poverty." He directed his executors to give her and her children £20 a year for clothes and other necessities.[120] Charles Brandon, duke of Suffolk, intervened in his daughter Mary's marriage to Thomas, Lord Monteagle, to protect her from abuse and reform his son-in-law's financial affairs. He agreed to cancel Monteagle's large debts to him after he swore to abide by Suffolk's ordinances for the management of his estates and household. Monteagle also promised to "honestly handle and entreat the said lady Mary as a noble man ought to do his wife, unless there be a great default in the lady Mary and so affirmed by the council of the lord Monteagle." The latter provision suggests that Monteagle had neglected and mistreated his wife.[121]

Cardinal Wolsey's ordinances for John, fourteenth earl of Oxford, in 1523 portray an irresponsible, young husband who dressed extravagantly, drank too much, engaged in "riotous behavior," quarreled with his wife, and neglected her sexually.[122] At the behest of the countess's father and brother, the second duke of Norfolk and earl of Surrey, Wolsey ordered Oxford to live with his father-in-law. In the three years before this drastic action, the countess had been overwhelmed by the burden of managing her husband's affairs in the face of his dereliction. She told Wolsey, "And it is thought by many that I may do much in my lord's causes. And [i.e., but] if I meddle in any causes further than I do, I perceive that I should never live in rest. Therefore, I meddle no further than his household causes." She begged the cardinal to appoint reliable officers to manage her husband's estates and advise him since she rightfully distrusted the councel he received from Sir John Vere, her husband's distant kinsman and heir apparent. As she was well aware, Vere and his friends had an interest in fomenting trouble between her and her husband to prevent them from producing a son who would displace Sir John in the line of succession. "They care little for his coming forward," she wrote, "so the inheritance might be safe for Sir John."[123] Wolsey responded by ordering Oxford to "lovingly, familiarly and kindly intreat and demeane himself toward the said countess his wife as [i.e., in order that] there may be perfect good concord and amity engendered, nourished and continued between them, as to the laws of God and for bringing forth fruit and children between them to God's pleasure doth appertain." The cardinal particularly directed him to ignore "simple or evil . . . persons, which, for particular malice or to attain favor, thanks, or otherwise, shall contrive seditious and slanderous reports between them."[124]

Men's misuse of their wives' property provides the most common example of the speciousness of the ideological fiction that husbands and wives were one. Incidents of this kind occurred even in marriages characterized by affection and cooperation, particularly when men who were heavily in debt found that selling or pawning their spouses' jewelry, plate, jointures, and inheritances was the most attractive option for staving off insolvency. Just such a situation arose between Margaret, countess of Bath, and her husband, despite their obvious affection for each other and generally effective partnership. What was unusual in the countess of Bath's case was not her husband's misuse of her property but her success in protecting herself during their marriage.

Most women had to wait until they were widowed to recover their goods, although by then it was often too late. Dame Elizabeth Bodulgate, widow of Sir Thomas, petitioned Chancery during her second marriage because she wanted to redeem her gold collar, which Bodulgate had pledged as security for his debts. She claimed that although she had repaid more than the value of the collar to his creditor, he would not return it to her.[125] Maud, Lady Willoughby, alleged that her third husband, Sir Gervais Clifton, had "wasted and destroyed" jewels, plate, and household goods worth more than £1,000 that she had brought into their marriage.[126] No evidence exists about the truth of the charges in these two cases, but men's wills indicate that such behavior did occur. Sir Richard Fitzlewis acknowledged, for example, that he had sold some of his wife's plate when he bequeathed her the remainder.[127] Sir Edward Grey left one of his second wife's silver basins and ewers to his heir, her stepson.[128] The matter-of-fact wording of Sir Thomas Brandon's legacy to his wife—"to my lady my wife half of all the stuff of household that I had with her"—reflects the lack of self-consciousness with which many men treated their spouses' goods as their own.[129]

Husbands over their heads in debt were often tempted to sell or mortgage land assured for their wives' jointures. In his 1544 will, Francis, earl of Huntingdon, recorded that he and his father had sold land worth almost £200 per annum from his wife's jointure, apparently with her consent, to pay his father's debts. Now, "in part and not full recompence . . . of the jointure alienated," he bequeathed a life interest in a number of manors to her. Although men often claimed that their spouses had consented to transactions of this sort, skepticism about how freely the women agreed is certainly in order, given men's physical and legal power over their wives. In the Huntingdons' case, the countess was evidently satisfied, whatever her feelings about the original sales, since her husband appointed her one of his coexecutors.[130] Coercion was more evident in the case of John Elmys and his wife. His father-in-law, Sir John Mordaunt, sued him in Chancery to prevent him from executing a fine that would destroy his daughter's title to her jointure. He claimed that Elmys had employed "importunate means" to secure her consent.[131]

In a more surprising case, given the constraints on women under coverture, Elizabeth, Lady Vaux, acted vigorously on her own to prevent her husband from selling land that would jeopardize her jointure. Her opposition to the sales brought her into conflict with both her spouse and Thomas Cromwell, who wanted to purchase some of the land. Cromwell's agent,

Thomas Pope, told him bluntly that her "coming to town for this time hath dashed the matter."[132] Lady Vaux's uncle, Sir William Parr, tried to persuade her to agree but admitted defeat: "More than I have done it neither lieth in my power nor wit to do."[133] Although Lady Vaux succeeded in forcing her husband to sign a bond in which he promised not to alienate any more of his property without the king's special license, he continued to sell his estates. She then turned to Parliament and ultimately secured an act that protected her by nullfying any future sales in advance.[134] To preserve her jointure, Lady Vaux had engaged in the same kind of informed, energetic activity that wives routinely employed on behalf of their husbands and marital families. But the price of her success was alienating her husband. A year later he was living apart from her, although he assured Cromwell, probably disingenuously, that it was not because of "any grudge between me and my wife."[135]

Even without the complication of debts, women's jointures often caused conflicts between couples because, whatever the assumption about the identity of their interests, in practice husbands and wives had very different stakes in them. In some cases, men neglected or openly refused to secure their spouses' jointures legally to avoid tying up their estates. Although Thomas, Lord Sandys, referred to his "great love" for his wife, he admitted that he had not yet fulfilled his "earlier promises and covenants" to provide for her twenty-eight years after their marriage. Only then did he finally sign an agreement to settle her jointure with her brother, the earl of Rutland, and Sir Anthony Browne, a member of the king's Privy Chamber.[136]

Conflicts about women's inheritances also reveal the speciousness of the common-law doctrine of the unity of husband and wife. While the law restricted men's claim to their wives' real property to a life interest in the income, some husbands sought fuller rights, even complete title, to the women's property. Sir Richard Grenville admitted in his will that he had sold some of his wife's inheritance and jointure to pay for his service to the crown. Although he claimed that she had agreed to the transaction, he bequeathed her some of his own land in compensation.[137] Sir Simon Harcourt charged correctly that his mother's second husband, Sir John Huddleston, had induced her to levy a fine on her inheritance so that it would pass to their eldest son rather than Harcourt. On his deathbed, Huddleston "having great remorse in his conscience . . . charged his son upon his blessing" not to take advantage of his mother's gift, but to release the property to the proper heirs.[138] It is unclear whether or not their son, also named John, complied with his father's request, but when Jane died seven years later, she was deeply worried about the descent of her land. She not only recounted that her husband "did me wrong in his life, like as he testified and knowledged and also thereof had remorse at his departing," but also recorded carefully in the presence of the abbot and prior of Hailes that her "last will and full mind" was that all her property except one manor should go to the Harcourts. She stated further that Huddleston had made an enfeoffment of some of her property to their son's use "without my consent and advice; and I never did agree thereunto, but ever denied [it]," and that John the younger had defrauded her again two years earlier by tricking her into signing a document that released title in her estates to him and his heirs after her death.[139]

In some cases, men's designs on their wives' inheritances occurred in the context of marriages that had failed completely, although it is usually impossible to tell if the disputes about the women's property were a cause or effect of the failure. In 1553, for example, Margery Acton asked the Court of Requests to order her husband, Sir Robert, to give her "some convenient portion of living for her sustenation and payment of her debts or else to accept her home again in his company and to use her as his wife." Margery, heir to 100 marks of land and leases, claimed that Acton had stopped supporting her six years earlier and sent her to live in an alehouse. Following a hearing, the court ordered him to give Margery £30 a year for the rest of his life.[140] Before he died, Sir Robert sold most of her inheritance and entailed his land to their children. In his will, he left Margery a third of his movable goods and £20 in plate; but even this bequest was conditional on her not claiming the right to reside in his house.[141]

In a similar case, Sir George Harper's first wife, Lucy Peckham, complained that her husband refused to support her because she would not give him half of her inheritance. As in the case of the Actons, the Harpers were living apart at the time of her suit, but the cause of their separation was quite different: Lady Harper had a long adulterous affair with Sir Richard Morison and gave birth to five of his children. Because she was a *feme covert*, her husband was entitled to collect the income from her estates and she was effectively penniless, although she had inherited considerable property. In the end, given her weak moral and legal position, Lady Harper agreed to transfer title to one of her manors to her husband. As an adulteress, she was in a tenuous position, but the fact that she was an heiress gave her some bargaining power and enabled her to avoid the worst consequences of her misconduct.[142] The property disputes between aristocratic couples about real and movable property discussed here consitute only a fraction of those recounted in contemporary records, but they give an accurate picture of the range of issues that caused contention and the wide variety of strategies women used to compensate for their legal disabilities. They demonstrate that whatever the doctrine of the law or the dogma of the church, in everyday life members of the aristocracy knew full well that husbands and wives had separate interests and that wives were at a serious disadvantage when they clashed with their spouses about the use of their property.

When men refused to respect their wives' jointures and inheritances, to support them adequately, or to refrain from mistreating them, women's first, and often most successful, line of defense was to turn to their natal male relatives. Their appeals for help were frequently effective, particularly when daughters sought assistance from their fathers. Heiresses also had some leverage because the law limited their husbands' rights in their inheritances to life use of the income. When their situation was desperate enough, as in Lucy Harper's case, for example, they could use their estates to bribe their husbands into agreeing to their living apart.

More surprising, in light of the doctrine of coverture, was women's success in petitioning the equity courts and Privy Council on their own when their husbands abused or declined to support them.[143] In these cases, they marshaled the legal knowledge and expertise they had acquired as household and estate managers on their own behalf. In this connection, it would be fascinating to know more precisely what Lady Vaux did in London to block the sale of part of her jointure to Thomas Cromwell.

When privy councillors and equity court judges protected married women's property from their husbands, they were acting on the virtually unchallenged consensus that men who received dowries from their wives' families or the use of their inheritances had a duty to maintain their wives. As fathers and brothers, they had a stake in compelling men to support their mates and to respect their jointures and inheritances. At the same time, as husbands, they were sympathetic to men's assumption that they were entitled to use the income from their wives' inheritances. From their rulings, they also apparently thought that women living apart from their spouses needed and deserved relatively modest livelihoods. As a result, they awarded Margaret Acton only £30 a year, although she possessed land, leases, and a crown office worth 500 marks. Similarly, although William Bulmer acquired 100 marks per annum through his marriage, the court gave his wife only 40 marks a year when they separated.[144] Men's responses to women's suits in their official capacity as judges and privy councillors thus reflected their diverse relationships with a wide range of female kin. The conflicting demands on them as fathers, husbands, brothers, and uncles meant that although they fully appreciated the necessity of assisting their female relatives against abusive and negligent mates, they had a decidedly limited view of the extent of the assistance to which the women were entitled. In extreme cases like that of Margaret Acton, they did not ultimately even prevent husbands from stealing their wives' inheritance.

When wives sought protection against spouses who abused or deserted them, endangered their livelihoods by wasting their own or their wives' estates, or threatened their jointures and inheritances, they complained in a context in which the law was clear about their rights, however limited, and in which their male relatives had emotional and material reasons for defending them. They were in a far weaker position when the cause of conflict between them and their husbands was marital infidelity. On the ideological level, the church was absolutely clear that couples had mutual rights in each other's bodies and equal obligations to be faithful to each other. In practice, however, aristocratic men benefited from a clear double standard in the area of sex, although wives were not always held to a standard of absolute fidelity either.[145] Fifty-one of 763 aristocratic men's wills contained bequests to the men's mistresses and/or illegitimate children, while many other men probably provided for their mistresses and bastards in other ways.[146] The declaration in William Catesby's will that he had "ever be[en] true of my body" to his wife was unique and may have been a deathbed effort to settle a quarrel between them before he died. His plea for forgiveness—"I heartily cry you mercy if I have dealed uncourteously with you"—reveals his guilt about some issue they both considered important.[147]

Available sources contain little evidence of aristocratic men being sanctioned for extramarital affairs, although the destruction of the records of the Court of Arches—the ecclesiastical court most likely to deal with noblemen and knights—in the Great Fire of London in 1666 may create a false impression about their immunity from punishment. One of the rare documented cases occurred when Sir William Compton was forced to take the sacrament to prove he had not committed adultery with Anne, wife of George, Lord Hastings, while his own wife was still alive. The pair had been involved in a scandal in 1510, shortly after Anne's marriage, when her brother, the third duke of Buckingham, heard rumors that Compton was courting her. When Buckingham discovered Compton in her room at court, he handed Anne over to her husband, who deposited her in a convent some 60 miles away.[148] No evidence exists about what the duke saw or whether or not the couple was guilty of adultery, but a strong tie between them certainly existed. When Compton wrote his will in 1523, he left Lady Anne a life interest in a piece of his land, a very unusual legacy to a woman who was not the testator's daughter, sister, or niece. He also directed his executors to include her in the group, made up otherwise of all the usual kin, to benefit from the prayers for which he was paying.[149]

Whatever happened in 1510, Lady Anne eventually developed a warm, loving relationship with her husband. In 1525, he wrote her one of the most affectionate and charming letters of the period. "Mine own good Anne," he began, "with all my whole heart, I recommend me unto you as he that is most glad to hear that you be merry and in good health. . . . And sorry I am to hear of the trouble ye be in for dread of me. Good trull, as ye love me, put that away, for I trust there is no cause. I do thank God I am well amended over that I was." In response to her offer to come to London because he was sick, he assured her "rather than I would wish you to take such a journey upon you, considering your feebleness and also the foul way, I ensure you I would be glad to come home afoot." After describing his illness and recovery and recounting the news, he closed with the wish that God would "send us shortly

[a] good meeting"; added a postscript about some lozenges he was sending; and closed "once again, farewell, good Anne."[150] Hastings's will points in the same direction: he named his wife as one of his coexecutors, gave her custody of all their children and the power to arrange their daughters' marriages, and left her life rights in all his movable goods and a substantial number of his manors.[151]

Sir Thomas Wyatt, who openly lived with his mistress, Elizabeth Darrell, was one of the few other aristocratic men punished at all for adultery. Following his imprisonment in the Tower in 1541, probably because of his close association with Thomas Cromwell, one of the conditions of his pardon and release was that he leave Darrell and take back his wife. He had repudiated her almost twenty years earlier for committing adultery. Whether or not Wyatt complied is unknown, but in either case he provided for his mistress and their son in his will.[152]

Aristocratic wives' complacency in the face of male adultery further supports the conclusion that men's extramarital affairs were common and broadly accepted. Henry, Lord Grey, and Sir Ralph Bigod even asked their spouses to raise their illegitimate sons. The women apparently agreed since both men included them among their coexecutors.[153] Margaret Paston bequeathed 10 marks to her son John's illegitimate child, and Constance Culpepper left her husband's bastard daughter a gown and kirtle.[154] Lady Elizabeth Scrope's bequest to the first marquess of Dorset's "daughter in base" of "my bed that the said lord marquess was wont to lie in and all the apparel that belongeth thereto and all the apparel of the same chamber" can plausibly be interpreted as a covert admission that she was the girl's mother.[155] In this environment, the duchess of Norfolk's rage at her husband's long-term affair with Bess Holland may have been exceptional and can explain, in turn, the depth of his reciprocal anger at her.[156]

When aristocratic women committed, or were credibly accused of committing, adultery, they were far more likely to suffer for their misdeeds. It was one of the points at which the structural inequality of married men and women came into play. Unlike aggrieved wives, husbands had the physical and economic power to punish their unfaithful spouses and bastardize their children if they suspected them of being illegitimate. About fifteen years after Sir Thomas Wyatt separated from his wife because of her alleged adultery, for example, he suddenly refused to support her any longer and sent her to live with her brother, George, Lord Cobham. Cobham tried unsuccessfully to secure a "reasonable living" for her with the help of his and Wyatt's mutual friends. He then turned to Thomas Cromwell for assistance.[157] Thomas, Lord Burgh, was convinced his daughter-in-law was guilty of adultery and had given birth to a bastard when her first child was born in 1537. After her husband's death in 1542, and despite her protests of innocence, he secured passage of an act of Parliament, convicting her of committing adultery during his son's lifetime and declaring her three children to be bastards. When Lord Burgh died in 1550, however, he left the eldest child, Lady Burgh's daughter Margaret, 700 marks, a large bequest that gives credence to her mother's claim that Margaret was legitimate.[158] The earl of Sussex also responded punitively when his wife was accused of undergoing a bigamous marriage with Sir Edmund Knyvett. According to a distraught letter she wrote her mother, he threw her out of the house without "money, men, women, meat, nor more than two gowns of velvet." In 1555, the earl obtained a statute that deprived her of dower in his estates. Despite her apparent disgrace, the countess survived surprisingly well. After Sussex's death in 1557, she married Andrew Wyse, a royal official in Ireland. Their daughter had enough status to marry a younger son of Sir Edward Fitton, Queen Elizabeth's vice-treasurer in Ireland.[159]

The countess of Sussex's experience reveals a crucial dimension of the context in which the Yorkist and early Tudor aristocracy judged and responded to female adultery. Despite the prescriptive emphasis on the chastity of wives and men's tendency to regard them as their property, they were not hostile to sex in the clerical sense or prudish and censorious in their behavior. When adulterous wives were punished, the penalties against them involved the loss of property in one form or other or the bastardization of their children, rather than in complete ruin of their character, abandonment by their lovers, or permanent banishment from aristocratic society. Male relatives who assisted them generally focused on financial issues, specifically the women's livelihoods, rather than on their or their families' honor, as in the case of George, Lord Cobham, and his sister Lady Wyatt. Even the bastardization of children was related to material issues since it was intended to prevent titles and estates from descending to other men's offspring.

Only the aristocracy's relative lack of interest in the moral implications of adultery can explain the outcome of Lucy Harper's long affair with Sir Richard Morison or the charges against Lady Sussex. Joan Courteney and Mary Darcy also escaped punishment for committing adultery. Joan, daughter of Sir William Courteney of Powderham, had a child by Henry Bodrugan during her marriage to William Beaumont, whom she married shortly after her husband's death.[160] Darcy gave birth to four children fathered by Sir Richard Southwell while each of them was married to someone else. When Darcy's first husband died, Southwell, also widowed by that time, married her. He provided carefully for their eldest son, Richard, a future member of Parliament, and made no distinction between his legitimate and illegitimate children in his will.[161]

The story of Anne, Lady Powis, the duke of Suffolk's daughter, who eloped from her husband with her lover, Randall Haworth, underscores all these points. In 1537 Suffolk asked Cromwell to force Lord Powis to support Anne and to discipline her so that she would "live after such an honest sort as shall be to her honor and mine."[162] Although Cromwell secured £100 a year for Anne, he either would not or could not persuade or force her to separate from Haworth. Three years later, Powis petitioned the Privy Council to punish her for "continually" and "daily" persevering in her "abomination and whoredom" and conspiring with Haworth to murder him, but his complaint had no discernible effect.[163] After Powis died in 1551, his wife married her lover.[164] Whether Suffolk was genuinely concerned about his or his daughter's honor or asked Cromwell to discipline her to strengthen his request that Powis support her is impossible to tell from the extant sources. But her misbehavior may account for the fact that he ignored her in his will, which contained generous bequests to her two half-sisters.[165] Lady Powis's conduct and apparent immunity from punishment provide eloquent testimony to the contrast between actual aristocratic mores and the ideal of the chaste wife.

The wide variety of marital relationships and circumstances discussed in this chapter demonstrates the impossibility of creating a simple or universal model of aristocratic marriage or wifehood in Yorkist and early Tudor England. Instead, the legal, economic, and ideological structures of patriarchy created a framework within which individual couples interacted. Within these parameters, the vocation of wifehood provided many women with personal satisfaction, an outlet for their energies and abilities, and some measure of de facto authority within their households. For the majority of aristocratic women, wifehood evolved into a satisfying career through which they made a crucial contribution to their families and class. The impact of their subordinate status on their performance of their wifely duties and their relationships with their mates varied from one couple to another. Patriarchal institutions and practices weighed most heavily on wives in troubled marriages, though they affected even such successful unions as that of the countess and earl of Bath.

At the same time, however pervasive patriarchal institutions and practices were from the point of view of individual women, male power and authority were effectively dispersed among a number of men—their husbands, fathers, brother(s), and one figure who stood outside the biological family—the king. The wives most likely to suffer because of their legal disabilities and economic dependence, those quarreling with their mates about property and those in failed or troubled marriages, could and did appeal to members of their natal families or to the king and royal government. Their appeals and suits exposed the discrepancy between everyday reality and prevailing legal and religious assumptions about the unity of husbands and wives. Ultimately these channels gave women some leverage against their spouses and enabled many of them to avoid the worst consequences of coverture. Not surprisingly, the two early Tudor wives treated most brutally by their husbands, Elizabeth (née Stafford), duchess of Norfolk, and Elizabeth (née Hussey),

Lady Hungerford, were particularly isolated because their fathers had been executed and attainted for treason. As a result, they were unable to secure help from the crown or from influential male relatives.[166]

The combination of aristocratic wives' critical contributions to their marital families, coverture, and economic dependence on their husbands shaped a class-specific definition of wifely obedience and love and the gradual transformation of most of their arranged marriages into cooperative, affectionate relationships. To a large extent, women earned their husbands' love through the effective performance of their practical duties. Ultimately, therefore, the career of aristocratic wivehood encompassed and shaped both the emotional and material dimensions of their lives.

CHAPTER 5. SINGLE WOMEN

AND COMPULSORY MARRIAGE

*A*RISTOCRATIC wives enjoyed the fullest careers open to women of their class except for the small number who combined wifehood with appointments at court. In a class in which the female marriage rate was just under 94 percent, their lives provided the dominant model of adult womanhood.[1] No comparable careers or opportunities existed for the tiny group of Yorkist and early Tudor aristocratic women who neither married nor entered convents. Whatever their personal qualities and capacities, never-married laywomen remained perpetual daughters and life-long dependents, residing in the households of their relatives or friends and functioning as gentlewomen servants and companions of their hosts. The scanty surviving information about them accurately mirrors their marginality in aristocratic society.[2] There is not a single example of a never-married aristocratic woman who accumulated large amounts of property, real or movable, or who occupied a central position in her immediate or extended kin network. The narrow scope and relative insignificance of their activities contrasts dramatically with those of their married and widowed sisters.

Until the dissolution of the monasteries in the 1530s, convents theoretically provided potentially fulfilling alternate careers for aristocratic women. But the tiny number who became nuns suggests that neither they nor their families considered the religious life an attractive alternative to marriage. Careers in Yorkist and early Tudor convents did not offer women the social esteem or material benefits of wifehood or extend their natal families' political and social networks, as their marriages did.[3] Within this context, little evidence exists about why specific aristocratic women became nuns.[4]

This chapter focuses specifically on never-married aristocratic laywomen, most of whom continued to live in the great households of their natal kin. The contrast between the scope of their activities and those of the wives and

widows who were the most important female members of their families provides further insight into the significance of marriage and wifehood among
the Yorkist and early Tudor aristocracy. In addition, identifying the circumstances in which young women's families and friends concluded that they
were unmarriagable or failed to find them husbands despite their apparent
eligibility illuminates the meaning of marriagability in their class and the
gradual process by which daughters who expected to marry evolved into
women who never would. The lives of never-married women also highlight
certain easily neglected aspects of life in noble and knightly households, such
as the relationships between siblings and the figure of the unmarried gentlewoman companion or servant. Finally, comparing the resources and opportunities of never-married women to those of widows underscores the assets—
material, experiential, and relational—that women accumulated through
marriage. Although both never-married women and widows were free from
the disabilities of coverture, there was no comparison in their respective
wealth, political and social influence, or ability to shape their lives. This difference was a measure of what women gained through marriage even though
they were legally subordinated to their husbands.

Despite the limitations of their position, never-married women were, of
course, members of privileged, wealthy families. Although they were never as
rich or powerful as aristocratic wives and widows, their parents provided
them with sufficient incomes to live in the style of their class in the households of their close kin. They also often enjoyed warm personal relations
with members of their families. Underscoring the contrast between their
situation and that of wives and widows is not, therefore, meant to suggest
that women were emotionally or materially neglected after it became clear
that they would never marry. The point is, rather, that they were excluded
from the significant familial and political careers of wives and widows that
form the central subject of this study.

A variety of factors, some individual, some familial, explains why a tiny group
of aristocratic women remained single. Most interesting were the women
who apparently chose not to marry, although evidence about them is indirect.
The wording of the generous bequest of Thomas West, Lord de La Warre, of
a dowry of 800 marks "or if she be not disposed to marry, eight yearly payments of 100 marks" to his eldest daughter, Eleanor, indicates that he thought
she might choose to remain single, and he wanted to ensure her financial security if she did. He did not provide comparable alternatives to the dowries
that he bequeathed to her two sisters.[5] Three decades later, George, Lord
Bergavenny, directed his executors to provide at their discretion for his daughters Ursula, Margaret, and Dorothy "if any of them intend to live and not to
marry."[6] Sir John Tyrrell left 100 marks to his daughter Frideswide for her
marriage or "living sole."[7] There is no record of her ever marrying.

Some women became unmarriagable when their fathers were convicted of treason. If they carried royal blood, the crown itself may have placed them in convents to ensure that they would not marry and produce sons to oppose the reigning dynasty. This was the case of Elizabeth, only daughter of Edmund de la Pole, earl of Lincoln and heir to the Yorkist claim to the throne, who died as a nun at the Minories in 1515.[8] Elizabeth Brackenbury, daughter of Sir Robert, who fought for Richard III at Bosworth, was living in the duchess of Norfolk's household in the precincts of the Minories when she died. She asked to be buried there in her will and directed her executors to repay money the duchess had laid out for her "of her charity."[9]

A few women were almost certainly unfit for marriage because of physical or mental disabilities or chronic illness. Sir Edward Ferrers directed his widow to use the land he was leaving to his daughter Alice, whom he expected to remain single, to support her until she died. After her mother died, Alice could administer her inheritance herself if she was still alive.[10] Sir Alexander Culpepper left his daughter Alice a small annuity for twenty years "if she lives so long," although he bequeathed dowries to her two younger half-sisters.[11] Her contemporary, Anne Corbet, daughter of Sir Richard and Lady Jane, claimed that "for diverse infirmities [she] was not meet to marry."[12] Evidently her condition was not obvious when her father bequeathed her a dowry of 300 marks in 1524. Twenty years later, her mother's will reflected her conviction that Anne would remain single. She left Anne a life interest in some land, plate, half her (i.e., the testator's) clothes, household goods, and half the profits from the sale of a valuable piece of jewelry. Her directions for the descent of the land indicate that she assumed Anne would never have children of her own.[13]

A number of other parents left their daughters annuities or small pieces of land to enable them to support themselves. They clearly anticipated that the young women would remain single, although they did not indicate whether their daughters preferred not to marry or were unfit to do so.[14] The expectation is most evident when they bequeathed assets of this kind to one daughter and dowries to her sisters. Sir Robert Nevill of Liversedge gave parcels of land worth £7 11s. per annum to his daughter Rosamund and £140 for the marriages of her two sisters.[15] Similarly, Sir James Wilford asked his executors to employ £200 for the support of his daughter Elizabeth, while he bequeathed a dowry in the same amount to her sister.[16]

Other fathers who bequeathed capital instead of dowries to their daughters clearly anticipated the possibility of their remaining single even though their wills contain no telltale bequests of dowries to their sisters. John, Lord Zouch, left his daughter Cecily £10 worth of land, which was to be "severed and divided" from one of his manors, and Sir Giles Strangeways bequeathed an annuity of 40 marks plus £100 in goods and money to his daughter Elizabeth.[17] When Sir Richard Gresham wrote his will, he gave his daughter Elizabeth, then

22, an equal share in the third of his goods designated for his children, according to the custom of London, plus some land in Yorkshire. The land could have served as a marriage portion, but Elizabeth was still single when she died two years later.[18] The provisions made by Jane, countess of Southampton, for her daughter Mabel, then in her late 20s, clearly recognized that Mabel might never marry.[19]

Still another group of aristocratic women remained single because the deaths and remarriages of their parents meant that no one focused on arranging matches for them in the crucial years when they were in their teens or early 20s. As a result of high mortality rates and frequent remarriage, many parents died or remarried and had second or third families to worry about before they had successfully concluded matches for their daughters from previous unions. The complicated families that resulted often included half-siblings and stepsiblings, who diverted the surviving parents or stepparents from finding matches for their daughters or stepdaughters even though the girls had adequate dowries. A few cases of this sort contributed to the tiny number of aristocratic women who never married. Anne Norris, the eldest daughter of John Norris by his first wife, is an example. Norris's third wife, Margaret Chedworth, was already a widow when they married. Within a year of Norris's death in 1466, she married her third husband, Sir John Howard. When Margaret went to live at Howard's manor in Suffolk, she took Anne, her stepdaughter, as well as her two children by Norris, with her. Norris had left Anne an adequate dowry of £100, but she was still single and living in the Howard household fourteen years later.[20]

Similar family circumstances probably account for the fact that Margaret and Eleanor Darcy, two of Elizabeth Wentworth's four daughters by her first husband, Roger Darcy, remained single. After Darcy's death, Elizabeth married Sir Thomas Wyndham, with whom she had one son. When Wyndham died in 1521, he bequeathed dowries of £200 apiece to his stepdaughters, although it is not clear whether he was making a new gift to them or simply transmitting money originally left to them by their father. Sometime after 1524, their mother married John Bourchier, first earl of Bath, as her third husband and once again survived her husband. When she died two decades later, Margaret and Eleanor Darcy, the offspring of her first marriage, were well into their 30s and still single. They apparently never married.[21] Muriel St. Clare Byrne, editor of The Lisle Letters, thought an analogous family situation accounted for the fact that Jane and Thomasine Basset, Sir John's daughters by his first wife, also never married.[22]

Both Margaret Chedworth and Sir Thomas Wyndham were well disposed to their stepdaughters, but this was not always the case. Bad relationships between young women and their stepparents almost certainly contributed to the fact that some of them never married. Mary Zouche, daughter of the eighth Lord Zouche and his first wife, complained to her cousin, Sir John

Arundell, that her stepmother mistreated her and her siblings and incited their father against them: "We see nothing that should be to our comfort or preferment in any cause, but as we were foundlings that had neither father nor friend to trust to . . . my lady my mother-in-law, the which never loved none of us all . . . causes our father to be worse to us than he would be." Mary asked Arundell to help her obtain a position in Katherine of Aragon's or Princess Mary's household, which he apparently did since Mary belonged to both Anne Boleyn's and Jane Seymour's households. In 1537 the king granted her a pension of £10 per annum until she married.[23] There is no evidence that she ever did.

Sir Thomas Wyndham took great care to ensure that his Darcy stepdaughters had no difficulty in securing their dowries, but a few stepparents, siblings, and stepsiblings were less conscientious about the property of women whose fathers and/or mothers were dead. The withholding or theft of dowries probably accounted for another small group of aristocratic women who remained permanently single. When Sir Thomas Brudenell died, for example, he left dowries of 300 or 400 marks apiece, depending on what his estate could bear, to each of his four unmarried daughters. Subsequently, his widow complained in Chancery that their son, Edmund, had stolen goods worth £2,000 from his father's estate, in consequence of which her younger children were "like to be unprovided for and utterly undone." Most likely, the long dispute that ensued caused or contributed to the fact that two of the girls, Anne and Lucy, remained single.[24] In the same decade, four of Sir Piers Dutton's daughters sued their brother Ralph in Chancery for withholding their dowries. They claimed that as a result, although they "might have been married and preferred according to their degrees," their marriages had been delayed, "to their great hinderance and utter undoing." The girls' quarrel with Ralph was probably the reason two of them, Alice and Margaret, never married.[25]

Because they never became mistresses of their own households, permanently single women almost always lived in the main residence of their natal families, whether the head of the household was their father, brother, or one of the men's widows. When Sir Thomas De La Launde wrote his will, for example, he bequeathed the featherbed she "lieth in" and an annuity of £3 6s. 8d., to his sister Anne, who had never married. The legacy of the bed strongly suggests that she was living in his household.[26] Clare Plumpton remained at Plumpton Hall after her father died in 1523, and it passed to her brother William; she was still living there with her widowed sister-in-law five years after William's death in 1547.[27]

Living in establishments of their own was not a viable or desirable alternative for never-married women for a variety of reasons. From a financial point of view, single women were not rich enough to maintain residences appropriate to their status, however generous their inheritances. In any case, the heads of their families were expected to assume responsibility for dependent relatives, an obligation that was particularly persuasive in the case of unmarried daughters and sisters. Members of the aristocracy who failed to demonstrate affection and concern for the well-being of needy or dependent close kin were openly criticized for "unnatural" behavior. Moreover, the size of their households made it easy for them to accommodate their single sisters and daughters in their homes. Nor were the women financial burdens since they paid their living expenses from their inheritances. Unmarried daughters and sisters also helped their mothers, stepmothers, and sisters-in-law to run their large, complex establishments. Their contribution was particularly important when the mistresses of the households were pregnant, ill, serving at court, or pursuing business in London. Although the aristocracy had other ways of securing the services of qualified gentlewomen, resident female kin familiar with the household and its members were particularly well qualified to step in.[28]

As residents of their natal families' households, never-married women were integral members of their families' larger social circle and often spent considerable time visiting other relatives and friends. Elizabeth Gresham, daughter of Sir Richard, died at her married sister's house, although she usually lived with her stepmother.[29] Dorothy Clopton was living at Long Melford with her father and stepmother when she wrote her will in 1508. But her reference to a ring and a blue velvet frontlet that Lady Broughton, a distant relative, gave her may well have referred to gifts she received when she was living or serving in the Broughton household.[30] Dorothy had also spent some time at Nettlestead, the home of the Wentworths, where she had left a velvet bonnet that she bequeathed to her sister Katherine, although there is no way of knowing the length or nature of her stay.

On rare occasions, whether by choice because it gave them more autonomy or because they had no other option, single women boarded with someone to whom they were not related. Sir John Dawtry actually gave his daughter Jane a choice about where to live. He directed his heir, Jane's brother, to give her an annuity of £6 13s. 4d. and a cloth gown costing 26s. or its equivalent each year until she married, which would allow her to live respectably in someone else's household. If, on the other hand, she decided to reside with her brother, he was to provide her with all her necessities rather than pay the annuity.[31] Isabel Bourchier, who was living in London when she wrote her will, had apparently been boarding for some time with John Halhed and his wife, Gertrude, whom she called her hosts. She was clearly on good terms with them. In addition to directing her executors to pay Halhed the money she owed him, she bequeathed £3 apiece to him and his wife and 20s. to their servant, Katherine Birche. She also left John a worsted kirtle from which to make a doublet, a tawny gown to Gertrude, and her smocks to Katherine. Most surprisingly, since she enjoyed good relations with her brother, the second earl of Essex, and her half-brother, Richard Grey, future earl of Kent, Isabel appointed the Halheds overseers of her will, perhaps because they were on the spot and in a position to supervise the distribution of her goods. Whatever the reason, her choice underscores her confidence in them.[32]

Whether never-married women lived in their natal homes, as most of them did, or boarded out, like Isabel Bourchier, they were expected to "find" or support themselves, that is, to pay for their room, board, clothes, and other necessities. "Finding" themselves was, in fact, a minimum requirement of adulthood among the aristocracy, whatever the individual's marital status or sex. In the case of wives, the assumption was that their dowries had purchased their lifelong support from their husbands' estates, as the provisions for their jointures make clear. Never-married women also used their dowries to pay their living expenses since most men took the precaution of directing their executors to give the money to the young women when they reached a specific age, even if they were still single. The age varied from the unusually low 15, when Sir John St. Loe (d. 1499) wanted his daughters to receive their marriage portions, to a high of 25, which was quite common.[33] The most frequent ages were 18 and 21.[34] In this way, parents did their best to ensure that even if their daughters remained single, they would not have to rely on the charity of their relatives.

A Chancery case between Anne Corbet and her brother Sir Richard illustrates how central the obligation to find oneself was in the relationship between never-married women and the heads of the households in which they lived. Anne sued her brother for withholding the legacy she had received from her father a quarter of a century earlier. He responded that their mother had spent the money, the substantial sum of 300 marks, for Anne's expenses in the intervening twenty-five years. Anne replied that during the last ten years of her mother's life "she did service to the said Dame Jane which was more worth than the charges she did set her said mother unto" and that she was therefore still entitled to the disputed money.[35]

The dowries or other inheritances single women used to support themselves were treated as capital, but the women probably did not invest the money themselves. Sir James Wilford directed his sole executor, his widow, to manage the money he left to their daughter.[36] Isabel Bourchier, a granddaughter of the first earl of Essex, inherited £200 from her grandmother. At first, her uncles, Sir Thomas Bourchier and Lord John Bourchier, invested the money for her. After Sir Thomas died, his widow continued to manage it, probably in her role as his executor. Dorothy Clopton, who never married, was one of the beneficiaries of her grandfather's provision that his sheep be divided equally among his grandchildren "to put it in provement to their profit and use." Since her grandfather was one of the great sheep owners of his day, she lived well on her share of the bequest for the rest of her life.[37] The dependence of never-married women on their relatives, whether male or female, to invest their inheritances for them reflected their inexperience in managing capital. Their situation was very different from the married or widowed female kin who acted on their behalf. The contrast reflected and determined their very different positions within aristocratic society.

Although single women didn't manage their inheritances, they almost certainly received the income from them or at least the portion not deducted by the head of their households for their room and board. This practice gave them control over the purchase of such items as clothing, jewelry, and gifts for their relatives and friends and the ability to distribute alms and reward their servants. As single women free from the disabilities of coverture, they had full legal rights over their inheritances and were able to bequeath them by will. Within their families, therefore, they transmitted property from one generation to another, although, they never had as much wealth to bequeath as aristocratic widows. Katherine Bigod, daughter of Sir Ralph, inherited £40 from her mother in 1477. At her death, she divided her estate among her sister, Anne, Lady Conyers, her sister's children, and one of her brothers.[38] When Isabel Bourchier wrote her will at the age of 23, she still possessed her entire inheritance of £200, a substantial sum that she divided between her brother, the second earl of Essex, and her half-brother, Richard Grey, future earl of Kent.[39]

More surprisingly, perhaps, given their relative lack of experience in business matters, a few parents named their unmarried daughters among their executors. In one case, Dame Elizabeth Scargill appointed her only daughter, Elizabeth, as her sole executor, but usually mothers and fathers included them in a group of coexecutors.[40] Their intention may have been to empower them to protect their inheritances should they have difficulty gaining possession of them. Whatever the motive, the appointments indicate that these parents had confidence in their daughters' practical abilities.[41]

Sparse evidence makes it difficult to know how women who never married spent their time. They undoubtedly participated in the activities characteristic of all aristocratic women—sewing, embroidering, playing musical instruments, attending mass and engaging in private prayer, dispensing alms, and visiting their friends and relatives. Some of them assumed managerial responsibilities in the households in which they lived or otherwise assisted their female relatives. Anne Norris, who lived with her stepmother after she married John Howard, functioned as a gentlewoman servant in the Howard household.[42] Clare Plumpton almost certainly acted as her stepmother's gentlewoman since Lady Plumpton agreed to support her in the settlement of the Plumpton estate between her husband, Sir Robert, and his heir, William.[43] Anne Corbet claimed that she had acted as her mother's servant during the last ten years of her life.[44] Honor Lisle's eldest Basset stepdaughter, Jane, remained in England after most of the family went to Calais and assumed the role of a gentlewoman servant. She closed up the house at Soberton after the Lisles departed and then settled in at Umberleigh, her stepmother's home in Devonshire, where she kept an eye on her stepmother's affairs.[45] These were skills all aristocratic daughters learned as adolescents, whatever their ultimate destiny, from their mothers or from the mistresses of the households in which they were placed.

What surviving documents reveal most clearly, however, is not single women's activities but their ongoing relationships with their kin. Most, though certainly not all of them—one only has to think of Mary Zouche or Anne Corbet and her brother—were surrounded by warm, supportive kin networks centered on their parents, stepparents, and siblings. On her death-bed, Elizabeth Gresham remarked, for example, that her sister and brother-in-law, Sir John and Christian Thynne, "hath been very good unto me this four years" and bequeathed all her movable goods to them.[46] Isabel Bourchier asked to be buried with her deceased sister, Cecily, Lady Ferrers, and divided her inheritance between her brother, Henry, earl of Essex, and half-brother, Richard Grey, future earl of Kent, whom she made her coexecutors.[47]

Never-married women often attached great importance to their relation-ships with their brothers, particularly the family heir. These relationships, which were frequently characterized by affection and trust, had a practical dimension since single women often lived with their brothers, who were ex-pected to assume financial responsibility for them if it became necessary. Cecily Zouche's warm relationship with her brother, Sir John of Codnor, and his wife is unusually well documented. On one occasion, Cecily loaned him £40, a substantial sum for a single woman. When he died in 1530, he be-queathed her a dowry of 100 marks, the same amount he gave his two daughters. He was evidently not simply transmitting money that their father had originally left her since Cecily commented that the bequest was a con-sequence of his great love for her.[48] Zouche's widow, Margaret, her sister-in-law, died the same year and gave her the fur from her damask gown.[49] When William Plumpton died at the age of 62 in 1547, he ensured his sister Clare's financial security by leaving her £40, twice the amount their father had given her twenty-four years earlier.[50] Sir Richard Jerningham included his sister Mary among his coexecutors, along with his wife and a clergyman, a sure sign of his confidence in her. He bequeathed her a standing cup and £10 for her pains, a generous reward to executors in the early sixteenth cen-tury.[51]

Dorothy Clopton's testament gives a particularly detailed picture of a never-married woman's kin network. Her beneficiaries included her father, stepmother, four brothers, three sisters (two married and one single), a sister-in-law, a female cousin, a brother-in-law, two nephews (her sisters' sons), and one couple, the Cloviles, whom she did not identify and who do not seem to have been kin. Dorothy's bequests consisted of jewelry or jeweled objects and clothing. By and large she gave clothing and coral beads to women and precious jewelry or objects to men. She left what appear to be the most valuable jewels—a serpentine bead, a gold brooch with an image in it, and a silver and gilt table (a flat ornament or piece of jewelry)—to her father, the person who needed them least, in recognition of his power as head of the family. She said openly that the purpose of her gift was to secure his assistance in distributing her legacies. She bequeathed another costly piece, a silver pommander, to one of her younger brothers, Robert; gave her stepmother a ring with a daisy she originally received from Lady Broughton; and left rings or beads to two other brothers and two nephews. All the other jewelry consisted of coral beads. Of these, she gave the most precious set, which was garnished with ten beads of gold, to her cousin Katherine Froxmere. Dorothy also distributed an impressive number of luxury garments. She carefully gave each of her sisters and her sister-in-law Anne Darcy a garment that she described as "the best" of its kind.[52] In addition to the ring mentioned above, Dorothy left her stepmother a blue velvet frontlet (another gift from from Lady Broughton) and her cousin Katherine Froxmere a set of minks that Katherine had originally given to her.

Dorothy Clopton had probably received much of the jewelry and many of the clothes she distributed from her own mother, who died many years before, although she also received some from her distant cousin, Lady Broughton. Never-married women who had been well provided for financially by their fathers were often the recipients of many of their mother's movable goods. Anne, countess of Arundel, bequeathed her daughter Katherine the bed and hangings she used in her mother's household, some gowns, and £100.[53] Dame Margaret Sutton's bequest to her daughter Jane included a "pounced piece," spoons, bedding, napery, other household goods belonging to the buttery and kitchen, an ambling horse, three kine, and some lambs. She was apparently trying to provide Jane with a source of income, as well as practical items she would need when she no longer resided in her mother's household.[54] Jane, countess of Southampton, not only added £400 to her daughter Mabel's dowry but also left her a life interest in some leases, £100 worth of plate, £80 worth of apparel, and an impressive collection of jewelry—the countess's best brooch, which was set with ten diamonds and a ruby; an enameled gold book; a chain of gold, enameled black and white; a long gold girdle; a gold cross with a crucifix set with three diamonds and a pearl pendant; and a gold ring with a ruby.[55] She clearly wanted to ensure that Mabel, then in her late 20s, would be able to live in a manner suitable to her status as an earl's daughter whether or not she married. Women's wills thus demonstrate that never-married women participated as both beneficiaries and testators in the endless circulation of jewelry and clothes among female kin and friends.[56]

A fairly consistent picture of the position and lives of never-married women thus emerges from wills and other contemporary documents. Parents, but particularly fathers, felt an obligation to provide livings for all their children, even daughters who did not follow the culturally preferred path of matrimony. This support usually took the form of dowries, whether they eventually married or not, which underscores the point that dowries functioned as women's inheritances. Despite these legacies, single aristocratic women never headed their own households, as widows did. Instead, they almost always lived in the homes of their kin, most often their parents, siblings, or stepmothers. Although they helped their relatives to run their households, they did not act as substitutes for the male head of the household in his absence or play an active role in managing his estates, as wives routinely did. Wherever they resided, their social worlds revolved around their families, with whom they usually enjoyed warm, ongoing ties. With one notable exception in the surviving documents, that of Mary Zouche, their relationships with their stepmothers seem to have been good ones, a point worth noting, given conventional stereotypes.[57] Their relationships with their siblings, both brothers and sisters, seem particularly strong, but their connections with other female kin are also worth noting. Their lives followed the pattern common to all aristocratic women before they married. Because of their single status, they effectively remained perpetual daughters and sisters. Although they contributed to their families financially on a modest scale and by their service in the households in which they resided, they never enjoyed the broad range of activities, control over resources, social recognition, or degree of autonomy open to wives, mothers, and widows. Nor did they occupy a significant role in their families' patronage networks. However much they were valued and loved as individuals, therefore, they did not occupy an essential place in the overall pattern of aristocratic life. This marginality meant that they functioned as living illustrations to the younger women around them of the necessity of marrying to achieve the fullest roles open to women of their class.

CHAPTER 6. MOTHERHOOD—

BEARING AND PROMOTING

THE NEXT GENERATION

*M*OTHERHOOD was a crucial dimension of aristocratic women's careers as wives. Their success in bearing children, particularly sons, ensured the survival of their husbands' lineages and constituted a crucial service to their spouses and in-laws. Although they could never become full members of their husbands' patrilineages, their children represented their marital families' future. Their position as the mothers of the next generation strengthened their relationships with their spouses and increased their leverage with their husbands' close kin. On the practical side, becoming mothers added substantially to the responsibilities they had already assumed as wives. In addition to the physical labor of reproduction, they supervised their children's educations and care and cooperated with their husbands to settle them in appropriate careers and marriages. Performing these tasks increased their influence over the use of their husbands' incomes and enhanced their power and authority in their households.

For the great majority of Yorkist and early Tudor aristocratic women, wifehood and motherhood functioned as two closely linked dimensions of their adult careers. Ninety-one percent of the wives of noblemen and knights bore at least one child.[1] On average, they gave birth to 4.42 children, but substantial numbers produced many more offspring. Almost 40 percent of the women had 5 or more offspring; just under 30 percent had 6 or more.[2] In addition, many aristocratic mothers gave birth to stillborn babies or babies who died in infancy or early childhood.[3] Because many of these births were not recorded, the figures given here are almost certainly underenumerations. According to standard genealogical sources, for example, William, Lord Paget, had 5 children, but he himself noted in passing that he had 9.[4]

This chapter focuses on aristocratic women's experience and activities as mothers, beginning with their pregnancies and ending with their relations with their adult children. It demonstrates that the structure and goals of aristocratic families created a class-specific, historically distinctive form of motherhood. With the exception of the last stages of their pregnancies and lyings-in, the priorities of aristocratic families meant that wives' relationships with their husbands, social and managerial functions, and duties at court took precedence over their obligations as mothers. Aristocratic mothers routinely delegated the physical care of their infants and young children to servants and placed little weight on the importance of daily contact with them. They concentrated instead on ensuring that their adolescent and adult children possessed the property and connections they needed to maintain their position in their class and contribute to their families' advancement in the next generation. Although these goals were clear and widely accepted, aristocratic mothers had to balance the inherent tension between the primogenital priorities of their familes and their commitment to promoting the welfare of all their other children. They also had to cope with the complications that ensued when they were widowed and remarried, particularly if they had offspring by their second and third husbands.

The centrality of the patrilineage to the organization of the aristocratic family and the descent of its land meant that both women and men took an active interest in the pregnancies and deliveries of their female kin and friends and reported the news of conceptions and births with pleasure.[5] In 1472, John Paston III told his brother with evident satisfaction that the duchess of Norfolk was pregnant and expected the quickening within six weeks.[6] A decade later, Richard Page wrote William Stonor that he was "glad for the good speed of my lady and that she is with child."[7] In the 1530s the countess of Rutland "greatly rejoiced" when she heard that her friend Lady Lisle was pregnant.[8] In the Lisles' case, their friends were particularly excited because Lord Lisle did not have a male heir and both he and his wife were relatively old for childbearing. Sir John Wallop, the English ambassador in France, wrote quite frankly that he and his wife, also childless, "conceive great hope thereby, considering not to be so long married as you two, and either of us being younger, man for man, and woman for woman."[9]

As Wallop's comment indicates, members of the aristocracy were open about their desire for children and their disappointment when women failed to conceive. To combat infertility, they circulated sacred and magical objects believed to encourage conception. In 1534, for example, Lord Lisle sent Sir William Kingston and his wife some "tokens . . . to the intent we may have some increase thereof."[10] Women themselves often prayed to St. Anne when they had difficulty conceiving. The cult of St. Anne was particularly strong in fifteenth-century East Anglia, where Katherine Denston, a member of the Suffolk Clopton family, commissioned Osbern Bokenham to write a poem dedicated to the saint to serve the "talismanic function" of enabling her to bear a son.[11] Denston's contemporary, the childless Norfolk heiress, Anne (née Harling), Lady Scrope, built a chapel dedicated to St. Anne at her parish church in East Harling, where she was eventually buried.[12] Her acute disappointment about her infertility was evident in her direction that five children raised at her expense at the grammar school she founded at Rushworth should be designated as "Dame Anne's Children."[13]

Apparently there was no taboo or embarrassment among the aristocracy about discussing pregnancies or continuing their public and social activities until their formal lyings-in began. In 1472 Margaret Paston wrote jocularly to her husband, "Ye have left me such a remembrance that maketh me to think upon you both day and night when I would sleep" and remarked that her pregancy was so advanced that "I am discovered of all men that see me."[14] Indeed, visible signs of pregnancy elicited positive comments about expectant women's "fair," "goodly," "big," or "great" bellies.[15] In 1534 Lady Whethill reported that Lady Lisle's neice, Elizabeth Staynings, was "still a suitor [at court] with a great belly."[16] The countess of Rutland attended her daughter Gertrude's wedding in April 1539 when she was about six months pregnant.[17] Although she remarked that she was "big with child" in early May, she did not return to Belvoir Castle for her lying-in until mid-June.[18] As their figures changed, women adjusted their apparel by wearing their bodices unlaced and covering the opening with stomachers. In May 1537, John Husee reported that Jane Seymour was "great with child, and shall be open-laced with stomacher betwixt this and Corpus Christi day."[19] Two months later, he noted that she "goeth with placard not laced."[20] When he heard of Lady Lisle's pregnancy, William Lock, a mercer, sent her a cloth-of-gold stomacher with the wish that "it may cover a young Lord Plantagenet."[21] Katherine Parr could barely contain her joy at the quickening of her baby. She not only described its movements to her fourth husband, Thomas Seymour, but also allowed one of her friends to feel them. "I gave your little knave your blessing, who like an honest man stirred apace after and before; for Mary Odell being abed with me had laid her hand upon my belly to feel it stir. It hath stirred these three days every morning and evening so that I trust when ye come, it will make you some pastime."[22]

However welcome the news, everyone knew that pregnancy and childbirth were dangerous and might result in the death of the mother and baby.[23] Although there is no way of knowing how many Yorkist and early Tudor aristocratic women died in childbed or soon thereafter and how many survived only after serious illness and pain, no one living in the period could have escaped personal experience or knowledge of such cases. The announcement of a pregnancy, therefore, inspired a stream of wishes and prayers for the safety of the expectant woman and her infant. Richard Page told Sir William Stonor, for example, that he prayed God would send Lady Stonor a "good time and good deliverance."[24] The fullest evidence of the response of an expectant mother's friends to her pregnancy appears in the Lisle letters: seven women and seventeen men sent their wishes that she would become "a glad mother" and have a "prosperous and merry delivery."[25] Some well-wishers also sent religious objects or medicines to assist her. Sir John Wallop gave Lord Lisle two bottles of water from Avignon "against my lady's lying-in . . . and specially when she draweth nigh the churching time. For she shall be so much the readier by 5 or 6 days, if she will use the virtue of the same."[26] Both the Bishop of Hereford and John Whalley gave her cramp rings, and John Husee sent a stock of holy water, a sprinkler, and a casting bottle from London.[27] Lady Lisle herself gave a pregnant friend a girdle, "which hath been about the body of St. Rose."[28] Sir William Clopton evidently believed that the cross he usually wore protected pregnant women and required the son to whom he bequeathed it to lend it to "women of honesty being with child."[29]

Women often expressed concern about the expectant mother's survival and suffering. In 1535, Madame de Bours told Lady Lisle that she had been with her sister-in-law, Madame de Riou, for ten or twelve days but that although she was "sore acrased," she was not yet brought to bed. Anthoinette de Saveuses prayed that God would grant de Riou "a gracious travail, and to her child a name and baptism." She explained anxiously to Lady Lisle that "it hath pleased God to take from me all my relatives. At this present I have no other but her, whom I love as if I were her sister."[30] When de Sauveuses heard that Lady Lisle was pregnant, she exhorted her to be "of good courage" and asked Jesus to assist her in her "hour of need," words conveying her conviction that childbearing was a dangerous ordeal.[31] Three years later, Lady Lisle's niece, the countess of Sussex, almost died after a miscarriage.[32] Personal knowledge of at least some difficult deliveries and maternal deaths probably made it hard for women to contemplate their own or their friends' pregnancies without anxiety.[33]

Although pregnancy was a public event, women alone presided over and controlled the actual delivery of the baby. From the beginning of the expectant mother's lying-in to the churching, the religious service that concluded it, they enacted a series of rituals and customs that constituted the most elaborate expression of female culture recorded in Yorkist and early Tudor sources. In his superb account of childbirth in the seventeenth century, Adrian Wilson suggested that the lying-in lasted for about a month, although it clearly varied greatly, depending on the state of the mother's health. An entry in the Rutland accounts indicated, for example, that the countess's lying-in in 1536–1537 lasted for fifteen days, while Anne, Lady Petre, did not even sit up until two weeks after she gave birth in 1548.[34]

In anticipation of their lyings-in, aristocratic women carefully prepared the room in which they intended to give birth and accumulated the appropriate wardrobe, setting the space apart physically and symbolically by covering the windows and blocking up the keyholes.[35] Once they took to their beds, they depended almost entirely on candles for light. The 1494 ordinances for a royal birth directed, for example, that all the windows except one should be covered, but that one was to be hanged so that the queen could have light "when it pleaseth her."[36] Lyings-in were occasions for conspicuous consumption. Thomas Cromwell spent the hefty sum of £44 15s. on his daughter-in-law's "lying down."[37] Honor, Lady Lisle, consulted the royal tailor about the clothes she needed. He responded that she needed damask, velvet and satin nightgowns, ermine bonnets, and white satin waistcoats trimmed with ermine.[38] Lady Lisle planned to use equally rich beds, carpets, and hangings to furnish her birth chamber, but in this case she sought to enhance her status by borrowing what she needed from the royal wardrobe and the countesses of Rutland and Sussex, her two highest ranking, close friends. Lady Rutland sent a "great chest" with stuff, but unfortunately John Husee itemized the contents in a separate list rather than in the letters that have survived.[39] Lady Sussex promised to send a bed of estate, some carpets, a rich counterpane of ermines bordered with cloth of gold for a bed, a lawn sheet, one or two pairs of fine sheets, and a traverse, but she could not do so until Lady Beauchamp, who was then using them, was churched.[40] Husee also borrowed six carpets and a red traverse of the queen's from the royal wardrobe.[41]

Shortly before they gave birth, perhaps when they felt the first signs of labor, women withdrew to their chambers and remained there for three or four weeks.[42] During this period, as the ordinances for a royal lying-in make clear, they lived solely in the company of women: "And if it please the Queen to take her chamber, she shall be brought thither with Lords and Ladies of estate . . . and they then to take their leave of the Queen. Then all the ladies and gentlewomen to go in with her; and after that no man to come into the chamber where she shall be delivered, save women."[43] Aristocratic women's closest friends and kin shared their lyings-in and valued the opportunity to assist them. Madame de Bours told Lady Lisle twice, for example, that she wished she could be with her when she was "brought to bed to do you any service that I can perform."[44] Mothers and mothers-in-law often assisted their daughters and daughters-in-law, a pattern facilitated by the fact that many young couples lived in one of their parents' households. The wife of William, Lord Paget, and their daughter Jane were both present when another daughter gave birth in her natal home.[45] Lady Ursula Stafford's first child was born at the castle of her father-in-law, the duke of Buckingham, in 1520.[46] Some mothers and mothers-in-law traveled considerable distances to be present at the birth of their grandchildren. The countess of Westmorland went from the Lake Country to Belvoir Castle, Lincolnshire, when her son and heir's wife, who was very young and still living with her parents, gave birth for the first time.[47] The countess of Bath made the shorter journey from Hengrave, Suffolk, to London to help one of her daughters until she was successfully "brought to bed."[48]

Expectant mothers who were already in charge of their own households were more likely to be attended by their own ladies-in-waiting or kin and friends who lived nearby than by their mothers or mothers-in-law, either because the older women had died or were superfluous. In 1519, Lady Anne Lestrange's aunts by marriage, Lady Elizabeth Woodhouse and Mrs. Banyard, attended her for three weeks. Two other women joined them a fortnight later.[49] In July 1539, the countess of Rutland's gentlewomen, who included her younger sister, Margaret; Katherine Basset, daughter of her good friend Honor, Lady Lisle; and Dorothy Lovell, a distant relative by marriage, probably attended her.[50] Whoever they were and whatever their relationship to the expectant mother, those participating in the birth did so under the direction of the midwife. None of the documents used in this study mention the presence of male physicians, although one assumes that they were present at royal births and may well have attended women who delivered their babies in London.

After birth, the lying-in consisted of three stages: during the first, the women remained in bed; during the second, they sat up and walked around but did not leave their chambers; and during the third, they stayed indoors but were no longer confined to their rooms. From the outset, aristocratic women turned their infants over to nurses, who cared for them in separate nurseries while the mothers convalesced. The nurses' duties almost certainly included breastfeeding. This practice enabled fathers to see the infants while their wives remained in seclusion.

The first stage of the lying-in lasted from three days to two weeks, depending on the new mothers' physical condition. Their chambers were still accessible only to women. Friends and neighbors participated vicariously by sending them gifts, mostly of food. In June and July 1539, for example, after the countess of Rutland gave birth to her last child, she received cherries, strawberries, and numerous edible birds from well-wishers.[51] The messages new mothers received while they remained in seclusion show that however strong the aristocracy's desire for heirs and the preference for sons, relief about the survival and health of the mother and child forestalled expression of any disappointment about the birth of girls. The letters reporting that Sir William and Dame Elizabeth Stonor's daughter Anne was "well amended" after giving birth didn't even mention the sex of her baby.[52] Decades later, both the husband and father of Elizabeth, Lady Dacre, responded with obvious pleasure to the news that she had given birth to a girl.[53] Robert Dacres was equally delighted when he told his brother-in-law, Sir Anthony Denny, that "my sister, your wife, is brought to bed of a fair daughter, God save her . . . she is in [as] right good health as a gentlewoman in that case may be."[54]

Since mothers remained in bed, they did not attend their children's christenings, which took place within a few days of the babies' birth because of high infant mortality rates. In 1472, John Paston III advised his brother John II to return from London even before the birth of the duchess of Norfolk's child so that he would be able to attend the baby's christening. He obviously did not think that there would be sufficient time for the journey if he waited until he received news of the baby's birth.[55] Sir William Petre followed customary practice when he had his five-day-old son baptized in 1548.[56] A slightly longer interval might occur if the parents wanted to ask the king or some other distant friend or patron to serve as a godparent. After his wife gave birth to "a fair boy," for example, Ralph Sadler asked Thomas Cromwell to be the infant's "gossip" and give him his name.[57] If the baby was weak, premature, or seemed likely to die for any reason, the women in attendance prevented even a short postponement of the baptism. In 1538, the duke of Norfolk planned to ask Cromwell and the king to be godfathers to his heir's first son, but he reported that because the infant was premature, "the women here would not suffer me to let the child be so long unchristened."[58]

Baptisms occasioned two different kinds of gift giving. In keeping with the general practice of giving gratuities to servants, the infants' godparents and other kin and friends rewarded the midwives and nurses responsible for their delivery and care. Henry VIII rewarded the countess of Worcester's nurse and midwife with £4 and £3 6s. 8d. apiece to the women who attended Sir Nicholas Harvey's and Lord Hussey's children and Lord Audley's grandchild.[59] Thomas Cromwell sent 30 to 45s. to the nurses and midwives of children of the earls of Derby, Sussex, and Hertford; Lady Knyvett; and Mr. Mewtas;[60] and the earl of Rutland gave 50s. at the christening of Lord Hussey's son; a pound at the baptism of Master Harvey's child, and 6s. 8d. at the christening of Sir John Chaworth's son.[61]

Godparents, friends, and kin also sent expensive presents to the children themselves, thereby marking them as owners of luxury goods at the outset of their lives. The gifts to the French Queen and duke of Suffolk's first son included a gold salt and cup from his uncle, Henry VIII; two plain silver and gilt pots from Katherine of Aragon; two silver and gilt flagons from Cardinal Wolsey; and two pounced silver and gilt pots from the bishop of Durham.[62] Henry VIII gave a gilt standing cup to William, Lord Howard's child, and Edward VI sent a gilt standing cup with a cover to the earl of Oxford's son.[63] The duke of Buckingham gave his daughter Mary, Lady Bergavenny, "certain pots" for her first child in November 1520 and a goblet with a cover, with the Stafford knot on it, to one of Sir Anthony Hungerford's younger sons.[64]

Sometime between three days and two weeks after their babies were born, and almost always after they were baptized, women entered the second period of their lyings-in, the "upsitting." During this period of ten to fourteen days, they remained in their rooms but were not confined to bed. Women often celebrated their upsittings, an important stage in their recovery, with feasts or parties attended by large numbers of their female relatives and friends. In 1548, fourteen gentlewomen visited Lady Anne Petre when she sat up two weeks after the birth of a son.[65] The arrival of two women at Hunstanton a fortnight after Lady Anne Lestrange's lying-in began in 1519 probably marked her sitting-up.[66] During the third and final stage of the lying-in, which lasted another week to ten days, women stayed indoors but no longer remained in their chambers.

Women's lyings-in ended ritually when they were churched. Although contemporary sources indicate that churching was routine among the Yorkist and early Tudor aristocracy, the only contemporary description I have found was of Queen Elizabeth Woodville's churching in 1466.[67] There is no way of knowing, therefore, whether aristocratic women conformed to such popular customs as wearing veils during the ceremony and going to church with the midwife and other women who had participated in their deliveries. According to the Sarum Use, the most popular form of the service in pre-Reformation England, the ritual took place at the church door and combined elements of thanksgiving and purification. It opened with the recitation of psalms 121 and 128 and concluded when the priest sprinkled the celebrant with holy water as they recited the words "Thou shalt purge me, O Lord, with hyssop." The priest then led the mother into church, presumably to take communion.[68] After the break with Rome, the first English Book of Common Prayer (1549) called the service "The Order of the Purification of Women," but the second (1552) referred to it as "The Thanksgiving of Women after Childbirth" and substituted psalms 116 and 127 for those used in the Catholic rites.[69] The Anglican service also moved the ceremony inside the church, which often had a special churching pew. The change reflected the Protestant view that the new mother was not ritually unclean and in need of purification.[70]

The entire period, from the day the mother-to-be retired to her lying-in chamber until her churching, was unique in the lives of aristocratic women since it moved them into a female space controlled by other women. On a practical level, the lying-in allowed women ample time to recover from the ordeal of childbirth. On a symbolic level, it functioned much like a classic initiation rite composed of the three stages of separation, transition, and reincorporation.[71] But this symbolic interpretation does not account for the specific form the rituals surrounding childbirth took and, particularly, the fact that they were collective and exclusively female.[72] Elaborating on Natalie Davis's suggestion that the lying-in reversed customary power relations between wife and husband, Adrian Wilson concluded that it "inverted the central feature of patriarchy, namely its basis in individual male property" in their wives' bodies and labor and "represented a successful form of women's *resistance* to patriarchal authority."[73] The lying-in not only deprived aristocratic husbands of control over their wives but also subordinated men who rarely took orders from women to their wives' attendants, as the duke of Norfolk acknowledged when he reluctantly agreed to the speedy baptism of his grandson. The lying-in also increased women's political power vis-à-vis their male kin because they had exclusive access to their families' female patrons at that time. During the Pastons' long-drawn-out effort to regain Caister Castle from the duke of Norfolk, for example, John Paston III told his mother that the duchess "would be right glad to have you about her at her labor" and asked her to be ready to leave immediately if she were summoned, "for I think your being here should do great good to my brother's matters that he hath to speed with her."[74] Ralph Sadler's remark that the taboo against choosing pregnant women as godmothers was a "superstitious opinion and usage amongst women" may well be read as a protest—albeit an unconscious one—against a form of female power he felt unable to defy.[75]

During the period of the lying-in, aristocratic women's reproductive labor took precedence over their other responsibilities as wives. But even in the birth chamber, the low priority the aristocracy attached to the physical care of babies and young children was evident in the speed with which new mothers turned their infants over to hired nurses. They attached far more importance to returning to their household duties and attendance at court than to caring for and spending time with their babies and young children, who remained in the care of nurses and other servants. Their priorities have inevitably raised questions about their conception of good mothering and the character and intensity of women's emotional bonds to their offspring.[76] Both female and male members of the aristocracy attached considerable importance to good mothering, which they described as "natural," an expression conveying their conviction that good mothering was a result of the biological connection between mother and child and part of God's design for his creation.[77] Contemporary use of the phrase indicates that good mothering had two distinct dimensions, one affective, the other practical: "natural" mothers loved their children, cared deeply about their physical and spiritual health, freely used their property on their children's behalf, and gave a high priority to arranging their marriages and securing advantageous preferments for them. But good mothering did not require women to have daily contact with their infants and young children. The aristocratic conception of good mothering was, in short, tailored to meet the demands of their lifestyle and familial and political duties.

Tenderness, loving concern, and devotion were unquestionably crucial characteristics of good mothering, and members of the aristocracy expected women to bond emotionally with their children. In his will, Sir Anthony Denny mentioned the "fervent, inward, and hidden affection that noble nature hath grassed in the honest mother towards her dear children."[78] Cardinal Pole expressed similar ideas in more homey language when he told his niece, the countess of Huntingdon, that he wanted "little Walter," her son and his godson, "for a while not to be from you, but continue under your wing as the little chicken under the hen."[79] At the same time, aristocratic mothers never forgot the practical dimension of their responsibilities for their children. In-deed, members of the Yorkist and early Tudor aristocracy assumed that they expressed their love for their offspring by devoting their energy and financial resources to ensuring their material well-being and worldly success. John Gre-vill articulated this idea clearly in a deed that enfeoffed his wife with all his movable goods for her use in raising their children. He explained that he "wholely referreth and putteth in trust the education and bringing up of them, with the advancement and setting forward of the same in worldly liv-ing, unto his said best beloved wife, for that he well knoweth that she being natural mother unto them will above all other creatures tender their bringing up, education, and setting forth."[80]

When mothers failed to treat their children generously, their behavior was deemed "unnatural." In 1538, Margaret, dowager marchioness of Dorset, who was quarreling with her eldest son, had to defend herself against the charge that she was an unnatural mother because she did not give him a sufficient al-lowance. She wrote anxiously to Cromwell that there were "many untrue and light reports of my unnatural and unkind dealings toward my son marquis, much to my slander and rebuke, which trouble me not a little considering how good mother I have always been towards him in heart and deed . . . for his commodity and wealth."[81] In an even more extreme case, Parliament ac-tually deprived Lady Elizabeth Draycott of control over her inheritance, be-cause she had left her husband and "conceived such mortal and unnatural hate toward her own natural children" that she was trying to disinherit them. The act explained that if she were allowed to fulfill her purpose, she would in-jure her family and encourage other ill-disposed women to "like offences of disobedience, obstinacy, and unnatural ingratitude towards their husbands and natural children contrary to the laws of God and the principles and rules of nature."[82]

Unlike Lady Draycott, most aristocratic mothers developed strong, loving ties to their offspring in their early years, even though they rarely participated in their infants' routine care and almost always left their children behind when they left home. Evidence of their feelings appears in their petitions to the crown for their children's wardships. At the same time, the crown's indif-ference to the feelings of mothers underscores one of the ways in which court politics shaped aristocratic family life. The failure of Sir John Russell's suit for the wardship of his stepdaughter is a perfect example of both dimen-sions of the maternal experience. His wife, Lady Anne, was distraught about the possibility of losing custody of her younger daughter by her first hus-band, Sir John Broughton, after their only son died. Sir Thomas Henage, a member of Henry VIII's Privy Chamber, warned Cardinal Wolsey, "My lady Russell takes the death of her son so sore that Russell fears, if she should not obtain your favor for the wardship of the younger sister, it will be her utter undoing."[83] Her husband explained, "I do desire her for nothing else but for my wife's pleasure. For she would be very loth that another should have her said daughter afore her. For it is all her joy in this world."[84] Despite these pleas, Wolsey kept the wardship for himself. It passed to Agnes, duchess of Norfolk, when he fell from power the next year.[85] Dame Anne Owen was equally disappointed when she petitioned for the wardship of "my natural son, John Owen, which is now but young and tender and of the age of ten years."[86] Her grief at being deprived of his care was clear two years later when she reminded Cromwell that she had placed John in his household "contrary to my own heart" in exchange for assistance in reaching a settlement with her husband's executors. She wrote plaintively, "If it might please your lordship, I would be very glad to see him."[87]

Women's love for their children was also evident in their open grief when they died. They had difficulty accepting these deaths despite high infant and child mortality rates. The chronicler Edward Hall reported that when Katherine of Aragon's son died in 1511, "like a natural woman, [she] made much lamentation, howbeit, by the king's good persuasion and behavior, her sorrow was mitigated, but not shortly."[88] Years later, Katherine Parr advised Lady Wriothesely not to mourn her son's death with "inordinate" or "excessive" sorrow, but added empathetically, "Yet, when I consider, you are a mother by flesh and nature, doubting how you can give place quietly to the same; in as much as Christ's mother, endowed with all godly virtues, did utter a sorrowful natural passion of her son's death."[89] Lady Wriothesley was not the only noblewoman who found the religious injunction to resignation hard to follow. Four months after the duchess of Suffolk's two sons died in 1551, she told her good friend William Cecil, "And truly I take this his [i.e., God's] last (and to the first sight most sharp and bitter) punishment not for the least of his benefits, in as much as I have never been so well taught by any other before to know his power, his love, and mercy, my own wickedness, and that wretched state that without him I should endure here. . . . But, as I must confess myself no better than flesh, I am not well able with quiet to behold my very friends without some part of these vile dregs of Adam to seem sorry for that whereof I know I rather ought to rejoice."[90]

Although separations from their children were a routine aspect of aristocratic life, mothers clearly missed them when they were apart and remained closely involved in their upbringing. In 1471, a servant of Thomas Stonor reported that the duchess of Suffolk had returned to her household at Ewelme because "she thought full long [to have been] from the young lord and young ladies, her children, that been there."[91] Another widow who could not bear to be parted from her children, Katherine Willoughby, duchess of Suffolk, accompanied her sons when they went to Cambridge to study.[92] John Smyth reported that "above all the ladies of her day," Anne, Lady Berkeley, was "noted to be the most tender hearted to her children; and to them so over and above reason indulgent, as not contentedly she admitted them out of her sight."

Her behavior was considered extreme, however, and her children "often complained of that want of learning which a juster education should have afforded their estates and parentage."[93]

Women who placed their offspring at court or in other peoples' households barraged their substitutes with advice. Cromwell's correspondence is filled with directives of this sort from the mothers of boys living in his household. Four years after she reluctantly sent her son to live with him, for example, Anne Owen recommended that he appoint Richard Pollard as the boy's tutor. She also asked him to allow the 14-year-old boy to dispense the money she sent for his room or board "to find himself and his servant" in order to teach him the financial skills of a gentleman.[94] Margaret, dowager marchioness of Dorset, asked Cromwell to discipline her eldest son, Henry, who was living at court in 1534: "When you shall happen to see in my son marquis either any large playing [i.e., gambling] or usual swearing or any demeanor unmeet for him to use, which I fear me shall be very often, that it may please you . . . in some friendly fashion to rebuke him."[95] Several years later, she wanted him to be "a very father" to her younger son Thomas and "call sharply on him for his diligent service to you."[96]

Mothers who left their children at home when they traveled were equally diligent in overseeing their care. When Elizabeth Stonor, wife of Sir William, heard that her daughter Katherine was "craysed and hath a disease on her neck," she asked her husband "to suffer her to come to London to me to the intent she may be helped thereof" and sent three servants to Stonor to fetch her.[97] A month later she told him to send all the children since the epidemic of the pox in the city was over.[98] He must have complied because she subsequently reported, "Your children and mine fare well, blessed be God, and they be to me a great comfort in your absence."[99] Decades later, when the countess of Bath was in London and her husband reported that "a sickness" had broken out at Hengrave, she responded with prompt instructions about where to move their children. Her expectation that he would do as she instructed was clear in her concluding remarks: "If you will follow these orders which I have appointed ye in, I will tarry . . . If not, I will make speed to come home."[100] Within the parameters set by the structure and pattern of aristocratic life, she was an involved and loving mother.

Many daughters and sons appreciated and reciprocated their mothers' love and care. Years after her mother died, Frances West remembered her mother's "special love and zeal unto her above other of her children."[101] Her contemporary, Edward, Lord Hastings, recalled "the great trouble, pains, heaviness, and labor that the said lady his mother had with him in his bringing up, and specially since the decease of his said lord and father, and the manifold motherly kindnesses to him hitherto showed."[102] Unfortunately, few letters from children or adolescents to their mothers survive, and those that do have a stiff tone that probably reflected their inexperience in writing letters, as well as contemporary conventions about how people should address their superiors, rather than strained or distant relationships. A letter from Jane Long to the countess of Bath, which opened with the conventional "my duty remembered in my most humble wise" and closed "your most obedient daughter," is a good example. Its brief content consisted almost entirely of conventional phrases and sentiments.[103] Anne, Mary, and Katherine Basset's letters to Lady Lisle were somewhat more open about their affection for their mother: they expressed pleasure when they had heard from her, asked for letters when they hadn't, and often said they wanted to see her.[104] Mary was the warmest and most spontaneous of the girls, at least in their correspondence. Her feelings often seemed to be pushing against the conventional phrases so prominent in their letters. Most notable was her wish—"I would be with you when you shall be brought to bed, to warm his swaddling clouts for the babe"—during her mother's false pregnancy.[105] Men also recognized the close ties between their wives and daughters. Thus, Sir Humphrey Starkey left his wife, Isabel, "a goblet of silver and gilt with a covering of silver and gilt, which goblet was her mother's." Sir Edmund Molyneux gave his three younger daughters their mother's clothes and a little casket with her jewels and other things in it. He also gave Dorothy her mother's best ring and ouche as she had wished.[106]

As their daughters and sons approached adolescence, the practical side of motherhood assumed a larger role in the duties aristocratic women carried out for their families. Their participation in securing appropriate preferments for them was important because they were responsible for mobilizing their natal kin and friends on their children's behalf. Whether they were able to do so or not was one marker of their usefulness to their marital families. Most often at this juncture, they and their husbands sought to place their children at court or in the households of more powerful, better connected families than their own, which required activating all their friends and relatives. Aristocratic mothers were also actively involved in finding suitable mates for their children and negotiating their marriage contracts, although they clearly had to act in consultation with their husbands, who provided the dowries and jointures necessary to finance them. In the well-known case of Margery Brews and John Paston, Elizabeth Brews met with John's widowed mother to work out terms acceptable to her husband.[107] Her contemporary Katherine, countess of Huntingdon, participated in the discussions about a proposed match between her 15-year-old daughter and the heir of the earl of Lincoln.[108]

Widows and wives with offspring from previous marriages had particularly heavy responsibilities for preferring their children since they almost always had sole or joint custody of them.[109] Recent widows often expressed anxiety about assuming this burden alone. Lady Elizabeth Savage, who was in a particularly vulnerable position after her second husband, William Brereton, was executed for committing adultery with Anne Boleyn, sent Cromwell a gelding, promised that she and her "poor children" would remember him in their prayers, and then stated the real point of her letter—"that it would please you of your goodness to have my poor suits in remembrance."[110] After Sir Thomas Englefield's death in 1537, his widow wrote to Cromwell plaintively, "I assure you there was never poor woman had a greater worldly loss than I and my poor children have of him. . . . For we be now left alone and comfortless, having no help . . . unless it may please your lordship of your pity and goodness to be good lord unto me and them."[111] Despite Lady Englefield's reference to herself as a "poor silly woman," her deceased husband, a justice of the Court of Common Pleas with considerable experience in such matters, had enough confidence in her to appoint her one of his coexecutors.[112] When Lady Englefield herself died six years later, she left careful instructions about how *her* executors should complete the education and preferment of their younger son John and unmarried daughter Susan. She also increased Susan's dowry.[113] There is no way of knowing whether women like Elizabeth Englefield and Elizabeth Savage had as little confidence in themselves as their letters suggest or whether they were simply employing the trope of the defenseless widow as a strategy for gaining Cromwell's sympathy and assistance. What is clear is that they were representative of a large group of widowed mothers who competently raised their children, protected the children's inheritances, and arranged appropriate preferments for them.

Mothers' involvement in arranging their children's marriages also increased after their husbands died. If they held their eldest sons' or inheriting daughters' wardships, they made an especially important contribution to the family's position in the next generation. Mabel Parr paid "great sums" to the earl of Essex to marry her only son to his only daughter and heir, a match that lifted the Parrs into the ranks of the upper nobility. Margaret Whorewood, the widow of a lawyer who ended his career as Henry VIII's attorney-general, married their only surviving daughter to the Throckmorton of Coughton heir, a social leap just as large as the one Dame Parr engineered for her son.[114] Honor, Lady Lisle, married her only son by Sir John Basset upward by matching him with Frances, the daughter of her second husband, Lord Lisle.[115]

Most mothers were, of course, responsible for finding mates for noninheriting sons and daughters rather than heirs and heiresses since they often could not secure the latters' wardships. Those who remarried were sometimes able to secure advantageous marriages for them with their stepsiblings. Such matches, thirty of which have turned up in the sources used in this book, may well have been one of the attractions of remarrying. But mothers usually had to look more widely. Margaret, countess of Salisbury, paid extraordinary sums to marry her daughter Ursula to the third duke of Buckingham's heir, giving her a dowry of 3,000 marks, settling land worth 700 marks on the young couple and their children, and promising to increase Ursula's dowry by

1,000 marks if she recovered land she claimed from the king.[116] In 1530, Elizabeth Lucy, who had far fewer resources than the countess, went to London to complete negotiations for her daughter Radegund's marriage, but she would not agree to a final settlement without Cromwell's advice.[117] Although she did not hold his wardship, Lady Lucy was also instrumental in securing her son Richard Catesby's consent to a marriage with his guardian's daughter.[118]

Margaret, countess of Bath, to give a last, particularly well-documented example, was responsible for finding mates for twelve children since each of her three husbands died before any of their offspring were married. Like Mabel Parr, she aimed high, marrying her eldest son, Thomas Kitson, first to Lord Paget's daughter and then to Elizabeth Cornwallis, daughter of Sir Thomas, a client of the duke of Norfolk and head of a distinguished East Anglian family.[119] In the case of Frances, probably her youngest daughter by Kitson, she employed the same strategy as Honor Lisle to marry her into the nobility: one of the conditions of her marriage to the earl of Bath was his agreement to a union between Frances and his eldest son. The countess lived to see her grandson inherit the earldom.[120] She also concluded matches with knights for her three other Kitson daughters.[121] When she died in 1561, her five remaining daughters were still single, but her correspondence shows that she had been looking for desirable husbands for them.[122] In her will, the countess added 600 marks apiece to the marriage portions Sir Richard Long had left their three daughters and 900 marks each to the dowries of her two daughters by the earl.[123]

In addition to arranging their children's marriages and preferments, the crucial task facing widowed or remarried mothers was defending their sons' and daughters' inheritances and their daughters' dowries and jointures. Their compelling interest in their offsprings' futures was a major reason that so many men appointed them as their sole or coexecutors. Threats to their children's inheritances came from many directions. In Henry VII's reign, for example, the widowed Elizabeth Birmingham petitioned Chancery because her father-in-law intended to disinherit her sons, his grandchildren, in favor of a son by his second wife.[124] The estates of inheriting daughters were particularly vulnerable because collateral males, especially their paternal uncles and first cousins, routinely challenged their rights on the ground that their inheritances should have descended in male tail. Mary Willoughby, widow of Lord Willoughby of Eresby, played a key role in defending the rights of Katherine, their only daughter, against her uncle Christopher. She had a powerful, indeed crucial, ally in Charles, duke of Suffolk, the king's brother-in-law and intimate friend, who held the girl's wardship. Suffolk, whose wife and heir died in rapid succession in 1533 and 1534, eventually married the young heiress himself.[125] In a classic suit involving a contest between the heirs general and the male heir, Isabel Harrington, widow of Sir James, claimed his estates for her ten daughters, the heirs general, against her husband's brother, who claimed they were held in male tail.[126] In truth, her husband's will stated quite clearly that some of his inheritance was entailed to his heirs male and some to his heirs general.[127] No record exists of how this feud was resolved.

Mothers also protected their daughters' dowries and jointures. Elizabeth Tailboys sued her brother for her daughter's dowry in a petition that exposed the complicated agreements and transactions that often accompanied aristocratic marriages. According to Lady Tailboys, the contested money was part of her own unpaid marriage portion.[128] Anne Bourchier offered to cancel her son-in-law's debt to her if he would assure her daughter's jointure according to the marriage contract she had signed with his father.[129] Ursula Hynde relied on a similar strategy and bequeathed her son-in-law a considerable amount of plate, a number of farm animals, and the featherbed in her chamber "with all that goes with it" if he gave his wife a particular manor as her jointure.[130]

Second and third husbands often supported their wives' suits on behalf of their children, which may have been an incentive for some widows to remarry.[131] Sir John Savage and his wife, Alice, fought for years on behalf of her four sons by Sir William Gresley. Gresley's brother, Sir George, claimed to be the rightful heir because Alice's children were born while Sir William's first wife was alive and were, therefore, illegitimate. Wolsey ruled in Sir George's favor but awarded each of the boys incomes from their father's estate.[132] Lord and Lady Lisle's tenacious efforts to preserve the Beaumont inheritance for her son by Sir John Basset and to prevent the current holders from wasting it, particularly by selling off the woods, are painstakingly documented in their letters and give an idea of the vigilance necessary to protect contested property.[133]

While protecting their daughters' and sons' inheritances and their daughters' dowries and jointures might seem like a straightforward task, in practice some mothers found it difficult to fulfill their obligations to all their children without quarreling with their eldest sons. Primogeniture and the pattern of giving heirs the largest and most valuable share of their fathers' movable goods meant that some eldest sons resented any but the most minimal legacies to their siblings. They also often regarded their fathers' provisions for their mothers as excessive. In addition, some heirs felt aggrieved if their mothers were heiresses and left all or some of their property to their younger sons and daughters. When women served as their husbands' executors, disputes about the men's provisions for their widows and noninheriting children often became intertwined.

Quarrels about all these issues developed in two successive generations of the family of the marquesses of Dorset. In 1504, Cecily, widow of the first marquess and sole heir of William, Lord Bonville, announced her intention of marrying Lord Henry Stafford, the duke of Buckingham's younger brother. Her son, the second marquess, worried that she would use her inheritance to endow her second, younger husband at his expense. Stafford, who paid Henry VII £2,000 for permission to marry Cecily, obviously expected the match to be profitable, which gives credence to his stepson's fears. Dorset also challenged his mother's right to continue as his father's executor. The king and royal council intervened to prevent their dispute from escalating. The settlement the crown dictated permitted the marchioness to administer her husband's estate until she had paid his debts but prevented her from claiming her dower until she had transferred the remainder of her son's inheritance to him. The award also severely limited her power over her own inheritance: she had to bequeath all of it to her eldest son when she died; until then, she could grant lands worth up to 1,000 marks per annum for a limited period of years. In effect, the govenment limited her rights as an heiress in favor of her eldest son and the practice of primogeniture.[134] Almost two decades later, Dorset and his mother were quarreling again, this time about their responsibilities for his seven surviving siblings. On this occasion, Cardinal Wolsey intervened and required each of them to contribute to the dowries of the marquess's four sisters. In addition, the dowager marchioness promised to create annuities drawn from her inheritance for her three younger sons.[135]

In the next generation, Dorset's heir, Henry, the third marquess, engaged in even uglier battles with his mother. Their feud probably began when Henry, who was still under age, renounced his betrothal to Katherine Fitzalan, the earl of Arundel's daughter, and incurred a fine of £4,000 for breach of contract.[136] Because of this enormous, unexpected financial burden, Lady Margaret, who had custody of all her husband's property during Henry's minority, feared she would "not be able to set forth my daughters in marriage, neither continue in the keeping of my poor house."[137] Insisting that her husband's estate was "right small" in comparison to his debts and the cost of supporting herself and their children, she tried to limit her expenses for Henry to the allowance specified in his father's will. In addition, she only consented to a marriage between Henry and the duke of Suffolk's eldest daughter on the condition that the duke would support the couple during Henry's minority.[138]

Lady Margaret's lack of generosity to Henry shocked her peers as unmotherly and inappropriate behavior toward a high-ranking nobleman distantly related to the king. In 1534 she felt compelled to answer the charge that she was an "unnatural mother" and offered to contribute to her son's advancement "as my small power is and shall be."[139] Four years later, she referred defensively to "untrue and light reports of my unnatural and unkind dealings toward my son marquis."[140] By this time, Henry, who had come of age, was so discontented that he brought his quarrel with his mother before the king's council. Lady Margaret belatedly admitted that his allowance was not "meet or sufficient to maintain his estate" and offered to increase it.[141] Whatever arrangements they made at this time, Henry remained aggrieved and his mother wisely decided to move out of the family seat. She discovered to her

Margaret Wotton Grey, marchioness of Dorset, by Holbein RL12209. The Royal Collection ©2001, Her Majesty Queen Elizabeth II.

horror, however, that he would not allow her servants to remove her personal possessions. In a plaintive letter to Cromwell, she referred to herself as a "poor widow . . . unkindly and extremely . . . handled by my son marquis" and appealed to his honor as a nobleman and knight of the garter to convince him to compel her son to release her goods.[142]

The conflicts between the dowager marchionesses of Dorset and their eldest sons in two successive generations are among the most dramatic and best documented of such quarrels between 1450 and 1550.[143] Although most families escaped such conflicts, the dominance of a primogenital inheritance system encouraged heirs to regard their widowed mothers and siblings as burdens on their inheritances. Nonetheless, fathers had little alternative to providing for their daughters, younger sons, and widows with heavy, long-term charges on their estates in the form of dowries, annuities, jointures, and dowers, effectively postponing for considerable periods the moment when their heirs would receive the entire income from their inheritances. The situation was further complicated because so many men appointed their widows as their sole executors or coexecutors. Since they were not members of their husbands' patrilineages, they had far less stake than the heirs in minimizing expenditures on behalf of their younger sons and daughters, and they went to great lengths to implement their husbands' provisions for them. They also had a compelling interest in protecting their own jointures and dowers. As we have seen in the case of Cecily, marchioness of Dorset, the situation was even more explosive when mothers who were heiresses remarried and might be tempted to use their estates to endow their second husbands and families. In these circumstances, the stage was set for conflict if mothers and their eldest sons did not have good preexisting relationships or the latter resented their responsibilities for their brothers and sisters.

Quarrels between mothers and daughters about their dowries and legacies were far less numerous, but they certainly occurred. In the 1470s, Richard, Lord Dacre, and his wife, Joan, sued her mother for conspiring to disinherit her and her sister. Their suit may have been part of the larger quarrel between the heirs male and heirs general over the Dacre estates.[144] Most disputes between mothers and daughters developed because women who were executing their husbands' wills had to accumulate the girls' dowries over considerable periods of time. In her petition to Chancery about the goods her father had left her, for instance, Sir Hugh Willoughby's daughter Isabel claimed that her mother had promised to give them to her "as soon as I have done with the marrying of your sister Eleanor and your brother Ralph" but had not fulfilled her promise decades later.[145] Alice Mynors anticipated that her daughter Elizabeth would be dissatisfied with the £20 she was leaving her "in full recompense of her child's part" of her father's estate. To ensure that Elizabeth and her husband did "not vex themselves or trouble mine executors," Alice gave Elizabeth an additional £10 in gold money, a gold cross worth £6, and woods that had cost her £40. She directed that if, nonetheless, Elizabeth and her husband were not contented, "but [decided] further to vex and trouble mine executors for the said child's part or other demands, then I will that they then neither of them shall have the value of one penny further than his [i.e., Elizabeth's father] will gives them."[146]

Widows who preferred their children successfully, arranged advantageous marriages for them, and protected their inheritances, dowries, and jointures assumed full responsibility for functions they had previously carried out jointly with their spouses, expanding but not fundamentally transforming their careers as wives. As long as they remained single, they maximized the coincidence of their interests and the interests of their children. When they remarried, however, coverture legally subordinated them to men who were not their children's fathers and created the possibility of conflicts between their functions as wives and mothers in a particularly threatening way. To complicate matters further, the common law created a significant exception to the disabilities that flowed from coverture by according wives the full legal rights necessary to administer their deceased husbands' wills. The rationale for this exception was that women were not personally incompetent but suffered from specific proprietary incapacities.[147] The majority of aristocratic wives in second marriages were therefore in the anomalous position of simultaneously being guardians of their offspring, fully empowered legal executors of their deceased spouses' testaments, and *femes coverts*. The potential for conflict between their roles was enormous, particularly if their new husbands also had offspring from previous marriages or they had more children together.

Mothers who remarried almost always took their minor and unpreferred children with them to their new homes unless their offspring were heirs and became wards of the crown. Even then, they and/or their new spouses often purchased their custody from the king.[148] Whether they were their stepchildren's legal guardians or not, stepfathers had a great deal of power over them and relatively easy access to their property because, in their roles as their deceased husband's executors, women often had custody of considerable wealth—money, plate, and jewels—that belonged to their sons and daughters. In addition, during their second marriages they often accumulated large amounts of cash for their children's dowries, educations, and preferment from their previous spouses' estates.

In many cases, women's second husbands helped them to carry out their responsibilities to the offspring of their first marriages. As we have already seen, stepfathers often joined their wives as plaintiffs in the petitions and suits necessary to secure their stepchildren's inheritances and legacies. But this is only one of the ways in which they assisted their wives in meeting the heavy demands on them after their children's fathers died. Since safeguarding large amounts of money, plate, and jewelry was difficult in a society without banks or other reliable financial institutions, many women entrusted their children's money and valuables to their new husbands. When Elizabeth (née Stonor) Compton Walsh married Sir Philip Hoby as her third husband, for example, she asked him to safeguard the money she had accumulated for the dowries of her daughters by her second husband, Sir Walter Walsh. As she anticipated, Hoby safeguarded the money and make it available when she needed it.[149] Other stepfathers helped their wives to arrange or finance their stepdaughters' marriages. Margaret (née Chedworth) Wyfold Norris, almost certainly required the assistance of her third husband, Sir John Howard, a Yorkist courtier and royal servant, to negotiate the advantageous match between her daughter, Isabel Wyfold, whose father was a London grocer, and Sir Henry Marney, a courtier.[150] William, marquess of Berkeley, gave his stepdaughter Anne a manor to finance her marriage to the heir of Richard, Lord Beauchamp, in 1481.[151]

These examples illustrate the ways in which remarriage could strengthen women's ability to discharge the maternal duties they carried into widowhood. But there was always a danger that their children's money and goods would become confused with their second and third husbands' possessions and cash, particularly if the men died before their children were preferred. Conscientious men tried to forestall this possibility by writing their wills very carefully to ensure that their stepchildren's property would be returned. They wanted to prevent lawsuits against their estates and avoid divine retribution for jeopardizing their stepchildren's well-being. Many of them stated explicitly that their legacies to their stepchildren included all the money and valuables they were holding on their behalf. In 1539, for example, Sir William Hawte gave his stepdaughters a lease to hold until their brother was 18 "in full recompence" of the revenue he had received from one of their father's manors.[152] George Giffard left his eldest stepson a silver and gold cup worth £6 13s. 4d. and an equivalent sum in cash to his two younger stepsons, noting carefully that these gifts were "besides all the money that I have paid for them, out of their children's parts of their father's goods, to the late king Henry the eighth and to king Edward the sixth, so that every of them may have their whole parts bequested them by their late father."[153] Sir Edward Grevill directed his wife, one of his coexecutors, to distribute the bequests of her first husband, Sir Thomas Dinham, to their children "at such time as shall be thought reasonable."[154]

Men who anticipated that their stepchildren would claim that all their property had not been returned to them frequently took the precaution of making their legacies to them conditional on their acknowledging that they had received everything due them. Sir John Tyrell left his wife's daughter £40 "upon condition that I nor mine executors be not troubled nor vexed for anything contained in the will of John Hopton, esq., her father."[155] Thomas, Lord Berkeley, left one of his stepdaughters, Katherine Rowden, £50 "in full recompence, satisfaction and payment" of the legacies due her under her father's and uncle's wills if she renounced further claims on his estate. But he also admitted that he had sold "and converted to my use" a gold chain and plate that her uncle had bequeathed her sister Frances because of his "great need." In compensation, he left her £140. Luckily for Frances, Berkeley was honest, had sufficient resources to repay her, and appointed her mother as one of his coexecutors. If he had been less conscientious and careful, she would have had few alternatives to the expensive and tedious process of the law to recover money that was probably intended to finance her marriage.[156]

Two Chancery suits illustrate the difficulties stepchildren might face in re-covering property and goods in their stepfathers' possession. In the first case, Harry Frensche petitioned on behalf of his wife, Elizabeth, daughter of Sir Christopher Harcourt, for a dowry bequeathed to her by her grandmother and delivered to her stepfather, Sir John Huddleston, when she was "of tender age."[157] In the second case, Sanchia Strelley, widow of John, was responsible for the dowry and other legacies that Strelley left to her daughter Anne and that she took with her when she married Sir John Digby. Years later, Anne and her husband, Sir John Markham, claimed that Digby had appropriated her dowry and the livestock her father had bequeathed to her. They also con-tended that Sanchia had brought a "great substance" of Strelley's other wealth with her when she married Digby, who also appropriated it. On her deathbed, Sanchia felt "great remorse in [her] conscience" and died "with sore lamentation" because she had not performed Strelley's will but Digby nonetheless refused to give Anne her dowry or the livestock. Digby himself died shortly afterward, and the Markhams sued his executors, two of Anne's stepbrothers, for the money and livestock, as well as the deeds to land that Anne, one of Strelley's coheirs, claimed as her inheritance. One of the broth-ers, Simon, responded that Anne had received the dowry and livestock many years before, that on her deathbed Sanchia had given Anne and her husband a chain and jewels worth far more than the goods and money they were de-manding from him, and that he was entitled to retain the deeds in question because they were related to an ongoing lawsuit. There is no way of deter-mining the truth of either the Markhams' or Digbys' contentions, but an act of Parliament did eventually partition John Strelley's land among his daugh-ters, including Lady Markham.[158] In these cases, unlike examples cited earlier, mothers had jeopardized their ability to fulfill their responsibilities to their children by remarrying. These very different outcomes demonstrate how dif-ficult the choices facing aristocratic widows were when they had to decide whether or not remarrying would benefit or endanger their children.

Mothers who remarried not only subjected their children to stepfathers but also often acquired stepsons and stepdaughters of their own. There is consid-erably more evidence of antagonism between stepmothers and their stepchil-dren than of conflict between men and their stepchildren because women in second marriages were likely to outlive their husbands, an explosive situation if they were major beneficiaries or executors of their spouses' wills. The rela-tionships between widows and their stepchildren were especially fraught when the men had married much younger women and had second families with them. The offspring of their first wives, particularly their heirs, often considered their stepsiblings interlopers who were supported and preferred at their expense.

Occasionally, stepchildren or their kin accused women of behaving like the classic wicked stepmother. In a petition to Chancery, John Cotton charged that his niece Anne, daughter of Sir Robert Cotton, had fled from the "manifold unkindnesses" of her stepmother, Dame Alice, into a convent after her father died, but not before Alice had tricked her into willing her property to her half-brother rather than to the plaintiff.[159] Mary Zouche's desperate letter to her cousin, Sir John Arundell, begged him to rescue her and her siblings from "the greatest thralldom of the world."[160] There is no way of knowing if these charges were justified. What is notable, however, is how few accusations of this kind surfaced in the material collected for this project.

Even if Mary Zouche's and John Cotton's allegations were true, they represent only one side of the story of the relations between stepmothers and their stepchildren, as the evidence about Margaret, countess of Bath, and Honor, Lady Lisle, demonstrates. When the Lisles moved to Calais, they took four of Lady Lisle's daughters by Sir John Basset and Frances, one of Lord Lisle's daughters by his first wife, with them.[161] Lord Lisle sent another daughter, Elizabeth, to live with her half-brother, John Dudley, and sent Bridget, the youngest, to board at St. Mary's convent in Winchester. Dozens of letters to Lady Lisle refer to her daughters and the stepdaughter resident at Calais in a way that strongly suggests she treated them all very much the same.[162] Two extant letters to her from her stepdaughter Frances have an easy chatty style and warmth that reflect their positive relationship.[163]

Although Lady Lisle's two other stepdaughters lived elsewhere, she was far more concerned about their welfare and actively involved in their affairs than their father. While Bridget, the younger of the two, was boarding at St. Mary's, Winchester, the abbess, Elizabeth Shelley, and the Lisles' friends and servants regularly reported to her about the child rather than to her father. Lady Lisle frequently sent them directions about Bridget's wardrobe and money for her expenses.[164] Eventually Sir Anthony Windsor removed Bridget from the convent because "she is very spare and hath need of cherishing." Lady Lisle, who was in England at the time, decided unilaterally to bring her back to Calais. Lord Lisle's only comment was that he was "sorry that ye will bring my daughter Bridget with you."[165] Lady Lisle apparently did not consider it necessary to supervise the care of Bridget's older sister, Elizabeth, who lived with Elizabeth's half-brother, nearly as closely, but even so Lady Lisle's servants assumed that she was interested in the girl's welfare and routinely reported to her about her stepdaughter. On one occasion, John Husee told Lord Lisle that Elizabeth needed a new gown, but it was his wife who followed up on the request.[166]

Lady Lisle also had four older stepdaughters from her first marriage, to Sir John Basset. Two of them, Jane and Thomasine, remained in England when she moved to Calais with her second husband. They were still single and long past the normal age of marriage.[167] Lady Lisle permitted Jane to live at her, Lady Lisle's, manor at Umberleigh; use her household stuff; and pasture some animals there. She also gave Jane venison from the park and, occasionally, a gown. Jane's uncle, Roger Dennis, acknowledged and thanked her for her generosity: "I am well assured ye are far better lady unto her than she can deserve."[168] Of her three other Basset stepdaughters, Margery, wife of William Marres, wrote to Lady Lisle once for assistance in recovering land that her father had sold in spite of the fact that it was part of her dowry.[169] There are no letters from Thomasine, who died unmarried in 1536, or Anne, wife of Sir James Courteney of Upcot.[170]

When Lady Lisle's contemporary, Dame Margaret Long, married the second earl of Bath as her third husband in 1548, she insisted that he send his five daughters elsewhere to live, although her three daughters by Sir Richard Long and one of her daughters by Sir Thomas Kitson resided with them.[171] Her correspondence contains little evidence about her relations to the girls. On the other hand, she was extremely attentive to her stepsons as they moved into adolescence and early adulthood and took charge of placing one of them, George, at Furnivall's Inn in 1556.[172] Apparently he did not prosper at the law since a few years later one of her servants suggested that she bestow a benefice in her gift on him "if he would be a priest."[173] Another stepson, Henry, wrote to her, not to his father, when he needed money, clothes, and a horse.[174] The countess had a much more difficult relationship with her third stepson, her husband's heir, Lord Fitzwarren, who married her daughter Frances, because of the conflict between her efforts to maintain amicable relations with him and her determination to protect her daughter and the couple's children against the consequences of his extravagance.[175]

As we have seen in the case of Lady Lisle and her Basset stepdaughters, aristocratic women's relationships with their stepchildren did not end when their fathers died. Indeed, some fathers counted on their children's stepmothers to care for them and safeguard their property after their deaths. In 1492, for example, Edward, Viscount Lisle, appointed his second wife, by whom he had no children, sole executor of his will; asked her to buy his 11-year-old heir's wardship; and empowered her to arrange his two daughters' marriages.[176] As he had hoped, she purchased the boy's wardship and custody of his inheritance and arranged advantageous matches for the girls.[177] When she died, she left her stepson an enormous bequest that included money, plate, hangings, most of her household goods, and everything her husband had given her "freely to mine own use."[178] John, Lord Latimer, asked his wife, Katherine Parr, to collect her stepdaughter Margaret's dowry from property designated for that purpose and the income set aside to support her until she married.[179] When Margaret died a few years later, she wrote in her own will that she would never be able to thank the queen sufficiently "for the godly education and tender love and bountiful goodness which I have ever more found in her," and left Katherine the bulk of her considerable estate.[180]

Margaret Nevill's will is not the only evidence of good relationships between women and their stepchildren. Of thirty-one stepmothers who wrote
wills, twenty-three included bequests to their stepchildren, although few of
them were as generous to them as Viscountess Lisle. Dame Ursula Wotton
left her husband's heir a diamond ring and £200 her stepson owed her.[181]
Margaret, countess of Bath, gave her stepdaughter Elizabeth the large sum
of 200 marks, an especially noteworthy gift since she had not wanted Elizabeth to live with her when she first married Elizabeth's father. Alice Cotton
left her stepdaughter Bridget, wife of Sir John Huddleston, a considerable
amount of plate, although she was accused of driving Bridget's sister Anne
into a convent.[182] Some women were particularly careful about leaving their
stepchildren objects that had belonged to the children's natural parents and
might have sentimental value to them. Lady Anne Grey gave one of her stepdaughters one of the best goblets of the girl's father, and Dame Dorothy
Hungerford bequeathed one of hers a goblet from the family of the girl's
mother.[183]

Other stepmothers cooperated with their stepsons to minimize the burden
their jointures and dowers placed on the stepsons' inheritances. A few of
them exchanged their property for annuities, effectively giving their stepsons
control over their inheritances while preserving their income.[184] Exchanges
of this sort eliminated a major source of potential conflict between them because men often wanted to improve their estates or to mortgage and exchange particular pieces of property but had no objection to their stepmothers receiving incomes equivalent to their jointures. In other cases, widows
exchanged dower lands scattered throughout their late husbands' estates with
their stepsons to create more consolidated blocks of land, making it easier for
each of them to administer their property efficiently.[185]

Despite amicable arrangements of this sort, the worst difficulties between
women and their stepchildren almost always grew out of conflicts about the
performance of their husbands' wills and the division of their property. Nonetheless, although men undoubtedly witnessed feuds of this sort throughout
their lives, ninety-two, or 72 percent, of 128 male testators who had children
from their first marriages appointed their second or third wives as their executors or coexecutors. Their primary motive was their desire to protect their widows and/or second families against their heirs by giving them substantial
power over their estates. A number of men expressed such concerns openly in
their wills. John, Lord Scrope, pointedly left his heir everything at Bolton Castle and all his cattle in Yorkshire on the condition that "he love, comfort, aid and
help to his power my right kind and loving wife." He also required him to sign
a bond for £1,000 in which he promised not to interrupt his stepmother's or paternal grandmother's jointures.[186] Sir John Raynsford declared firmly, "I will
and charge my said son John Raynsford upon my blessing that he strive not
with my said wife nor with mine executors . . . for anything contained in this

present testatment and last will" on pain of forfeiting everything bequeathed to him.[187] Sir Edward Walsingham tried a different strategy to ensure that his children would treat their stepmother well: he left her all his "jewels, trenchers and rings," with the exception of three chains, "much trusting to her gentle remembrance towards my children as they shall show cause to her."[188]

Litigation between widows and their stepsons usually involved property that the widow claimed as her jointure but that the heir said should descend to him immediately. Chancery petitions often focused on the accusation that the defendant had illegally seized the deeds to the contested property and then fraudulently asserted ownership.[189] A Chancery decree by Thomas, Lord Wriothesely, settling a case of this kind between Elizabeth Tilney, Sir Philip's third wife, and his heir, awarded the manor of Shelley and the other disputed property to her, but the award contained numerous qualifications and provisos, illustrating the difficulty of finding solutions acceptable to both parties and likely to secure their compliance.[190]

Disputes easily spread from the specific issue of the widow's jointure to the movable goods her husband had left her and her position as his executor. Thomas Stonor's second wife, Katherine, maintained that his heir, Sir Walter, would neither permit her to execute the deed to her jointure nor honor his father's deathbed gift of all his movable goods to her. She argued that he had been present when his father was dying and promised he would honor his father's wishes. To bolster her case, she noted that she and Thomas were married for twenty-two years and that she had contributed an inheritance worth 100 marks to their property.[191] In a letter to Thomas Cromwell in 1539, John, first earl of Bath, complained that his father had left him "sundry weighty charges without allowance or otherwise" and named his stepmother as his sole executor. Bemoaning the fact that "no child [was] so unnaturally entreated as I am," he blamed her for taking advantage of her presence when his father was making his will "cruelly to incense my lord my father against me . . . no part of his goods to bequeath me, considering she hath five hundred marks of my inheritance to her jointure."[192] Bath's summary of his father's will was actually inaccurate: the movables his father left to his widow consisted entirely of plate, jewels, and other goods she owned before their marriage, and she was only one of three coexecutors.[193] The earl's real grievance was probably about the generous jointure his father had left her. In any case, his letter articulates the issues that produced litigation between widows and their stepsons.

The children of first marriages were most likely to interfere with the settlements of their fathers' land and performance of their wills when they had had offspring by their second or third wives. In combination with their widows' jointures, the cost of supporting and preferring their second and third families represented a long-term burden on their estates, which some heirs regarded as intolerable. Cromwell arbitrated a dispute between Dame Jane Calthorp, second wife and sole executor of Sir Philip, and his heir, which exemplifies these issues. Her stepson, also named Philip, was furious at how much of his inheritance his father had tied up for the performance of his father's and then his widow's will over and above his stepmother's jointure. His father's generosity was almost certainly rooted in his concern about the three children he had with Jane, all of whom were still young when he wrote his will. Cromwell's settlement of the case indicates that Philip had illegally seized three of his father's manors and taken the profits from them since his death. He therefore ruled almost entirely in Dame Jane's favor. In addition to her jointure, he gave her possession of the disputed manors for life and the right to use the profits for her own will for seven years. He also ordered Philip to give Jane the income Philip had collected from them since his father's death. All Philip gained were some other manors for which he had to pay Jane rent and a disputed annuity of £18. Cromwell required Philip to sign a bond with four sureties to ensure his compliance.[194]

Even more protracted quarrels between women and their stepsons developed when fathers tried to divide their inheritances permanently between their two families. Such a feud developed because Sir Thomas Brews, who died in 1482, settled a valuable part of his estate on himself; his second wife, Elizabeth; and their male heirs and then changed his mind when his heir married. His second wife never accepted his decision even though he compensated their children with purchased property of equal value. After Sir Thomas's death, she sued her stepson William for trespassing on his inheritance. When William also died, she seized all the deeds to his estates and illegally took possession of his chief manor. The quarrel now passed to William's two daughters and coheirs and their husbands, Thomas Hansard and Roger Townshend II. Roger's father sued Elizabeth for illegal dispossession in 1491 on his 13-year-old son's behalf, but the dispute was not settled finally until 1502.[195]

Whether they were wives or widows, most aristocratic women were mothers. Their ideal of good motherhood, what they called "natural motherhood," balanced affection and worldly concerns in much the same way as their vision of successful wifehood. Good mothers loved their children, but they expressed their love by working to ensure their economic and political fortunes rather than by caring for them and interacting with them on a daily basis, just as good wives worked tirelessly on behalf of their husbands, even though they spent much of their time apart. In complex households and families—like those of Sir Robert and Lady Margaret Howard in the fifteenth century, the Lisles in the 1530s, and the earl and countess of Bath in the 1540s and 1550s—in which both spouses had offspring from one or more previous marriages, securing their children and stepchildren's futures drew on all aristocratic women's skills, connections, and material resources. The success of their activity on behalf of their children constituted an important dimension of their lifelong careers as wives and widows and made a crucial contribution to the survival and prosperity of their families and class.

CHAPTER 7. WIDOWS—

WOMEN OF PROPERTY AND

CUSTODIANS OF THEIR

FAMILIES' FUTURES

*W*IDOWHOOD was the culmination of aristocratic women's careers as wives and mothers. Like wifehood and motherhood, it was a stage in most of their lives: 70 percent of 751 male testators who married at least once had surviving wives.[1] Freed from the disabilities of coverture, widows continued to perform tasks they had first assumed as wives and mothers, but with a new degree of independence and authority. Where they had functioned as junior partners during their marriages, they now acted on their own. If they were heiresses, they controlled their inheritances and the income it yielded for the first time. They were the only aristocratic women who headed their own households. In addition, most widows assumed new responsibilities as executors of their husbands' wills and guardians of their minor and unmarried children.

Many historians of the aristocracy have argued that widows were a burden on the landed estates of their marital families; that there was a correlation between their long lives, the political and economic decline of their families, and the extinction of peerages; and that men resented widows' claims on their patrimonies and went to great lengths to reduce them to a minimum.[2] In the most extreme version of this opinion, Rowena Archer describes the effect of long-lived dowagers on the fortunes of the nobility as "monstrous," blames them for the "swallowing up of one peerage by another," and argues that only the widow with a reasonable jointure who survived "just long enough to see her child through his minority, following her husband to the grave within a small space" had a "mild, possibly even beneficial" effect on her marital family, "provided she was a caring guardian of her son's inheritance."[3]

This chapter supports the opposite point of view. It demonstrates that most widows managed the real and movable property in their possession profitably, whether they held it on their own behalf or on behalf of their heirs and other children. When they died, they carefully distributed their own land and goods to the next generation of their families. The impact of their achievements and choices, especially on their children and grandchildren, was even greater because of their longevity: 63 percent of 351 aristocratic widows survived their husbands by more than ten years; 37 percent, by more than twenty.[4] Collectively their activity ensured the survival and continued prosperity of their class.

Widows' position in their marital families as they carried out these tasks was extremely complicated. Their husbands situated them at the center of their patrilineages by leaving them large amounts of property beyond their jointures and dowers and naming them as their executors and guardians of their children. In contrast, their in-laws and stepchildren often viewed them as interlopers, exercising illegitimate power over their families' property and future. Occasionally sons also took this position. These incompatible perspectives produced innumerable quarrels, lawsuits, and appeals to the crown.

To make matters more difficult, the women's own definition of their families was far more complex and fluid than their husbands'. While they shared their spouses' commitment to their children and grandchildren, their decisions about how to provide for the children were complicated by the fact that more than half of them married more than once and many had children by more than one husband. When they distributed their own resources or exercised discretionary power as executrices, therefore, they often had to choose between the offspring of two different patrilineages or between their children and stepchildren.

Furthermore, because of their longevity, many widows survived long after their children and even their grandchildren had become financially secure adults. When they bequeathed their estates, they were freer than their husbands had been to define their families broadly and flexibly. Their beneficiaries often included natal and affinal kin, as well as direct descendants. They were particularly generous to their siblings and their sisters' children. Their bequests prove that although women served the interests of their marital families, they maintained ties with their families of origin and were especially close to their sisters. The most affluent widows also remembered their affinal relatives. In the largest sense, the wills of long-lived widows demonstrate that rather than passing through familes—from their natal to their marital families and then from one marital family to another—aristocratic women accumulated familes as they moved through their life cycles and maintained significant ties with large, complex kingroups that they defined in bilateral terms.[5]

At any time between 1450 and 1550, aristocratic widows owned or administered a significant portion of their families' wealth. Although surviving documents do not permit quantifying this assertion or estimating the total amount of wealth they owned or controlled individually or as a group, the evidence supporting it is overwhelming.[6] They administered a huge amount of real and movable property as their husbands' executors and guardians of their children. Seventy-seven percent (403) of 523 knights and noblemen with surviving wives selected them as executors or supervisors of their estates. Thirty-five percent of the 403 named them their sole executors.[7] An even larger percentage—86 percent of 114 fathers—appointed their widows as guardians of their noninheriting minor children.[8] Since their wives and children were almost always their main beneficiaries, selecting their widows to fill these offices was a natural choice. The likelihood that women would survive their spouses for years was another advantage as many fathers died while their children were quite young. At the same time, the high percentage of childless men who appointed their widows as their sole executors or coexecutors, 83 percent of the 45 in my group of 523, indicates that aristocratic men's decisions were dictated as much by their general confidence in their wives as by their concern about their offspring. For most aristocratic widows, administering their husbands' wills was an extension of their careers as wives.

The extent of men's confidence in their wives' reliability and practical skills is evident in the decision of many husbands who included their wives among their executors to ensure that the women controlled the performance of their wills. The simplest expedient was to name them their "chief" or "principal" executor.[9] Alternatively, some men restricted the power of their widows' coexecutors. Sir Thomas Montgomery directed his other executors to limit themselves to advising his widow.[10] Sir Thomas Arundell empowered his wife to "add and [di]minish this my will at all times as it can by her best be thought."[11] Other testators trusted their widows more than anyone else but worried that the women would die or remarry before they settled their estates. Such men often appointed a number of executors but limited their power as long as their wives were alive and single. Sir John Danvers ordered his son Richard, one of his two executors, "to meddle with no manner of administration during his mother's life but with her advice,"[12] and Sir Philip Champernon directed his two other executors not to "have any part or meddling with my goods or chattels unless my said wife die afore my will be performed."[13] In addition, in a few cases, the testators' other executors resigned their offices and made their widows their de facto sole executors.[14]

Even aristocratic men who had appointed their wives to be their sole executors took the trouble to explain the broad discretionary power they wanted them to exercise. Sir John Sapcotes granted his widow and sole executor complete authority to dispose of his plate, goods, and chattels with the exception of his gold chain, a silver cup worth £10, £20 in cash, and his "ancient" silver plate. He gave her use of the "ancient" plate during her lifetime but directed that it should descend to their eldest son, his heir, at her death. In the case of everything else, Dame Sapcote was free to do as she wished, leaving Sapcote's heir entirely dependent on her for a share in his father's other goods.[15] Similarly, Sir Andrew Lutterell permitted his widow to "use and administer" all his movable and immovable goods at her discretion as long as she remained single.[16] A third testator, Sir Thomas Denys, gave his wife absolute freedom to dispose of £500 worth of his goods and use of the residue.[17] In conjunction with the high percentages of women appointed as their executors or coexecutors, clauses such as these testify to the extent that most aristocratic men considered their wives better suited than anyone else to rear and prefer their children, manage their estates, and transmit their real and movable property to the next generation.[18]

Whatever their role in the execution of their husbands' wills, widows were almost always among their primary beneficiaries. In combination with their jointures and dowers, their husbands' legacies to them meant that they had large incomes and possessed enormous amounts of luxury goods for the rest of their lives. Although most of the land they held passed to their husbands' heirs when they died, they could usually bequeath much, if not all, of their movable property in their wills. Their wealth enabled them to maintain the style of living in which they had lived during their marriages and preserved their position as important figures in their families.

The foundation of the aristocratic widow's wealth was her jointure or dower, each of which gave her a life interest in a portion of her husband's land. Contemporaries referred to the income from this land, which was meant to support only the widow, as her living. Men with dependent and unmarried children always provided for them separately. The value of women's jointures, expressed in contemporary documents as the annual income they yielded, varied considerably. Data on eighty-three jointures indicate that between 1450 and 1490, they ranged from £10 to £1,333 6s. 8d.; between 1491 and 1520, from £13 6s. 8d. to £1,333 6s. 8d.; and between 1521 and 1550, from £20 to £1,000.[19] The median jointure was worth £60 between 1450 and 1490; £66 13s. 8d. between 1491 and 1520; and £133 6s. 8d. between 1521 and 1550. Virtually all the women with jointures under £50 were the daughters and wives of knights; none was the daughter or wife of a peer.[20] These figures highlight the huge differences in wealth within the aristocracy. They also raise questions about the ability of the twenty-nine widows in the group of eighty-three with jointures of less than £50 to maintain their status and standard of living. In practice, their jointures look far less inadequate in the context of knights' total incomes. In the fifteenth century, the incomes of knights ranged from £40 to £400, but anything over £200 was quite exceptional.[21] Even in Henry VIII's reign, few knights had incomes of more than £300 to £400. Those that did were almost always courtiers and the group from whom new peers were chosen.[22] The smallest jointures noted above—£10 or £13 6s. 8d.— were therefore probably adequate for the widows of knights whose total income was only £40. At the other end of the spectrum were the thirty widows with jointures of £100 or more, who were unquestionably wealthy by contemporary standards. They were able to accumulate luxury goods—expensive clothing, jewelry, and silver and gold plate—to hoard cash, and occasionally to invest in land. At the very top of this group were nine widows with jointures of more than £500 a year.

Whatever the size of their jointures and/or dowers, most aristocratic widows had other sources of income and owned or had the use of other assets. Eighty-four percent of 523 men with surviving wives left them property over and above their dowers or jointures. A small number—59 men, or 11 percent—included real estate among these extra bequests. It is difficult to discern a pattern in the men's decision to give their widows additional land since the composition of their families varied greatly. Their widows were divided almost equally between first and second wives; three testators were in third marriages.[23] The second wives were divided equally, in turn, between those who had children with their husbands and those who did not. None of the men had offspring with their third wives, and eight had no children at all. Given this diversity, the testators' decisions evidently reflected the specific needs and emotional dynamics of their particular families rather than widespread structural imperatives.

These grants of land over and above their wives' jointures are surprising in the context of the historical scholarship that treats widows as burdens on their marital families and assumes that men resented these claims on their patrimonies.[24] In practice, however, as these examples suggest, some husbands placed greater weight on their relationships with and responsibilities to their wives and younger children than on their heirs' immediate possession of their inheritances. Most of these testators—forty-one of the fifty-nine—evidently felt that they had balanced the interests of their wives, sons (or other heirs), and patrilineages sufficiently by limiting their widows to life interests in the additional real property they gave them. Like the women's dowers and jointures, the land would descend to the men's heirs as soon as their widows died. More surprisingly, nineteen men actually bequeathed the property to their widows with rights of inheritance, which permitted their wives to alienate the land permanently from their husbands' patrilineages if they had different heirs. Situations like this arose if wives in second marriages had children by their first husbands or if the women had no children at all.[25] Although historians have often assumed that heirs resented and would try to obstruct any temporary or permanent reduction of their inheritances, only one of the heirs of the fifty-nine testators challenged his father's bequest in court.[26] Both the behavior of these testators and that of their heirs strongly suggests that historians have overemphasized men's hostility toward widows' claims on their husbands' real property and the primacy they attached to the interests of their patrilineages.[27]

While only a minority of aristocratic husbands left their wives land in addition to their jointures, almost all of them provided their widows with a manor or other dwelling to live in. In a group of fifty-one widows, thirty-six, or 71 percent, lived and/or died in a dwelling that had belonged to one of their husbands. Five others were heiresses who were residing on their own property. The evidence does not indicate how the remaining ten widows acquired their homes, but some or all of them may well have been their husbands'.[28] These figures suggest that most aristocratic women did not have to use the income from their jointures or dowers to purchase or rent homes.

In many, perhaps the majority of cases, widows' jointures included a manor or house they could inhabit after their husbands died. But many men altered the arrangements made at the outset of their marriages—usually making them more favorable to their mates—through deeds or enfeoffments executed subsequently or through provisions in their wills.[29] The new settlements often reflected their desire to permit their widows to remain in the manors they had inhabited together but which were not part of their wives' original jointures. The men's willingness to give their widows possession of their chief mansions usually marked the end of long marriages marked by affectionate relationships and successful working partnerships. In other cases, husbands who provided houses for their wives toward the end of their lives were taking account of their spouses' preferences, altered family circumstances, or changes in their land holdings.

One hundred and seven, or 21 percent, of 523 male wills granted manors or other houses, often in London, to their wives. Sixty-six of these houses were additions to the women's dowers or jointures.[30] More than half of these legacies gave the widows possession of their husbands' chief mansions. These bequests are another instance of men's placing their wives' interests over those of their heirs. In effect, they postponed their heirs' entrance into one of the most symbolically important parts of their inheritances in order to permit their widows, many of whom would survive them for years, to remain in their marital homes.

Although only a minority of aristocratic husbands added land to their wives' jointures and dowers, an overwhelming majority, 81 percent of 523, left them movable goods, often in enormous quantities. In the Archdiocese of Canterbury, where the vast majority of the Yorkist and Tudor population lived, men acquired complete testamentary power over their goods in the fourteenth century.[31] As a result, if men wrote a will, it excluded their wives from claiming any of their movable goods except their paraphernalia from their spouses' estates, and it permitted their husbands to bequeath any goods their wives owned at the time of their marriage or received after it. Most aristocratic widows depended, therefore, on legacies from their husbands for the clothing, jewelry, silver and gilt plate objects, furniture and household goods, horses, and livestock necessary to maintain their standard of living. In contrast, women's traditional right to one-third of their spouses' movable goods survived into the late seventeenth century in the Archdiocese of York, Wales, and London.[32]

Aristocratic men's wills prove that the vast majority of them were generous about taking care of their wives in this respect. Fifteen percent of 523 testators gave their wives all or a fixed portion of their goods and chattels, but most men bequeathed their movable property category by category— clothing, jewels, plate, cash, household stuff and implements, livestock, and so on. More than a third of them gave their wives gold or silver plate and household goods and utensils. They also left them jewelry and clothing (22 percent), "ready money" or coin (21 percent), livestock (16 percent), horses (8 percent), grain and timber (7 percent), and farm equipment (2 percent). Some husbands (8 percent) carefully returned the apparel, jewelry, plate, and other goods their wives had brought into their marriages with them. A third also left their wives the residue of their estates.[33]

Dame Elizabeth Brown (d. 1487) and Dame Alice Clere (d. 1538) are two examples of the many aristocratic women who grew rich through their marriages. Neither was the widow of a peer or an heiress, characteristics that distinguished a minority of aristocratic women. Elizabeth Brown, daughter of Agnes and William Paston, married Robert Poynings, Lord Poynings's second son, in 1458 with a dowry of £200.[34] Her husband died at the second battle of St. Albans three years later and left her land worth £42 6s. 8d. as her dower or jointure.[35] A decade later, she married Sir George Brown, who was executed for rebellion in 1483. Dame Brown held land worth £60 from this marriage.[36] When she died in 1488, she left almost her entire estate—plate, jewels, apparel, and household stuff, over 300 items altogether—to her daughter Mary as a dowry. The bequest listed 45 pieces of silver or silver and gilt plate; jewelry made with diamonds, emeralds, pearls, and sapphires; 6 girdles (i.e., belts) made of luxury fabrics; a "great bed of estate"; a "great counterpoint of tapestry work"; and 5 gowns and a kirtle trimmed with fur.[37]

Half a century later, Alice Clere was even richer when she died. Dame Clere, daughter of Sir William Boleyn, married Sir Robert as his second wife sometime after 1506 with a dowry of 500 marks (£333 6s. 8d.).[38] After her husband died in 1529, she held over twenty manors as her jointure.[39] They probably included Ormesby, the Cleres' chief mansion, since Sir Robert bequeathed to her all the chapel stuff there, as well as sufficient sheep, horses, farm equipment and implements, corn, and swine to occupy it profitably. In addition he left her £60 worth of plate, half his household stuff, and a house in Norwich with the advowson of the church and most of its contents.[40] When Dame Clere died nine years later, her primary concern was endowing her younger son, Thomas, with sufficient land and money to live in the style of his class. Her bequests to him included £700 for the purchase of land or a ward to marry, silver or silver and gilt plate worth £60, a pair of gold beads with precious stones that her niece Queen Anne Boleyn had given her, and three luxury beds. Dame Clere had acquired the freehold of the manor of Fretenham, perhaps by purchase during her widowhood, which she left to Thomas in compensation for 1,000 marks still due to him from his father's estate. She also left jewelry to three nieces and a stepdaughter and divided the residue of her goods between her two sons.[41] In both cases the wealth Alice Clere and Elizabeth Brown distributed in their wills was one of their rewards for successful careers as wives. When they themselves died, they each left the bulk of their property to a favorite noninheriting child instead of to the family heir, choices that exemplify aristocratic women's tendency to use their wealth to mute the primogenital bias of the law.

One of the challenges to aristocratic widows was securing legal possession of the real property and goods due them under their marriage contracts and husbands' wills. For most widows, gaining possession of their jointures and dowers was relatively routine. The execution of most jointures at the outset of their marriages meant that they held the land on which they expected to live in joint tenancy with their husbands at the time of the latters' deaths and did not need to initiate a legal process to take possession of it.[42] As a result, legal and official sources usually do not record this transition, although inquisitions post mortem occasionally noted that the widows of the king's deceased tenants were already legally seissed of some of their land.[43] In less favorable circumstances, women's jointures were unexecuted when their husbands died and they had to secure a legal estate in them from their feoffees. A similar situation existed when their spouses left them land in their wills.[44] Some of these women had to sue their husbands' feoffees in Chancery to force them to transfer the land to them.[45] Whether their jointures were executed or not, widows might also encounter substantive challenges to their titles to them. Still a third group of widows, those who claimed common-law dower on some or all of their husbands' land, had to petition the crown for a writ of right of dower to gain possession of their livings.[46]

Widows who encountered difficulties in taking possession of their jointures could seek relief in a variety of venues. Women with connections at court often appealed directly to the king or his leading ministers. Others instituted suits in the courts of Chancery, Star Chamber, Requests, or the Duchy of Lancaster. Although it is impossible to determine the number or percentage of Yorkist and early Tudor aristocratic widows who encountered problems of this kind, the evidence suggests that it was relatively small compared to the number of peers and knights with surviving wives who died in the period.[47] Of 551 cases in Chancery, Star Chamber, Requests, and the Duchy of Lancaster in which aristocratic women were plaintiffs or defendants between 1450 and 1550, 120 involved competing claims to their jointures. The small number of these conflicts—not much more than one a year—supports the argument that members of the aristocracy did not, by and large, regard their widows as burdens on their estates and inheritances or attempt to undermine their rights.

However small their numerical significance, looking more closely at these lawsuits is useful because they highlight the most difficult relationships widows encountered as they renegotiated their position in their families.[48] Of fifty-nine disputes between widows and their relatives, women were the mothers of the heirs in only nine. This figure underscores the fact that women solidified their membership in their marital families, and, therefore, their claims to its property, by bearing sons. It also indicates that sons usually accepted their mothers' right to the jointures carved out of their inheritances.

Trouble was much more likely to occur when the widows were not the heirs' mothers, a situation that weakened their position in their spouses' families. The most conflictual relationships were those between women and their stepsons, brothers-in-law, and fathers-in-law, which accounted for over 70 percent of the fifty-nine suits. Lacking the affective ties and normative expectations that undergirded the interaction of mothers and sons, stepsons and brothers-in-law were much more likely to regard widows as interlopers on their estates. Women's relationships with their stepsons were particularly fraught.[49] On an emotional level, stepsons may well have resented the women who took their mothers' place in the family. On a practical level, second and third wives were often younger than their husbands, holding out the prospect that they would occupy their jointures or dowers for decades. In addition, if they had children of their own, their offspring would also have claims on their stepsons' inheritances.

Securing their jointures was not the only difficulty widows encountered as they assumed their new responsibilities and roles. They sometimes also faced obstacles in taking possession of the real and movable property designated for performance of their husbands' wills or collecting the income from land enfeoffed for that purpose. Two family situations were most likely to produce these conflicts. The first occurred when men with many young children had to use the income from their land to support and prefer them for years, even decades. Their heirs then faced the unwelcome prospect of long delays before they gained possesion of their inheritances. Fathers in this situation also often permitted their executors to employ their most precious movable goods, particularly their plate and jewels, for the children's benefit, ensuring that many of the most valuable items would be sold long before their heirs received the residue. The other explosive situation arose when men who had daughters only owned land that descended in male tail. Fathers in this situation almost always charged the property that would pass to their heirs, usually their brothers or nephews, with the heavy cost of their daughters' dowries. Well aware that their heirs were likely to resent this burden on their estates, they tried to protect the girls by appointing their wives as their executors. But arrangements of this kind were almost destined to lead to quarrels between the women and their brothers-in-law or nephews. A few mothers responded by contesting their brothers-in-law's claims to be their husbands' heirs altogether.[50]

In practice, many of the conflicts between aristocratic widows and their husbands' heirs raised several of these issues at once. The women's adversaries challenged the women's rights to their jointures, their position as their husbands' executors, and their use of the land and goods designated to perform their husbands' wills. Three exemplary cases illustrate the scope, length, and bitterness of these feuds. The first developed between Elizabeth Whethill, widow of Sir Richard, and her eldest son, Robert. Robert was furious at his father's generous provision for his three unmarried sisters and two younger brothers and the broad discretionary power he gave his widow over his estate. Sir Richard had evidently expected trouble to erupt between his heir and widow and tried to forestall it by making his bequests to Robert conditional on his being "sworn on the Holy Evangelists for the performance of this my last will and over that [to] be loving and kind to his mother, brethren and sisters."[51] Despite this requirement, Robert and his father-in-law, Sir Richard Grenville, attempted to prevent the will from being implemented on the grounds that his father's land in the Marches of Calais could not be divided as he directed and that his legacies to his younger sons and daughters were excessive.[52]

In response, Dame Elizabeth appealed directly to Thomas Cromwell for protection. She defended the will in terms of her procreative and material contribution to the family during her marriage of forty-six years: she had given birth to fourteen children and brought her husband money, goods, and land worth more than 1,000 marks. Given her successful career as a wife, "now to be left with nothing were against all reason and conscience." She also reminded Cromwell of the trouble she had experienced when her husband was imprisoned and held for ransom.[53] In a subsequent letter, Dame Whethill reported that her attempt to settle her dispute with Robert out of court had failed because he refused to let her occupy a farm that she and her husband had always used to supply their household. Her son wanted to divide it with her and live in half the house "unto the which I will not agree, considering his unnatural handling of me that am his mother."[54] Cromwell upheld Sir Richard's will unambiguously. Although he recognized Robert as his father's heir, he gave Dame Whethill possession of the disputed farm in return for an annual rent of £5 20d., and ordered Robert to give his mother 50 marks, an annuity of 100 marks as her jointure, and £40 of household goods. In addition, Robert had to provide substantial dowries for two of his sisters, support two of his younger brothers and one of the girls, and permit the boys to receive the profits of the land their father had bequeathed to them.[55]

Despite Cromwell's clear ruling, Dame Whethill and her eldest son continued to quarrel. Edward Lee, archbishop of York, petitioned Cromwell on her behalf months after he had issued his award.[56] In January 1539, Dame Whethill herself reported to Cromwell, "I am yet in great trouble with my son."[57] Even her death in 1545 did not close the matter. In 1547, Robert sued her surviving executor, his brother-in-law John St. John, for possession of the land his mother had held on behalf of his siblings. He was almost certainly angry that she had completely ignored him when she distributed her estate, although her decision was inevitable, given their previous quarrels. St. John responded that Dame Whethill had fulfilled Cromwell's award, which Robert misrepresented in his suit; that Robert had not paid his sisters' dowries; and that at the time of her death Dame Elizabeth did not possess goods worth £500 belonging to her husband that should have descended to his heir. St. John also noted that he had performed Dame Elizabeth's will "long time before" the bill against him.[58]

The second feud erupted between Dame Elizabeth Holford, widow of Sir John, and her two stepsons, Sir John and George, who resented her role as their father's executor and his provision for their three young half-brothers. Dame Holford alleged in the Court of Star Chamber that they had attacked the manor in which she was living with their half-brothers; endangered the children's lives; robbed her of £200 of goods, 28 oxen and 22 kine, and over 200 marks of coin; and expelled her from her jointure.[59] In their responses, they not only accused her of falsely pretending to be their father's executor but also claimed that she was "never coupled in lawful matrimony" with him.[60] In addition, they challenged her right to her jointure in Chancery.[61] Both courts ruled for Dame Holford and recognized her as her husband's lawful executor. On pain of forfeiting a bond of £100, they required her stepsons to return the goods they had seized or the equivalent value in cash and to permit their stepmother to enjoy her jointure and dower.[62] Their decisions implicitly recognized the validity of her marriage to their father.

The third quarrel pitted Dame Isabel Harrington, widow and executor of Sir James, who had no sons, against his brother Nicholas. Nicholas sued her for the "evidences, charters, and muniments" related to his brother's land on the ground that it was held in male tail and should descend to him rather than to his daughters.[63] Dame Harrington responded that the land was not held in male tail and should pass to her husband's heirs general, their eight surviving daughters. She asserted further that Sir James's land was enfeoffed to her for life for the performance of his will and then for her own use. Dame Harrington claimed that she was retaining the disputed evidence to ensure that the will was executed and that the documents should go to the heirs general after her death.[64] Although no Chancery decree in this case survives, Sir James's will sustains Dame Harrington's central contention that his land was enfeoffed for performance of his will and her use during her lifetime. But the will also made clear that some of his land was entailed to his male heirs and only part was to be divided among his daughters after his wife died.[65]

Like the three suits discussed here, litigation about women's jointures and the property they held as their husbands' executors usually involved widows and their male relatives, most frequently their stepsons and brothers-in-law.

But occasionally mothers-in-law and daughters-in-law ended up in court because they claimed the same land as their jointures. In the best documented of these cases, Jane Courteney and her second husband sued Lady Florence Fitzwarren for her jointure from her first husband, Thomas Fulford. Lady Fitzwarren was Fulford's mother by *her* first husband, Sir Humphrey. Three members of the Fulford family supported Jane's claim that her father had paid 500 marks to Sir Humphrey as her dowry in return for settling the disputed land as Jane's jointure. Lady Fitzwarren responded that Sir Humphrey's father had previously enfeoffed the contested land as her jointure and that her prior rights defeated her daughter-in-law's claim. Jane then argued that if Lady Fitzwarren's assertion were true, she should return Jane's dowry since Lady Fitzwarren was Sir Humphrey's executor. Lady Fitzwarren replied that she had already completed performing her husband's will and no longer had any of his goods to distribute.[66]

Since we do not have a decree in this case, we cannot determine how Chancery resolved the issue or where it thought right lay. Nonetheless, the suit is a clear example of the issue most likely to disrupt relationships between widowed mothers-in-law and daughters-in-law and underscores women's dependence on their fathers (or other guardians) to ensure that the land assigned as their jointures at the outset of their marriages was not encumbered by prior enfeoffments. The litigation also illustrates the way in which widows moved from one marital family to another without severing their ties to any of them. By the time this case went to court, both women who were claiming a lifelong interest in the Fulford estates were remarried. Yet three Fulford men testified for Jane Courteney, demonstrating the durability of her connection to them. Their willingness to help her was particularly notable because she was the younger of the two women and likely to occupy the disputed Fulford land for a longer period than her former mother-in-law.

The four lawsuits examined here reveal the determined opposition some widows faced when they tried to execute their husbands' wills or take possession of their jointures. They defended their rights vigorously, drawing effectively on the legal knowledge, court connections, and business skills they had acquired during their marriages. Although widows often described themselves as helpless and desolate in their petitions, the record paints a very different picture. In fact, the awards in the minority of cases in which the outcome of their suits is known prove that they were remarkably successful litigators: not one of the women in this admittedly small group lost her case completely, although some of them had to submit to arbitration and accept compromise settlements. Successful careers as wives were the basis for their effectiveness as widows.

Opposition from their sons, stepsons, and in-laws caused many of the difficulties widows had taking possession of their jointures and the land and goods designated for the execution of their husbands' wills. But their relatives were not responsible for all their problems. The crown also often placed obstacles in their path. When fathers died and left minor sons who became wards of the crown, their widows could not enter their jointures or dowers without royal permission. Although securing the necessary writ was often a routine matter, difficulties arose when the king had a political or financial interest in delaying the proceedings.[67] Henry VII withheld Lady Edith Darcy's jointure lands for over a year after her first husband, Ralph, Lord Nevill, died in 1500 and left a minor heir.[68] He relented only after her second husband, Sir Thomas Darcy, promised to supply him with 200 well-equipped men on a day's notice to defend the border town of Berwick-on-Tweed.[69] Anne, countess of Derby, and Henry VIII signed an indenture that appointed her dower almost two years after her husband had died. The agreement indicates that in the intervening period she had petitioned the Courts of Chancery and of the Duchy of Lancaster, as well as the king and his council.[70]

Women's success in suits of this kind often depended on their connections at court. In 1535, Anne, Lady Berkeley, who had been widowed almost a year earlier and given birth to her husband's heir posthumously, petitioned Cromwell for assistance in securing a writ for her jointure from the Master of the Wards.[71] Lady Anne, who had earned Henry VIII's favor by attending Anne Boleyn at their wedding, specifically asked him to "move the king's highness" on her behalf.[72] But however much she counted on the king's friendship, she knew that Cromwell's favor was essential for her suit to succeed and that she would have to offer him something for his support. She therefore assured him that she had not forgotten the annual fee she owed him, although the wording of her letter implied that she might not be able to pay it until she received her jointure.[73] In spite of her appeal to Cromwell's self-interest and at least one journey to London to see him in person, the matter was still pending in August 1536, almost two years after Lady Berkeley was widowed, although she did eventually secure the land due to her.[74]

The experiences of the countess of Derby and Ladies Darcy and Berkeley illustrate the difficulty aristocratic widows had in gaining possession of their jointures when the king had claims on their husbands' estates. The crown never relinquished its rights easily, and successful suits required time, energy, and appropriate gifts to the petitioners' friends at court. Women were in an even more precarious position if their husbands died as felons or traitors because punishment for these crimes included forfeiture of the men's real and movable property. Under the common law, the forfeited goods included their wives' clothing, jewelry, and other personal possessions, as well as their dowers. In theory, women's jointures and inheritances were exempt from forfeiture since they possessed legal estates in them during their marriages. But wives whose husbands were in exile or prison after they were attainted did not have even this security because the government routinely excluded them from their jointures and inheritances to prevent them from using their income to assist their spouses. To a greater or lesser degree, therefore, depending on their specific situations, the wives and widows of felons and attainted traitors depended on the king for their incomes and repossession of their goods.[75]

Although historians have traditionally maintained that aristocratic widows did not suffer for their husbands' crimes, their fate was actually far more complicated and unpredictable.[76] The Yorkist kings treated the widows of attainted men particularly harshly after their final victory over the Lancastrians in 1471. Katherine Vaux did not have "wherewithal to live and to support her children" until the king restored her jointure to her seven years later.[77] Edward IV agreed to a statute that treated his sister-in-law, Anne, countess of Warwick, as if she were legally dead and permitted the transfer of her huge inheritance to his younger brothers, her two sons-in-law, the dukes of Gloucester and Clarence during her lifetime.[78] Gloucester's treatment of Elizabeth, the aged countess of Oxford, widow of the twelfth earl, is another chilling example of the fate of an heiress whose husband was attainted when members of the royal family coveted her estate. Gloucester's brutal behavior when he badgered her into surrendering her inheritance to him undoubtedly contributed to her death in 1474.[79] The Yorkists were equally punitive in their behavior to the countess's daughter-in-law Margaret, wife of the thirteenth earl of Oxford. According to historical tradition, Margaret, who was not an heiress, had nothing to live on but charity and her needlework after her husband was attainted in absentia in 1475. There is no record of a grant to her until 1481, when she finally received an annuity of £100 from the crown.[80]

The experiences of these women must, of course, be set against the relatively good fortune of such women as Eleanor, countess of Northumberland; Anne, widow of Aubrey De Vere; and Katherine, duchess of Buckingham, who were granted substantial incomes within months of their husbands' attainders.[81] Richard III even agreed not to attaint William, Lord Hastings, after he was murdered so that Hastings's widow, Katherine, the king's "well-beloved cousin," could enjoy her husband's estates. He also granted her wardship of her minor son and custody of his inheritance.[82] The point is not that all aristocratic women were impoverished after their husbands were attainted in the Yorkist period, but rather that the possibility always existed. Attainders deprived them of the legal protection and property rights on which they normally relied. Instead, at a critical juncture in their lives, they depended on the mercy of kings who had just condemned their husbands as traitors.

Although the accession of the Tudors ultimately led to greater dynastic stability than existed under the Yorkists, Henry VII's reign was marked by rebellions, plots, and pretenders, which produced as many attainders as that of Edward IV.[83] In contrast to his immediate predecessors, however, Henry generally refrained from punishing the wives and widows of the men he attainted. The experience of the Howard women, the duchess of Norfolk and the countess of Surrey, contrasted dramatically with that of the countesses of Oxford under Edward IV. Henry not only respected the duchess's jointures from her two previous marriages but also permitted her to take possession of her jointure from the duke, which included his chief mansion at Stoke-by-Nayland. The countess of Surrey was in a weaker position because her husband was imprisoned rather than executed after he was attainted, which deprived her of her jointure. But Henry did not copy Richard III's (i.e., Gloucester's) example in the case of Elizabeth, countess of Oxford, and permitted Lady Surrey to retain her inheritance, as well as her jointure from her first husband.[84]

Edward IV's and Henry VII's statutes and patent rolls portray the widows of attainted men as passive recipients of royal acts of mercy, but surviving evidence occasionally allows us to look behind the official record and reveals that these widows were just as active in defending themselves as women whose husbands had died within the law. Here again, widows exploited the connections and knowledge they had acquired as wives to rescue some of their property in the wake of their husbands' forfeitures. Elizabeth, the ill-fated countess of Oxford, tried to save her inheritance by conveying it to feoffees and protesting in Chancery that she had not transferred it to Richard III of her own free will. Although her efforts proved futile at the time, her action helped her heir, the thirteenth earl of Oxford, to regain possession of his inheritance after Henry VII ascended the throne.[85] Ellen Delves, from a much less powerful family, was equally tenacious in defending her jointure. Both her husband and son had died while fighting for Henry VI in 1471. When Henry VII reversed her son's attainder in 1485, she became involved in a three-way struggle over the Delves' estates that involved her son's coheirs—his two daughters and their husbands, Sir James Blount and Sir Robert Sheffield—and her husband's brother Ralph, who insisted that he was the heir because the land was held in male tail. Some of the most powerful men on Henry VII's council settled the quarrel the following year and assigned Dame Delves her jointure.[86]

Henry VIII's peaceful ascent to the throne meant that for the first time in decades a reign did not begin with a rash of attainders. The conviction of the third duke of Buckingham for treason in 1521 was the only attainder before the break with Rome. But after 1533 the rise and fall of court factions in response to religious reform and the king's successive marriages produced a series of convictions for treason and forfeitures that ended only with the king's death in 1547. In addition, in 1541, Thomas, Lord Dacre of the South, forfeited his property after he was convicted of murder.[87]

The widows of Henry VIII's victims were no more likely than their Yorkist predecessors to accept the loss of their property passively. Instead, they activated their personal and family networks to support their petitions for restoration of their land and goods. The response of Lady Elizabeth Carew and her family to the execution of her husband, Sir Nicholas, a member of the Privy Chamber and one of the religious conservatives executed in 1539, is particularly well documented. Lady Carew had been raised at court because her parents, Sir Thomas and Lady Margaret Bryan, both held offices in the royal household. Her brother, Sir Francis, was a member of the Privy Chamber and one of the king's closest friends.[88] In the early, halcyon days of the reign, Elizabeth and her future husband were members of the king's inner social circle and performed regularly in the masques and dances that were among his favorite pastimes.[89] Henry almost certainly arranged their marriage: he attended their wedding and endowed them with a gift of 50 marks' worth of land.[90] In those years, the king showered Lady Carew with "beautiful diamonds and pearls and innumerable jewels."[91]

After the execution, Lady Carew and her relatives mobilized immediately to petition the king for an adequate living for her and her children. Although no record of his intervention exists, her brother, Sir Francis Bryan, almost certainly spoke to the king on her behalf. Her mother, then Prince Edward's governess, petitioned Cromwell within days of Sir Nicholas's death. She reported that the king had promised Elizabeth land in Sussex worth £120 a year but complained that there was no suitable residence for her there. She wanted the king to grant her daughter the manor of Bletchingley, which Henry had given to the Carews in 1522, in addition to the Sussex property. Lady Bryan also reminded Cromwell to secure any land returned to her daughter in male tail so that she would have "somewhat to comfort her poor children withal, which hath no succor but of the king's grace and you."[92]

Lady Carew herself wrote to Cromwell the same day, begging him to be her "mediator . . . for my living and my children's." Like her mother, she focused on practical details, displaying a thorough understanding of her financial and legal situation. She pointed out that although she had a jointure of only £20, she could not claim common-law dower from her husband's estates because of his attainder. To relieve her poverty, Lady Carew pleaded for two manors, Bletchingley and Wallington, which the king had given to her and her husband jointly, plus the land in Sussex. Confirming her mother's comment that she was not used to living frugally, she noted that altogether the property was worth only a little over 300 marks, "the which I ensure your lordship, I cannot live honestly under."[93]

Cromwell agreed to assist Lady Carew and met with her in person at least once. After their meeting, she reported that royal servants who were receiving the income from her husband's forfeited estates had given her £32 but that the money was inadequate for her needs. Furthermore, the house she was inhabiting in Wallington was "in great decay," unlike the manor at Bletchingley, which had "a very fair house . . . and all things necessary about it." Lady Carew expressed reluctance to repair Wallington until she was sure she would be allowed to remain there. She was, she confessed, particularly worried because one of the king's gentleman ushers had sent a servant to Bletchingley in anticipation of receiving it from the crown.[94]

Lady Carew's fears about losing Bletchingley proved to be justified. The "splendid" house and huge park remained in the king's hands until he granted them to Anne of Cleves as part of their divorce settlement in 1540.[95] Although few women had a longer personal relationship with the king or better-placed relatives than Lady Carew, she lost the estate she wanted most. Her disappointment must have been even sharper because Henry had originally given it to her and her husband jointly. On the other hand, he granted her and her male heirs the rest of the property for which she had petitioned: Wallington in Bedington, Surrey, and the land in Sussex.[96]

None of the correspondence mentioned the fate of Nicholas Carew's movable property, which included his wife's clothing and jewelry, as well as their household goods and gold and silver plate. Lady Carew may have been referring to it obliquely when she assured Cromwell, "I have not and will not meddle with nothing that is my own until such time that I have knowledge of the king's pleasure and yours." Lady Carew's will, written two years later, indicates that the king had allowed her to keep at least some of their precious possessions. Her bequests included almost 300 marks of plate, £40 in cash, her wedding ring, two diamond rings, an emerald ring, a crimson satin doublet, and two gold tablets. On the other hand, none of the jewelry sounded like the magnificent pieces that had so impressed Eustace Chapuys, the Imperial ambassador.[97] Here, as in the case of her husband's land, the king apparently kept the choicest objects for himself.

The extant evidence about Lady Carew and her family in the wake of her husband's attainder provides an unusually detailed and vivid picture of the intense behind-the-scenes activity that preceded the restoration of some of her property. But she was only the best documented of the widows who recruited their friends and relatives to support their petitions after their husbands' property had been forfeited to the crown. Her contemporaries, Lady Anne Fortescue and Mary, Lady Dacre, responded with equal vigor after their husbands' executions.[98] All three women were in much weaker positions legally and politically than widows whose husbands had died within the law, but they reacted to the crises in which they found themselves in much the same way: they drew on their knowledge of the legal system and marshaled their kin networks and court connections to salvage whatever they could of their property. Their practical, energetic activity demonstrates how effectively the experience, knowledge, and relationships they had accumulated during their marriages prepared them to meet even the severest challenges of widowhood.

Once they gained possession of their jointures and the land enfeoffed for the performance of their husbands' wills, aristocratic widows were responsible for ensuring that it retained its capital value and produced the expected income. Most of them were able to discharge these tasks competently because they had participated in managing the family estates while their husbands were alive. Only a handful of women surrendered their dower and jointure lands for annuities or rent from their husbands' heirs instead of supervising the property themselves. The exchanges were often arranged to settle disputes between them and their husbands' heirs. In 1478, for example, Katherine, third wife and widow of Sir Roger Lewkenor, agreed to rent her jointure lands to her stepson Thomas for 100 marks. The indenture they signed contained elaborate stipulations to protect Dame Lewkenor if Thomas withheld the rent, an indication of the hostility between them.[99] Twenty years later, mediators intervened to settle the "variance" between Margery Strickland, widow of Sir Thomas, and her stepson. She gave him control of her jointure lands in return for an annuity of £50. Once again the agreement contained careful provisions in case he defaulted.[100] To protect the two women further, both indentures were recorded in Chancery, which enabled them to enforce the settlements more easily if their stepsons withheld their income. Other widows probably exchanged their jointures for annual payments to avoid the kind of conflict that developed in the Lewkenor and Strickland families. Margery Blount agreed to take an annuity of 100 marks from her father-in-law, Walter, Lord Mountjoy, after her husband, his heir, predeceased him, and Ladies Florence Clifford, Joan Berkeley, and Cecily Berkeley accepted annuities from their stepsons.[101]

Although settling or avoiding disputes with their husbands' heirs was the primary reason that aristocratic widows exchanged their jointures for annuities, some women preferred such arrangements for more idiosyncratic reasons. In 1486, a year after her husband died, Alianore Shirley released her jointure to her son Ralph in return for an annuity of £80, two bucks in the summer, two does in winter, and his promise to give each of his four sisters marriage portions of 100 marks. Dame Shirley, who had been married for almost thirty years and had given birth to at least a dozen children before her husband died, may well have been too old, too sick, or too tired to manage her jointure and raise her daughters' dowries.[102] Anne Willoughby, widow of Sir Edward, told her husband's brother and heir, Sir John, that she would consent to any arrangement he wanted about her jointure in appreciation of the "great pains you took with me here in my great troubles." She told him to choose whether he wanted "to take the whole lands and appoint me 40 marks yearly" or "to appoint me such lands as I shall have that I may put order in it for my most profit." She trusted him, she said, to be a "good brother to me as I have always found you in times past."[103]

In a more unusual situation, in 1507, Anne Herbert, widow of Sir Walter, gave her brother, Edward Stafford, third duke of Buckingham, control of her jointure, which included Raglan Castle in Wales, because Raglan was located in an unruly area from which it was difficult to extract revenue. To make matters worse, her husband, an illegitimate son of William, earl of Pembroke, had seized the castle forcibly from his legitimate half-brother William (d. 1479) and prevented it from passing to the latter's only daughter, Elizabeth. Rather than dealing with these difficulties herself, Lady Anne, then only in her 20s, returned to her brother's household at Thornbury and put him in charge of her affairs. He secured a grant from the crown that confirmed her rights, despite Elizabeth's superior claim to the property, and administered her jointure for her until she remarried two years later.[104]

Half a century later, in November 1556, Lady Anne Berkeley released all her rights in Calloughdown, the Berkeley's chief mansion, to Henry, her heir, although she had held the estate as part of her jointure for over two decades.[105] The transfer was almost certainly part of the settlement made on her son's marriage to the duke of Norfolk's sister Katherine since the Howards would have insisted that her jointure include an appropriate residence in the event that she was widowed. As it turned out, the young Berkeleys spent most of their time at court. Their absence permitted Lady Anne to remain at Calloughdown, where she managed the family estates until her death eight years later.[106]

Unlike these women, the majority of aristocratic widows managed their jointures and the land they held on behalf of their husbands' beneficiaries themselves. By the mid-fifteenth century, tenants, either leaseholders or copyholders, farmed most of the aristocracy's arable land. Leaseholders paid entry fines and annual rents for their land; copyholders owed a combination of traditional dues, most of which had been converted into money payments, according to the custom of the manor. Whatever their tenants' status, aristocratic widows related to them as rentiers. As estate managers, the widows concentrated on maximizing and collecting their rents; finding tenants for vacant tenaments; exploiting their woods, mills, bakehouses, dairies, and poultries; and keeping their property in good repair. Although, like men of their class, aristocratic widows hired dozens of estate officials to assist them, most of them directed their employees personally, supervised the leasing of unoccupied tenaments, kept careful track of their revenue, and monitored the behavior of their servants and tenants. The record of their activities includes scores of letters, as well as such documents as the receipts signed by Dame Elizabeth Say in 1490; Dame Eleanor Townshend's book of transactions from the same decade; a recognizance signed by Margaret, countess of Salisbury, in 1513; and accounts signed by Mary, duchess of Richmond, in 1546.[107]

This material demonstrates conclusively that widows paid careful attention to administrative details and even relatively small sums of money, to preserving their legal rights, to keeping careful accounts of their income and expenditures, and to safeguarding the deeds, rentals, valors, and enfeoffments that proved their rights to their land. In 1540, for example, Margaret, dowager marchioness of Dorset, became involved in a suit about a property in Leicestershire between William Hickling, who claimed it as his freehold, and Thomas Siston, who said he held it as copyhold from her. During litigation in the Court of Requests, the marchioness produced a deed from Richard II's reign, a rental from 1485, and three witnesses to support Siston.[108] Her ability to defend her interests depended on her possession of the necessary written records and illustrates why landowners went to such lengths to protect their "evidence and muniments." As Margaret Paston warned her eldest son shortly after her husband's death, "Your father, whom God assoil [i.e., absolve, pardon of sin], in his trouble season set more by his writings and evidence than he did by any of his movable goods. Remember that if they were had from you, ye could never get no more such as those be for your part etc."[109]

On a day-to-day basis, women's records of their income were equally important. Dame Eleanor Townshend, who had a life interest in her son's inheritance as well as in her jointure, had her estate officials keep her accounts in English so that she could examine them herself, although her husband had kept them in Latin and her son would do so after her death.[110] Two letters from 1526 and 1527 record Dame Anne Rede's anxiety about calculating the profits from her land. After going over "certain books of account" with her brother-in-law, she sent them to Henry Gold, her brother's man of business, because he had "better skill" in such matters than she. Dame Rede asked him to "cast the said accounts," as well as "other books which lieth in my casket with you concerning the last Michaelmas rent." She was certain she was "behind for a great part" of the money owed her. Once Gold "made the account perfectly," she intended to examine it carefully and take whatever action was necessary to collect the revenue due to her. She was particularly worried because the rentals of her jointure indicated that they were worth £3 less than the £100 owed her. She was negotiating with her stepson Leonard about making up the deficit and gave Gold careful directions about how to proceed.[111] Three months later, as she prepared for a hearing before the royal escheator to adjudicate the dispute, she asked Gold "to make in readiness my books . . . so that no fault may be laid on me at the time."[112]

Like other members of her class, Dame Rede depended on her servants and kin to collect her rents physically and deliver them to her. She had particular confidence in Henry Gold in this area. In April 1527, she told him, "And where ye are purposed to ride into Buckinghamshire about my business, ye should do me a great pleasure so to do and bring with you home my rents."[113] On her very deathbed, Jane Roos begged her nephew to send her the discharge necessary to permit her bailiff and other servants to collect the money due from her property at Cramwell. She also wanted his assurance that he would deliver the income from the property to her executors for the next six months, even if she died immediately, since they needed the money to perform her will. Ever conscious of the technicalities of the law, she repeated three times that she wanted the documents certified by both his seal and sign manual.[114]

Widows were almost as preoccupied with leasing their estates on favorable terms as collecting their income. Sometimes they rented small pieces of property to tenants who worked the land or operated their mills themselves. In 1446, for example, Agnes Paston rented a mill to one lessee and some land and a meadow to another.[115] Six decades later, Mary, Lady Hastings, granted a number of leases to small pieces of property that yielded such modest annual rents as 7s., 18s., and 26s. 8d., and Dorothy Ferrers rented land to a tanner.[116]

Tenurial relationships of this kind frequently led to litigation. When they did, tenants often claimed that the suits should be heard in Chancery or Star Chamber because their widowed landlords would overawe the local common-law courts. During Henry VIII's reign, Nicholas Patrick, who leased a piece of property in Derbyshire from Dame Elizabeth Giffard for 28s. 8d. per annum, maintained that he could not sue her at the common law because she was "a woman of great power and riches and hath many friends and kinfolk in the country there."[117] Similarly, in 1547, Richard Leche alleged that he was too poor to defend himself against Dame Dorothy Fulford's common-law suit against him about a tenament worth 17s. a year because she was "greatly friended and allied."[118] Whether the tenants' claims in these particular cases were true or not, allegations of this kind were clearly credible and testify to the power widows gained in their localities as large-scale landowners and members of important regional networks.

Instead of managing their estates directly, some aristocratic widows adopted the alternative strategy of leasing out whole manors or large blocks of land to other members of their class, gentry below the rank of knight, or substantial yeomen. Their tenants either used the land for demesne farming or sheep grazing or sublet it in smaller units to those who actually worked the land. In 1464, for example, Eleanor, Lady Hungerford and Moleyns, leased her manor of Whitley, in Wiltshire.[119] Twenty-four years later, Margaret Bourchier, Lady Fitzwalter, granted one of her manors to Sir Thomas Lovell. Lovell renewed the lease for five years before vacating the property.[120] In 1551, Dame Eleanor Percy, widow of Sir Thomas, leased Horton, Northumberland, to her brother, Thomas Harbottell, for twenty-one years, simultaneously assisting her natal family and relieving herself of direct responsibility for the property.[121]

Although aristocratic widows received most of their income from rent, they also engaged in demesne, dairy, and sheep farming. Wills contain the best evidence of this dimension of their activity. Fifty-seven, or 21 percent, of 266 women's wills include bequests of grain, cows, oxen, sheep, or farm equipment. In 1467, Dame Maud Eure divided most of her sheep, oxen, and cows between her two sons but gave "all my husbandry [i.e., farm equipment]" at Wotton specifically to Harry."[122] Dame Agnes Scott left her daughter, Isabel Poynings, two working oxen and all her instruments of husbandry as long as Isabel remained at Scott's Hall.[123] Dame Elizabeth Englefield divided "milche beasts," sheep, oxen, beef and other cattle, wheat, malt, and corn equally between her two sons.[124]

The evidence rarely reveals the degree of aristocratic widows' involvement in their farming enterprises, but it does show that some of them were active in their daily operation. A few specifically mentioned their agricultural servants in their wills, which probably indicates that they had some personal contact with them.[125] John Smythe of Nibley, who knew Lady Anne Berkeley personally, recorded that "country housewifery seemed to be an essential part" of her activities and that she "would betimes in winter and summer make her walks to visit her stable, barns, dairy house, poultry, swine troughs and the like."[126] On one occasion, she leased a tithing barn from St. Augustine's monastery in Bristol to store her grain.[127] Dame Elizabeth Gates managed the demesne farm of her son Sir John while he pursued a career at court in the 1540s. In December 1545, she reported in detail about the wheat and malt harvested on his behalf and inquired where he wanted his "Lent corn, as peas and oats, sown."[128]

Many aristocratic widows engaged in sheep farming on an enormous scale and made significant profits from wool sales. When Eleanor, countess of Arundel, died in 1455, she had wool worth more than £100 at her manor of Heytesbury.[129] Dame Eleanor Townshend never kept less than 8,000 sheep during her widowhood.[130] In the 1550s Dame Elizabeth Spelman left one of her younger sons, Erasmus, 200 sheep and over 1,000 to her grandson Thomas, the eldest son of her deceased heir.[131] Dame Elizabeth Unton, a second wife without children, left the younger of her two stepsons over 1,500 sheep. Her estate also included wool worth £40.[132]

Whether they depended entirely on their income from rent or also engaged in demesne, dairy, and sheep farming, aristocratic widows employed dozens of servants to assist them in overseeing their property and collecting and auditing their income. Choosing these men carefully and securing their loyalty was a key dimension of successful estate management. But it was also a valuable form of patronage. In conjunction with women's wealth, it contributed to their familial and local power. The highest ranking, most affluent noblewomen often filled their most important positions—stewardships and receiverships—with knights, who received substantial fees for their service. These appointments created or perpetuated the women's ties to key figures in their localities and counties. In 1460, Anne, duchess of Buckingham, commissioned Sir William Berkeley as master of her deer and overseer of her parks, warrens, forests, and chases in Gloucestershire; the next year, she rewarded him "for his good and gratuitous services" with the stewardship of the manor of Thornbury.[133] Henry VII's mother, Margaret Beaufort, commissioned Sir

Richard Cholmeley as steward of her manor of Cottingham, Yorkshire, and Sir John Hussey as steward of Maxey Castle, Warwickshire and Deeping, Lincolnshire.[134] Elizabeth, Lady Scrope; Katherine, duchess of Norfolk; and Cecily, duchess of York, all appointed Sir John Howard as one of their stewards and paid him substantial fees.[135]

Aristocratic widows with fewer resources turned to their relatives—frequently, but not always, distant kin from less affluent families—for their estate officials. They clearly hoped that kinship would increase their servants' trustworthiness. Their recognition of these blood ties suited both the minor gentlemen who needed supplements to their landed income and the noble and knightly widows who needed reliable employees. It is in this connection that the most expansive definition of the aristocratic family—a whole world of "cousins"—becomes visible in the records. In the mid-fifteenth century, Elizabeth Clere called on her "cousin" John Paston I to assist her in defending her grazing rights in an enclosed pasture.[136] Decades later, Margaret Fitzwilliam thanked her "cousin" Sir Thomas Wentworth for his "labor and pain" in resolving a dispute between her and her tenants.[137] Isabel Plumpton employed Robert Girlington, a distant relative from a minor gentry family, to hold her courts and act as her general man of business, as well as William Woodruffe, whom she called her "loving friend and kinsman" in her will.[138]

Aristocratic widows also went outside their kin groups for servants, hiring lawyers, auditors, clergymen, and crown officials who possessed the necessary practical skills and/or connections to assist them. John Knight, a professional auditor, worked for Margaret Beaufort, as well as for the earls of Nottingham and Derby.[139] Margaret, countess of Salisbury, appointed Sir Christopher More, a remembrancer in the Court of Exchequer, as her surveyor. She undoubtedly found (or expected) his position in the royal bureacracy to be useful when she had business at court.[140] Dame Anne Rede's servant Henry Gold was also the chaplain and man of business of her brother, Archbishop Warham. Gold was not unusual in combining clerical and secular activities. During her long life, Margaret Beaufort, countess of Richmond, employed dozens of clerics in her household and on her estates. As in the royal bureaucracy itself, this practice enabled her to reward her servants at the church's expense rather than her own. Hugh Oldham was appointed receiver for Lady Margaret's west country estates in 1492 and became her receiver-general in 1501. She secured two rectories for him in 1493 and 1494 and the Bishopric of Exeter a decade later.[141] Another clergyman, Hugh Ashton, who assisted Oldham, became Lady Margaret's receiver-general in 1501. With her assistance, he eventually became Archdeacon of Richmond.[142]

As the countess of Richmond's promotion of Oldham and Ashton indicates, aristocratic widows incorporated their estate officials into their patronage networks so that the fees for their offices were only one—and often not the largest—benefit they derived from their service. In 1473, for example,

Dame Katherine Arundell awarded two small manors in Cornwall worth £12 per annum to Richard Tomyowe for "the good service that he had done for my husband and me in days passed and the charges that he must do for me hereafter."[143] In 1536, Margaret, dowager marchioness of Dorset, granted one of her stewardships in Leicestershire to the son of a lawyer whom she retained.[144] Other widows remembered their favorite estate officials in their wills. Joan, Viscountess Lisle, left a gilt cup, a cloth gown, and £10 to her receiver in 1500; Dame Anne Barnardiston gave 13s. 4d. to her bailiff in 1559; and Jane Wriothesely, countess of Southampton, bequeathed £10 to her surveyor in 1574.[145]

Relationships between aristocratic widows and their estate officials were not always as satisfactory as these legacies suggest. The women supervised their servants closely enough and were well informed enough to act decisively when they were concerned about the revenue the officers collected, the accounts and estate records that came into their possession, and their officers' failure to carry out their duties. In 1488, Margaret Beaufort resorted to the law to compel one of her receivers to make his account with her "as he ought to do." She charged he had "suddenly departed from us otherwise than according to the trust that was put in him."[146] Elizabeth, Lady Fitzwarren, charged that one of her baliffs and receivers had failed to give her 100 marks that he had collected the year before he died. When his widow refused to pay the money or make the account that was due, she sued her in Chancery.[147] Servants also accused their employers of breaches of contract or trust. When Elizabeth, duchess of Suffolk, prosecuted Sir Thomas Hansard for trespassing on her property and stealing her tenants' cattle, he responded that he was exercising his legal right of distress because she had not paid his wages.[148] Another disgruntled employee, John St. Clere, sued Elizabeth, countess of Bath, for depriving him of his office as receiver of her estates in Devon and Cornwall. The countess counterclaimed that St. Clere had failed to post the recognizance that was a condition of his office.[149]

Whether aristocratic widows administered their estates directly or leased whole manors or large blocks of land, the success or failure of their management had a major impact on the long-term fortunes of their families, particularly since over 60 percent of them survived their husbands by more than a decade. The revenue from the dower lands of Anne, duchess of Buckingham, increased by 40 percent (from £884 to £1,245) between 1460, when she was widowed, and 1473, when the heir, her grandson, came of age. Luckily for the young duke, the crown had also assigned his other English estates to her during his minority; they also increased in value.[150] Dame Eleanor Townshend was an equally capable manager. When Sir Roger died in 1493, he gave her a life interest in most of the Townshend estates, which were worth £230 to £240 per annum. In the six years before she died, she added £55 of purchased land to them, raising her son's income over 20 percent.[151]

Sir John Spencer (d. 1522) and Lady Isabella Graunt Spencer (d. 1558). Great Brington, Northants. By courtesy of the Conway Library, Courtauld Institute of Art.

Dame Townshend was not the only aristocratic widow to invest in land, the quintessential mark of successful estate management. The women's purchases constitute persuasive evidence of their contribution to the long-term well-being of their families. Their purchases ranged from large investments such as the manor Elizabeth, duchess of Suffolk, bought for 700 marks to the small tract Dame Dorothy Ferrers acquired for £18.[152] Some widows, Dame Margaret Shelton and Lady Jane Corbet, for example, left their acquisitions to their eldest sons, thus permanently endowing the senior family line.[153] Dame Margaret Capell's and Elizabeth Spelman's bequests of recently purchased land to their eldest son's heirs had the same effect.[154] But in other cases, aristocratic women bought land to endow their younger sons, thereby modifying the primogenital priorities of their class. Dame Elizabeth Hussee actually purchased a manor from her heir to bequeath to his younger brother.[155] Dame Alice Cotton and Dame Joan Denny bought land for their younger sons, while Dame Jane Constable helped her younger son Marmaduke found a cadet branch of the family by jointly purchasing the manor of Wassand with him.[156]

Whether they were buying land, grazing huge flocks of sheep, engaging in demesne farming, leasing their land, or cultivating their families' networks when they appointed their estate officials, aristocratic widows contributed to the survival and continued prosperity of their families and, collectively, of their class. Their large numbers, longevity, and extensive landholdings meant that the majority of knightly and noble families who retained their position over more than one or two generations depended on their competence, energy, and dedication for considerable periods of time. Overall, long widowhoods were a benefit, not a danger, to their husbands' patrilineages.

Two examples chosen from many possibilities—the Spencers and the Barnardistons—illustrate this point. The Spencers were one of the most successful, upwardly mobile families of the early Tudor period. The first Spencer to achieve a knighthood, Sir John, purchased two manors, Althorp and Wormleighton, in the first decade of the sixteenth century. He died in 1522, leaving a widow who survived him for thirty-six years. His relatively short-lived heir, Sir William, died in 1529 or 1532; his widow survived until 1549. Although the two widows held a significant portion of the Spencer estate for the entire second quarter of the century, the Spencers flourished economically and rose socially. The third-generation Spencer knight, another Sir John, marrried three of his daughters into the nobility.[157]

The Spencers' contemporaries, the Barnardistons of Kedington, Suffolk, also acquired their first knighthood in the early Tudor period and supported two long-lived widows without notable detriment to their fortunes, although they never accumulated the wealth of the Spencers or intermarried with the peerage. Dame Elizabeth, widow of the first Barnardiston knight, Sir Thomas, survived her husband by twenty-three years. His son, another Sir Thomas, died twenty-two years before his wife. Yet the family remained prosperous, and the third Sir Thomas Barnardiston married a woman from the politically influential Walsingham family.[158]

Whether they acted on their own or in concert with others, aristocratic women executing their husbands' wills assumed a wide variety of responsibilities in addition to securing and managing land and goods designated for that purpose. Their duties included arranging and paying for their husbands' funerals, building their tombs, fulfilling their religious bequests, collecting their debts and paying their creditors, raising and preferring their children, and distributing their legacies. Unfortunately, because the Court of Arches, the Archbishop of Canterbury's probate court in London, burned in the Great Fire of 1666, the inventories and accounts necessary to study their activities systematically no longer exist. Nonetheless, enough material survives to prove that as a group aristocratic widows were conscientious, effective administrators of their husbands' wills.[159] Since it is impossible to determine who was acting in a group of coexecutors, the evidence marshaled here to support this statement draws entirely on the wills of men who appointed their widows as their sole executors or on legal records and letters that make it clear that the women were functioning independently.

Widows' activities as their husbands' executors began immediately after the men's deaths, when they arranged and paid for their funerals and oversaw construction of their tombs. Most men indicated where they wanted to be buried, demonstrating an overwhelming preference for the parish church where their chief residences were located. Dames Margaret Carew, Alice Saville, Jane Knightley, and Elizabeth Barnardiston are examples of the many sole executors who carried out their husbands' directions in this respect.[160] A few testators, Sir William Coffin and Sir Anthony Knyvett, for instance, left the choice of their burial place to their sole executors.[161] Although a few men built their monuments before they died, most sole executors also supervised construction of their husbands' tombs.[162]

In some cases, building men's tombs took years. John Paston's wife and heir argued for over a decade about who should pay for it. In 1471, five years after he died, his widow, Margaret, wrote to her younger son, John III, "It is a shame, and a thing that is much spoken of in this country, that your father's grave stone is not made. For God's love, let it be remembered and purveyed for in haste."[163] Two years later, her eldest son, John II, blamed her for the disgraceful state of affairs. "I pray you," he wrote his brother, "remember her for my father's tomb at Bromholme. She doth right not; I am affeared of her that she shall not do well."[164] Still nothing was done. In 1476 the Prior of Bromholme, where Paston was buried, reminded his younger son "of the ill speech which is in the country now of new that the tomb is not made. And also . . . the cloth that lieth over the grave is all torn and rotten and is not worth 2d."[165] Finally, twelve years after John I's death, Margaret and John II agreed to sell a piece of gold cloth to pay for the monument. He promised her that "if it be sold, I undertake or [ere] Michelmas that there shall be a tomb and somewhat else over my father's grave . . . that there shall none be like it in Norfolk, and as ye shall be glad thereafter to see it."[166] Margaret was nervous about entrusting him with the expensive cloth and warned him, "If you sell it to any other use, by my truth, I shall never trust you while I live."[167]

Fulfilling their husbands' religious bequests was closely related to women's responsibility for their funerals since the services almost always involved distributing alms and performing other acts of charity. Before the Reformation, these bequests were explicitly or implicitly linked to prayers for the souls of the deceased. In addition to distributing alms on the day of their burial and at their month-minds, aristocratic men left money to their parish churches, favorite religious orders, and the universities, for the repair of highways and bridges and the marriage of poor maidens, and to endow almshouses, hospitals, and chantries for perpetual prayers for their souls. After the government dissolved the religious orders and the Church of England eliminated the doctrine of purgatory, aristocratic men continued to make those traditional pious bequests that were still permitted, at least in the decades covered in this book. In addition, by the 1540s a few aristocratic men, influenced by the movement for reform, funded new kinds of religious benefactions. Charles, Lord Mount-joy, and Sir Robert Payton both directed their sole executors to establish sermons in their name.[168] Religiously conservative men resumed their gifts to monasteries and convents when they were reestablished in Mary's reign.[169] Overall, the wills of peers and knights support scholars who emphasize the slow pace of religious change but recognize that a small group was increasingly committed to reform.[170]

Most aristocratic men directed their widows to make a relatively small number of religious bequests that were easy to carry out.[171] But particularly devout men often placed a considerable burden on their widows because of the large number or complexity of their legacies for spiritual purposes. Humphrey, first duke of Buckingham, directed his sole executor to distribute 200 marks to clergymen who attended his funeral and the residue to the poor within eight days of his burial. In addition, he wanted her to establish two chantries for him. His instructions for the foundation at the College of Pleshy, Essex, were exceedingly elaborate and involved building an almshouse for seven men and a new chapel, where the prayers were to be said.[172] Sir John Manyngham's will contained detailed instructions for the establishment of prayers for his soul, the distribution of alms, and bequests to a dozen or more religious orders.[173]

Founding chantries, hospitals, and almshouses involved widows in the complicated legal process of amortizing land to support these institutions and supervising their construction. As Michael Hicks's essays on Margaret, Lady Hungerford, demonstrate, there was no certainty that testators' wishes would be carried out.[174] Everything depended on whether their executors identified their own spiritual well-being with their husbands' wishes. As the sole executor for Robert, Lord Hungerford, Margaret not only accepted responsibility for carrying out his religious bequests but also assumed his unfulfilled obligation to endow a hospital at Heytesbury for his father. That there was real choice involved in her decision is evident in her concurrent refusal to endow a chantry and almshouses at Bath for her own father, William, Lord Botreaux.[175] Margaret Leynham, Margaret Choke, and Joan Vernon are three of the many sole executors who built the chantries their husbands provided for in their wills.[176] Elizabeth Cutte, who neglected to build her husband's almshouses and chantry, sought to avoid a spiritual penalty for her failure by directing her executors to complete the task for her.[177]

Sometimes widows who were trying to found their husbands' chantries faced opposition from the testators' heirs, who resented financing them out of their inheritances. Quarrels between William Paston's widow and sons prevented the fulfillment of his wish that a chantry and obit be endowed for him at the Cathedral Priory in Norwich. The prior who recounted the matter forty years later had no doubt about his widow's desire to fulfill her husband's wishes. He claimed that she had financed prayers for her husband as long as she lived because her sons prevented amortization of land to support them and stole the goods deposited in the monastery to pay for them until the endowment was completed.[178] Dame Elizabeth Barnardiston, sole executor of Sir Thomas's will, also faced opposition from their eldest son when she tried to establish her husband's chantry. She eventually sued him in Chancery for refusing to enfeoff the lands his father had bequeathed to endow it.[179] She didn't secure a licence from the crown to found the chantry until 1517, fourteen years after her husband died.[180] Nonetheless, the chantry was not built at her death nine years later, and she provided for it in her own will. Dame Barnardiston's decision to appoint the Prior of Walsingham as her sole executor probably means that her son still opposed endowing the chantry. This time it was established.[181] Dame Elizabeth also funded an obit for her husband and herself with income from a manor she had purchased in Cambridgeshire. The endowment was also to be used to support a scholar known as "my Lady Barnardiston's child."[182]

Dealing with their husbands' debtors and creditors often taxed the skill and tenacity of women performing their husbands' wills. Collecting the money owed them was an immediate concern because many testators included their debts among the assets to be used to implement their wills. Yet in many cases widows did not have written proof of the money owed or had such old obligations that they had to collect the money from the debtors' heirs or executors. Margaret Fleming's effort to recover £230 owed to her late husband, Sir Thomas, from the estate of Robert Wade illustrates how complicated the process could be when the debtors themselves were dead. Dame Fleming alleged that before he died, Wade had enfeoffed property to pay the obligation but that his feoffees had refused to satisfy her nonetheless. Wade's feoffees admitted that he had borrowed the money, but they claimed they could not repay it because Wade's heir had sued them for possession of the estates enfeoffed to perform his will and the case was still undecided.[183] Even when the debtors were alive, reaching a settlement with them was rarely a simple matter. Margaret, dowager marchioness of Dorset, sued Arthur, Lord Lisle, for £150 he owed her husband. One of Lisle's lawyers wrote to him that none of them had any record of the liability and asked what they should do.[184] Her contemporary, Elizabeth Strelley, sued George Bykerstaffe for the £10 he owed her husband's estates for building stone he had purchased a decade earlier.[185]

Satisfying their husbands' creditors was an equally pressing matter because failure to pay one's debts was a mortal sin. The widows of men who died in debt were therefore assuming essential spiritual, as well as worldly, obligations on their behalf. Sir Thomas Elyot explicitly connected payment of his debts with the "weal of his soul."[186] Some anxious testators instructed their executors to pay their obligations before their other legacies or to satisfy their neediest creditors first.[187] Men whose estates were heavily burdened with debts often designated specific assets to be used to pay them. Sir Henry Guildford told his widow to sell all the lands he had purchased in Kent for that purpose, and Sir John Jenyns ordered his widow to use the residue of one of his farms to pay his obligations.[188]

However good their intentions, widows often found that paying their husbands' debts was an onerous task because they lacked the information necessary to determine which claims against their husbands' estates were legitimate. Less than 5 percent of their wills listed their debts or recorded that they had provided their executors with separate schedules of their liabilities.[189] A few other testators mentioned specific obligations.[190] Not surprisingly, therefore, aristocratic widows were frequently defendants in suits for payment of their spouses' debts. In response, they often denied knowledge of the obligations and maintained that the alleged creditors did not have written proof of their claims. In one such dispute, witnesses in the Court of Requests supported the plaintiffs against Dame Anne Skeffington when she relied on this defense.[191] Widows also responded to suits of this kind by claiming that they had already paid the obligations in question or that they had settled their husbands' estates and no longer had any of their assets to distribute.[192] When a former park keeper of her husband sued her for unpaid wages, Alice, Lady Burgh, maintained that he had not appeared when she issued a public proclamation asking all Lord Burgh's debtors to come forward shortly after her husband's death. By the time of his suit, she declared that she no longer had sufficient funds to pay the alleged wages and that she had already spent more money satisfying her husband's creditors than she had received to perform his will.[193]

Whatever their widows' intentions, some aristocratic men's estates could not cover their debts, a situation almost certain to lead to litigation. In these circumstances, wives were understandably reluctant to act as sole executors. Dame Anne Harcourt, widow of Sir William, articulated these issues clearly in her petition to the Court of Chancery after her husband died in 1474. "Your said suppliant," she wrote, "dreading . . . that his goods will not stretch for to pay his debts . . . dare not as yet to take upon her the charge of administrator of the said goods." At the same time, she feared that if she refused to take on the office, "she might lose all such goods as were bequeathed unto her." Her friends and lawyer shared her indecision. To make matters worse, she was already being sued by one of her husband's alleged creditors as if she were his executor "whereof whether [it] ought to be due or nay, it is utterly unknown to your said suppliant."[194]

In practice, at least by the sixteenth century, Chancery protected widows from liability for their husbands' debts when the debts exceeded their estates. In 1549, for instance, the Lord Chancellor ruled that Elizabeth, widow and executor of Robert Burgoyne, owed the £27 10s. claimed against her but that she could not pay it out of his goods and lands "without some moderation for

time of payment and reduction in principal." Accordingly, he reduced her liability and established a new payment schedule. He also decreed that her new
husband, Sir Richard Lytton, was not liable for Burgoyne's debt.[195] Nonetheless, some women did pay their husbands' creditors out of their own property, perhaps because they regarded doing so as necessary for the good of
their own or their husbands' souls. When Dame Mary Fitton died in 1557, she
recorded with satisfaction that she had spent £62 of "mine own proper goods"
to satisfy her late husband's creditors.[196] Sir William Coffin tried to save his
widow and sole executor from such scruples by explicitly directing her to
"charge herself no further" than his goods to pay his debts.[197]

Women with connections at court often turned to their friends on the
Privy Council for assistance in dealing with their husbands' creditors. Dame
Mary Guildford, widow of Sir Henry, a member of Henry VIII's Privy Chamber, asked Thomas Cromwell for help of this kind in 1534. She reported that
she had already followed his advice and given one of the creditors, Marcus
Auger, "new stuff" worth £50 but that Auger was still unsatisfied. Two other
creditors, Adam Sampson, to whom her husband owed £100, and Master
Monday, to whom he owed £930, had rejected her settlement offers. If Cromwell could not convince them to reconsider, she would let them sue her since
"then I think it shall appear to them that they shall not receive as much as I
have offered them, wherefore they will the gladdlier come to an end with
me."[198] Two years later, Auger and Sampson still claimed that Dame Guildford owed them money. Weary of their incessant petitions, Cromwell pressed
her to come to some agreement with them.

But Mary Guildford was not easily pressured. She reminded Cromwell that
her husband had owed Henry VIII "far above all the goods that he left behind
him." After she had paid his debts to the king and royal serjeant of the cellar,
the king had released the residue of her husband's estate to her "freely,"
which, she "reckoned," discharged her from the extremity of the law in respect to her husband's other creditors. Nonetheless, she had been trying to
satisfy those willing to "come to any reasonable end" in good faith and offered to send Cromwell the record of her transactions. She also promised to
follow his advice about "the residue of the creditors" but reminded him that
she was a "poor widow" and needed some "small part" of her husband's estate for herself.[199] Subsequently, Dame Guildford met with Cromwell in person and agreed to pay Sampson 100 marks, but their dispute was still unset-
tled two months later. By this time, her friends were again urging her to let
her husband's creditors sue her since they would discover that she had already
offered or given them "more than I trust there could have been recovered on
me by law."[200] This unusually detailed record reveals how time-consuming
and vexatious responsibility for their husbands' debts could be. It makes
Dame Harcourt's reluctance to adminster her indebted husband's estate easy
to understand.

In addition to arranging their funerals, paying and collecting their debts, and carrying out their religious bequests, aristocratic widows distributed a wide variety of legacies to their husbands' relatives, friends, and servants. The burden of dividing their money and goods varied enormously from testator to testator, depending on the number and complication of their bequests. But whether the men's wills were simple or elaborate, their primary focus was almost always on providing for their widows (a subject discussed earlier in the chapter) and their children and grandchildren. Relatively few collateral kin appeared among their beneficiaries and the bequests to them were usually relatively small. The process of carrying out their provisions for their children and grandchildren often took years to complete because so many men died while their children or grandchildren were minors and unmarried.

When William, Lord Hastings, wrote his will in 1481, for example, he had four minor children. He assigned custody of his daughter Anne, his two younger sons, and two of his wards—George, earl of Shrewsbury, and his brother Thomas—to his wife, Lady Katherine. Since Anne was already betrothed to the young earl, Hastings directed his executors to use the income from Shrewsbury's inheritance to maintain Thomas and the young couple until the earl came of age and assured Anne a jointure of at least 200 marks. Hastings bequeathed land to each of his sons and instructed his executors to support them from their respective shares. When the boys turned 18, the executors were to convey their inheritances and any income remaining from their portions to them. His executors' other major task was to divide his plate, jewels, and household stuff among his wife and four children and to retain the latters' portions until they were 18. He also ordered them to sell his third wardship and employ the proceeds to perform his will.[201]

Although Hastings appointed a group of four executors, including his wife, his murder in 1483 transformed the situation. When his widow appealed to Richard III for mercy for herself and her children, he pledged to be their "good and gracious sovereign lord" and to protect Katherine "as our well beloved cousin and widow." More specifically, he promised not to attaint her husband; to grant her the wardship of Edward, her eldest son, and custody of his land; and to permit her and her husband's other executors to perform his will.[202] A formal indenture between Lady Hastings and her eldest son, Edward, in 1489, when he was 14 or 15 years old, demonstrates that she had assumed primary responsibility for fulfilling her husband's will. Edward acknowledged the "great trouble, pains, heaviness, and labor" his mother had taken on his behalf since his father's death. The agreement also recorded their mutual satisfaction about their recent division of Hastings's plate, jewels, and household stuff. For the future, Lady Hastings and her son undertook to share equally the cost of redeeming those "parcels" still in pledge for payment of their debts. Edward also consented to his mother's use of the land in enfeoffment for performance of his father's will for another three years. Significantly, the indenture contained no mention of Lady Hastings's coexecutors.[203] She also completed her daughter Anne's marriage to the earl of Shrewsbury.[204]

Securing their sons' wardships and finding husbands for their daughters were among the most important tasks widows assumed on behalf of the next generation. Many of them already had experience in these areas since women in second marriages often purchased the wardships of their eldest sons by their first husbands and wives routinely participated in arranging their daughters' marriages. What was new was their sole responsibility for performing these functions. In practice, these tasks were so connected to women's roles as mothers that even widows who were coexecutors took initiative in these areas. Margaret Bedingfield, Cecily Baynham, and Mabel Parr are all examples of coexecutors who purchased their eldest sons' wardships on their own.[205] Dame Parr also arranged her daughter Katherine's marriage.[206] Since so many husbands—27 percent in a group of 523—had unmarried daughters when they died, widows who negotiated and financed the girls' matches contributed significantly to the unusually high marriage rate of their class, whether they acted as sole executors or coexecutors.

Aristocratic men who died later in their lives than Lord Hastings often assigned heavy responsibilities for their grandchildren to their widows. This decision positioned the women at the center of their martial families for long periods of time and empowered them to play a significant part in shaping the fortunes of their spouses' patrilineages for two generations. Sir William Capell, who appointed his wife and son-in-law as his coexecutors in 1515, specifically entrusted his widow with the huge amount of cash and plate he bequeathed to his grandsons. He empowered her to use it on their behalf and to distribute the residue to them when they were 22.[207] Four decades later, Sir William Drury wrote his will just after his heir, Robert, had died. His heir was the oldest of Robert's four sons, all of whom were minors. Sir William also had two unmarried daughters. He gave Elizabeth, his widow and sole executor, responsibility for carrying out his arrangements for the next two generations of the family. Before his death he had purchased the wardship and marriage of Robert Drury, from the Rougham branch of the family, as a husband for his daughter Elizabeth, but he left her a dowry of 200 marks in case the plan failed. He also bequeathed his other daughter, Dorothy, a dowry of £200.[208] Elizabeth married Robert of Rougham as her father wished, and his widow arranged Dorothy's marriage as he expected.[209] Sir William also asked her "to see to the bringing up of my said son Robert's children." Although most of his estates would descend to the eldest boy, he left some land to the younger three "to the advancement and preferment of their living," directing his wife to assure the property to them and their heirs male in reversion after her death.

Although most of their wealth passed to their widows, children, and grand-

children, almost a third of the knights and noblemen with survivng children and grandchildren also remembered their sons-in-law, siblings, nieces,
nephews, parents, brothers-in-law, sisters-in-law, stepchildren, aunts, uncles, or
vaguely described "cousins" in their wills. Distributing these bequests further
reinforced women's membership and importance in their marital families and
helped them to preserve ties that would be useful to their children and grandchildren. In addition to her heavy responsibilities for her children, for example,
Katherine, Lady Hastings, had to raise and pay a large bequest of 100 marks to
her husband's married sister Elizabeth Donne; 200 marks each for the dowries
of his nieces, John Brokesby's daughters; and 100 marks for the marriage of another niece, Anne, daughter of Sir Thomas Ferrers of Tamworth Castle.[210] Edward Grey, Viscount Lisle, Sir William Uvedale, and Sir Henry Hussey included
paying annuities to their younger brothers among their sole executors' duties.[211] Still other men directed their wives to complete the performance
of wills they themselves had been executing before they died. In effect, their
widows became executors for their husbands' grandparents, parents, and siblings.[212] Sir Thomas Frowick's wife, Elizabeth, assumed his role as administrator of the goods of his older brother, Sir Henry, and assumed the wardship
of Henry's children.[213] Sir John Constable's widow and sole executor, Elizabeth, raised dowries for his two sisters and acted as their guardian until they
married.[214]

The men who empowered their widows to assume critical functions for
their families after they died relied on the skills the women had developed
during their marriages. Executing their husbands' wills was a logical extension of their careers as wives and mothers. It also reinforced their membership in their marital families and amplified their responsibility for the future
prosperity of their husbands' patrilineages. Collectively, their labor as executors was a key factor in preserving the stability of their families and class. To
avoid the uncertainties about the relative participation of executors who were
acting together, the discussion here has focused on the achievements of
women appointed as their husbands' sole executors or on documents clearly
showing that women appointed as coexecutors were acting independently.
There is enough evidence of the latter kind to caution historians against assuming that the men in a group of coexecutors were the ones actually doing
the work.

Widowhood was the most powerful stage in aristocratic women's life cycles.
Freed from the disabilities of coverture, they headed their own households,
owned and managed huge amounts of property, and occupied key positions
in their marital families as executors of their husbands' wills and guardians of
their children. In addition, they had unprecedented control over their own
persons. With few exceptions, they could choose whether to remain single or
to marry again.[215] Under feudal law, the king had the prerogative of marrying

the widows of his tenants-in-chief, a group that included the vast majority of noblemen and knights. When Chancery issued writs of dower, therefore, it required the recipients to swear not to marry without the king's permission.[216] In practice, however, the widespread use of enfeoffments extinguished the king's feudal rights and protected widows from the exercise of this royal power. Furthermore, when the crown retained its feudal privileges, widows often purchased licenses allowing them to marry whomever they wanted.[217] Occasionally, the king granted them this permission without payment as a mark of particular favor.[218] In other cases, couples bought licenses that sanctioned their matches or purchased pardons for having ignored the king's prerogative after they married at will.[219]

In addition to circumventing the king's feudal rights where they still existed, aristocratic widows had to cope with pressures from the king and key figures at court who wanted to arrange their marriages for political reasons or to enrich their relatives and servants. One of the most notorious matches of this kind was the marriage between Edward IV's 20-year-old brother-in-law, Sir John Woodville, and Katherine Nevill, the 60-year-old dowager duchess of Norfolk.[220] In the same reign, Margaret, countess of Richmond, whose son was heir to the Lancastrian claim to the throne, sought safety by marrying Thomas Stanley, earl of Derby, who controlled the northwest for the Yorkists.[221] After Henry VII ascended the throne, his uncle Jasper Tudor, newly created duke of Bedford, married Katherine, the widowed duchess of Buckingham and aunt of the new queen, Elizabeth of York.[222] The king undoubtedly supported or initiated all these matches since they involved members of the royal family or claimants to the throne.

In Henry VIII's more settled reign, arranging the marriages of aristocratic widows functioned as a routine form of court patronage. In 1527, both Charles Brandon, duke of Suffolk, and Cardinal Wolsey sought to reward a favored servant with a marriage to Sir Walter Strickland's widow, Katherine.[223] In the 1530s, Thomas Cromwell pressured Lady Margaret Audley to marry the king's servant George Aylesbury,[224] while Cecily, Lady Dudley; Dorothy, Lady Mountjoy; and Thomas Wriothesely, a rising figure at court, all petitioned Henry VIII and Thomas Cromwell to support Edward Sutton's suit for the hand of Anne, Lady Berkeley. Sutton, the impoverished heir of John, Lord Dudley, was a distant relative of the king.[225]

Although some widows consented to these matches, they could refuse them without danger. In the three cases just mentioned, Katherine Strickland did marry Wolsey's servant, but neither Lady Berkeley nor Lady Audley agreed to the proposed matches.[226] Lady Audley responded firmly, "For any intent or purpose of marriage, either to the said Aylesbury or any other living creature, as yet I have none. And if it shall chance me hereafter to have any such fantasy or mind, which I pray God I may not have, I do assure your good lordship, it is not he that I can find in my heart to take to my husband, of all creatures alive."[227] In a similar vein, Lady Berkeley told Cromwell, "I cannot with my heart bear fair unto Mr. Dudley . . . my stomach cannot lean there, neither as yet to any marriage." Despite her recalcitrance, she begged Cromwell to "continue my good lord" and to intervene with the king "so that I may stand in no displeasure with his grace."[228] Lady Berkeley was still single when she died almost thirty years later.[229]

The other threat to aristocratic widows' right to remain unmarried was outright violence in the form of abduction and forced weddings, a crime especially likely to affect heiresses. In 1487, Parliament passed An Act Against Taking Away of Women Against Their Will, the only early Tudor statute exclusively directed toward women.[230] Despite its general title, the preamble stated explicitly that the act's purpose was to protect women of property, especially heiresses. It declared that abducting them, formerly a misdemeanor, would now be a felony, a capital offense. There is no way of knowing whether the statute was responding to a specific abduction or an increase in kidnappings of this sort or was a product of the government's broad campaign to discourage violence.[231] But two notorious cases involving widows had occurred soon after Henry VII's accession: the kidnapping of Jane (née Statham) Sacheverell in November 1485 and of Margaret (née Beaufitz) Ruyton in September 1487.[232] What is clear is that the act made little difference. After its passage, it was cited in only four cases and proved to be useless in punishing those responsible for the most notorious abduction of the reign, the kidnapping of Margaret Bassett after the death of her first husband.[233] Significantly, when Dame Anne Salvan, widow of Sir Ralph, sued Stephen Miles for kidnapping her in the 1530s, she pursued him in Star Chamber rather than at the common law.[234]

The majority of aristocratic widows were relatively free, therefore, to consider the advantages and disadvantages of remaining single. If they chose to remarry, they would once again be *femes coverts*, reside in households headed by their husbands, and risk the possibility of their spouses' appropriating and misusing the property they held on their own and their children's behalf. The men would control the income from their land, including their jointures and dowers, and gain absolute rights over their money, jewelry, plate, and other goods. Even if they protected themselves with prenuptial contracts, they had no way to enforce them against their husbands. By the time they were widowed again, it was often too late to recover their possessions or secure adequate compensation from the men's estates.

In light of these potential dangers, aristocratic women's remarriage rate is surprisingly high and requires explanation. Thirty-nine percent of the widows of 193 peers and 24 percent of the widows of 194 parliamentary knights remarried at least once. If one takes into account the fact that many of these women were already in their second or third marriages, their lifelong remarriage rate was much higher—58 percent for peers' widows, and 85 percent for the widows of parliamentary knights.[235]

The possibility of using prenuptial contracts (whatever their defects) to protect themselves and their children certainly encouraged aristocratic widows to remarry. As wealthy women with considerable value to their prospective husbands, they had the leverage to insist on favorable agreements. As we saw in the case of Margaret, countess of Bath, in chapter 4, their legal knowledge and business acumen served them well at this juncture. Although few of these contracts survive, evidence of them appears regularly in men's wills. Of 523 husbands who predeceased their wives, 48 left them the movable property their wives had brought into their marriages or legacies they had promised their wives before their weddings. At least 32 of these women had been married before and had probably inherited the goods being returned to them from their first husbands. Some wills stated openly that the testators were honoring prenuptial agreements. Sir Richard Shirley referred explicitly to "such covenants as I made at such time as I took her to wife,"[236] and Sir Edward Wotton noted that he was "bound" to leave his wife £400 in money or the equivalent in goods.[237] The expansive bequest of Walter, Lord Mountjoy, to his wife, Anne, duchess of Buckingham—"all such goods as were her proper goods the day afore our marriage or that she hath bought since or to her given by any person"—suggests strongly that a prenuptial agreement gave her separate rights to her movable property. A surviving account indicates that she also administered and used the income from her jointure and dower estates independently.[238]

Widows also used prenuptial contracts to protect money they were accumulating to finance their children's marriages and careers and goods they were holding on their children's behalf until they came of age. Thomasine Barrington's agreement with her second husband, John Hopton, carefully specified that an annuity of 20 marks a year should be accumulated from her inheritance to be used for her children by William Sidney. It also gave her complete control of their daughter Thomasine's dowry.[239] Similarly, the marriage agreement of Margaret, countess of Bath, with the earl of Bath required him to give her three daughters by Sir Richard Long the dowries their father had bequeathed them if he survived her and she left him sufficient money and goods for that purpose.[240]

Once they protected themselves against the legal disadvantages of coverture, large numbers of aristocratic widows found the prospect of remarrying appealing. In a class with an extraordinarily high female marriage rate, wifehood was the normative role for adult women and remarrying may well have seemed to be the natural choice. More specifically, ambitious women could use the wealth and status they had gained during their first marriages to secure husbands of still higher rank the second time around. Margaret, countess of Bath, is a striking example of this phenomenon. The sole heir of John Donnington, a Middlesex gentleman, her first husband was a successful London mercer, Thomas Kitson; her second husband was Sir Richard Long, a

Lady Jane Skennard Knightley. Fawsley, Northants. By courtesy of the Conway Library, Courtauld Institute of Art. Photography by Bruce A. Bailey.

member of Henry VIII's Privy Chamber; and her third was the earl.[241] The countess's social ascent was dramatic, but she was not alone in using remarriage to rise within the aristocracy. Of forty-three widows who married peers as their second or third husbands, 81 percent were making hypergamous matches.[242] The comparable figure for 132 widows who married parliamentary knights was 62 percent.

Another potential advantage of remarriage was that aristocratic women's second and third husbands could help them defend their property rights and perform their previous spouses' wills. Since their new mates benefited from the income and movables the women brought into their marriages, the men had every reason to do so. Nonetheless, the figures on aristocratic women who were litigating in the Courts of Chancery, Star Chamber, and Requests suggest that securing male assistance was not an overwhelming inducement for them to remarry. Only a third (108) of 315 aristocratic women were married when they were plaintiffs or defendants in these courts.[243] Of 215 women who were litigating specifically about their jointures, dowers, or duties as executors, 45 percent—a higher proportion but still not a majority—went to court with second or third husbands. The majority of widows evidently had sufficient resources, legal knowledge, and self-confidence to litigate on their own, although legal difficulties may have encouraged some of them to remarry.[244]

Even when their second husbands were parties to their legal actions, securing their support was not necessarily why aristocratic widows had married them. Dame Jane Knightley, widow of and sole executor for Sir Richard, became involved in a series of bitter lawsuits against her brothers-in-law after her husband died without a male heir. The entry on her husband in Bindoff's *Commons 1509–1558* notes that she "was harrassed by financial difficulties and by her brothers-in-law" and "married as her second husband, Sir Robert Stafford, who defended her rights." The implication was that she married Stafford to secure his assistance. Yet a letter from Sir William Parr to Thomas Cromwell, who had another candidate for her in mind, emphasized her "forward fantasy" for Stafford.[245] Had Dame Jane been remarrying solely for practical reasons, she might have done better to accept Cromwell's candidate, but she followed her personal inclinations instead.

Like Jane Knightley and unlike first-time aristocratic brides, peers' and knights' widows were able to marry for love. Most of them had, after all, been exposed to the culture of the court and romance literature that idealized such marriages.[246] As we have seen, Ladies Berkeley and Audley successfully resisted matches proposed by the king and his favorites by referring to the inclinations of their hearts, evidence that this argument was persuasive when widows employed it. In the same way, men who were courting aristocratic widows knew that they had to secure their affection. In 1547, for example, the earl of Bath received a letter from Margaret Long, whom he was courting, with "great thanks," but he complained that "the latter end of your said letter is very quick." He expressed disappointment that she had refused a token from him. Nonetheless, he repeated his determination "never [to] have no woman to his wife, unless he have your Ladyship."[247] Edward Dudley visited Anne, Lady Berkeley, himself during his unsuccessful attempt to win her hand. He reported that she had received him "after the most loving sort" on his first visit. But "at my coming with the king's letters I was nothing so well welcomed, but where it was so familiar before, it was much stranger." Lady Berkeley clearly had no intention of being pressured into a second marriage and resented Dudley's attempt to use his connections at court for this purpose.[248]

Other aristocratic widows explained their second matches in emotional terms when they acted against the practical advice of their contemporaries. Two well-documented cases occurred within the royal family itself. Henry

VIII's sister Mary, widow of Louis XII of France, defended her elopement with Charles Brandon, duke of Suffolk, on the ground that the marriage was "the thing which I desired most in the world."[249] Two decades later, his sister-in-law, Mary Boleyn Carey, eloped with a younger man, William Stafford, infuriating Henry and his then queen, Anne Boleyn, who had hoped to arrange a more advantageous match for her. In a letter begging Cromwell to intervene with them on her behalf, Mary attributed her imprudence to the fact that her husband was young, that her "love overcame reason," and that she was "in bondage" to him. But she remained unrepentant and rejoiced she had been "at liberty" to choose a husband herself. She declared that she "had rather beg my bread with him than to be the greatest Queen christened. And I believe verily he is in the same case with me." She reminded Cromwell that "old books" recounted tales in which kings and queens pardoned those who had offended them "for as just causes."[250]

Although few letters are as explicit as Mary Boleyn's, other evidence demonstrates that women put great weight on their feelings when they considered whether or not to remarry. A number of widowed heiresses—Katherine Willoughby, duchess of Suffolk; Mary, Lady Hastings; Anne (née Wentworth), Lady Maltravers, for example—married one of their servants as their next husbands, although contemporaries regarded their decisions as imprudent if not positively disgraceful.[251] Frances, duchess of Suffolk, scandalized Queen Elizabeth when she chose Adrian Stokes, secretary and groom of her chambers, who was from yeoman stock and fifteen years her junior, as her second husband.[252] In the same decade, Frances, the daughter of Margaret, countess of Bath and widow of the heir to the earldom, ran off with her stepfather's land agent, William Barnaby. Barnaby was almost certainly the recipient of a letter from Frances to an unnamed person in which she referred happily to their mutual love and affirmed that "whatsoever promises before this time hath been between us of my part undoubtedly shall be performed."[253]

In light of almost universal disapproval, the number of aristocratic widows who selected husbands of lower rank and smaller fortunes than their own supports the argument that they were relatively free to choose their next mates. A third of the widows of seventy-six peers who remarried between 1450 and 1550 picked men who were neither noblemen nor knights, while 45 percent of the widows of forty-seven parliamentary knights chose gentlemen or esquires. Evidently, once they had achieved the highest rank to which they aspired, they felt free to follow their inclinations when they remarried. Furthermore, although these marriages were usually love matches, they also had practical advantages since the women's higher rank and greater wealth almost certainly strengthened their power vis-à-vis their new husbands. The widows who married downward were always wealthy enough to sacrifice financial considerations to secure husbands they loved in less intensely patriarchal relationships.

Whatever their motives, aristocratic widows who remarried were very different from wives in first marriages. In some ways, they retained the power and privileges of widows. As executors of their husbands' wills and guardians of their children, they continued to manage huge amounts of movable and real property. If they signed prenuptial contracts before their weddings, they retained the right to use the income from their jointures and dispose freely of their movable goods. Even carrying out the central duties of wives and mothers was more complicated for women in second and third marriages, as we saw in chapters 4 and 6. Because of the prevalence of remarriage, wifehood and widowhood were life-cycle stages that most aristocratic women entered and exited more than once and experienced differently on each occasion.

Whether they remarried or not, aristocratic women who were executing their husbands' wills played a crucial role in transmitting property to the next generation of their husbands' patrilineages and arranging the marriages and careers of their children. But carrying out their husbands' instructions was not the only way in which they shaped the futures of their natal and marital families. Aristocratic women themselves had a great deal of property to bequeath if they died as widows or owned goods protected by prenuptial contracts. Although their jointure and dower lands reverted to their husbands' heirs and they often had only life rights in some of the movable property left to them, most of them also held real estate and goods "for their own proper use" that they could distribute in their wills. In addition, many widows accumulated land, money, plate, and jewelry by investing rather than consuming the incomes from their jointures. Most important, given the signifiance of land in securing aristocratic fortunes, were the women who purchased land to increase their heirs' patrimonies or endow their younger sons.

Like their husbands, therefore, the widows of knights and peers influenced their families' futures and forcefully expressed their feelings about their relatives in their wills. Here, more freely than at any other point in their lives, they could record their vision of the family and indicate whether and in what ways it differed from the vision of their male kin. The discussion of their bequests that follows is based on the wills of eighty widows and their spouses, a sample that makes it possible to compare the choices of husbands and wives.[254] In the most general sense, aristocratic widows' definition of their primary family was remarkably like their husbands'. All the women with surviving children and/or grandchildren designated them as their major beneficiaries. Without exception these were the kin for whom they felt most responsible financially and to whom they were most attached emotionally. Often, in fact, they seemed to be thinking in terms of a family strategy in which their bequests complemented their husbands', and their joint goal was to secure the futures of all their children. In this sense, their bequest patterns were another aspect of their careers as wives, which were built around their acceptance of their husbands' goals for their families. Within this general context, however, some differences between the women's and men's bequests do appear in their wills. These differences reflect the women's somewhat different relationship to their husbands' patrilineages, particularly if they were married more than once; their stronger ties to their female kin; and their somewhat weaker commitment to concentrating their families' wealth on their eldest sons.

Many aristocratic widows favored their younger sons and stepsons over their husbands' heirs when they distributed their property. In 1489, for example, Dame Margaret Darcy left all the household goods she had purchased from her husband's estate to Thomas, one of her younger sons. She remembered each of her other children, including the family heir, with a single piece of jewelry.[255] Anne, Lady Roos, established an annuity for her younger son, John. Like Dame Darcy, she limited her legacies to her heir to a single piece of jewelry.[256] Cecily, marchioness of Dorset, a wealthy heiress, gave each of her three younger sons life rights in portions of her inheritance, the most she could do for them under the terms of a legal agreement she had signed with her heir twenty years earlier.[257] Still other mothers purchased land with rights of inheritance for their younger sons, the most desirable way of securing their futures. Dame Alice Cotton bequeathed such land to Edward Griffin, her younger son by her first husband, and to Robert Cotton, one of her younger stepsons.[258] There is no way of knowing whether these bequests reflected a family strategy or the women's own desire to mute the primogenitural emphasis of the common law.

In some cases of this kind, however, the wording of their wills does indicate that the women's bequests to their younger sons were the result of joint estate planning with their husbands. Dame Alice Clere left Thomas, the younger of her two sons, the manor of Fretenham, which she described as hers, to satisfy his father's legacy to him. She also gave him £700 to purchase additional land or a ward to marry, further redistributing wealth from the heir to his younger brother.[259] That same year Dame Elizabeth Englefield bequeathed real estate she had purchased to her only younger son, John, in accordance with her late husband's wishes. She also bequeathed most of her plate and goods to him.[260] Dame Eleanor Kempe, the mother of fourteen, purchased land for John, evidently her favorite among her five younger sons. She also distributed most of her household goods to her younger sons, although she bequeathed clothing and plate to her married daughters and a diamond ring and pair of gilt salts to her heir.[261] Twenty years earlier, her husband had concentrated on providing dowries for their daughters.[262] On the other hand, Dame Elizabeth Unton, widow of Sir Thomas, specifically ignored her husband's wishes. Unton had left her the manor of Wadley with all the stock and sheep on it and directed that she should leave the farm and animals to his heir when she died. Nonetheless, Dame Unton, who had no children of her own, gave three times as many sheep to Thomas, her younger stepson, as to his elder brother.[263] Her will provides no insight into her motives, but the rarity of such evidence suggests that most widows thought in terms of family priorities articulated by their deceased husbands.

Aristocratic women's own preferences were more evident when they increased their daughters' dowries, effectively transferring substantial amounts of cash or its equivalent in plate and jewels from their eldest sons to their daughters. Given the enormous amount of money that husbands had already devoted to their daughters' marriage portions, it is likely that these gifts reflected the women's own decisions. In 1490, for example, Sir Thomas Delamere directed his executors to divide 200 marks between his daughter Jane and his younger son George. Four years later, his widow's will added 100 marks to Jane's dowry.[264] Mabel Parr and Constance Culpepper both doubled the marriage portions their husbands had left their daughters. Dame Parr added a large amount of jewelry and a luxury bed to this generous legacy.[265] Their contemporary Dame Joan Denny left an additional 500 marks to each of her five daughters, raising their portions from the ample 600 marks their father had left them to a level adequate for the daughters of barons. Her only gift to her eldest son was his father's gold chain. She also delayed transfer of the rest of "her" land to him for a decade to permit performance of her will.[266] Finally, Margaret, countess of Bath, bequeathed an overwhelming portion of her movable goods to her unmarried daughters, although she remembered all her surviving children in her will. She left her two daughters by the earl 900 marks apiece and 600 marks each to her three daughters by Sir Richard Long. She stated explicitly that these bequests were over and above the dowries the girls' fathers had left them.[267]

Aristocratic widows' inclination to favor their daughters over their eldest sons was also evident after the girls' marriages, when they bequeathed to their daughters large portions of their luxury goods—plate, jewelry, and expensive beds and clothing. Like their additions to their unmarried daughters' dowries, these legacies enriched their married daughters at the expense of their eldest sons. When Sir Henry Heydon died in 1503, for example, he divided most of his movable goods between his widow and heir. Seven years later, she carefully distributed most of her jewelry and plate and many of her household goods to her surviving married daughters, their husbands, and their children. She left a relatively small legacy, some household goods and "my worser" silver basin and ewer, to a younger son, and the household goods at "my place in Kent," but no plate or jewels, to the Heydon heir.[268] Mabel Parr left her daughter Katherine, then married to Edward Borough, the heir of Thomas, Lord Borough, an enormous amount of jewelry and a purple satin bed "panyd with cloth of gold" over and above her marriage portion, a gift that substantially reduced the movables that would descend to her only son. The jewels included two items that would usually have gone to the eldest son as heirlooms: a tablet with pictures of the king and queen and beads "dressed with gold which the said Queen's grace gave me."[269]

In the context of a general pattern in which both aristocratic women and men gave the bulk of their estates to their children and grandchildren, the most distinctive female bequest pattern appeared in the wills of widows who left property they inherited from their second or third husbands to children from their first marriages. Of twenty-six remarried women who had children by their first husbands, eleven distributed much of their movable property in this way. Because many widows married upward, aristocratic mothers were often able to add substantially to the inheritances of their children by their first husbands after they were widowed for a second or third time. Their decision to redistribute property from one of their marital families to another provides further evidence that women remained members of all their families rather than leaving one behind as they joined another. What is even more striking is aristocratic men's willingess to permit their widows to alienate significant amounts of their movable property, particularly plate, money, and luxury items, away from their own patrilineages. They could, after all, have restricted their wives to life rights in these goods to preserve them for their own children, but chose not to do so. They apparently accepted their wives' continued commitment to the offspring of their previous marriages and were willing to support it with their own property. In a society and culture that put so much emphasis on the patrilineal family and on preserving wealth from one generation to another, their behavior is hard to explain except as an expression of their confidence and affection for their wives or the result of prenuptial agreements that are invisible in their wills.

Women's decision to use their legacies from their second husbands on behalf of the offspring of their first marriages does not seem to have been affected significantly by whether or not they had children with their second spouses: of the eleven widows being considered here, six did and five did not. When Dame Katherine Reed, who had no children by her second husband, Sir Edmund, died in 1498, she left her plate and household stuff to her sons by her first husband and her two precious girdles to their wives. Among the goods were plate and four luxury beds that she had inherited from her second husband.[270] Similarly, Dame Elizabeth Speke, who received £100 and 20 marks of plate from her second husband over and above the plate she had brought into their marriage, gave most of her jewelry and plate to her two sons by her first husband, William and Walter Colshill, and William's wife. Her only reference to her second husband's heir, her stepson George, was a warning that he was claiming some of her goods as his own.[271] Although Dame Reed and Dame Speke married upward after their first husbands died, women who married laterally, socially and economically, also often favored the offspring of their first marriages. Jane Ormond, daughter and coheir of Sir John, married three knights in succession, Sir Thomas Dynham, Sir Edward Grevill, and Sir William Fitzwilliam of Milton. She had ten children by Dynham but none by her other husbands. Dynham left her 1,000 marks and all his movables in the expectation that she would use them on their children's behalf. Both Grevill and Fitzwilliam had numerous children by their previous wives. Although Grevill did not leave his widow any of his goods, Fitzwilliam, her third husband, gave her some plate, 500 marks in cash, and half the residue of his movable property. When she died, Dame Fitzwilliam divided the bulk of her goods, plate, clothes, jewelry, household stuff, and horses among her sons and daughters by Dynham, completely ignoring the Grevills and Fitzwilliams.[272]

Women who had children by their second or third husbands often bequeathed property they inherited from them to the offspring of their first marriages. Dame Katherine Hawte, the thrice-married daughter of a London merchant, had three daughters by her first husband, Walter Writtel, and four or five sons and a daughter by her second, John Green. Her third spouse, Sir Richard Hawte, who had a son by a previous marriage, bequeathed all his goods and land to his second wife when he died in 1492. In her will, written the next year, Dame Hawte concentrated on providing for her children by Green, who were still underage, directing her executors to sell land and houses that she and Hawte had purchased together to support and educate them and leaving them each substantial cash bequests. By this time Dame Hawte's daughters by Walter Writtel, her first husband, were all married, and she left them only small bequests from her movable goods. But she did carefully direct her executors to use the Writtel lands she held for them as their father had provided two decades ago.[273]

Dame Constance Culpepper, widow of Sir Alexander, divided her movable property among the children of her two marriages. As Culpepper's sole executor and recipient of the residue of his goods, she controlled a great deal of his estate. She divided her luxury goods between George Harper, the only offspring of her first marriage, and Thomas, her elder son by Culpepper. She also gave Thomas, who was his father's heir, the household goods and farm equipment and animals belonging to his inheritance. Her legacy to John, her second Culpepper son, was much more modest. Like many widows, she was extremely generous to her two unmarried daughters, Margaret and Katherine Culpepper, doubling their cash dowries and giving them considerable wealth in the form of jewelry and plate. Most interesting, she divided a gold chain that she had received from her brother, Sir Edward Chamberlain, between the girls rather than turning it into an heirloom for either of her inheriting sons. Her bequests to her two married daughters were much smaller than her legacies to their sisters, which was consistent with the fact that they had already received their dowries, but even here she left them more money than she gave their younger brother John. In addition, she left gifts to dozens of other relatives, including her stepdaughter Alice, her sons-in-law, her grandchildren, nieces and nephews from her birth and marital families, and various Culpep-per cousins, illustrating the way widows with grown children used their wills to mark their larger, bilaterally defined kin networks.[274]

All the aristocratic women whose wills we have discussed here had off-spring by at least one of their husbands. Like the men of their class, they left the bulk of their property to their children. Within that context, the choices they made among their heirs, younger sons, and daughters affected the future shape of their families. Very different choices faced the minority of aristo-cratic widows who had no children or had outlived both them and their grandchildren. These women had to look exclusively to collateral relatives when they distributed their land and goods. In these cases, they tended to concentrate their bequests on a relatively narrow group of their natal kin—their siblings and siblings' children—but what is especially notable is their par-ticular attention to women in these categories. Here, more clearly than any-where else, we find dense, enduring female networks that provided a resource and alternative family for childless aristocratic wives and widows. The phe-nomenon of movable goods, especially jewelry, plate, and clothes, passing from one woman to another over a number of generations is particularly strong when the childless women had no brothers.

Dame Agnes (née Danvers) Say, who had four husbands and five daughters but no sons, headed a women-centered kin network of this kind.[275] When she died, all her beneficiaries were women except for her brothers Henry, William, and Robert and the executors and overseer of her will. In addition to her daughters, all of whom were married, she was particularly concerned about an unmarried granddaughter, Constance Brown, to whom she left £100, goods worth 100 marks, and, most important, land and tenements in the suburbs of London. She was closest to Elizabeth Waldegrave and Margaret Leynham, her daughters by her second husband, Sir John Fray, and relied on them to complete a chantry she was endowing and to distribute the residue of her estate for the good of her soul. She also chose Margaret and a clergyman, probably her confessor, as her confidants to help her clear her conscience in connection with "a matter about the sum of £10." She divided her plate among her daughters and the residue of her goods among her daughters, her brother Robert, and her granddaughter Constance. She also left some land with rights of inheritance to her daughter Elizabeth Waldegrave, whom she included among her executors.[276]

In the next generation, one of Dame Say's favorite daughters, Margaret Leynham, wife of Sir John, died childless. Her husband, who had predeceased her, left her almost all his goods, chattels, debts, and land. When she wrote her will three years later, she left all her property except her religious bequests to her sisters, their children, and her maternal kin, the Danvers. Most impor-tant was the disposition of her land. She left manors with rights of inheri-tance to her sisters Elizabeth and Katherine and life rights in a manor to one of her nephews, John Brown, and his wife, Agnes. The beneficiaries of her plate, jewelry, and other luxury goods included her sisters Elizabeth and Katherine, her half-sister Alice, Alice's two sons, Elizabeth's son and three daughters, and the sons of her deceased sister Agnes. When her sister Katherine died, she transferred her legacy to Katherine's daughters. She also bequeathed £10 of goods to one of her Danver uncles and gilt cups to two others.[277]

An even more extensive female network centered on the eight daughters of Sir Richard Scrope of Bentley, a younger son of Henry, Lord Scrope of Bolton and Masham.[278] When Sir Richard wrote his will, he directed that if he had no son and his wife remarried (both of which happened), the manor of Bentley, his main property, should be sold for his daughters' benefit. Presumably he intended the profits to be used for the dowries of those who were still single since he made no other provision for them. His only other legacy to the girls was a piece of plate for Anne, who became a nun.[279] Of the seven sisters who married, one, Elizabeth, Viscountess Beaumont and then Countess of Oxford, died childless and another, Margaret, duchess of Suffolk, had an only daughter, Elizabeth, who became a nun at the Minories.[280]

Sir Richard's widow, Eleanor, married Sir John Wyndham as her second husband. Like many aristocratic women in her situation, she arranged a marriage between a daughter by her first husband, Eleanor, and her second husband's heir, Thomas. Her second husband assisted her first family by purchasing Bentley and two other Scrope manors and bequeathing the sale price, £1,000, to three of her Scrope daughters, Katherine, Mary, and Jane, for their marriages.[281] When Dame Wyndham died twenty years after her first husband, her Scrope daughters were among her main beneficiaries. She left much smaller legacies to her children by Wyndham.[282]

The surviving wills of three of the Scrope sisters—Margaret, duchess of Suffolk; Elizabeth, countess of Oxford; and Lady Mary Jerningham Kingston—document their continuing ties to one another and to their respective children over the next four decades.[283] The duchess, the first to die, lived with her childless niece, Lady Elizabeth Pechey, and her husband, Sir John, at Lullingstone, Kent, and made her largest bequests to them.[284] But she also remembered five of her sisters, giving the countess of Oxford her image of St. Michael with pearls and precious stones; Jane Brews, a standing cup of silver, all gilt; Frances St. Clere, all her pearls; Mary Jerningham, some table linen; and Anne, a nun at Barking, a silver pot.[285]

Two decades later, when another sister, Elizabeth, countess of Oxford, wrote her will, the connections among them were still strong. Indeed, the countess, whose main residences were at Castle Hedingham and Wivenhoe in Essex, visited at Felbrigg and Norwich in Norfolk regularly to see her sisters and other members of the Scrope family.[286] The countess bequeathed to her sister, Lady Mary Kingston, a silver basin and ewer, chaced with gilt, "of the newest making"; a gold goblet engraved with two of her husbands' badges; and a gold book set with pearl. She was even more generous to another sister, Jane Brews, whom she gave a silver basin and ewer chaced with gilt "of the oldest sort . . . having my Lord of Oxford's arms in the bottom"; a great goblet with a silver cover, partially gilt, "which she lately gave me"; a gold cross that had belonged to their father; a bed and counterpoint of black velvet and scarlet cloth embroidered with gold letters; and some bed clothing and accessories. She divided her samplers equally between Mary and Jane. She was somewhat less generous to a third sister, Lady Frances Clere, who received a silver and gilt cup, £4 in cash, a bed of black velvet and satin, a counterpoint, and some bed clothing and accessories. The countess also bequeathed plate or jewelry to two of her brothers-in-law—Mary's second husband, Sir William Kingston, and Sir John St. Clere—and eleven nieces and nephews, her sisters' children. She was particularly generous to Elizabeth St. Clere, who bore her name and was probably her goddaughter. In addition to leaving her some plate, she contributed £100 to her dowry.[287]

Dame Mary Kingston, the third Scrope sister whose will has survived, had both children and grandchildren, unlike the countess of Oxford. When she died in 1549, her major beneficiaries were her son by her first marriage, Henry Jerningham, and his daughter Mary. Nonethess, her legacies also perpetuated her ties to her natal family. She gave one of her surviving sisters, Jane Brews, a gold hoop and a book covered with purple velvet, and Lady Frances St. Clere, the other, a black velvet gown, a tawney satin kirtle, and a pair of beads. She also bequeathed a black velvet kirtle to Frances's daughter Elizabeth and a gold brooch to Jane's son John.[288]

As testators, executors of their husbands' wills, guardians of their children, and managers of huge amounts of real and movable property, aristocratic widows made crucial contributions to the stability and prosperity of their families. Freed from the disabilities of coverture, they performed roles they had first assumed during their marriages and continued to promote the prosperity of their immediate families, as they had during their husbands' lifetimes. To succeed in their expanded roles, they drew on the business skills, legal knowledge, and familiarity with their families' estates and finances that they had acquired during their marriages. Their new situation transformed them from experienced wives into competent widows. Yet they could not have succeeded in either of these roles without the assistance and emotional support of a broad group of friends and kin. It is to this wider world outside their households that we will turn in the next chapter.

CHAPTER 8. BEYOND

THE HOUSEHOLD—

FAMILY AND FRIENDS,

PATRONAGE AND POWER

*A*RISTOCRATIC women spent most of their lives in castles or manors that belonged to their marital families, promoting the interests of their husbands, children, and grandchildren. The minority of wives without children concentrated on their siblings, particularly their sisters, and their siblings' children. On the surface, their lives appeared to be spatially confined and narrow in scope, but in reality their interests and connections extended far beyond the walls of their homes and their immediate lineal descendants. In fact, aristocratic wives depended on their natal kin and their networks for the material resources and political influence necessary to perform their duties as wives, mothers, and widows. Their families of birth also provided them with a safety net if their marriages failed. They in turn served as advocates for their natal and marital families when they sought assistance from each other, thus contributing to the power and prosperity of both. As women evolved from young brides into mature wives, most of them also developed friendships and patronage relations with their husbands' nonresident, collateral kin and members of the local aristocracy. These connections further extended their networks and reinforced their spouses' political connections to local families. Collectively these horizontal ties constituted a form of nonmaterial capital that enabled them to carry out their primary responsibilities and enhanced their power in their families and neighborhoods.

Aristocratic women's natal kin were the most important members of their extended networks. As heads of their natal families, their fathers remained involved in their affairs long after their weddings, helping them to perform their functions as wives and mothers and defending their financial interests. The correspondence between Eleanor, countess of Rutland, and her father, Sir William Paston, displays the mixture of affection and practical assistance that characterized successful relationships between aristocratic wives and their fathers. In 1529, the countess asked her father to assist her husband in two different matters, illustrating the ways in which men benefited from their wives' ongoing relationships with their natal families. The countess was particularly anxious that he use his position as one of Sir Thomas Lovell's executors to the greatest possible advantage of her husband, who was Lovell's nephew and one of his beneficiaries. She also wanted Paston to "make much" of her cousin George Paulet "for my lord favoreth him much and I am much beholden to him, as I shall show you at my next meeting with you."[1] Subsequently she reported at length about her negotiations for a marriage for one of her daughters. She was not optimistic that they would succeed and remarked that "howsoever it goeth, I trust by your good help, and with the help of my lord, to provide her of another as good as he." Her comment revealed both her father's ongoing involvement in her affairs and her assumption that he would continue to assist her.[2] In return, the countess, who held a position in the queen's household, told her father the latest information from court, an important function in a period when letters were the major source of news.[3] Paston's continuing role in his daughter's life was evident years later, when her husband was dying. In addition to comforting her, he reminded her not to "fully cast away yourself" because it would "not only displease God but also hinder my lord and your children and many other." He promised that he and her mother would come to her "as fast as we may."[4] A few months later, Lady Rutland, who was her husband's chief executor, sought her father's help to probate and perform his will.[5]

Given the eclectic character of surviving documents, it is usually difficult to observe the development of aristocratic wives' relationships with their fathers over time. The evidence about Sir Walter Stonor and his only daughter, Elizabeth, is exceptional in this respect and records their interaction for more than two decades. When Elizabeth's first husband, Sir William Compton, died in 1528, he had not established the jointure he had promised her in their marriage contract. Elizabeth and her second husband, Sir Walter Walshe, sued his estate in Chancery, but the matter was not settled when Walshe also died, in 1538.[6] During her second widowhood, Elizabeth returned home, and her father replaced Walshe as her advocate at court. He discussed her affairs with Cromwell, promising that she would grant Cromwell an annual fee in return for his favor. When Stonor sent him the fee for the first year, he reminded Cromwell to be her "good lord" and protect her from "great wrongs."[7] After Elizabeth's third marriage, to Sir Philip Hoby, she and her husband rented their chief residence, the manor of Wreysbury, Buckinghamshire, from her father.[8]

Despite her father's support for her during the previous two decades, Lady Hoby was reluctant to spend the Christmas holidays with him at Stonor in 1549 because of his "unkindness" to her. One issue between them was religious. Sir Walter told his daughter's servant, Richard Scudamore, "that he knew very well how to order himself and that my lady was much given to the Scriptures and that she always was arguing and contending with him in the same, and which thing he could in no wise bear and specially at her hands." The other difficulty involved Stonor's "sweetheart Mistress Margaret," whom Lady Hoby feared he would marry. Stonor assured Scudamore that he was "bound in conscience by his promise" and "never intendith to marry." Indeed, he was going to compel "his man" Rous, who had slandered Margaret, to marry her himself "to make amends thereof and to satisfy the world." Scudamore apparently defended his mistress successfully since her father finally declared, "If it pleased my lady to come unto him to make merry and not to meddle with him or any of his household she should be as welcome as ever she was." His declaration evidently satisfied her, and she agreed to "keep her Christmas" at Stonor after all.[9]

The interaction between the countess of Rutland and Lady Hoby and their fathers occurred in relatively ordinary circumstances. In contrast, material about the Talbot earls of Shrewsbury exhibits men's responses when their married daughters found themselves in emergency situations. The first crisis involved Mary, daughter of George, the fourth earl, and wife of Henry Percy, sixth earl of Northumberland. By 1528, only four years after their marriage, the couple's relationship had broken down irretrievably.[10] Northumberland complained about his wife's "malicious acts" and "imaginations of untruth," while her father worried that he was abusing and might even poison her. Northumberland was outraged at Shrewsbury's suspicions and refused to permit his father-in-law's servants to see or speak to his wife. When the countess's brother-in-law, William, Lord Dacre, asked the duke of Norfolk to defend her, Northumberland told Norfolk that he, Northumberland, "would never come in[to] her company [again] as long as he lived."[11] The couple may have separated shortly thereafter, at least temporarily, since Mary delivered a stillborn child at her father's home in April 1529.[12] In 1536, Shrewsbury noted that his daughter had been living with him for two and a half years.[13] At about the same time, Northumberland announced that he was bequeathing his entire inheritance to the king since he had no children and he and his wife were "not likely to come together." He did not want his brothers, whom he accused of behaving "unnaturally" to him, to inherit his property.[14]

Once her marriage disintegrated, Shrewsbury offered his daughter a home and tried to persuade her husband to provide her with an adequate income.[15] He claimed that Northumberland had agreed to give her 200 marks a year, but when Shrewsbury reproved him for failing to keep his promise, Northumberland retorted sharply that his father-in-law had no grounds for complaint since he had never paid his daughter's dowry.[16] The issue was not settled when Northumberland died in 1537. Shortly before he himself died the next year, Shrewsbury carefully framed his will to ensure that his heir, Francis, would support his sister and continue the struggle to secure an adequate income for her from her late husband's estates.[17] Since Northumberland had given his estates to the crown, Francis had to petition Henry VIII for her income. By 1542, the countess, who was living as a dependent in her brother's household, was desperate and went to court to plead her case in person. The scene at Greenwich must have been a dramatic one, beginning with Lady Northumberland's humble plea—"I beseech your majesty be good and gracious lord unto me"—and explanation of her plight. In response, Henry pointedly reminded her that her father had not paid her dowry and "marveled" that "being so great a wise man" he had not settled the matter "in his time." Nonetheless, he referred Mary's petition to the Privy Council, which granted her an annuity of 100 marks, half the jointure she expected, in March 1543.[18]

The fourth earl of Shrewsbury also assisted his other married daughter, Elizabeth, Lady Dacre, after her husband was indicted for treason in May 1534. When Lady Dacre decided to go to court to petition Henry VIII on his behalf, "according to her duty," Shrewsbury asked Cromwell to advise her since "she hath not been accustomed or brought up in any affairs or uncomfortable business, but after the homely fashion of the country."[19] She apparently pursued her suit so vigorously that the king ordered her to stop her appeals until after her husband's trial.[20]

Decades later, Shrewsbury's heir, Francis, the fifth earl, faced a similar problem when his daughter Anne's husband, John, Lord Bray, was arrested for plotting against Queen Mary. In June 1556 she went to court to plead for his life and his release from imprisonment. Her father gave her letters to assist her in gaining access to the queen and paid her expenses while she was in London. Robert Swift, one of his most trusted servants, accompanied her and sent the earl detailed reports about her progress. By July, Lady Bray had secured permission to see her husband and actually spent twelve days with him in the Tower of London, but she had not yet spoken with the king or queen and was determined to continue her suit. There is no way of knowing how much her efforts contributed to the queen's decision not to execute her husband.[21]

Wills support the positive picture of aristocratic fathers' relationships with their married daughters that emerges from evidence about the countess of Rutland, Lady Hoby, and the Talbot family. One hundred and thirty of 763 testators left their daughters bequests over and above their dowries, usually a few pieces of plate or jewelry or relatively small sums of money. Although most men clearly felt that they had fulfilled their financial obligations to their daughters when they paid their marriage portions, they used their wills to express their affection for them and mark the women's continued membership in their natal families. Sir Richard Harcourt bequeathed a silver and gilt cup with a cover to his daughter Alice Besilly; Sir Robert Wotton gave his daughter Margaret, marchioness of Dorset, a gold ring with a turquoise; and Sir

William Sidney left £20 apiece to his two married daughters.[22] Most revealing were fathers who gave their married daughters sentimentally significant items that embodied and perpetuated their daughters' emotional ties to their parents. Sometimes these bequests consisted of precious objects that had belonged to their mothers. In 1496, Sir Thomas Burgh gave his daughter Elizabeth, wife of Richard, Lord Fitzhugh, a gold enameled book that her mother "was wont to wear."[23] Sir Brian Stapleton left his daughter Jane a gold ring "which was the last token betwixt my wife [her mother] and me."[24] In other cases, their gifts recorded their own relationships with their married daughters. In 1505, Sir Robert Lytton bequeathed pieces of his gold chain "for a remembrance" to his two daughters.[25] Thomas, earl of Arundel, left his daughter, the countess of Lincoln, his "great ring with a turquoise,"[26] and Sir Edward Montague gave each of his four married daughters 66s. 8d. to make a ring or tablet "to wear for my sake."[27] Occasionally, men connected to the court left their daughters precious objects they had received from the king or queen. Since these gifts carried enormous social and political prestige, they transmitted the testators' high status to their daughters. Sir David Owen bequeathed a jewel rose he wore at Katherine of Aragon's coronation to his daughter Elizabeth, and the fourth earl of Shrewsbury chose standing cups he had received as New Year's gifts from Henry VIII for his two daughters.[28]

Not all relationships between fathers and their married daughters were as affectionate and supportive as those discussed here. As we saw in chapter 3, men did not always pay their daughters' dowries promptly or protect their jointures adequately. Nor were they all as helpful as the earls of Shrewsbury when their daughters petitioned the crown for their jointures or their husbands' lives. Thomas Howard, third duke of Norfolk, openly quarreled with his daughter Mary, duchess of Richmond, widow of Henry VIII's illegitimate son, because she did not think he was persistent enough in petitioning the king for her jointure. Norfolk was understandably reluctant to risk antagonizing Henry in the year his niece, Anne Boleyn, was executed for adultery. He was shocked, however, to discover that the duchess had consulted lawyers on her own "and be put in such comfort by learned men that her right is clearly good, and that she hath be delayed so long (as she thinketh) for lack of good suit made to the king's highness by me." He remarked disapprovingly to Cromwell, "My lord in all my life I never commoned with her in any serious cause or now, and would not have thought she had be such as I find her, which as I think is but too wise for a woman."[29] Although the duchess signed one of her letters to her father "your humble daughter," she was anything but that and told him bluntly that it was his fault her suit had not yet succeeded.[30]

Furious at Norfolk's continued delay, the duchess took matters into her own hands and determined to go to court to petition Henry VIII herself. In January 1538, she told Cromwell openly that she had little confidence in her father's efforts on her behalf and asked for permission to appeal to the king in person.[31] By April, her father was so worn out with her "weeping and wailing" that he told Cromwell he would "follow her mind" and bring her to London, if Cromwell assured him the king would not be offended.[32] The duchess's visit to the court, which lasted from at least May 13 until July 15, proved to be a success.[33] The following March the king granted her a large amount of monastic property and the reversion of a number of manors.[34]

When aristocratic fathers died, they expected their heirs to assume their responsibilites for their married daughters. On his deathbed, for example, Sir Richard Wentworth exhorted his son, Thomas, Lord Wentworth, "not only to be a brother [to your sisters] as you are in very deed but also to be to them and every one of them as a father." As administrator of his father's will, Wentworth was responsible for finding husbands for his five sisters and paying their dowries. One of them died unmarried and the youngest, Thomasine, forfeited her dowry when she eloped and married without her brother's consent, but Wentworth did pay portions for the other three.[35] Many brothers found paying their sisters' dowries a heavy burden. Thirty-five years after his father's death, Thomas Darcy still had not repaid money he had borrowed for his sisters' marriages,[36] while Sir Richard Cornwall paid only part of his sister Maude's marriage portion before he died.[37]

Arranging and financing their sisters' marriages was not the only "paternal" responsibility brothers assumed for them. After his sister Anne's marriage, for example, Henry, third marquess of Dorset, tried to convince Sir John Willoughby to increase her jointure. Anne was married to Sir John's nephew and heir, son of his brother, Sir Edward. Dorset considered the jointure already settled on her, 100 marks, "small recompence" for her dowry of £1,000, all of which had been paid. He was worried because Sir John was "a man of many years" and Sir Edward was about to depart for the king's wars. "Yf it should chance you both to dye, as God forbid, the gentilwoman should be right meanly furnished" and would have little remedy since her husband was a minor and would become the king's ward. One of Dorset's lawyers delivered the letter with a proposal to remedy the situation without reducing Sir John's income or costing him any legal fees.[38]

In still another situation, George, Lord Cobham, responded forcefully when Sir Thomas Wyatt the elder, who had charged his sister Elizabeth with adultery years before, suddenly stopped supporting her and sent her to live with her brother. Cobham asked a number of his influential friends at court—Sir John Russell, Sir William Hawte, and Thomas, Lord Cromwell—to intervene with Wyatt to "give her something reasonable towards her living, she now being destitute of help," but all to no avail.[39] Nonetheless, Cobham and his friends bided their time and seized their opportunity four years later when Wyatt was arrested and imprisoned in the Tower. One of the conditions of his release was that he give up his long-term mistress and return to his wife.[40]

Not all brothers were as dependable and prompt in responding to their sisters' difficulties as Wentworth, Dorset, and Cobham. Lady Elizabeth Manners's jointure was not assured until at least twenty-eight years after her marriage to Thomas, heir of William, Lord Sandys. For almost three decades, therefore, she was dependent on her common-law dower if she were widowed, a dangerous alternative in a period when most aristocratic estates were enfeoffed and exempt from claims of dower. The problem developed because Lady Sandys's father, George, Lord Roos, had died before her jointure was settled.[41] The responsibility for protecting her therefore fell to her brother, Thomas, Lord Roos (created earl of Rutland in 1525). Apparently Rutland could not prevail on her father-in-law to fulfill his obligations and was reluctant to sue him. In 1541, however, one year after Lord Sandys died, Rutland and Sir Anthony Browne brought an action in Chancery against Elizabeth's husband, now the second Lord Sandys, and secured a recognizance of £10,000 against him. As a result, he signed an indenture to settle his wife's jointure as he and his father had promised in their marriage contract. Given mortality rates and life expectancies, Lady Sandys was lucky she had not been widowed earlier.[42]

Another brother, Sir Henry Clifford (created earl of Cumberland in 1525), responded inadequately when his sister, Lady Anne Clifton, could not collect the income from her jointure after she was widowed. Well aware of her brother's friendship with Henry VIII and his connections at court, Lady Clifton asked him to petition Cardinal Wolsey, then at the height of his power, on her behalf. She expressed "great marvel" at his "unkindness, that ye would not be here your self at this time, nor none for you," and commented bitterly that his neglect had convinced her husband's kin that her friends "set little price by me."[43] Lady Clifton's remarks make clear that members of the aristocracy expected women's brothers to assist their sisters when they were in trouble and that the women's position in their marital famlies was jeopardized if the men's support was not forthcoming.

Brothers who assumed their fathers' responsibilities for their married sisters accentuated the hierarchical dimension of their relationship. But aristocratic wives were far more than lifelong dependents on their brothers. After they grew into their roles as mature wives, they were able to reciprocate their brothers' patronage and favors and develop genuine friendships with them. Henry, sixth earl of Northumberland, and his sister Margaret, wife of Henry, first earl of Cumberland, enjoyed a relationship that mingled just this kind of warmth and practical assistance. However difficult his relations with his wife and brothers, the earl was genuinely fond of his sister, whom he visited often and entertained in turn.[44] This friendship enabled Margaret to function as a link between her husband and brother. On one occasion, for example, her brother appointed her husband's servant to an office in one of his forests, according to his "desire and my good sister's your bedfellow."[45] His comment underscored Margaret's role in securing patronage for her husband's client.

Many other wives functioned as intermediaries between their husbands and brothers and facilitated the exchange of favors anticipated at the time of their marriages. After Lady Anne Stafford Herbert's marriage to George, Lord Hastings, for example, Hastings appointed her brother, Edward, third duke of Buckingham, steward of all his Welsh properties, an office that strengthened the duke's position in the Welsh marches.[46] Buckingham made his wife's brother, the fifth earl of Northumberland, steward of his property in Holderness, Yorkshire. In return, Northumberland appointed Buckingham steward of his estates in Somerset. Since the center of Buckingham's influence was in the West Country and Wales and Northumberland's was in the North, the exchange increased both men's control over outlying parts of their respective estates.[47] Like the countess of Cumberland, wives often called on their friendships with their brothers when their husbands sought favors from them. Elizabeth, Lady Dacre, wrote to her brother, Francis, fifth earl of Shrewsbury, for her spouse when two of his servants brought a suit before him. She specifically requested that "they may have a readier dispatch therein and the rather at my contemplation."[48] Her wording indicates that she attached considerable importance to the credit she would gain with her husband if her suit succeeded. In another instance, Lord Bergavenny relied on his wife, Frances, to obtain a stay of a writ permitting seizure of his lands in Sussex from her brother, the earl of Rutland.[49] When brothers granted their sisters favors of this kind, they contributed to the success of their sisters' careers as wives.

Married women and their brothers also collaborated as equals when they had mutual interests. Sir William Sandys (later created Lord Sandys) and his sister Lady Edith Darcy cooperated to finance the marriage of one of their younger sisters.[50] Lady Elizabeth Lucy and her brother Thomas Empson joined in a series of legal actions against Richard and William Fermor about land in Northamptonshire and Bedfordshire and were codefendants in a suit brought by the Prioress of Swadesley.[51]

The correspondence between Dorothy Josselin, wife of Thomas, an Essex landowner knighted in 1546–1547, and her brother, Sir John Gates, a member of Henry VIII's Privy Chamber, provides one of the fullest extant records of friendship and mutual assistance between a married woman and her brother. Dorothy managed her brother's affairs in Essex, while he acted as her advocate at court. Gates was particularly well placed to assist her because he and a more distant relative, Sir Anthony Denny, controlled the dry stamp, which replaced the royal signature on official documents in the closing years of Henry VIII's reign.[52] Both Dorothy and her brother benefited from their relationship.

Throughout the correspondence, Mistress Josselin appeared to be more assertive and shrewder about business than her spouse. She almost always wrote in the first-person singular and spoke of their joint concerns as hers.

When the earl of Oxford ejected her husband from his office as keeper of Stansted Park in 1542, she sent Gates a detailed narrative of what had occurred and discussed the maneuvers necessary to secure his reinstatement.[53] In one letter, Dorothy openly criticized her husband for attempting to settle the issue informally because she thought he would get a more favorable resolution from the crown. Ultimately, the influence of Dorothy's natal family prevailed, and the king commanded Oxford to reinstate Josselin or send two representatives to the Privy Council to explain why he had not done so.[54]

One of Mistress Josselin's chief interests was investing in real estate and wardships. On two occasions, she needed her brother's assistance to purchase land from the crown because there was always brisk competition for such property.[55] She also wrote to him at length about purchasing a wardship from a Mr. Darcy. Dorothy was annoyed because Darcy had raised the sale price after she and her husband had begun negotiating with him. She also worried about their losses if the ward died before they collected any income from his inheritance. Once they had agreed on the purchase price and Darcy had promised to return their money if the ward died before his fourteenth birthday, Dorothy delayed closing the deal until her brother checked the value of the child's property and made certain it was not tied up by will, jointure, or mortgage.[56] These precautions reflected her familiarity with the intricacies of land transactions and experience in protecting her interests.

In return for Gates's assistance and advice, Dorothy handled his business in Essex. After reporting on the death of a local landowner, for example, she added, "If his land can do you pleasure, being copyhold, let me have knowledge about what ye would have done therein and I shall be glad to accomplish your desire."[57] There was no question about her competence to do so. She was equally efficient about helping Gates recruit soldiers for the war with France in 1544 and providing him with the supplies he needed. She expressed regret that she would not be able to see him before he embarked, commenting, perhaps because she was pregnant, that "by that time, I am sure I shall not endure to take so long a journey."[58]

In contrast to the Josselin-Gates correspondence, which catches the interaction of a married woman and her brother in the 1540s, extant documents record the evolution of relations between Elizabeth, duchess of Norfolk, and her only brother, Henry, Lord Stafford, over three decades. In 1529, Lord Stafford fulfilled a classic fraternal role when he participated in the recovery of land for his sister's jointure.[59] Within a few years, however, when the Norfolks' disintegrating marriage caused a public scandal at court, Stafford criticized her harshly for refusing to acquiesce when her husband moved his mistress, Bess Holland, into their chief residence.[60] Stafford, who was trying to recover land his father had forfeited when he was attainted in 1521, was dismayed at the prospect of losing Norfolk's friendship and support. He condemned the "continual contentation" that caused the duke "nothing to tender the preferment of any of her friends." What made matters worse was that his sister was also defying the king. Instead of listening to the "gentle advertisement that his highness hath sent to her divers times," she had earned his "high displeasure, which is to every true heart death" and a "continual hinderance" to "her poor friends . . . whereof our Lord knows they have no need."[61] Never forgetting that their father had been convicted for treason on verbal evidence alone, Stafford was terrified by his sister's "wild language," which extended to criticizing Henry's divorce from Katherine of Aragon.[62] He flatly refused to open his home to her, as both her husband and Cromwell requested, on the ground that her presence would put him and his family in "great jeopardy."[63]

Despite Stafford's disapproval of his sister's behavior, they reconciled after she and her husband separated in 1534.[64] Although the duchess complained about her "imprisonment" in the manor Norfolk had rented for her and claimed that no gentlewoman or man could visit her "but such as my Lord appoints," a warm letter she sent her "good brother Stafford" indicated that his daughter Susan was living with her. Stafford, who had thirteen children, apparently wanted to send another of his daughters to her. The duchess agreed, expressing her preference for Dorothy, "for I am well acquainted with her conditions already."[65] Even at the low point of her life, the duchess was able to provide practical assistance to her brother. Years later, when she died, the duchess made Stafford's wife one of her main beneficiaries and named her brother her sole executor and residual heir.[66] For his part, Stafford wrote an epitaph for her tomb in the Howard Chapel in Lambeth Cathedral in which he addressed her as his "good lady and sister dear" and said that she was "to me, both far and near, a mother, a sister, a friend most dear."[67] Together the will and epitaph represent the combination of sentiment and material benefits characteristic of successful relations between brothers and their married sisters.

Aristocratic men's friendship and cooperation with their sisters encouraged many of them to develop warm relations with their sisters' husbands and to collaborate with them in pursuit of their mutual interests. As a result, some husbands—30 in a group of 763 testators—included their wives' brothers among their executors. This arrangement simultaneously marked their mutual affection and trust and maximized the likelihood that provisions for their widows would be carried out as expeditiously as possible. In 19 of these cases, the men's widows were also among their executors, creating a situation in which aristocratic men gave their marital kin a dominant voice in distributing their estates, as sure a sign as any that they thought of kinship in bilateral terms when they considered how best to protect their children and grandchildren. Wives who succeeded in facilitating and encouraging such relations between their spouses and brothers helped lessen the impact of law and custom that supported a patrilineal definition of family.

Surprisingly in this context, few aristocratic men and their married sisters—less than 8 percent of both sisters and brothers—remembered each other in their wills, and even fewer included them among their executors. As we have seen repeatedly, members of the aristocracy distributed the bulk of their real and movable property to their spouses, children, and grandchildren. The contrast between these choices and their mutual support during their lives reveals how situational and fluid their definition of family was. While they were alive, aristocratic siblings could usually rely on each other. In a context in which families tended to rise and fall together, their interaction reflected a subtle mixture of self-interest and affection. But when they faced death, their definition of the family contracted, and unless they had no children of their own, they excluded their brothers and sisters, their nearest collateral kin, from the distribution of their property.

Although married women's relations with the successive heads of their natal families, their fathers and eldest brothers, are more visible in the extant documents, they also nurtured their ties to their mothers and sisters, which were often characterized by considerable warmth. As we have seen, mothers often traveled long distances to assist at their daughters' lyings-in. But this was not the only reason they visited each other. In 1488, for example, Alice, Lady Fitzhugh, told John Paston III that she could not leave her daughter—whose husband, Francis, Lord Lovel, had disappeared the year before, after the Battle of Stoke—even though it meant foregoing an advantageous business deal.[68] Decades later, in a more ordinary situation, Dame Maud Parr journeyed from Hertfordshire to Lincolnshire to visit her daughter Katherine, recently married to Edward Burgh.[69] Sir Thomas and Lady Elizabeth Burgh cohabited in the house of her mother, Lady Anne Owen, after the birth of a daughter whose legitimacy was later contested.[70]

When they could not travel to see each other, mothers and daughters expressed their mutual affection by exchanging gifts. Sometime between 1543 and 1551, for example, Frances, Lady Burgavenny, gave her mother, Eleanor, dowager countess of Rutland, some "gear," a word used generically for clothing. The countess thanked her in "gentle letters" and reciprocated with a white linen cap called a creppyn. Frances then requested some green silk for a shirt for her husband.[71] Their contemporary, Lady Dorothy Pakington, received a cup, almost certainly made of silver or silver gilt, from her mother, Margaret, countess of Bath, whom she thanked verbally through a servant.[72] Many mothers—94, or 35 percent, of 266—remembered their married daughters in their wills. Not only were they generous to them, but they also often gave them personal, emotionally charged items that embodied their mutual love as well as their daughters' continued membership in their natal families. Agnes Say gave her daughter Margaret Leynham a cup she had originally received from Margaret's father, and Margaret Capell bequeathed a diamond ring, "which was the first ring her father gave me," and a gold collar and gold heart, "which were both my lady my mother's," to her daughter Elizabeth Paulet.[73]

Like the men of their class, aristocratic mothers also expressed their affection for their married daughters by assisting them in practical matters. On the everyday level, Margaret, countess of Bath, recommended a servant to her daughter Catherine, wife of Sir John Spencer.[74] In a more serious situation, her daughter Dorothy begged her to answer a letter from her husband, Sir Thomas Pakington. "For she sayeth," the countess's servant reported, "at his coming he will blame her and say she did never remember the same and she cared not."[75] Pakington clearly assumed that if she took the trouble, his wife would be able to prevail on her mother to grant him the favor he had requested. Mothers were particularly solicitous and generous when their sons-in-law's improvidence, insecure inheritances, or political misfortunes jeopardized their daughters' comfort and security. Shortly after her daughter Isabel's marriage to Sir Robert Plumpton, who was being ruined by the feud over his inheritance, Lady Edith Nevill returned a bond he had given to her husband to relieve them of one of his debts.[76] Dorothy Codrington received legal assistance from her mother and stepfather when her husband died without assuring her jointure.[77] Widows frequently went to court or left conditional bequests in their wills to protect their daughters' inheritances and jointures, as we saw in chapter 6. In more desperate situations, mothers—Elizabeth, Lady Latimer; Cecily, dowager marchioness of Dorset; and Dame Jane Corbet are examples—arranged livings for their daughters from their own properties.[78] Lady Margaret Bryan, who spoke tenderly of her daughter Elizabeth, "being so kind a child to me," spared no trouble in petitioning Thomas Cromwell for her after her husband, Sir Nicholas Carew, was attainted for treason.[79]

As the years passed, aristocratic mothers also aided their daughters by helping to prefer their granddaughters. The countess of Salisbury's willingness to take her granddaughter, Margaret Stafford, one of her daughter Ursula's thirteen children, into her household must have been a great relief to Ursula and her financially beleaguered husband, Henry, Lord Stafford. Three of Margaret's female first cousins, daughters of her uncles Arthur and Geoffrey Pole, also lived with the countess, which had the additional advantage of facilitating the creation of a network among the next generation of Pole women.[80] Similarly, the three daughters of Katherine, Lady Daubney, lived with their grandmother, Agnes, duchess of Norfolk; their first cousin Catherine, Henry VIII's future wife, was also a member of the household.[81] Some grandmothers, 24 of 266, contributed substantial sums to their granddaughters' dowries, the most important possible contribution to their future prosperity. A far larger number, 68, bequeathed cash or movable goods to them. Whatever the nature of their legacies, women were more likely to choose their daughters' daughters as beneficiaries than their sons' daughters.[82]

The relations between mothers and their married daughters were not always, of course, conflict free. Cecily, marchioness of Dorset, was extremely slow about paying her daughters' dowries, although she subsequently provided a living for the neediest of them, Cecily, Lady Dudley.[83] Dame Dorothy Verney tried unsuccessfully to use a fraudulent will to gain possession of her only daughter's inheritance.[84] But cases of this kind were relatively rare. Of 551 suits involving aristocratic women in the courts of Chancery, Requests, and Star Chamber, mothers and daughters litigated against each other fewer than a dozen times. Women were much more likely to protect their daughters than to withhold their dowries and inheritances.

The interaction between married sisters resembled their relations with their mothers, mixing friendship and practical mutual support. In this context, they do not appear to have distinquished between siblings and half-siblings, evidence of the success of families created by successive marriages. Sisters often visited each other when they were ill and supplied each other with game for their households. In 1538, when Elizabeth, Lady Dacre, fell ill after her churching, her husband summoned her sister, the countess of Northumberland, because her presence would be a "consolation and comfort" to her.[85] A few years later Anne, Lady Powis, visited her half-sister, Eleanor, countess of Cumberland, who was ill with "jaundice and the ague."[86] Honor, Lady Lisle, who had three sisters, was closest to Mary, wife of Thomas St. Aubyn. By far the richer of the two, Lady Lisle sent Mary a variety of gifts, including a doe for her daughter's wedding and beads that Thomas described as "fair and goodly" and "like none that could be found in Cornwall."[87] In addition, Lady Lisle supplemented the St. Aubyns' income by appointing Thomas overseer of her property in Cornwall.[88] Both the Lisles, who needed trustworthy estate officials while they were in Calais, and the St. Aubyns benefited from the arrangement, which strengthened the links between Lady Lisle's natal and marital families.[89]

Another way in which aristocratic women used their resources as wives on behalf of their natal families was to promote their younger sisters. Many single women joined their older sisters' households when the time arrived for them to be "put out." Sir Robert Plumpton's daughter Eleanor lived with her sister Anne after the latter's marriage to Germain Pole.[90] Two of the sisters of Eleanor, countess of Rutland, Elizabeth and Margaret, lived with her at different times after her marriage.[91] Elizabeth Gresham, daughter of Sir Richard, died at the London home of her sister, Lady Christian Thynne, wife of Sir John, in 1552. On her deathbed, she bequeathed all her goods to them because they "hath been very good unto me this four years."[92] Edith, Lady Darcy, and her husband, Thomas, not only negotiated a marriage for her younger sister while she was living in their household but also agreed to pay 100 marks toward her dowry.[93] A quarter of a century later, the dowager countess of

Westmorland thanked her daughter Anne, wife of the second earl of Rutland, for "furthering" the marriage of Anne's sister. Her letter implied that the ceremony was going to take place in Anne's household.[94]

Despite these kinds of warm, mutually supportive relations, few widows, only 29 (11 percent) of 266, remembered their sisters in their wills. They were even less likely to include them among their executors, and then only when they had no children.[95] Women's legacies to their sisters usually consisted of specific pieces of clothing or jewelry or treasured books, the same kinds of objects mothers gave to their daughters. The most generous bequest to a married sister was the childless Elizabeth Pechey's gift to Agnes Redman, whom she named one of her coexecutors. It included plate, pewter, household goods, and furniture, including "the bed that I lie in wholely as it standeth."[96] More common were such legacies as the gold ring with a sapphire that Bridget, Lady Marney, left to her sister and coexecutor, Dame Dorothy Spring; the gold flower with a ruby and two half-pearls that Dame Jane Nevill gave to her sister Elizabeth, Lady Welles; and the £10 that Dame Elizabeth Hussey left to each of her sisters.[97]

The horizontal extension of aristocratic women's kin networks to their siblings almost always incorporated their siblings' spouses. Sisters- and brothers-in-law routinely turned to each other for practical support and often developed warm relations. When the jointure of Elizabeth, duchess of Norfolk, was resettled in 1529, for example, two of her sisters' husbands were among her feoffees.[98] Grace, countess of Shrewsbury, wife of Francis, the fifth earl, visited his sister, Elizabeth, Lady Dacre, and her daughter Anne, countess of Cumberland, at Skipton Castle in the 1550s, probably during one of Anne's lyings-in. Lady Dacre thanked her for the "great pains" she had taken with her daughter. Shortly afterward, Lady Dacre wanted to borrow £10 from her brother, but instead of writing to him directly, asked the countess "to be a mean" to him for the loan.[99] Lady Shrewsbury intervened successfully, and a week later Lady Dacre wrote to thank her "very good brother" for the money.[100] During her years at Calais, Honor, Lady Lisle, and Margaret, widow of her brother, Sir Roger, exchanged friendly letters and tokens.[101] In 1533, she took a distant relative, John Worth, into her service at Margaret's request.[102] As we have already seen, Lady Lisle was on exceedingly good terms with her sister Mary's husband, Thomas St. Aubuyn.

A similar pattern of friendship and mutual patronage marked the relations of aristocratic aunts and their siblings' children. Dorothy, Lady Mountjoy, and her sister Eleanor's son, Sir Thomas Arundell, saw each other regularly. In response to a note about his plans to visit her, she responded warmly that "you shall be right heartily welcome, trusting that it will please you to bring with you my lady your wife. . . . And although I cannot make her so good cheer as she hath made me, yet shall she be right heartily welcome."[103] But her relationship to her nephews was not limited to social occasions. She actively supported the suit of her sister's son, Edward Dudley, to marry the widowed Anne, Lady Berkeley, as a solution to his financial woes.[104] Aunts and their nieces and nephews also served as resources for each other in even more dire situations than Dudley's. After the earl of Surrey was executed in 1547, his sister, Mary, duchess of Richmond, raised his children.[105] Four years later, following the execution of Edward Seymour, Lord Protector, the king's council placed four of Seymour's daughters in the care of his sister, Elizabeth, Lady Cromwell, and the fifth in the home of his other sister, Lady Dorothy Smith.[106] Once they reached adulthood, nephews also assisted their aunts. After her husband's death at the Battle of St. Albans, for example, Elizabeth Poynings's nephew, John Paston II, joined his father and uncles in helping her to defend her property.[107] In another kind of family crisis, George, earl of Shrewsbury, assumed custody of his father's sister, Margaret Vernon, described as a lunatic, after she was widowed.[108]

The relations of Honor, Lady Lisle, with her siblings' children demonstrate the importance to her natal family of an aristocratic woman who married upward and had friends at court. Between 1533 and 1535, for example, she mobilized her court connections on behalf of her sister Philippa's daughter, Elizabeth Staynings, whose husband was in prison for debt and whose creditors were threatening to foreclose on land he had mortgaged. Her efforts saved Staynings's inheritance and secured his release from prison. A few years later, when he died of the plague, Lady Lisle invited his widow to live with her at Calais.[109] She also patronized her nephew Diggory Grenville, a younger son of her deceased brother, Sir Roger, appointing him as one of her liveried servants and assigning him an important role in managing her English estates while she was at Calais.[110] Diggory, the father of five sons, placed the second, Nicholas, in the Lisles' household and subsequently asked them to take the third.[111] Diggory also acted as an intermediary with the Lisles for his clients and friends.[112]

Lady Lisle's relationship with Diggory's older brother, Sir Richard, head of the Grenville family, was much more tumultuous. Sir Richard assisted his aunt in her lengthy struggle to secure the Beaumont lands for her son John Basset.[113] When he became Marshall of Calais in 1535, however, he reported obliquely to Cromwell, "And where it was thought by you, ere I came to Calais, to have found great kindness in some persons, I assure you I have found the contrary, and do find most in the feminine person, right as I shewed you."[114] Despite his complaint, the Lisles appointed him steward of one of their manors, and Lady Lisle granted an office on one of her estates to a clerk of the court of Common Pleas "at the desire of mine especial good master Sir Richard Grenville."[115]

Tensions between Lady Lisle and her nephew developed in 1537 when they disagreed about two serious matters involving Sir Richard's daughters. Grenville, whose daughter Jane was married to Robert Whethill, supported him in his feud with his widowed mother, while the Lisles were partisans of Dame Elizabeth.[116] The Lisles also became involved when Sir Richard opposed his daughter Margaret's marriage to Richard Lee, a protégé of Thomas Cromwell and Surveyor at Calais. Grenville objected to Lee because of his low social origins and relative poverty. After the couple contracted to marry *per verba de praesenti* without Sir Richard's consent, Cromwell defended Lee and tried to secure a reconciliation between Sir Richard and the young couple. The Lisles followed Cromwell's lead. Lady Lisle even gave Margaret refuge in her household during the period between her betrothal and formal marriage.[117] When the quarrel was finally settled, almost certainly because of Cromwell's threats and determination, he thanked Lord Lisle for his "great gentleness for my sake extended to my friend Master Lee." He added that since "Master Marshal is [now] so honestly minded towards him for my sake, I require you to forget all unkindness between the said Marshal and you."[118] As Cromwell hoped, Grenville and the Lisles were reconciled. Two years later, when Sir Richard and his wife were at court, he reported that Lady Lisle's daughter Anne, one of the queen's Maids-of-Honor, was "very merry, and that I was so bold to bring her to my wife, whose bedfellow she was a four or five nights while I was in the Court."[119] Cromwell's intervention in the quarrel reminds us that kinship did not automatically translate into agreement on family matters and that there is no way of separating personal relations within aristocratic families from the crown's political interest in maintaining peace among their members.

On the whole, aristocratic women were no more likely to leave property to their siblings' children than to their brothers and sisters. Thirty-one (12 percent) of 266 female testators left legacies to their siblings' children, about the same frequency with which they remembered their siblings. Their bequests to them also usually consisted of the same kind of gifts—small amounts of cash, jewelry, single pieces of plate, and luxury clothing.[120] A few women even left legacies of this kind to their nieces' and nephews' spouses. Eleanor, countess of Arundel, bequeathed £10 and a silver salt cellar to Sir Maurice Berkeley, her nephew and brother's heir, and a book of matins covered with velvet to his wife.[121] Similarly, Dame Constance Culpepper gave a little gilt pot with a cover to her brother's son Ralph Chamberlain and a gilt spoon to his spouse. She had originally received both items from Ralph's father. She also left two silver spoons to Ralph's brother George and a gold ring with a turquoise to his wife.[122]

The one significant exception to this bequest pattern appeared in the wills of aunts without children of their own. In these cases, many aristocratic women regarded their sisters' offspring, their closest female-connected kin in the next generation, as appropriate heirs to or beneficiaries of their estates and contributed substantially to their futures. Here we see evidence of the female networks that constitute a minor, but important, note in the lives of

women who devoted most of their energy and resources to serving their husbands' patrilineages. Elizabeth, Lady Scrope of Upsall and Masham, coheir of
John Nevill, marquess of Montague, adopted her sister's daughter Lucy as her
heir on the condition that she agree to the match her aunt had arranged for
her. A year after she wrote her will, Lady Scrope added a codicil that showed
that the wedding had already taken place. Accordingly, in addition to inheriting her aunt's land, Lucy was named residual heir of Lady Scrope's movable
goods. Since Lucy had two brothers, neither of whom were mentioned in
Lady Scrope's will at all, Lady Scrope's arrangements clearly indicated her
preference for promoting a female over two males who stood in the same relationship to her.[123]

Another childless heiress, Ursula Knightley, coheir of the fourteenth earl of
Oxford, left her estate to her sister, Dame Elizabeth Wingfield, and her children. She appointed Wingfield's widowed daughter, Elizabeth Naunton, sole
executor of her will and gave her use of some of her land for twenty years
to perform it. She recorded that she had already given Dame Naunton
movables, chattels, and plate "for many considerations me moving." In addition, she assigned life rights in her estates in Suffolk and Essex to her sister
Wingfield and directed that they should descend to Wingfield's eldest son, Sir
Robert, when she died. She also provided pensions to her sister's four
younger sons for twenty years.[124]

Childless aunts who were not heiresses also made substantial contributions
to their nieces' and nephews' futures. A number of them left land they had acquired from their husbands or purchased during their widowhoods to their
siblings' sons.[125] Another aunt, Elizabeth Talbois Greystock, contributed 20
marks and a gold collar to one of her nieces' dowries.[126] Dame Mary Gates
gave enough cash to the younger sons of her sister, Martha Carew, to increase
their livings substantially.[127]

With the children of their siblings, we come to the outer limit of the
women and men who usually occupied significant places in aristocratic
women's natal kin networks. What is most striking is how narrow their hori-
zonal connections were. Their bequest pattern underscores a point made
numerous times in this study—that knightly and noble families defined themselves first and foremost in linear terms and distributed their property accordingly when they died. At the same time, aristocratic wives and widows maintained close relations, built on affection and mutual self-interest, with the
restricted group of natal kin discussed here. Their fathers and eldest brothers
were crucial in protecting their interests vis-à-vis their marital families and
helping them to perform their complex roles. They also regularly exchanged
favors with their mothers and sisters and were particularly useful to their families of birth when they married upward. Although their ties to their natal kin
were always subordinate to their relationships and obligations to their husbands and children, these connections contributed to their ability to carry out

their primary responsibilites. Their natal families also provided an alternative source of resources and links to the next generation if their marriages failed or they had no children of their own.

When aristocratic women married, they acquired a whole set of connections to their husbands' families. Unlike their ties to their natal kin, however, their relationships to their marital families were structually and emotionally complex. On one hand, as young wives, they brought their fathers-in-law and husbands large cash dowries and the basis for new or renewed political alliances with their own fathers and brothers. Once they had children, they occupied a central place in their marital families as mothers of the next generation. Decades later, as widows, they assumed central positions in their husbands' patrilineages as they administered their husbands' wills, raised and preferred their minor children and stepchildren, managed large amounts of property on their own and their offsprings' behalf, and arranged the transmission of their own considerable wealth to the next generation.

On the other hand, while their husbands positioned them at the center of their families and entrusted them with much of their wealth, their in-laws often had a very different point of view, as we have seen in our discussion of their jointures, their inheritances from their husbands, and their activities as executors of their spouses' estates. Resentment against their claims on their husbands' property was particularly acute when they were childless or only had daughters. For second wives, the situation was further complicated by the presence of stepchildren. Conflicts rooted in their ambiguous structural position in their marital families produced dozens of lawsuits between them and their husbands' parents, paternal uncles, and brothers, as well as between them and their stepchildren. These disputes raise serious questions about aristocratic wives' ability to overcome the contradictions inherent in their relationships to their marital kin and the degree to which they could depend on their in-laws as they carried out their responsibilities as wives, mothers, and widows. Their inability to transcend these difficulties increased the importance of their continued ties to their families of birth.

In the early years of their first marriages, the majority of young aristocratic wives lived with their husbands' parents, a situation that could last for decades since it often ended only when both their fathers- and mothers-in-law died or their widowed mothers-in-law remarried. Only noblemen and the richest knights had separate dower houses for their widows. Coresidence gave women an opportunity to develop warm relationships with their husbands' parents and unmarried siblings and establish their position in their husbands' families. In the case of their fathers-in-law, however, there is little evidence that they were able to overcome the structural barriers between them. Strikingly few men, only 6 of 763, mentioned their daughters-in-law in their wills.

Although most fathers-in-law carried out their contractual obligations by assuring the women's jointures, their testaments contain few signs of affection for them. Sir William Paston was exceptional when he increased the jointure of his widowed daughter-in-law, Mary, "for the affection and good will that I bear to" her and "that she hath so many children" by his son Erasmus.[128] Overall, the relationship between fathers- and daughters-in-law rarely transcended the men's tendency to define their family in patrilineal terms. This conclusion is consistent with the fact that most of the evidence about their interaction comes from the records of lawsuits between them.

In contrast, many aristocratic wives did establish warm relations with their mothers-in-law. The long periods they spent together in their husbands' absences and during the younger women's pregnancies and lyings-in encouraged intimacy between them. In addition, the early years of women's first marriages functioned like apprenticeships, in which their mothers-in-law taught them how to manage their large households and oversee their estates. Lady Anne Lestrange's accounts indicate, for example, that she was beginning to involve her daughter-in-law Ellen, who had married her eldest son, Nicholas, in 1528, in agricultural activities at Hunstanton.[129]

Aristocratic women's wills reflected the affection they felt for their daughters-in-law. Forty-nine of 266 testators left them bequests, eight times the comparable figure for 763 men. The difference reflects the bonding that occurred between the women when they coresided and women's weaker commitment to their husbands' patrilineages. Their legacies to their daughters-in-law consisted of the same kinds of objects—jewelry, clothes, small amounts of cash, and plate—that they gave their sisters and nieces. Occasionally they noted that they thought the bequests would have special emotional significance to them. In 1487, for example, Dame Elizabeth Uvedale left her son Robert's wife "a hoop of gold with which I was wedded to the said Sir Thomas Uvedale his father."[130] One mother-in-law, Dame Elizabeth Fitzjames, even included her son's wife among her executors.[131] In two cases, widows who predeceased their mothers-in-law left remembrances to the older women.[132]

Some aristocratic women were just as close to their sons-in-law. As in the case of daughters-in-law, their relationships were often a product of coresidence since a small number of young couples resided with the wife's family rather than the husband's. For example, three of Sir John Howard's daughters lived with him and his second wife, Lady Margaret, after their marriages.[133] Henry, Lord Morley, and his wife, Elizabeth, resided with her mother, Elizabeth, duchess of Suffolk.[134] In other cases, coresidence began at the other end of aristocratic women's life cycles. Catherine, countess of Westmorland, lived in a London mansion that belonged to her son-in-law, Henry, second earl of Rutland, after she was widowed.[135] Although the Rutlands divided their time between London and Belvoir Castle, they almost certainly lived together intermittently. Lady Anne Petre's mother, Alice Keble, had a room at Ingatestone, her son-in-law's chief manor, from 1550 until her death.[136]

Whether they coresided or not, mothers- and sons-in-law had many common interests since the women's daughters benefited from their husbands' advancement and enrichment. Women with connections at court often used them, therefore, to promote the men's interests. In 1539, Jane Roper petitioned Cromwell on behalf of her daughter's husband for the office of attorney to Anne of Cleves.[137] The following year, Dame Katherine Blount asked Cromwell to be a good lord to her son-in-law, Richard Lacon, who was appealing to the council about his dispute with Sir Richard Brereton.[138] In 1558, Sir Thomas Cheyne recognized the benefit he had reaped from the patronage of his wife's powerful mother, Anne, the elder countess of Bedford, by bequeathing her £100 "in consideration of her great friendship and love . . . towards me and mine, as the hope I have in the continuance thereof."[139]

Aristocratic widows' wills demonstrate their attachment to their sons-in-law and confidence in them. Forty, or 15 percent, of 266 remembered them in their wills, and a small number, 18, or 7 percent, named them among their executors. Both figures are high in comparison to the number of their bequests to their brothers or sisters and the frequency with which they included their siblings among their executors. Their choices reflected their expectation that their daughters would benefit from their bequests to their sons-in-law and the general tendency of members of the aristocracy to think of the family in vertical terms. A few mothers-in-law enriched their daughters by giving their sons-in-law productive assets such as sheep, other farm animals, and farm equipment.[140] But most mothers-in-law simply left their sons-in-law tokens of their affection, often in the form of jewlery, such as the heart of gold Isabel Sapcote gave her son-in-law, William Stavely, and the gold hoop Margery Waldegrave left her daughter's husband, Sir John St. John.[141] Some of the objects had dynastic, as well as personal, significance. Dame Anne Bourchier gave her son-in-law, Roger Appleton, a silver and gilt spoon with her arms on it, and Elizabeth Whethill left her daughter Elizabeth's husband her best brooch and signet ring.[142] Dame Margaret Capell's generous bequest to her son-in-law, William Paulet, included three gilt goblets embossed with her arms, her long chain of gold with a cross set with a ruby, an emerald ring, a ring with a pointed diamond, a gold salt cellar, and £10 in cash.[143]

While aristocratic wives' relations with their parents-in-law were their most important connections in their marital families in the early years of their marriages, they become increasingly involved in the lives of their brothers- and sisters-in-law as they grew into their mature roles as managers of their families and households. Their husbands' siblings often lived with them when they were young. Later on, wives often helped to arrange their brothers- and sisters-in-law's marriages. Most important, as supervisors of their husbands' affairs, they made payments of all kinds to them whatever their ages. Although her husband's sister, Elizabeth, did not live with them, for example, Margaret Paston was intimately involved in the long-drawn-out, frustrating process of arranging Elizabeth's marriage. In 1453, after speaking with Elizabeth herself, she wrote to her husband, exhorting him to pursue a possible match. A year later she raised the subject again.[144] She was also in close contact with her brother-in-law, William, who resided in London. A letter from William to Margaret in 1458 indicated that they both benefited from their relations. Two of Margaret's sons were living with their uncle, while Margaret collected William's income in Norfolk for him.[145] After her husband's death, Margaret and William collaborated in a wide variety of business matters.[146]

Three generations later, Margaret's great-granddaughter Eleanor married Thomas, first earl of Rutland. During the period the countess kept the Rutland household accounts, one of her husband's unmarried sisters, Anne, resided with them. The earl also had a dependent younger brother, Richard, who lived elsewhere, and two married sisters, Catherine, wife of Sir Robert Constable of Everingham, and Elizabeth, wife of Thomas Sandys, who became second Lord Sandys in 1540. The countess was closely involved in all their lives and made numerous payments to them, sometimes at her husband's direction, sometimes on her own initiative. In 1528, for example, she paid the quarterly installment on Richard's annuity and 20s. to his married sister Elizabeth Sandys, at "my Lord's commandment."[147] Two years later, her husband directed her to pay for a velvet bonnet for Elizabeth. But there were no notations of this sort when she spent £3 15s. for some goldsmith's work for his sister Anne; bought her 8 ounces of pearls for a frontlett; gave Elizabeth Sandys another 23s.; or gave the earl's sister, Catherine Constable, 20s. for her travel expenses after she visited the Rutlands.[148] Nor were the countess's expenditures for her sisters-in-law limited to small sums of this sort. She also paid Anne's and Margaret's dowries, which involved transferring huge sums of cash.[149]

Occasionally the vagaries of death meant that aristocratic wives or widows assumed responsibility for raising their husbands' nieces and nephews. After Sir Henry Willoughby was killed during Kett's rebellion in 1549, his sister-in-law, Frances, duchess of Suffolk, raised his daughter Margaret, whom she introduced at court.[150] Similarly, Lady Elizabeth Frowick, wife of Sir Thomas, agreed to raise the children of her brother-in-law, Sir Henry Frowick. When Sir Henry wrote his will in April 1505, he appointed her husband as one of his coexecutors. Since he assumed that Sir Thomas would acquire his sons' wardships and rear his unmarried daughters, he left his sister-in-law 100s. "to be good lady and aunt" to them.[151] Less than a year later, in anticipation of his own death, Sir Thomas assigned the boys' wardships and marriages and administration of his brother's remaining goods to his wife, Lady Elizabeth.[152] By the time Dame Frowick herself died a decade later, she had developed a close relationship with one of Sir Henry's daughters, Elizabeth, by then married to Sir John Spelman. She bequeathed her bed, some clothing, and a gold chain with a cross to Elizabeth and left one of Elizabeth's daughters, her goddaughter and great-niece, a silver and gilt cup with a cover, two tablecloths, a ring, and £20 toward her marriage. As an heiress, Dame Frowick also had land to bequeath. She gave most of it to her only daughter, Frideswide, as we would expect, but left the residue to Elizabeth Spelman's husband, whom she appointed as one of her coexecutors.[153]

Dame Frowick was unusual in her generosity to her brother-in-law's family, probably because she was an only daughter with an only daughter of her own. Dame Mary Gates was the only other widow in a group of 266 female testators who left significant legacies to the children and grandchildren of her husband's siblings. A childless widow who survived her husband by almost thirty years, she responded to her atypical situation by treating her brother-in-law Geoffrey's children as her own. In her will she noted that she had already "disposed" of £300 on behalf of his son Anthony. Another son, Geoffrey, actually lived with her. When she died, she gave him the furniture from the room in which "he hath heretofore used most commonly to lodge" and the hangings in the great chamber that had the Gate arms on them. She also divided £50 equally among his children, her great-nephews and nieces. In addition, she contributed substantial sums to the dowries of two other great-nieces, Christian and Frances Wentworth.[154]

Atypical situations—in one case, the combination of childlessness and a long widowhood; in the other, responsibility for raising her brother-in-law's children—created unusally close relations between Mary Gates and Elizabeth Frowick and their husbands' siblings and their children. In most other cases, aristocratic women's relations with their husbands' brothers and sisters and their children were a by-product of their responsibilities as wives and did not create the kind of ties that influenced the distribution of their property in their wills. Only a tiny group of widows—9 of 266—mentioned their brothers- and sisters-in-law in their wills. Of these, only 1 other, Jane Talbot, another childless widow, made a significant bequest to one of her husband's siblings, leaving £40 and all of the household stuff at her home in London to her husband's sister, Elizabeth Mowbray, duchess of Norfolk, whom she also appointed as her chief executor.[155]

Much more evident in surviving documents were the hostilities that ensued when widows faced challenges from their in-laws about their jointures, their children's inheritances, or their management of property that would eventually descend to their husbands' heirs if they were not the women's sons. Although such difficulties were most frequent between widows and their stepsons and brothers-in-law, they also occurred with their nephews by marriage. Dame Elizabeth Pechey's dealings with her husband's heir, Percival Hart, his sister's son, were poisoned by his impatience and suspicion after her husband left her life rights in virtually all his real and movable property.[156] Thirteen years after she was widowed, Dame Pechey referred to Hart as her enemy and claimed that he would do anything to ruin her. One of the issues between them was an annuity she had given him voluntarily and then canceled because it was a "great hinderance" to her. For his part, Hart accused his aunt of selling movables and plate he was supposed to inherit, and appealed to Cromwell to prevent her from wasting his inheritance. Dame Pechey worried about Cromwell's proposed solution, that she sign a bond to Hart, because she feared that he would use it against her. On the other hand, she was "loth to have any further ado with him . . . in my old age, when I live in rest and serve God."[157]

Whether their individual relations with their in-laws were good or bad, taken as a whole the evidence of wills underscores the limits to aristocratic women's incorporation into their marital families. In their role as wives, they assisted their spouses to carry out their obligations to their families. But when their marital relatives distributed their property, the persistent view of the women as outsiders prevailed. Only 9 of 763 men left bequests to their brothers' wives. Women's wills demonstrated remarkably similar priorities. The two closest marital relationships, those between women and their daughters- and sons-in-law, reinforce this point since they reflected the pervasive vertical definition of the family. Furthermore, when aristocratic widows bequeathed property to their children's spouses, they also assisted the sons and daughters who were the primary focus of their concerns. Their relations with their other in-laws were very different and did not easily transcend the contradictions inherent in their position in families that defined themselves patrilineally. However consistent husbands were in positioning their wives and widows at the center of their plans for the future of their immediate descendants, the women remained at least partial outsiders in the eyes of their parents- and siblings-in-law.

In addition to the comparatively narrow group of natal and marital relatives who formed the core of their family networks, most married aristocratic women maintained ties with at least some of their distant relatives—aunts, uncles, great-aunts and great-uncles, great-nieces and great-nephews, and a host of others whom they called cousin. Some of the last were first and second cousins, but in other cases the term applied to such distant kin it is impossible to reconstruct the connections today. Contemporaries often referred to these more distant relatives collectively as their friends. Like the men of their class, aristocratic wives and widows gave priority to them when they took adolescents into their households, distributed fees, hired estate officials or household servants, and responded to requests for their intervention at court. In turn, they called on these connections when they themselves needed assistance. From the point of view of women's primary commitment to their spouses, children, and grandchildren, these networks constituted valuable resources and contributed to their success as wives, mothers, and widows. At moments of crisis the effectiveness of these networks could even have a major effect on their families. On the other hand, women with children rarely remembered relatives of this kind in their wills. In the totality of their lives and conception of their families, these horizontal connections could not compete with their devotion to their husbands and immediate lineal descendants.

Margaret Paston's letters provide an unusually vivid and detailed picture of such a network in their record of her lifelong relations with her distant cousins, the Mountfords, Cleres, and Calthorps.[158] In 1460, for example, Margaret and her husband, John I, assisted her mother's sister, Elizabeth Mountford, to purchase her daughter's wardship after her husband was executed.[159] The Pastons themselves regularly turned to the Calthorps and Cleres, even more distant relatives, for assistance as they struggled to protect their property and continue their social ascent. Margaret Paston's great-aunt, Eleanor Mautby, had married the Sir William Calthorp who died in 1421. Eleanor's grandson, another Sir William, was heir of the Mautby lands after Margaret's own children.[160] The relationship between the families was warm and mutually supportive: Anne Paston, Margaret's daughter, lived in the Calthorp household after her father's death, and Margaret and Lady Elizabeth exchanged herbal remedies.[161] Even more important, Lady Calthorp helped Margaret's younger son, John III, settle his feud over his inheritance with his uncle William II.[162]

The Cleres, to whom the Pastons were connected through Sir John Fastolf, played an even larger role in the Pastons' affairs, although their relationship was still more removed.[163] Margaret, her husband, John I, and their children were particularly close to Elizabeth Clere and her son Robert, who was knighted in 1494. The two families were in constant contact and regularly supplied each other with news.[164] They also assisted each other in a myriad of practical matters. In the 1440s, Elizabeth Clere, wife of Robert, esquire, of Ormesby, actively promoted a match between Stephen Scrope and Elizabeth Paston, Margaret's sister-in-law. Drawing on her considerable knowledge of the law, she reminded Elizabeth's brother, John I, to examine the indentures for the marriage of Scrope's daughter by his first wife and advised him to support the match only if a son by Elizabeth would inherit his land. She also expressed alarm about Agnes Paston's mistreatment of Elizabeth and her refusal to permit her to see or speak to any of her potential suitors.[165]

Relations of this kind between the two families continued for the rest of the century. In 1453, Margaret borrowed a necklace from Elizabeth Clere when she was presented to the queen because she was ashamed to wear her own jewelry "among so many fresh gentlewomen."[166] Ten years later, the Cleres sold the manor of Horninghall, or Caister Clere, to William Paston II,

and Mistress Clere served as one of his feoffees.[167] In 1474, when the Calthorps could no longer keep Margaret's daughter Anne, she asked her
younger son, John III, to inquire about placing her with the Cleres.[168] The
Cleres also loaned the Pastons money on a number of occasions.[169]

While the wealthier Cleres assisted the Pastons financially, John I reciprocated by acting as his cousin Elizabeth's lawyer and business agent.[170] She
trusted him enough to choose him as her representative when she agreed to
settle her quarrel with Brian Stapleton by mediation.[171] Her relationship with
John was so well known in East Anglia that on one occasion Lord Scales asked
him to intervene in a quarrel between her and one of his servants.[172] At the
end of the century, the Cleres and Pastons crowned their long friendship with
a marriage between John III's daughter Elizabeth and Sir Robert Clere's son
William.[173]

Margaret Paston's relations with the Cleres and Calthorps served as a resource in her family's relentless struggle to rise socially and defend its property. Connections of this kind functioned differently for high-ranking women
from established families. In contast to the Pastons, they incorporated distant
kin into their patronage networks. Thus the Pastons' contemporary, Elizabeth Mowbray, duchess of Norfolk, extended her favor to her first cousin,
Richard Roos, esquire, in return for his service.[174] On one occasion, when she
thanked him for carrying out some business for her at great "cost and charge
. . . and importune trouble," the duchess reminded Roos to call on her if
there were anything she could do to reciprocate. On another, she agreed to
arrange (and presumably finance) the marriages of two of his daughters.[175]
Her assistance was probably responsible for Mary Roos's advantageous match
with Hugh Denys, a member of Henry VII's Privy Chamber.[176] High-ranking
women often appointed kin from more modest families as their household
servants or estate officials. Joan, Lady Clinton, daughter of Sir Ralph Mignell,
employed her goddaughter Joan Mignell,[177] and Gertrude, marchioness
of Exeter, chose her young kinsman William Pierreponte as one of her gen-
tleman-waiters.[178] Margaret, dowager marchioness of Dorset, employed a
cousin as steward of one of her manors in Leicestershire. After he died, she
expressed regret that his son had neglected to ask for the office before she
granted it to someone else.[179]

In addition, aristocratic women with connections at court accepted their
obligation to act as intermediaries with the crown and its leading officers for
their less affluent and prominent distant kin. In 1524 Dame Mable Parr asked
Thomas, Lord Dacre, to help a cousin "in such causes as he hath to [i.e., in]
your parts."[180] Ten years later, Elizabeth Nevill petitioned Cromwell on behalf of a cousin who was seeking an appointment as a royal judge. She told
him, "I had rather to spend a hundred marks than he should be disappointed," indicating that she and her husband were prepared to reward Cromwell well if her suit succeeded.[181] Katherine Willoughby, duchess of Suffolk,

continued to patronize William Naunton, her husband's second cousin, after the duke's death in 1545. She was responsible for Naunton's election to Parliament in 1547 and supported him in his dispute with Richard Fulmerton about a royal office, probably the marshalship of the King's Bench that he assumed in November 1550.[182] Referring to Naunton as her friend and cousin, she petitioned William Cecil, then the Lord Protector's secretary, for the office on at least four occasions.[183] When her suit finally succeeded, she responded fulsomely, "What you have done for me in my cousin Naunton's cause, even so much as when I shall think on it, I shall blush that I am no ways able to requite your gentleness, but with my hearty thanks."[184]

Aristocratic women were not, of course, always patrons in these relationships and often turned to their distant kin for favors. When the third duke of Norfolk renegotiated his wife's jointure in 1529, for example, her mother's brother and an uncle by marriage were among her feoffees.[185] The feoffees for Constance (née Talbot) Blount's jointure included a second cousin and paternal uncle.[186] Dame Jane Fitzwilliam appointed her grand-nephew by marriage, Sir Richard Sackville, as one of her coexecutors. She was apparently very close to Sackville, who had a bed in her household and was probably one of her most reliable servants. In her will, she bequeathed him a black velvet gown, a counterpoint, a gelding, a fine gold bracelet, and preference in the purchase of any of her goods that were sold, an unusually generous bequest to such a distant kinsman.[187]

Although kin unquestionably dominated married women's ties outside their households, they also cultivated connections with other aristocratic families in their neighborhoods or local regions. Since these families tended to intermarry and most marriages in the late fifteenth and early sixteenth centuries were patrilocal, women's neighborhood networks overlapped with their ties to their marital kin but were not limited to them. What is distinctive about these networks is that they were based on geographical proximity and often drew their members into the affinities of noblemen who dominated the region. As mistress of Hunstanton, located in the northwest corner of Norfolk, for example, Lady Anne Lestrange, wife of Sir Thomas, lived within easy traveling distance of many of her husband's relatives. Some were close connections like his sister, Katherine, wife of Sir Hugh Hastings; others were similar to Edmund Wyndham, son of Sir Thomas, whom the Lestranges called cousin because they had marital relatives in common. Lady Lestrange's husband also had marital relatives in common with the third duke of Norfolk and belonged to his affinity. Within this extensive circle, Lady Lestrange developed her own relationships with such women as her husband's sister, Katherine Hastings, and two of his aunts of the half-blood, Lady Elizabeth Woodhouse and Mistress Anne Banyard, who visited Hunstanton regularly and participated in Lady Lestrange's lyings-in.[188] Her connections with these women reinforced her husband's relations with their spouses, which strengthened his regional political significance and enhanced his value as a member of the duke of Norfolk's affinity.

Lady Lestrange's contemporary Eleanor, countess of Rutland, also cultivated her ties to knightly and gentry families from the area around her main residence, Belvoir Castle, Lincolnshire. As one of the queen's ladies-in-waiting, she divided her time between Belvoir and the court and developed some of her most important relationships within the royal household. Nonetheless, she maintained ties to a number of knightly families, the Strelleys and Markhams, for example, from the nearby area of Nottinghamshire. The countess appointed Isabell Strelley, probably a daughter of Sir Nicholas, one of her gentlewoman servants. Her eldest son, Henry, and her son-in-law, George Talbot, attended Henry Strelley's wedding in 1539.[189] Members of the Markham of Cottam family also appear frequently in the Rutland accounts. Lady Markham sent the countess numerous gifts during the summer and fall of 1539.[190] The following January, Lady Markham also sent presents to Lady Margaret Nevill, the countess's daughter-in-law, when she gave birth to her first child at Belvoir.[191] The wives of Sir John Byron and Sir Brian Stapleton, two other Nottinghamshire knights, also visited Belvoir or sent gifts that year.[192] Many of the heads of these families were the earl's clients and served in his retinue during the wars in Scotland in 1541.[193] The countess's relations with their wives reinforced the bonds between their families and cemented loyalties that were indispensable in maintaining the earl's political and military power.

Although kin and neighborhood connections were essential dimensions of all aristocratic women's careers as wives, the networks of women with and without children functioned somewhat differently. In the case of mothers, women's horizontal ties were never as important as their commitments to their children and grandchildren. In contrast, childless women looked to their collateral relatives for alternative connections. In addition, because they did not have to concentrate on their immediate lineal descendants, they often developed closer relations with many more of their collateral kin than women with sons and daughters to promote. Anne, Lady Scrope, an only daughter who married three times but had no children, is a particularly vivid example of a woman who created and benefited from networks of this kind. Lady Scrope spent most of her life in East Anglia, where she inherited land from both her father, Sir Robert Harling, and her mother, Joan Gonville, heir of the family that endowed Gonville College, Cambridge. Her chief residence was her ancestral home at Harling, Norfolk, where her first husband, Sir William Chamberlain of Gedding, Suffolk, was buried in 1462. Although she survived him for over thirty years, her attachment to him remained strong. In 1479, when she wrote her first will, she bequeathed the reversion of one of her manors to Thomas Chamberlain and his wife "for the love she bore her first husband."[194] Two decades later, she asked to be buried with her first husband "according to my promise made unto him afore this time."[195] She also left some land to her sister-in-law, Dame Elizabeth Chamberlain, widow of her husband's brother Sir Robert, and to their son "for the good love, will and confidence" she had in them.[196]

Lady Scrope's second marriage, to Sir Robert Wingfield, controller of Edward IV's household, brought her into the inner circle of the Yorkist court.[197] His huge family—he was the second of twelve siblings; his elder brother alone had sixteen children—connected her to many of the most important knightly families in East Anglia. Although Lady Anne was disappointed that she and Wingfield had no children of their own, she adopted one of his nephews, his godson and namesake, "which I have brought up of a child since he was three years of age," as her partial heir. Twenty years after her second husband's death, she left this nephew one of her manors.[198]

Lady Scrope's third marriage, to John, Lord Scrope of Bolton, linked her to still another network of East Anglian families, which revolved around the Howards of Stoke Nayland and the Wyndhams of Felbrigg. Lady Anne cultivated these connections by employing Sir John Howard, later the first duke of Norfolk, as steward of her East Anglian properties.[199] The Scropes lived, at least part of the time, at Harling, since Lord John wrote his will there and was buried at Thetford, the Howard mausoleum, less than 10 miles away.[200] Although their marriage was a relatively short one, Lady Scrope became attached enough to her third husband's family to leave his grandson John, his heir's younger son, two manors in Cambridge.[201]

Lady Anne Scrope's closest blood relative was a first cousin, Margaret, who married Sir Edmund Bedingfield. She sold Bedingfield the reversion of most of her inheritance for 1d. in 1477; when Lady Anne died, it passed to Bedingfield's heir.[202] Although this gift perpetuated the connection between her blood relatives and her inheritance, Lady Anne excluded the Bedingfields when she distributed her considerable movable wealth. Her will attests to her strong attachment to her successive marital families and the Norfolk aristocracy among whom she lived. In addition to dozens of Scropes and Wingfields, her beneficiaries included scores of people to whom she was related through her husbands' families—Lovells, Jerninghams, Echinghams, Brewses, Radcliffes, Bigods, Wyndhams, Howards, Knyvetts, Calthorps, Pastons, Cleres, Heydons, Hevinghams, Boleyns, and Southwells. Some of the relationships, her ties to the Pastons, for example, were so distant that we would hardly reckon them as kin at all. Lady Scrope's freedom to choose the heirs of her inheritance and the beneficiaries of the substantial movable wealth she accumulated through her three marriages made her the central figure in an influential network that extended through much of East Anglia.

Lady Scrope's contemporary, another childless widow, Anne Montgomery, also built a network based on the confluence of geography and kinship. But unlike Lady Scrope, Anne Montgomery was neither an heiress nor a particularly wealthy woman. Her greatest assets were her personal magnetism, practical competence, and trustworthiness. Montgomery's parents, Sir Robert Darcy of Malden and Elizabeth, daughter of Sir Thomas Tyrrell of Heron, connected her to two distinquished Essex and Suffolk families.[203] When she was quite young, she married John Montgomery, esquire, a client of the twelfth earl of Oxford, the leading Lancastrian nobleman in the region. Montgomery was executed in 1463 for plotting with the earl against Edward IV.[204] Dame Montgomery, who never remarried, spent the next twenty-five years in northeast Essex and the area just across the border in Suffolk, surrounded by a close-knit circle of her kin and the late earl of Oxford's followers. Although she retained her jointure, there is no evidence that she maintained an independent residence during her long widowhood, perhaps because she could not afford to support a household appropriate to her rank and connections.[205] Her ties to her kin and her considerable influence over them depended, therefore, on her personal qualities rather than on control of the resources and patronage available to mistresses of large aristocratic households. By 1479, Anne was in the service of Elizabeth Mowbray, duchess of Norfolk, to whom she was distantly related by marriage.[206] The duchess lived in Essex much of the time and was powerful enough around Malden, the family seat of Anne Montgomery's natal family, the Darcys, to intervene in a parliamentary election there in 1472.[207] In 1488, Anne moved with her patron to the Minories in London and remained there until her death ten years later.[208]

Throughout her life, Montgomery remained in close contact with her natal and marital kin and their affines, a pattern that survived her move to the Minories. She appears in a surprising number of their wills, including that of her nephew, Thomas Darcy, esquire, who gave her partial control of his daughters' marriages, and that of his widow, Margaret, who left her 10 marks.[209] Anne's brother-in-law, John Clopton, included her portrait in the famous stained-glass windows he comissioned for the parish church at Long Melford, Suffolk.[210] When he died, he gave her one of his most precious possessions, his "agnus with all the relics there." He valued the reliquary so much that he asked her to leave it to one of his children or grandchildren "after her day . . . for there be many great relics therein." Most surprising, he included her among his coexecutors, the only woman in a group of seven, although men rarely appointed sisters-in-law to this office.[211] In Clopton's case the choice was a particular mark of confidence since he had served as an executor for at least nine people and was well aware of the responsibilities involved.[212]

Sir Thomas Montgomery, another of Anne's brothers-in-law, also mentioned her in his will, indicating that they had remained in contact although her husband had been dead for a quarter of a century. In addition to including her among the beneficiaries of the chantry he was establishing, Sir Thomas confirmed an indenture in which Anne agreed to release all her rights to his

manor in Charlton, Hampshire, to Alice Langley, his sister and heir. Anne fulfilled the agreement seven years later in anticipation of her own death.[213]
That same year, a more distant kinsman, Thomas Froxmere, appointed his
wife and "my cousin Anne Montgomery" as his coexecutors, directing them
to use the profits from all of his land except his wife's jointure for nine years
to support, educate, and marry his three minor children. If his wife died
within that period, he wanted Anne to receive and use the income from his
entire estate for these purposes.[214]

During the decade she lived at the Minories, Anne Montgomery belonged
to a circle of aristocratic women who gathered in and around the duchess of
Norfolk's "great house" in the convent precincts. The circle included the
duchess's sister-in-law, Jane Talbot, widow of Sir Humphrey, and Elizabeth
Brackenbury, coheir of Sir Robert, a follower of Richard III who died at
Bosworth.[215] Both the duchess and Dame Talbot outlived Anne and asked to
be buried near her, a final tribute to the profound influence she had on those
with whom she came in contact.[216]

Aristocratic women's collateral relatives, particularly those who lived in their
neighborhoods, dominated their extended networks. The importance of kinship as a basis for sociability and patronage was evident in the contemporary
practice of using the term *cousin* to designate people whom we would not
reckon as relatives at all. Nonetheless, some women did establish friendships
and exchange favors with people, most often neighbors, to whom they were
not related by blood or marriage. Occasionally they referred to such people as
their *gossips*. Although such friendships did not make a major contribution to
their careers as wives, mothers, and widows, their existence provides further
evidence of aristocratic women's integration into their neighborhoods. In this
broad sense such friendships almost certainly contributed to their husbands'
local position. They also functioned as an additional resource for widows.
Thus, Dame Constance Culpepper left her Kentish neighbor and friend, Lady
Anne Grey, gold beads, rings, and a gold button for a partlett,[217] and Sir John
Porte's second wife, Dorothy, frequently visited her Derbyshire neighbor,
Lady Cavendish.[218] In June 1558, Sir William Sharington of Lacock, Wiltshire,
invited his neighbor, Lady Christian Thynne, who lived about 15 miles away at
Longleat and whom he called his gossip, to his mansion at Lacock. He added
that he hoped they would exchange visits "more times than once before
Michaelmas."[219] Dame Jane Hungerford, who lived at Charlecote, Warwickshire, included her gossip, John Spenser, esquire, and his wife and daughter,
who lived relatively close by at Hodmell, among her beneficiaries. Evidently,
she was very close to Spenser, whom she appointed as her sole executor, ex-
cluding her son, Sir Thomas Lucy, owner of Charlecote, although her legacies
to Sir Thomas contain no hint that they were estranged.[220]

Aristocratic women were the recipients of gifts from friends and neighbors of this kind, as well as gift givers. Sir Richard Jerningham, a younger son of the family located at Somerleyton, Suffolk, bequeathed 20 marks to Lady Anne Knyvett, wife of Sir Edward of Wymondham, Norfolk, and widow of Robert Lestrange. Their family seats were about 20 miles apart.[221] Thomas, Lord Audley, Henry VIII's chancellor, left £10 9d. to his friend Lady Julian Waldegrave, who lived at Bures, Suffolk, about 20 miles from his mansion at Audley End, Essex.[222] Lady Julian's husband, Sir William, bequeathed a gold brooch he wore on his hat to his friend Lady Anne Cornwallis, who lived at Brome, near the border with Norfolk.[223]

Collectively, these complex networks of kin, neighbors, and friends meant that few aristocratic women were isolated in their households or completely dependent on their spouses for resources. Rather, the natal connections they brought with them when they married and those they cultivated with their marital relatives and neighbors linked them to the wider world in which their families exercised and pursued wealth and power. These networks were an important resource as they promoted their husbands' and children's careers and often permitted them to function in regional institutional settings we tend to think of as male. In 1536, for example, Dame Katherine Blount "labored" for the election of her eldest son, George, as knight of the shire for Shropshire. Dorothy, Lady Mountjoy, attended the local assizes in Edward VI's reign, and Lady Elizabeth Copley, the only elector at Gatton, Surrey, sent her son Thomas to three Marian Parliaments.[224] Some of the highest ranking, most ambitious women operated outside their households on an even broader scale and emerged as major power brokers in their regions. Margaret, countess of Shrewsbury, for example, was responsible for much of the violence attending the fifteenth-century feud over the Berkeley inheritance. She imprisoned James, sixth Lord Berkeley, and his sons until they signed deeds and bonds worth £35,000 to secure their release; participated in the siege of Berkeley Castle; and incarcerated James's wife, Lady Isabel Berkeley, in Gloucester Castle, where she died in 1452.[225]

Alice, duchess of Suffolk, was equally disruptive in East Anglia. After she was widowed in 1450, she and her son, who married Edward IV's sister Elizabeth, were among the Pastons' most implacable enemies. Together they maintained two of the most lawless men in late Lancastrian and Yorkist East Anglia, Sir Thomas Tuddenham and Sir John Heydon.[226] It was Heydon who convinced Lord Moleyns to seize Gresham, one of the Paston manors, in 1448.[227] Two years later, a parliamentary petition included the duchess among those responsible for the diminished resources of the crown and lack of effective law enforcement.[228]

Despite her unpopularity and evil reputation, the duchess of Suffolk remained active in East Anglian politics and allied with the Pastons' adversaries until her death in 1475.[229] In 1459, she supported a marriage between John

Wyndham, another enemy of the Pastons, and Sir John Heveningham's widow, much to the Pastons' consternation.[230] The next year, she tried unsuccessfully to influence Edward IV to appoint a sheriff favorable to her interests and hostile to the Pastons.[231] According to Margaret Paston, the duchess and her son were widely disliked because they maintained "all the traitors and extortioners" in the county.[232] As far as she was concerned, they deserved their notoriety. In 1465, the Suffolks laid claim to Hellesdon and Drayton, two manors originally belonging to Sir John Fastolff but now in the Pastons' possession. The dowager duchess accompanied her son and his wife when they took up residence at Cossey, their manor just across the river from Hellesdon, to prepare for the duke's attempt to seize it forcibly in July.[233] Although the attack failed, the duke assaulted Hellesdon successfully the following October, destroying the house and lodge.[234] Shortly afterward, Margaret reported, "The old lady and the Duke is set fervently against us."[235]

For the remainder of the decade, the duchess of Suffolk and her son were involved in the disorders endemic in East Anglia and retained possession of Hellesdon and Drayton. At some point, the duchess petitioned Thomas Bourchier, archbishop of Canterbury, one of the feoffees for Hellesdon, to give her and her heirs title to it, fraudulently claiming that John Paston II had agreed to the transfer.[236] To make matters worse, Paston learned in October 1468 that the duchess planned to seize Cotton, another of his manors that had previously belonged to Sir John Fastolff.[237] The following January, the earl of Oxford reported that the duchess intended to hold a court at Cotton at which her supporters would deliver seisin (i.e., possession) of the manor to her.[238] Her role in disturbances in the region was so serious that the crown actually intervened to bring her under control. In 1468–1469, Queen Elizabeth Woodville wrote to ask her to "common" with the lords in regard to matters the king had previously discussed with her "so [that] no default be founden" in her.[239] The letter may have been connected to Edward IV's subsequent journey to East Anglia to reestablish law and order. During his visit, the duchess remained far away at her manor at Ewelme, Oxfordshire, so that if she were summoned, she could "feign excuse because of age or sickness" and avoid appearing.[240]

The duchess of Suffolk's contemporary Elizabeth Mowbray, duchess of Norfolk, was also a powerful political presence in East Anglia, although she did not cause disorder and was well inclined toward the Pastons. John Paston III entered the service of her husband, the fourth duke, in the early 1460s.[241] His mother thought, incorrectly as it turned out, that the duchess might assist them when the duke of Suffolk attacked Hellesdon in 1465.[242] Later that year, however, the duchess did prevent Gilbert Debenham from attacking the Pastons at Cotton by informing her husband and his council about the impending assault.[243] In September 1472, she supported John Paston II's election to Parliament from the borough of Malden, Essex.[244]

After 1469, when the duke of Norfolk beseiged and captured Caister Castle, the most important of Fastolff's properties in Paston hands, the duchess was the focus of much of their effort to convince him to relinquish it. Her prominence in their calculations and regular participation in the meetings of her husband's council attest to her steady involvement in regional politics.[245] Despite her good will, she was unable to convince her husband to part with Caister. Indeed, in 1475, the duke dashed any hope John III still retained that he would return it by declaring in the king's presence that he would rather die than surrender it. Paston was so angry he left Norfolk's service.[246] Only the duke's death the following January broke the seven-year deadlock. Free to follow her own inclinations at last, the duchess acted as the Pastons always thought she would and returned Caister to them in less than six months.[247]

The dowager duchess's role in East Anglian affairs continued for over a decade after she relinquished Caister Castle. She was a good friend to William Paston II and supported him vigorously when he quarreled with his nephews, John II and John III, about their inheritance.[248] In 1479, she offered William sixty men to back up his claim to estates that his mother had been holding at her death.[249] Both John III's wife, Margery, and their distant kinswoman Lady Elizabeth Calthorp realized that no settlement was possible without the duchess's consent. After Lady Calthorp spoke to the duchess on John III's behalf in 1481, she reported that an agreement was possible without resorting to the law.[250] A few days later, John's wife, Margery, learned from a cousin who belonged to the duchess's council that she was "near weary of her part" in the quarrel. He advised Margery to approach the duchess herself because "one word of a woman should do more than the words of twenty men," as long as she was careful to "speak none harm of mine uncle [i.e., William]." If her husband, John III, agreed, Margery was willing to approach the duchess in the company of Lady Calthorp, her mother, and her mother-in-law and beg her to be her husband's "good and gracious lady." She was confident of success as long as John agreed to a resolution that preserved the duchess's honor as William II's patron.[251]

Despite Margery's optimism, the quarrel dragged on until 1486 or 1487, when John III and William II finally submitted their dispute to arbitration. Sometime between 1488 and 1492, Sir Henry Heydon, one of the arbiters the Pastons had chosen, reported that they had finally come to an agreement.[252] Although the duchess had retired to the Minories in London in 1488, he warned John that her consent to the settlement was essential: "I advise you . . . in any wise that ye nor any your servants have none words in this matter but that it is agreed by mine lady you [are] to have peacable possession."[253]

A few years later the duchess, still involved in East Anglian affairs, asked Paston, by then Sir John, and five other leading Norfolk knights and gentlemen to intervene with Sir Henry Grey on behalf of his nephew and heir, Thomas Martin, her servant and late husband's kinsman. She had heard that

Grey was planning to disinherit Martin and wanted them to dissuade him from doing so.[254] Paston and his fellows apparently succeeded since Grey's inquisition post mortem in October 1496 listed Martin as his heir, and the duchess thanked Paston for his efforts.[255]

Historians associate the kind of role the duchesses of Norfolk and Suffolk played in fifteenth-century East Anglia with the endemic disorder that resulted from the weakness of the monarchy. But noblewomen continued to exercise this kind of power long after the Tudors ascended the throne. The activities of Anne, Lady Berkeley, in Gloucestershire in the 1530s and 1540s are a case in point. Lady Berkeley, who was widowed less than two years after her marriage, gave birth to her second child and only son, Henry, after her husband's death.[256] From then on, she dedicated herself to safeguarding his inheritance during his long minority. She even tried to enlarge it by repossessing property her father-in-law had left to her husband's younger brother Maurice. In June 1534, a group of her servants entered the mill and pond at one of the manors, Mangottsfield, Gloucestershire, and carried away 40 shillings' worth of fish. Although the intruders were subsequently fined, she rewarded their leader by appointing him her receiver, surveyor, auditor, and woodwarden.[257] Her aggression ignited a bitter feud and series of breaches of the peace in which another brother-in-law, Sir Nicholas Poyntz, who was married to her husband's sister, vigorously defended Maurice. In 1537, she complained in Star Chamber that Sir Nicholas and a band of sixty men had occupied her manor at Burton for two days and nights and had taken fish worth £20 from the pond before destroying it.[258] Her adversaries also attacked Mangottsfield, apparently then in her possession, destroying the mill and spoiling the fish. On still a third occasion, Poyntz and Maurice Berkeley jointly invaded her park at Yate, killed many of the deer, and even discussed setting one of her hayricks on fire in the hope that the flames would spread to the stable and house. Lady Berkeley responded on both occasions by resorting again to Star Chamber.[259] In 1541, she also complained to the Privy Council.[260] Since the feud showed no sign of abating, Lady Berkeley finally appealed directly to Henry VIII, whose favor she had won during her brief period at court in the early 1530s.[261] He responded by appointing her to a commission to inquire into the disturbances. Lady Berkeley sat on the bench in the sessions hall at Gloucester, impaneled a jury, heard evidence, and convicted and fined the defendants, including Sir Nicholas and her brother-in-law Maurice.[262]

In the same period in the North, many of the most energetic aristocratic women shared their husbands' regional political responsibilities. Elizabeth, Lady Dacre, wife of Lord William, kept watch on the borders with Scotland and reported to him in great detail when he was away from home.[263] In 1537, Catherine, countess of Westmorland, acted decisively to prevent rebellion from spreading to her locality during the Pilgrimage of Grace and its aftermath. On January 18, 1537, she sent a copy of Sir Francis Bigod's letter that was inciting insurrection to her husband, who was in London, to forward to Thomas Cromwell and begged him to return home immediately.[264] When neither he nor the Bishop of Durham appeared, she took matters into her own hands. As Thomas Tempest reported with admiration to the duke of Norfolk, she "stayeth the country . . . I assure your lordship, she rather playeth the part of a knight than a lady."[265] A few months later, the duke approached her, as well as her husband, when he tried to persuade Westmorland to accept the wardenship of the east and middle marches, a clear recognition of her influence over her husband and the fact that she would share his responsibilities if he accepted the office.[266]

Women such as the countess of Westmorland; Anne, Lady Berkeley; and the fifteenth-century duchesses of Norfolk and Suffolk expanded their regional political role to the fullest possible extent. Their activities depended on their ability to mobilize the members of their household, their husbands' councils, their tenants, and the local aristocracy. They were, of course, unusual in the personal initiative and energy they exhibited and the extent of the familial power they could mobilize. But they were not unusual in looking beyond their households to carry out their duties to their families and friends. Scores of their contemporaries joined them in looking beyond the walls of their manors and castles as they promoted the careers and fortunes of their husbands, children, and kin. Their natal, marital, and neighborhood networks gave them the resources they needed to discharge these functions and, if necessary, to protect themselves in unsuccessful marriages. Rather than containing them, therefore, their marriages and households provided them with the material and personal assets required to dominate their neighborhoods and promote their families in the most capacious, possible way.

CHAPTER 9. THEIR BRILLIANT

CAREERS—ARISTOCRATIC

WOMEN AT THE YORKIST

AND EARLY TUDOR COURT

*T*HE VAST majority of Yorkist and early Tudor aristocratic women achieved lifelong vocations through marriage, but the minority, from families with close ties to the reigning dynasty, could also aspire to careers at court. Such careers offered them the only opportunity to fashion identities and roles outside their natal or marital families. Appointments to the queen's household also gave them a nonfamilial source of income since Ladies-in-Waiting and Maids-of-Honor received annual fees and nonmonetary perquisites, privileged access to royal patronage, and annuities or pensions when they retired. Nonetheless, careers at court were an addition to, rather than a substitute for, women's careers in the family since virtually all those who held offices in the royal household married before, during, or after their appointments. Their positions increased the resources at their disposal to carry out their duties as wives, mothers, and widows at the same time that it gave them status outside their families.

The queen's Maids-of-Honor, who were unmarried by definition, obtained their offices when they were around 16 through the political influence of their natal families and their possession of the necessary physical attributes and social accomplishments. When they married, many of them were promoted to positions as Ladies-in-Waiting and remained at court even after they had children. Other women entered the royal household as Ladies-in-Waiting after their marriages because they were relatives of the queen or married to members of the king's Privy Council or Privy Chamber. Ladies-in-Waiting who developed independent ties with the queen and proved their usefulness as one of her attendants often retained their offices after they were widowed or remarried. Positions in the royal household, therefore, gave aristocratic women the opportunity for sustained, even lifelong, employment.

However they secured their initial postions, the queen's servants gradually acquired the knowledge and experience necessary to ensure the smooth functioning of her household. Over time, their tenure at court came to depend as much on their expertise as on their family connections. Their importance as professional servants of the crown was especially clear during the 1530s and 1540s, when the personnel in the queen's household remained relatively stable despite Henry VIII's rapid change of wives. Experienced Ladies-in-Waiting and Maids-of-Honor introduced each of his queens to the elaborate ceremonial surrounding their daily lives and helped them to carry out their new responsibilities. They provided continuity on the female side of the court in a period of exceptional instability.

Conceptualizing aristocratic women's service in the royal household as careers and attributing political significance to their contribution to the public, ceremonial side of the monarchy challenge the dominant perspective in the field of Yorkist and early Tudor court studies. David Starkey's innovative and stimulating work pays little attention to the queen's household and servants,[1] while Steven Gunn, writing on Henry VII's courtiers, stated categorically that "there is no sign that they [i.e., women at court] were regarded as important figures in their own right, nor that any woman could do much to forge her own career at court."[2] Historians writing on particular queens or, more rarely, other high-ranking women constitute the major exceptions to this generalization, but their work has not had a major impact on interpretations of the court as a whole.[3] This chapter demonstrates that the activities of women with offices in the royal household constituted careers in the fullest sense of the word and that their participation and presence were essential for the court to perform its central social, ceremonial, political, and diplomatic functions.

The emergence of careers in the royal household as viable options for aristocratic women was connected to the development of the court as the political center and visual symbol of the monarchy, itself one of the most conspicuous results of the reestablishment of effective kingship in Yorkist and early Tudor England. Contemporaries distinguished the court from the royal household as early as Edward IV's reign, although the court had no organization of its own and the household remained its structural core.[4] This lack of bureaucratic definition accurately reflected the court's multiple functions and fluid, even elusive, character: the court was at once a political and domestic entity, a place, and a fluctuating group of the king's servants and friends.[5] Its location depended on the presence of the king and his entourage; its members included all those attending or with the right of access to him.[6] From a domestic point of view, the function of the court was straightforward: it was the king's residence. As a political institution it was complex and multidimensional: it was the site of council meetings and formal royal audiences, the central point for distributing the crown's vast patronage, the setting for dynastic and state ceremonies, and the forum for displaying the king's magnificence through elaborate ritual and conspicuous consumption.[7]

The growth of the court depended on the increasing power and resources of the monarchy, particularly the expansion of the royal demesne. Its expansion gradually transformed the relationship of crown and aristocracy during the late fifteenth and early sixteenth centuries.[8] As the king's income and landed estate grew, members of the aristocracy turned to him ever more insistently for the land, offices, and fees necessary to maintain their positions in the counties and to raise their social and political status vis-à-vis their peers. Increasingly, only grants from the crown and the profits of royal office could carry ordinary members of the gentry, often the kin or clients of the court aristocracy, from relative obscurity to social and political prominence and transform their modest wealth into great fortunes. Ambitious members of the aristocracy therefore spent considerable time, energy, and resources in seeking positions in the royal household, maintaining their ties with the king and leading power brokers at court, and participating in state celebrations and the rituals of royal family life. In this context, direct contact with the king and his intimates was the key to worldly success. Conversely, admission to the court and participation in its public spectacles was a marker of social and political prestige.[9]

Aristocratic women joined their male kin in turning their political energies toward the Yorkist and early Tudor court as enthusiastically as they pursued their families' interests at the local and regional level. They sought offices in the royal household for themselves or their daughters and then used these positions to gain access to royal patronage. As a result, they benefited from the reestablishment and expansion of effective central government, which extended their political horizons from their households and "countries" to the court and added a new dimension to their political activity. This conclusion challenges the most influential work about the impact of the growth of the early modern state on women, which has emphasized the link between centralizing and expanding government in the period and the reinforcement of patriarchy.[10] In England, however, what was at stake in the consolidation of the monarchy was not the augmentation or intensification of patriarchal power per se but its movement from periphery to center, from unruly members of the aristocracy to the king and his ministers. Women's greater presence and activity at court was consistent with this kind of state building, which was specifically directed at shifting the balance of authority and power between the king's government and the noble and knightly familes who traditionally controlled the countryside. Indeed, the crown's interest in accelerating this process made it receptive to petitions from aristocratic women with court connections who accused their male relatives and neighbors of breaking the law and behaving riotously.

Like the court itself, the "court ladies" of the Yorkist and early Tudor periods are a difficult group to define. In the broadest sense they fell into three categories: first, the women who held offices in the royal household as servants of the queen and royal children; second, women who lived at court because their husbands held postions there; third, women who came to court for relatively short periods to celebrate great state occasions and major events in the life of the royal family. Whatever the extent and character of their residence at court, these women entered its precincts as members of a relatively small number of interrelated families with close ties to the reigning dynasty, forming an inner circle within the aristocracy. Its members developed personal relationships with the king and his favorites and secured patronage for themselves, their kin, and their servants. Their family connections and ties to the royal family and favorites also encouraged them to align themselves, more or less openly, with the shifting factions that characterized court and dynastic politics, despite the ideological marking of political activity as male. Within this large group, it was the women in the first category, those who held offices in the queen's or royal children's households, who had careers at court and who form the subject of this chapter.

The growth of a more elaborate and sophisticated court culture—first in imitation of Burgundy, then increasingly, of France—that accompanied the expansion and centralization of the monarchy played a significant role in increasing women's importance at court by creating new opportunities for them to gain access to the king and his favorites. The centerpiece of this new culture was the disguising, or masque, an early theatrical form that originated in Henry VII's reign and included active parts for women, unlike the traditional tournaments that confined them to the role of spectators.[11] The most sophisticated disguisings were dramatic productions that incorporated simple plays and carefully rehearsed dances united by a common chivalric theme and performed by elaborately costumed, masked courtiers and court ladies.[12] From women's point of view, particularly that of the young, unmarried women who participated in masques most frequently, what was crucial was that disguisings required considerable rehearsal. Participating in them involved the kind of informal contact with the king usually restricted to men who belonged to or had easy access to his Privy Chamber. Like these men, female maskers who caught the king's eye gained his favor and the material benefits that went with it.

Disguisings evolved slowly from fifteenth-century tournament processions, in which ladies led knights onto the field, into the sophisticated and elaborate masques produced by Ben Jonson and Inigo Jones at the Jacobean court. Appearing first at the court of Burgundy, these processions increasingly sacrificed the martial character of the tournament to display, elaborate costumes, and dramas performed on mobile stages called pageant carts or pavillions. Although the Burgundian example affected the tournament on a modest scale in Edward IV's reign, its influence reached an unprecedented height when Henry VII created his second son duke of York in 1494.[13] That year also saw the first disguising performed independently of a tournament at the revels celebrating Twelfth Night.[14] Seven years later, spectacular productions with dramatic themes, disguisings, and dances followed the four state banquets that celebrated Prince Arthur and Katherine of Aragon's wedding. They were completely independent of the tournaments held earlier in the day.[15]

From then on, disguisings functioned as autonomous court spectacles. They incorporated various combinations of pageant carts, elaborate and fanciful costumes, a loose narrative built around chivalric themes, speeches in the form of dramatic arguments, mock combats or sieges, and final resolution in the form of a dance. When the performance was completed, the masked players often danced with members of the audience. Although the first full-fledged disguisings were staged to celebrate major events in the life of the royal family, they became a regular form of entertainment at Henry VIII's court. For two decades or more, the king was an enthusiastic sponsor and participant in the masques and revels produced to frame tournaments, celebrate holidays, entertain ambassadors and other guests at state banquets, or simply to amuse him and his favorites. They were one of the main subjects of Edward Hall's contemporary chronicle of the period, indicating their importance in the public image of the court and the conduct of diplomatic relations.

Women played essential roles in disguisings because their chivalric themes centered on ladies who needed to be rescued from imprisonment or forced to accept the suits of their lovers. Women also performed in the carefully rehearsed dances that resolved the plot and concluded the productions. Following the formal entertainment, they often invited members of the audience to dance with them. On some occasions, their choice of partner was carefully planned to support the king's diplomatic goals. In 1518, for example, at the conclusion of the disguising to honor the French ambassadors and the signing of the Treaty of Universal Peace, the "lady maskers took each of them a French gentleman to dance and mask with them . . . these lady maskers spoke good French, which much delighted these gentlemen, to hear these ladies speak to them in their own tongue."[16] During Henry VIII's visit to France in 1532, Anne Boleyn chose the French king as her partner to signal her position as the king's future wife.[17] Thus, when they performed in court masques, women contributed to the development of court culture, furthered the king's diplomatic objectives, and earned the favor that had drawn them to court in the first place. Their participation functioned as both an avenue of access to the king's goodwill and a sign of the favor they had already achieved.

Under both the Yorkists and early Tudors, the queen's household was a separate department, physically and organizationally, within the *domus regie mag-*

nificencie, which contained both the public precincts of the court and the private lodgings of the royal family. As its name indicated, the function of the *domus regie magnificencie* was to display the king's wealth, power, and status—his magnificence—in every dimension of its activities.[18] A great deal of attention was paid to formality, rank, and conspicuous consumption on both the queen's and king's side of the court. The Black Book, issued to regulate Edward IV's household, stated explicitly that the queen's service "must be nigh like unto the king and that for her ladies and other worshipful men and gentlewomen, their services and liveries . . . as it is to the king's household men."[19]

The queen's household was organized as a mirror image of the king's, with the three private rooms, or chambers, in which she lived—Watching (or Great) Chamber, Presence Chamber, and Privy Chamber—lined up one behind the other. One entered the queen's suite through the first of the three rooms, the Watching Chamber, which led directly into the Presence Chamber and, finally, into the Privy Chamber. Servants of the crown guarded the entrance to each of the rooms and allowed fewer and fewer people access as they moved from the outer to the inner parts of the household. The Presence Chamber served as the queen's formal dining room and the place where she entertained the king and other important visitors.[20] Edward IV was the first king to convert the Privy Chamber into extensive lodgings, or suites, for members of the royal family. Henry VII and Henry VIII went a step further and turned the Privy Chamber into a separate department within the household. A similar development took place on the queen's side of the court.[21] Her private suite corresponded to the king's and included privy and bed chambers, privy wardrobe, and privy kitchen.[22] Early Tudor queens probably also followed the kings' example in eating many of their meals privately. John Husee's report of the conversation in which Jane Seymour promised to take one of Lady Lisle's daughters into her service has an intimate quality that strongly suggests it took place in her Privy Chamber rather than in the Presence Chamber, where meals were more public and formal.[23]

The queen's privy lodgings were closed to virtually everyone but those of her servants specifically granted the right of admission and the king and those accompanying him. Other members of the court and suitors who wanted to see her or her attendants had to await them in the Presence Chamber. As Husee reported on one occasion, "I returned to the Queen's chamber to give thanks to Mistress Margery [Horsman] . . . which as then was returned into the Privy Chamber, so that since I could not speak to her."[24] Katherine of Aragon's reaction to the unexpected arrival of Henry VIII and twelve companions in 1510 suggests that even the king rarely appeared unannounced and almost never with a large company. They "came suddenly in a morning into the Queen's Chamber, all appareled in short coats, of Kentish Kendal, with hoods on their heads, and hose of the same, every one of them, his bow and arrows, and a sword and a bucklar, like outlaws, or Robin Hood's men, whereof the Queen, the Ladies, and all other there, were abashed, as well for the strange sight, as also for their sudden coming."[25]

The administrative structure of the queen's household paralleled the king's and was headed by her own Lord Chamberlain.[26] Although he and many of those working under him—Vice-Chamberlain, Master of the Horse, Carvers, Cupbearers, Servers, Gentlemen, Yeoman Ushers, and Groom Porters—were male, the queen's side of the court was a somewhat insulated female space within the royal household. The queen spent much of her time in the Privy Chamber in the company of her ladies, gentlewomen, and maids; ordinarily she also dined with them apart from the king and his servants even when they were lodging in the same palace.[27]

As the Yorkist and early Tudor court expanded, so did the households of the queens. At the beginning of the period, Elizabeth Woodville appointed fourteen women to serve her: five Ladies-in-Waiting, two of whom were noblewomen; seven Maids-of-Honor; and two other female servants.[28] In addition, Elizabeth Darcy served as "lady mistress" of the nursery.[29] In 1502–1503, Elizabeth of York, Henry VII's consort, paid wages to eighteen aristocratic women, two of whom were noblewomen.[30] She also gave a pension to her sister Katherine, who lived at court a good deal of the time and frequently dispensed funds from the queen's privy purse.[31] In the first year of Henry VIII's reign, Katherine of Aragon's household included thirty-three aristocratic women, eighteen of whom were the wives or daughters of peers.[32] After that, the queen's household remained relatively stable in size. At the end of the reign, Katherine Parr's household included thirty-three women from aristocratic families; ten were married to peers.[33] Aristocratic women also supervised the nurseries and households of Henry VII's and Henry VIII's children.

Women who performed their tasks in the queen's household successfully and possessed valuable social skills retained their positions during multiple reigns and served successive queens and royal children. Mary Roos Denys, Elizabeth Stafford Fitzwalter, Elizabeth Pechey, Anne Percy, Eleanor Pole Verney, and Anne Verney Weston attended both Elizabeth of York and Katherine of Aragon.[34] The duchess of Norfolk belonged to Katherine of Aragon's household for sixteen years; Lady Maud Parr served her for over ten.[35] Many of the queen's attendants even survived the factionalism surrounding Henry VIII's matrimonial adventures, providing an element of continuity in the institution of queenship during a turbulent period. Jane Seymour and Margery Horsman served both Katherine of Aragon and Anne Boleyn. Horsman also served Jane Seymour after Seymour married Henry VIII.[36] Mary (née Scrope) Jerningham Kingston belonged to Katherine of Aragon's household from 1509 until at least 1527 and then participated in Anne Boleyn's coronation, Edward VI's baptism, and Jane Seymour's funeral. By 1538, she was a member of

Princess Mary's household. Two years later, she was appointed to attend Anne of Cleves.[37] Jane Parker first appeared at court in the 1520s; later, as Lady Rochford, she attended her sister-in-law Anne Boleyn and then served in the households of Jane Seymour, Anne of Cleves, and Katherine Howard.[38] Anne Basset, sworn as Jane Seymour's maid in September 1537, attended all three of Henry VIII's subsequent wives.[39]

Long service was equally characteristic of the women who headed the royal nursery. Henry VII appointed Lady Elizabeth Darcy, who had previously held this postion under Edward IV, to head Prince Arthur's nursery by 1488.[40] Lady Jane Guildford began her career as a Lady-in-Waiting to Henry VII's mother, Margaret Beaufort. She subsequently served his wife and then became the governess of both his daughters.[41] Margaret Pole, countess of Salisbury, another member of Katherine of Aragon's household, became Princess Mary's governess around 1520 and held the position until 1533.[42]

After years, even decades, of service, the positions of women like these ceased to depend on their husbands or their natal families. Anne Basset's place in the queen's household was so secure that it survived the arrest of her mother and stepfather in 1540. Indeed, Henry VIII showed particular concern about her welfare when he dissolved Katherine Howard's household the following year, ordering the queen's maids to "repair each of them to their friends there to remain, saving Mistress Basset, whom the King's Majesty, in consideration of the calamity of her friends, will, at his charges, specially provide for." After Henry VIII's death, Anne received an annuity from the crown, a clear recognition of its responsibility for a long-term servant who depended on her position but was superfluous when an unmarried, minor king ascended the throne. In 1553, Queen Mary appointed Anne to her Privy Chamber and granted her a life annuity of 40 marks.[43] Anne Basset and women like her can be described as career servants of the crown as accurately as men in comparable positions on the king's side of the court.

The political and economic value of appointments in the queen's household meant that competition for them was keen. As the countess of Salisbury once warned, successful suits to place a daughter at court required both "time and leisure."[44] Like men on the king's side of the royal household, women obtained their offices through family influence and almost always functioned there as members of dense kin networks, even after they had developed independent identities as servants of the crown. At any given moment, a small group of interconnected families dominated the royal households. Most of these families were related to the king and queen, to other members of the royal household, or to the king's current favorites. In addition, many of the queen's maids married the king's servants and favorites. These court couples usually retained their offices and continued to serve the royal family. Their children often intermarried also, extending their parents' and families' presence at court into the next generation. In this way a self-perpetuating group of court families developed within the aristocracy.

English-born queens almost always brought their favorite female relatives to court with them. In the 1460s, Elizabeth Woodville's five Ladies-in-Waiting included her sister Anne, Lady Bourchier; her sister-in-law Elizabeth, Lady Scales; and her first cousin Lady Alice Fogge. In the early years of Henry VII's reign, a number of Queen Elizabeth of York's female relatives—her sisters Anne and Cecily, her cousins Margaret of Clarence and Elizabeth Stafford, and her aunt the countess of Rivers—lived or spent a great deal of time in the royal household.[45] Two decades later, her sister Katherine Courteney was living at court and her cousin Elizabeth Stafford was one of her Ladies-in-Waiting.[46] Katherine of Aragon's household included five of Henry VIII's kin: Gertrude Courteney, marchioness of Exeter; Lady Elizabeth Stafford and her sister Anne; Margaret Pole, countess of Salisbury; and Mary Bourchier, countess of Essex.[47] At the end of the reign, Katherine Parr's attendants included her sister Anne, Lady Herbert; her first cousin, Lady Maud Lane; and a more distant cousin by marriage, Lady Elizabeth Tyrwhit, as well as Henry VIII's daughters; his daughter-in-law, the duchess of Richmond; and three of his nieces, Lady Margaret Douglas; Frances, marchioness of Dorset; and Eleanor, countess of Cumberland.[48]

The second group of Ladies-in-Waiting and Maids-of-Honor came from families with long traditions of service to the crown or with connections to such families. They constituted an even larger portion of the queen's servants than her relatives and were the women most likely to develop lifelong careers at court. Lady Jane (née Vaux) Guildford and Lady Margaret (née Bourchier) Bryan are two examples of women whose lengthy tenure in the royal household was rooted in their families' close multigenerational ties to the Tudor dynasty. Lady Jane's natal family, the Vauxs, supported the Lancastrians and Tudors throughout the fifteenth century. Her mother had been Margaret of Anjou's lady-in-waiting and remained with her until she died in exile.[49] After Henry VII's accession, Lady Margaret Beaufort raised Jane's brother Nicholas, who was created Lord Vaux in 1523. Jane married Sir Richard Guildford, controller of Henry VII's household, in the king's and queen's presence sometime before 1489. After she was widowed in 1506, she served all the female members of Henry VII's immediate family—his mother, wife, and both his daughters. When Lady Jane retired in the mid-1510s, Henry VIII granted her the substantial annuity of £60. Her only son, Henry, was a member of the king's Privy Chamber and Master of the Revels.[50]

Lady Margaret Bryan was the daughter of Sir Humphrey Bourchier and granddaughter of the first Lord Berners. Both her paternal grandparents were members of Elizabeth Woodville's household.[51] Margaret's brother, the second Lord Berners, a major literary figure in Henry VIII's circle, was also a leading servant of the crown.[52] Her two husbands also came from court families. The first, John Sandys, eldest son of Sir William, died young, but his brother William was a great favorite of Henry VIII, who visited him three times at the family seat in Hampshire and created him Lord Sandys.[53] Margaret's second husband, Sir Thomas Bryan, was Knight of the Body to both Henry VII and Henry VIII and Vice-Chamberlain of Katherine of Aragon's household.[54] Lady Bryan herself first served Katherine of Aragon and then became the governess of all Henry VIII's legitimate children.[55] The Bryans' prominence at court continued into the next generation. Their only son, Francis, was one of Henry VIII's closest friends, and both their daughters married members of the Privy Chamber.[56] Familial contexts of the kind exemplified in the lives of Jane Guildford and Margaret Bryan gave women in the queen's household greater access to royal patronage and favor than they would otherwise have had. At the same time, their positions reinforced their families' influence and gave them opportunities to establish their own identities as servants of the crown.

The third group of women in the queen's household, her maids, obtained their positions through the patronage of her Ladies-in-Waiting and the Gentlewomen of her Privy Chamber. When Lady Lisle began her campaign to place two daughters from her first marriage, Anne and Katherine Basset, in Jane Seymour's household, John Husee, her agent in London, told her firmly that it was "no meet suit for any man to move such matters, but only for such Ladies and women as be your friends."[57] Lord Montague's response to her request for assistance was that he would ask his mother, the countess of Salisbury, "to do her best" in the matter; he also advised Lord Lisle that "it will sooner take effect" if he wrote to his mother directly.[58] This method of recruitment gave the queen's servants control over a crucial area of court patronage and considerable power within the inner circle of court families. As Lady Lisle discovered, parents who wanted their daughters to become the queen's maids had to cultivate and reward the senior members of her entourage. Since the queen's ladies favored the daughters of their friends and kin, this method of recruitment reinforced the tendency of established court families to perpetuate their power in the household.

To forward her suit, Lady Lisle obtained the active assistance of two relatives at court, the countesses of Rutland and Sussex; two other members of the queen's Privy Chamber, Mistresses Horsman and Coffin; the queen's sister-in-law, Anne, Lady Beauchamp; and two other influential noblewomen, the countess of Salisbury and marchioness of Exeter. Endless gifts of wine, hawks, cherries, quails, conserves, and personal tokens accompanied the steady stream of letters she sent to remind them to pursue the appointments.[59] In June 1536, when Jane Seymour's household was first being formed, she sent tokens to the countesses of Salisbury and Rutland and to Mistresses Arundell and Horsman in an unsuccessful effort to secure places for her daughters among the new queen's maids.[60] The following spring she resumed her suit because she expected the marriage of one of the maids to create a vacancy in the queen's entourage. Between March and September, when Anne finally secured the coveted appointment, her mother sent tokens and presents to the countesses of Sussex and Rutland, Lady Beauchamp, and Mistress Coffin. In June, Lady Rutland thanked her for cherries, peascods, and "many other gifts." In another letter, she sent "hearty thanks" for a pipe of Gascon wine and two barrels of herring and assured Lady Lisle she would do everything she could to further her suit.[61]

The Lisles also approached and rewarded three men, Thomas Heneage, William Coffin, and the earl of Sussex, who were in daily contact with the queen's servants and could influence them indirectly.[62] Coffin and Heneage were members of Henry VIII's Privy Chamber; Coffin and Sussex's wives belonged to Jane Seymour's household. At Husee's prompting, Lady Lisle sent Sussex French and Gascon wine. When it arrived, he was so pleased, receiving it "wondrous thankfully," that Husee felt it would have been worth three times the price.[63] On another occasion, Coffin expressed "most hearty thanks" for a hawk the Lisles sent him and promised to do his "uttermost" on behalf of Lady Lisle and her daughters.[64] The men's role in promoting Lady Lisle's suit by influencing the queen's servants underscores the continual interaction between the two sides of the court and women's role in the patronage networks that flourished there.

In the end, the crucial offering proved to be a steady supply of quails for the queen herself, who developed a craving for them during her pregnancy.[65] On May 20, Sir John Russell, a member of the king's Privy Chamber, wrote to Lord Lisle at the king's commandment, ordering him to send "some fat quails" to court as soon as possible. "The Queen," he explained, "is very desirous to eat some but here be none to be gotton."[66] The first shipment arrived four days later. Husee reported that the king and queen were "right glad of them" and expected the shipments to continue.[67] Lisle complied, and quails continued to arrive during June and July.[68] Despite Husee's continual complaint that they should be fatter, his efforts produced the desired reward. On July 17, he announced triumphantly, "The Queen being at dinner, my Lady Rutland and my Lady Sussex being waiters on her Grace, her Grace chanced, eating of the quails, to common [i.e., speak] of your ladyship and of your daughters; so that such communication was uttered by the said ij [i.e., two] ladies that her Grace made grant to have one of your daughters; and the matter is thus concluded."[69] After more than a year of persistent, expensive effort, the countesses of Sussex and Rutland and the quails had succeeded.

Despite the queen's grant, two barriers remained. Since the queen did not know the Basset girls, she refused to proceed until she had seen Anne and Katherine in person to "know their manners, fashions and conditions, and take which of them shall like her Grace best."[70] Furthermore, before the appointment could be finalized, the king had to give his consent.[71] His ultimate authority in the selection of her maids underscored the fact that they were expected to contribute to the magnificence of *his* court and serve his political and diplomatic objectives, as well as to attend his wife. Lady Lisle sent her daughters to be inspected in late August. A few weeks later, Anne, whom the king and queen preferred, received the coveted office.[72]

Yorkist and early Tudor kings considered physical beauty young women's primary qualification for their appointments as Maids-of-Honor because their appearance was a crucial element in the impression their courts made on their contemporaries and a major topic in reports about them. A foreign visitor to the queen's chamber during Edward IV's reign commented specifically, "Nor have I ever seen such exceedingly beautiful maidens."[73] Edward Hall noted "the beauty of the English ladies" who accompanied Katherine of Aragon when she entered London for her marriage to Prince Arthur in 1501.[74] Two decades later he praised the "beautiful train of ladies" who assisted Katherine to receive Charles V when he visited England.[75] Gasparo Spinelli, a Venetian who attended festivities at Greenwich in 1527, wrote that the "beauty and apparel" of the women who were attending the banquet "caused me to think I was contemplating the choirs of angels" and that the eight "damsels" who performed in the disguising were of "such rare beauty as to be supposed goddesses rather than human beings."[76] In a revealing gesture, when Henry VIII took Anne Boleyn to meet Francis I in 1532, he removed the visors from the English female maskers to display "the ladies' beauties" to the French king.[77] As the king told Anne Basset bluntly in 1540 after he repeated his refusal to appoint her sister Katherine as one of the queen's maids, he "would have them that should be fair, and as he thought meet for the room."[78]

In addition to being beautiful, English kings expected Maids-of-Honor to be skilled at dancing, singing, playing musical instruments, and if possible, speaking French. Elizabeth of York, who later married Henry VII, danced with her father, Edward IV, and the duke of Buckingham during a court festivity when she was only 6.[79] Her daughter Mary fulfilled the ideal of the accomplished aristocratic woman in her youth and set the standard for women who aspired to become the queen's maids. In 1506 when she was only 11, she danced with another woman and played the lute to entertain Philip of Castile and her father. A contemporary noted that "she was of all folks there greatly praised that of her youth in everything she behaved herself so very well."[80] The chronicler Edward Hall focused on similar accomplishments when he explained why Henry VIII fell in love with Elizabeth Blount, then one of Katherine of Aragon's maids, describing her as "a fair damsel . . . which . . . in singing, in dancing, and in all goodly pastimes, excelled all others."[81] Likewise, according to a French observer, Anne Boleyn was "a fresh young damsel" who could sing and dance "passing excellent" and speak French "ornately and plain" in the years she attracted Henry VIII.[82]

A fourth group of women owed their appointments at court to their marriages to members of the king's household. Of twenty-two married women in Anne of Cleves's household, ten (45 percent) fell into this category.[83] Since only two of them were specifically identified as members of the queen's Privy Chamber, the others were probably part of the larger group who attended her in the Presence Chamber and participated in court ceremonies.[84] Of the ordinary members of Katherine Parr's household, just under two-thirds, fifteen of twenty-four, owed their positions to their husbands. Although no comparable lists exist for Henry VII's reign, a number of the women who appeared regularly at court, Ladies Daubney and Bray, for example, almost certainly owed their position to their spouses.[85]

Women who came to court with their husbands often developed their own identities and influence there since their spouses served in the king's households for long periods. Katherine Willoughby, who married the duke of Suffolk as his fourth wife at the age of 14, almost certainly arrived at court as a result of her marriage. By the time the duke died in 1545, however, she had become one of Katherine Parr's closest friends and had an independent position in Parr's household, where she emerged as a forceful advocate of religious reform.[86] Knights' wives with less powerful personalities also developed careers that survived their husbands' death. The widowed Katherine Edgecomb belonged to both Anne of Cleves's and Katherine Howard's households.[87] Mary Kingston served Anne of Cleves after Kingston's husband died in 1540; six years later she was still listed as an extraordinary member of Katherine Parr's household and retained the right to lodge at court.[88] She even received two small grants of monastic property during her widowhood.[89]

The final group of women in the royal household arrived not as the queen's servants but as the daughters or gentlewomen of her ladies. Young and unmarried, many of them participated actively in the social life of the court and made distinguished matches without ever assuming offices in the queen's service. Lady Margaret Bryan brought her two daughters and Lettice Peniston, whom she was raising, to court while she was Katherine of Aragon's servant.[90] Her daughters married two of Henry VIII's closest friends, Nicholas Carew and Henry Guildford, and were enthusiastic dancers and maskers at court during the first decade of his reign.[91] Lady Carew was a particular favorite of the king, who showered her with "beautiful diamonds and pearls and innumerable jewels."[92] Two other members of Katherine's household, Elizabeth Boleyn and Maud Parr, also brought their daughters to court.[93] Mary Boleyn married a member of Henry VIII's Privy Chamber, Sir William Carey, and later became the king's mistress. Her sister Anne performed in a court masque soon after she returned from her long residence in France in 1522. She became one of Katherine of Aragon's maids in 1527 and her successor in 1533.[94] Anne Parr served as one of Jane Seymour's Maids-of-Honor and had a long career attending Henry VIII's wives, including her sister Katherine.[95]

Mary Bullen Wife to W.ᵐ Carey Esq

A Woman said to be Mary Boleyn, wife of William Carey. Unknown artist, Private Collection. Photograph: Photographic Survey, Courtauld Institute of Art.

The queen's ladies, gentlewomen, and maids received substantial economic and political rewards for their service. Although in most cases the profits of their positions could not compete with those of the king's servants, Maids-of-Honor who became Henry VIII's wives or mistresses were exceptions to this generalization. Anne Boleyn, Jane Seymour, and Katherine Howard were all in their predecessor's households. Henry's two known mistresses, Mary Boleyn and Elizabeth Blount, were Katherine of Aragon's servants.[96] Henry rewarded Blount well after the birth of their illegitimate son, the duke of Richmond: he arranged her marriage to Sir Gilbert Tailbois, raised her husband to the peerage, granted the couple the manor of Rokeby, and endowed Elizabeth with a life interest in a significant portion of the Tailbois estates.[97] He was also generous to Mary Boleyn and her husband, William Carey, granting them land on a number of occasions between their marriage in 1520 and Carey's death in 1528. Carey also became keeper of Henry's palace at Beaulieu and other royal properties. After he died, his widow continued to collect his

annuity from the crown.[98] Although we tend to see women who received titles, land, and the advancement of their families in return for their sexual relationships with the king as engaged in a unique kind of exchange, they were
not very different from men like Charles Brandon or William Compton,
whose intense friendships with the king brought them and their families similar rewards. In a personal monarchy, such exchanges were at the heart of politics. Indeed, the opportunity to create personal relationships with the king
and queen that could be turned into land, office, and status was what drew
women and men to court in the first place.

The majority of the queen's Ladies-in-Waiting and Maids-of-Honor were
not, of course, involved sexually with the king and received much more modest compensation for their services, although it was still significant by contemporary standards. They received room, board, and stabling for their
horses at court; official liveries at Christmas and Whitsuntide; and special
clothing for coronations and royal funerals.[99] Since their high rank meant that
they themselves required gentlewomen servants, members of the queen's
household brought their own attendants to court with them. They were also
entitled to room and board at the crown's expense.[100] Because the numbers
of these servants and the consequent cost to the crown had an inevitable tendency to grow, the government periodically embarked on reforms to reduce
the size of the royal household. Edward IV's Black Book limited the number
of gentle servants allowed to members of the king's household on the basis of
their rank and office. It was much vaguer about the queen's servants, stating
simply that they should have "in service and livery somewhat less in everything" than equivalent officers on the king's side of the court.[101] The Eltham
Ordinances of 1526 were much more specific about the number of servants
and horses the queen's servants were permitted to keep. The numbers reflected their rank and whether or not their husbands were also at court.[102] In
the 1530s Ladies of the Privy Chamber could keep two gentlewomen in the
queen's household; Maids-of-Honor could keep one.[103] These limitations
were apparently unenforceable, and the Ladies-in-Waiting were tacitly allowed to keep one more gentlewoman than their official allotment. In 1537,
for instance, the countess of Sussex refused to take her cousin, Katherine Basset, into her chamber because she already had one servant more than she was
permitted.[104]

In addition to payments in kind, members of the queen's household received annual fees or wages. Their fees were calibrated to their rank, preserving a hierarchy among the queen's attendants that corresponded to the status
of their respective families. Elizabeth Woodville paid her Ladies-in-Waiting
£40 per annum if they were noble and £20 if they were not. Her Maids-of-
Honor earned between 5 marks and £10. Fees in Elizabeth of York's household ranged from the high of £33 6s. 8d. granted to Elizabeth Stafford, daughter of a duke, to the low of £5 given to Anne Brown, daughter of a knight.[105]

In 1529, Katherine of Aragon paid Elizabeth Blount, a knight's daughter, £5, and Lady Anne Grey, the first marquess of Dorset's daughter, £13 2s. 8d.[106] Jane Seymour granted two of her Maids-of-Honor, Mary Zouche and Anne Basset, £10.[107] Although no contemporary reckoning of the total monetary value of offices in the queen's household exists, the government provided Anne Basset with an annuity of £26 13s. 4d., more than twice her fee, at Edward VI's accession, which may represent the real value of her position.[108]

Monetary fees and payments in kind represented only a portion of the benefits of a position in the queen's household. Many of its members also received valuable gifts and grants from both the king and queen. On a number of occasions, Henry VII and Henry VIII gave clothing, one of the most expensive items in the aristocratic budget, to their wives' attendants. In 1497, for example, Henry VII gave Lady Anne Percy, one of Elizabeth of York's ladies, two gowns, a kirtle, a bonnet, a doublet, and some smaller items, the better part of a new wardrobe.[109] His son, Henry VIII, gave Mary Jerningham, one of Katherine of Aragon's gentlewomen, a tawny velvet gown trimmed with fur.[110] Wine was apparently another favorite gift. Edward IV and Henry VII rewarded Lady Elizabeth Darcy's long tenure in the royal nursery with the grant of an annual tun of wine to be received at the port of London.[111] Henry VIII made a similar gift to Eleanor Verney, who had served his parents and sisters, and to Lady Margaret Bryan.[112] Henry also sent New Year's gifts to many of the queens' servants and occasionally granted them wardships and land.[113] The kings' gifts indicated that they attached considerable value to the service their queens received from their ladies and gentlewomen and to the women's contribution to the success of the court as the political and visual center of the monarchy. In some cases, their gifts also reflected the kings' personal relationships with women who resided in the royal household for long periods of time.

Documents from the 1540s indicate that Katherine Howard and Katherine Parr also rewarded their household servants with valuable gifts. An inventory of Katherine Howard's jewels taken after her arrest noted that she had given a girdle of gold or goldsmith's work to Lady Baynton and a pair of beads to Lady Margaret Douglas as New Year's gifts, a second pair of beads to Lady Mary Carew as a wedding present, and still a third pair as a token to Lady Rutland.[114] Katherine Parr gave velvet gowns to three kinswomen in her household, Ladies Anne Herbert, Elizabeth Tyrwhit, and Maud Lane.[115] On other occasions she sent bucks, a prestigious gift, to her favorites.[116] Shortly after her marriage to the king, she used her influence with Henry to secure land worth just under £1,000 per annum for her widowed cousin and Lady-in-Waiting, Maud Lane.[117]

Henry VII and Henry VIII also often awarded annuities or pensions to the queens' ladies and maids. They were the most valuable monetary benefits available to the women over and above their regular fees and perquisites.

Henry VII granted Mary Roos, one of his wife's ladies, an annuity of 40 marks in 1496, which Henry VIII increased to £53 6s. 8d. The crown was still paying it in 1540.[118] This was only one of the cases in which Henry VIII was particularly generous to women who had served his parents and sisters. He awarded pensions ranging from 10 marks to £60 per annum to Elizabeth Catesby, Jane Guildford, Elizabeth Pechey, Katherine Vaux, Dorothy Verney, and Eleanor Verney for this reason.[119] After Katherine of Aragon's death, he granted an annuity of £40 to one of her attendants, Margaret, Lady Grey.[120] Soon after Jane Seymour died, he gave her maid, Mary Zouche, £10 a year "until [she was] married or otherwise provided for."[121] The wording of many of the grants indicates that they were awarded when the recipient retired from the queen's household.

For Maids-of-Honor, the most valuable form of royal patronage was not monetary at all but rather the king's and queen's assistance in arranging or financing their marriages. Royal support enabled them to make better matches, that is, to marry men of higher social and political status and greater wealth than their families could have arranged for them. Given the importance of first marriages in establishing aristocratic women's material and social positions for the rest of their lives, this was an incomparable benefit. In 1511, Henry VIII attended the wedding of Lady Anne Percy, who had served his mother and wife, to William, earl of Arundel, and gave her 100 marks as a present.[122] In the same year, the queen provided her maid, Anne Weston, with a dowry of 200 marks when Weston married another of the queen's servants, Ralph Verney the younger.[123] Three years later Henry financed the marriage of the queen's gentlewoman Mabel Clifford to William Fitzwilliam, one of his Gentleman Ushers, with the grant of a manor in Staffordshire and an annuity of £100.[124] The royal couple were even more generous to the queen's favorite Lady-in-Waiting, Mary Salinas. Katherine negotiated the contract for Salinas's marriage to William, Lord Willoughby, in 1516 and gave her a dowry of 1,100 marks "in tender consideration of the long and right acceptable service to her grace done by the said Mary Salinas to her singular contentacion and pleasure." In addition, the king granted her the reversion of four manors in Lincolnshire as a wedding present.[125] Two years later, Henry promised land worth 100 marks per annum to Sir Thomas Fettiplace and Elizabeth Carew, daughter of Sir Richard and sister of his favorite, Sir Nicholas.[126]

Patronage of this kind continued throughout the reign, although less frequently than one might expect since Henry VIII's later queens held their positions for relatively short periods. Anne Boleyn and the king probably sponsored Anne Savage's marriage to Thomas, Lord Berkeley, a few months after their own wedding to reward her for attending the queen at their ceremony.[127] In March 1537, John Husee reported that the marriage of one of Jane Seymour's maids, Jane Ashley, to Peter Mewtas, a member of the king's Privy

Chamber, was being delayed because "it dependeth on the King's goodness to look towards their living, and that, men thinketh, will be at leisure." Despite Husee's pessimism, Henry fulfilled his promise and the couple were married by the fall.[128]

Whatever their marital status, women in the queen's household benefited from the opportunities that regular contact with the king and his favorites gave them to secure royal patronage for themselves and their families, friends, and clients. In 1522, for example, the king restored all the forfeited goods, chattels, and lands of one Gawain Lancaster "on the supplication" of Lady Maud Parr, then a member of Katherine of Aragon's household.[129] Women in the royal household often competed successfully in the market for the crown's wards. Maud Parr; Maud Lane; Jane, countess of Southampton; and Katherine, duchess of Suffolk, all succeeded in purchasing their sons' wardships,[130] while Anne Weston, Katherine Edgecomb, and the countesses of Salisbury and Devon bought wardships to secure mates for their children or to resell for profit.[131] In other cases, women's petitions touched on more delicate matters. In 1538, after Sir Nicholas Carew was executed and attainted for treason, for example, his mother-in-law and widow, both longtime figures at court, successfully petitioned the king for an adequate living for his widow and children.[132]

Lady Lisle's daughter, Anne Basset, became her mother's regular intermediary with the king within a few years of her arrival at court, justifying the financial investment her mother had made to secure her appointment. On one occasion, she reported that she had "declared unto the King's Highness all things, as your ladyship willed me to do, so that his Grace took the same in right good part, accepting your good will and toward mind therein."[133] At another time, she wrote that she did not dare ask the king to send her mother a token "for fear lest how his Grace would have taken it" and that despite her efforts, he had once again refused to appoint her sister Katherine to the queen's household.[134] Anne's judgment about approaching and responding to Henry was obviously sound. By 1542, she stood so high in his favor that a Spanish observer attributed her stepfather's release from the Tower of London to his affection for her, a clear example of the fact that the maids could and did acquire political influence through their personal relationships with the king.[135]

Although Edward IV's Black Book said explicitly that the queen's service "must be nigh like unto the king," drawing conclusions about the duties of her female servants from ordinances for the king's household is not straightforward.[136] The Eltham Ordinances of 1526 carefully listed the duties of the Gentlemen, Ushers, and Grooms of the king's Privy Chamber but did not do so in the case of the queen's Ladies, Gentlewomen, and Maids.[137] Although they undoubtedly performed some of the functions of the men in the king's Privy Chamber, it is difficult to draw conclusions about their respective positions. When John Husee reported that Anne Basset had been appointed one of Jane Seymour's maids, he noted precisely that she would occupy "the room of a yeoman usher."[138] Yet it is unlikely that she had the same responsibilities as the king's Yeomen Ushers, whose primary function was to regulate entrance into the outer chambers of his household, a task unsuited to women.[139] In fact, a detailed list of Katherine of Aragon's servants indicated that she had two male Yeomen and Gentlemen Ushers of her own, as well as male Grooms and Pages in her Privy Chamber.[140] Hence Husee's comment probably referred to Anne's status and rewards rather than her responsibilities.

All the queen's female servants attended her personally, spending much of their time with her in the Privy Chamber and elsewhere in the court and accompanying her when she moved from palace to palace or went on her summer progress. Presumably they helped her to dress, carried out other intimate tasks inappropriate for male servants, and provided her with companionship.[141] The highest ranking of her ladies, the wives or daughters of the nobility, served her at table.[142] If, as seems likely, the situation was similar on the king's and queen's side of the court, members of her Privy Chamber spent much of their time waiting on the queen's pleasure for tasks to perform. While they did so, they were expected to "have a vigilant and reverent respect and eye" in order to recognize by her "look or countenance what lacketh, or is . . . [her] pleasure to be had or done."[143]

In the long hours they spent together, the queen and her ladies devoted considerable time and energy to planning their wardrobes and those of her maids. The enormous amount of attention that contemporary chroniclers and foreign visitors paid to their clothing reflected its importance in contributing to the visual splendor of the court and representing the queen's status as the highest ranking female in the kingdom.[144] Because particular fabrics and colors were recognized signifiers of status, English sumptuary legislation carefully regulated what men could wear, according to their rank, but explicitly exempted women and household servants. As dependents, they were expected to dress in accordance with their husbands' or employers' degree rather than their own.[145] Queens required their ladies and maids to wear the luxury fabrics and colors appropriate to their mistresses' status. In this cultural context, to dress inadequately was to risk one's position at court. In 1476, for instance, Elizabeth Stonor told her husband that Edward IV's sister, the duchess of Suffolk, was displeased because Stonor's sisters were "no better arrayed" and that "without they be otherwise arrayed . . . she may not keep them."[146] Decades later, Katherine Basset could not accompany her mistress, the countess of Rutland, to Jane Seymour's funeral because she lacked an appropriate black gown.[147]

The *Lisle Letters* provide the most detailed evidence about the effort and money expended on the wardrobes of the queen's attendants. From the day

Anne Basset entered Jane Seymour's service and her sister Katherine entered the service of the countess of Rutland, John Husee's letters to their mother were filled with directions about the clothes they needed. He informed her immediately that Anne "must have such apparel as is . . . written in the . . . book . . . 'pointed by my Lady Rutland and Sussex.'" A velvet bonnet and frontlet were absolute necessities and could not wait.[148] To ensure that Anne was properly dressed until her new apparel arrived, Lady Sussex had already given her a crimson damask kirtle and sleeves. Two weeks later Husee wrote that Anne needed a black satin gown, another of velvet, and a bonnet or two with frontlets and an edge of pearl. At Lady Sussex's command, he had even ordered a worsted gown without awaiting her mother's consent. He reported further that the queen and her ladies had criticized Anne's smocks and sleeves because they were "too coarse" and asked Lady Lisle to send finer material for new ones. Fortunately, the countess of Sussex had decided to have Anne's old gowns made into kirtles (i.e., skirts or skirts and bodices) to save some expense.[149]

For Anne, these clothes were only the beginning. Within weeks, she required a black velvet gown turned up with yellow satin for Edward VI's christening, a new satin gown for the queen's churching, and a lion tawny velvet gown for Christmas.[150] When Jane Seymour died, Anne and the other members of her household assumed "mourning gear."[151] Nonetheless, she still needed a new lion tawny satin gown for Christmas because "it was uncertain how long the King's pleasure should be that they [the dead queen's servants] should wear black." Lady Sussex maintained firmly that "it was not meet that she should be without ij [i.e., two] changes of silk besides her velvet gown."[152]

Although Katherine attended the countess of Rutland at court, she dressed less grandly than her sister because her mistress was a countess rather than the queen. When Husee began to assemble her wardrobe for Christmas, for example, he noted, in clear contrast to Anne's requirements, "My Lady Rutland will in no wise that I make her a satin gown, but only a gown of tawny chamlet, with velvet of the same color turned up."[153] There is no better illustration of the association between rank and fabric and the practice of household servants dressing in accordance with their employers' degree rather than their own. Nonetheless, even Katherine required some new clothes. Husee purchased a pair of tawny satin sleeves for her almost immediately.[154] To supplement a velvet gown from Lady Sussex, her black satin gown had to be refurbished and two of her old gowns made into kirtles. Like Anne, she needed a new bonnet and frontlets and better cloth for her sleeves and smocks. She also had to have a kirtle of white taffeta, a pair of sleeves of white satin, a frontlet of crimson velvet lined with crimson satin, a gold brooch for her collar, and sleeves and a French white partlet for Christmas.[155] The cost of these wardrobes to Katherine's and Anne Basset's mother, Lady

Lisle, represented a considerable expense over and above her initial expenditures on securing their places in the queen's household, and is another indication of the value she and her contemporaries attached to women's careers at court.

In addition to planning their wardrobes, the queen and her women spent considerable time doing fancy needlework, an essential accomplishment for aristocratic women whether they were at court or not. Margaret Beaufort made an embroidery that showed the descent of the St. Johns, to whom she was related, as a wedding present for John St. John in 1498.[156] Elizabeth of York worked on a sampler in the last year of her life.[157] Katherine of Aragon and her women helped to make standards, badges, and banners for Henry VIII's wars in the early 1510s.[158] Henry's next queen, Anne Boleyn, was just as skilled with a needle.[159] She and her ladies filled Hampton Court with their handiwork.[160]

The queen's ladies and gentlewomen often gave members of the royal family clothing they had sewn or finished themselves. In 1533, the countess of Rutland purchased gold and silk to embroider a pair of sleeves and a frontlet for New Year's gifts for the king and queen. The next year she gave Anne Boleyn six plights of fine lawn for sleeves with bands of pearls of gold, "besides working the same." She sent Henry a shirt collar, "embroidered," in 1537.[161] Lady Guildford, Lady Kingston, and Mistress Heneage all gave Henry VIII shirts they had made as New Year's gifts.[162] After Princess Mary was reconciled with her father in 1536, members of the queen's household often gave her needlework as gifts. In 1543 she received "wrought" sleeves from the duchess of Suffolk, the countess of Hertford, and Lady Edgecomb.[163]

In a lighter vein, the queen and her servants amused themselves by playing cards, dice, chess, and ninepins and engaging in early forms of bowling.[164] They almost always gambled when they indulged in games of this sort.[165] Even Henry VII's mother, the pious Lady Margaret Beaufort, played chess and cards for money.[166] His wife, Elizabeth of York, gambled at dice.[167] A famous anecdote in which Katherine of Aragon remarked to Anne Boleyn, "You have good hap to stop at a king, my lady Anne, but you are not like others, you will have all or none," places the two rivals playing cards in the queen's chamber.[168]

The queen's ladies and maids were equally, if not more, enthusiastic about dancing. Virtually all the contemporary accounts of activities in her chamber mentioned their dancing together whether they were by themselves or entertaining visitors. When Henry VII and Prince Arthur visited Katherine of Aragon shortly after her arrival in England, "she and her ladies let call their minstrels, and with right goodly behavior and manner they solaced themselves with the disport of dancing."[169] After Elizabeth of York met Katherine for the first time at Baynard's Castle in London, they enjoyed themselves "with pleasant and goodly communication, dancing, and disports."[170] In addition to functioning as recreation, dancing in the queens' quarters was almost certainly the occasion for teaching their daughters and other young girls at court this "essential courtly skill" in a familiar and private setting.[171] All the royal princesses were able to perform for visitors when they were still quite young: Elizabeth of York was 6 when she danced with her father in front of Louis Gruthuyse, Henry VII's daughter Mary was 11 when she danced with one of her mother's ladies for Philip of Castille, and Henry VIII's daughter Mary was only 6 when she danced for the Imperial ambassadors.[172]

Members of the queen's household also diverted themselves by listening to and playing music. Lady Margaret Beaufort and the Yorkist and early Tudor queens all maintained their own minstrels, professional musicians who played the lute, harp, and rebec.[173] In addition to providing music for dancing, the minstrels probably put on informal concerts and taught the royal children and other young people at court. The early Tudor princesses were all accomplished performers. Henry VII bought lutes for his daughters when they were quite young. During her progress northward for her marriage to James IV of Scotland, Margaret, then 14, played the clavichords and lute for her future husband.[174] At the age of 11, her sister Mary was proficient enough to entertain Philip of Castille on the lute and claregalles.[175] Henry VIII's daughter Mary was even younger when she played the spinet for the Imperial ambassadors in 1522; she was also skilled on the lute, harpsichord, and virginals.[176]

As we have seen, musical skills were among the requirements for appointments as the queen's Maids-of-Honor, and ambitious members of the aristocracy paid close attention to their daughters' musical educations. Contemporaries commented favorably on Elizabeth Blount's singing and Anne Boleyn's ability to sing to her own accompaniment on the lute and to play the harp and rebec.[177] Katherine Howard also played the virginals and lute.[178] Their accomplishments drew attention because of their intimate relationships with the king, but they were hardly unique among young women groomed for careers at court. Lady Lisle's daughter Mary studied the lute and virginals when she was being educated in France for appointment to the queen's service; she also wanted to learn to play the spinet and regals.[179] Dorothy Long, the daughter of Sir Richard, a member of the Privy Chamber, played the lute.[180] Given their proficiency, the queen's ladies and maids undoubtedly played instruments and sang for their amusement or to entertain their mistress. But they also used their musical skills to contribute to ceremonies and performances at court, which gave their accomplishments public, as well as private, importance. At one of the disguisings to celebrate Katherine of Aragon's and Prince Arthur's marriage in 1501, for instance, twelve "ladies and women of honor" played on such instruments as the clavichord, dulcimer, and harpsichord "so sweetly" that one observer thought it the best music "that ever was heard in England of long season." Another observer described the women, who also sang, as having "angelic voices."[181]

Although the queen and her attendants spent a great deal of time in her chambers, they played highly visible roles on diplomatic and ceremonial occasions at court. Beautiful, high-born damsels were an essential feature of the magnificent court of the late medieval and early modern imagination. On a practical level, too, they contributed to the atmosphere of friendship and goodwill that facilitated diplomacy. When they moved from the queen's Privy Chamber to the public areas of the court, therefore, their appearance and accomplishments took on political meaning and contributed to the success of the Yorkist and early Tudor monarchies. Their presence in luxury fabrics and dazzling costumes at royal christenings, weddings, coronations, banquets, and tournaments was essential for creating and sustaining the image of the court as magnificent, while their performance with the king and his favorite courtiers in disguisings and other court entertainments played an essential part in fifteenth- and sixteenth-century diplomacy. From their personal points of view, participating in these events gave the queen's attendants direct access to the king and to royal patronage, the primary benefit they and their families anticipated from their positions. The queen's maids gained the additional advantage of appearing advantageously in highly visible positions at the center of the aristocratic marriage market.

Evidence about the ceremonial and celebratory life of the court, and even more about the participation of the queen and the members of her household in it, is extremely uneven for the Yorkist and early Tudor periods. Nonetheless, it is clear that Queen Elizabeth Woodville and her household contributed to the visual splendor and decorum of Edward IV's court. Leo of Rozmital, brother of the queen of Bohemia, arrived in England in 1466 and observed the state dinner following the queen's churching. Gabriel Tetzel, who recorded the event, waxed enthusiastically about the room where she dined, probably her Presence Chamber, an "unbelievably costly apartment"; the lavishness of the food served her; and the formality and length, three hours, of the meal. The queen sat alone on a golden chair. Her mother and the king's sister were present but stood at some distance until she was served the first fish course, and kneeled to reply if she addressed them. The ladies and maidens serving her stayed on their knees the whole time she ate. Most remarkably, "everyone was silent, and not a word was spoken." During the dancing that followed, Queen Elizabeth remained seated and her mother continued to kneel before her. At one point, the king's sister entertained the guests by performing "a stately dance" with two dukes. When all the dancers were tired, the festivities concluded with a concert by the king's choir.[182]

Six years later, when Louis, Lord Gruthuyse, who had sheltered Edward IV during his short exile in the Netherlands, visited England, the king took him to meet the queen on his first evening at Windsor Castle. The men found her and her ladies playing games and dancing, again probably in her Presence Chamber. The next day the queen invited him to "a great banquet" followed

by dancing. At the conclusion of the evening, the king, the queen, and her attendants conducted him to the luxurious apartment prepared for him in a
manner worthy of romance literature.[183]

Queen Elizabeth and the members of her household were enthusiastic
participants in chivalric, courtly culture. In the spring of 1466, when her
brother, Anthony, Lord Scales, was visiting her, for example, her ladies tied a
garter of gold and pearls around his thigh and dropped a little roll of parchment tied with golden thread into his hat, which was lying on the floor. Scales
took the parchment to the king, who opened it and read the challenge. The
ladies wanted Scales to be their champion in a two-day tournament against a
noblemen "of four lineages and without reproach," in which he would fight
on horseback with spears and swords the first day and on foot with spears,
axes, and daggers the second. The king gave his approval and Scales challenged Anthony, the Bastard of Burgundy, to what became one of the most
famous tournaments of the period. It was held in London in June 1467. At its
conclusion, the king and queen and scores of noblewomen attended the banquet celebrating the combatants' valor.[184]

Despite his reputation for thrift and seriousness, Henry VII was as sensitive
as Edward IV to the importance of a magnificent court in establishing the
legitimacy of his dynasty. Festivities at court continued to center on chivalric
themes and required the participation of his wife, Elizabeth of York, and her
ladies. In 1488, on St. George's Day, for example, the queen and her mother-in-
law, Lady Margaret Beaufort, attended services at Windsor dressed in the same
gowns of the garter as the king and lords and joined in the subsequent proces-
sion around the cloister. On Twelfth Night 1494, the king and queen, her ladies,
and the French and Spanish ambassadors watched the most elaborate disguising yet held at the English court. The production, which interrupted an inter-
lude being put on by the King's Players, included three costumed figures, St.
George, a lady, and a dragon; a speech; and an anthem by the singers of the
King's Chapel. When the miniplay was completed, twelve disguised gentlemen
and ladies, probably members of the queen's household, performed an elaborate series of dances.[185] Later that year, the court celebrated Prince Henry's
creation as duke of York with a series of tournaments. Three of the queen's
maids, Ladies Elizabeth Stafford, Anne Percy, and Anne Nevill, participated in
the pageantry surrounding the fighting. Each evening after supper and dancing, they presented the winners to the king's elder daughter, Margaret, who
awarded the prizes. On the third and last day of the jousts, they also led three of
the knights into the ring. For this occasion, they wore white damask gowns
with crimson velvet sleeves and circlettes of gold and precious stones on their
heads.[186] Sixteen years later, Elizabeth and her attendants accompanied Henry
VII and the male members of the court to Calais to meet Archduke Philip of
Burgundy. Following a rich banquet, the archduke danced with "the ladies of
England" before he took leave of the royal couple.[187]

From the outset, Henry VIII's reign saw an increase in the frequency and lavishness of court festivities. The king's enthusiasm about participating in tournaments and disguisings and his acute awareness of their importance in maintaining his image vis-à-vis his continental rivals meant that they grew in number and scale after he ascended the throne. At the same time, the growing efficiency and bureaucratization of government, the spread of printing, and the growing hold of the monarchy on the sixteenth-century imagination produced a dramatic increase in the quantity and quality of contemporary accounts—ambassadors' reports, chronicles, and financial records—of events at court. As in the previous reigns, women were essential participants because performances at court continued to be based on chivalric and romantic themes. The Westminster Tournament of 1511, held in honor of the queen to celebrate the birth of the king's first (and very short-lived) son, marked a major event in the life of the royal family. The festivities included an elaborate pageant and masque performed by the king, five of his closest friends, and six women. The guest list included a number of foreign ambassadors, which underscored the diplomatic significance of such spectacles.[188]

Throughout Henry VIII's reign, his queens and their household servants played an essential role in the conduct of foreign relations. Their presence created an amicable environment that encouraged successful negotiations and deflected attention from irreconcilable differences that were being conveniently ignored. They also provided pleasant diversions for members of foreign delegations who had little to do while ambassadors and other key figures were conducting business behind closed doors. Festivities in 1517, 1518, and 1522 are among the best documented of these occasions. In July 1517, Henry VIII brought the Imperial ambassador to Katherine of Aragon's chamber after dinner and "made her and all those ladies pay him as much honor as if he had been a sovereign." For the occasion, the queen had arranged "amusements of every description, the chief of which, however, and the most approved by his Majesty, was the instrumental music of the reverend Master Dionysius Memo."[189] A few days later, the king sponsored a tournament and hosted a banquet at Greenwich. Many of the women seated at the head table were or had been members of Katherine of Aragon's household.[190] When the banquet was over, the "chief ladies" joined in the dancing.[191]

In the following year, while the king and Cardinal Wolsey were negotiating the Treaty of Universal Peace with the French ambassadors, other members of the French delegation "danced and passed the time in the queen's chamber with [her] ladies and gentlewomen."[192] When the agreement was finally signed, Cardinal Wolsey hosted an elaborate banquet. The entertainment included a disguising led by the king and his sister, the French Queen. Of the eleven other women who performed that day, four (Lady Guildford the younger, Lady Carew, Elizabeth Blount, and Lady St. Leger), were members of the queen's household and five others (Anne Carew, Anne Brown, Anne

Wotton, Mary Fiennes, and Margaret Bruges), were probably Maids-of-Honor or young women who were living in her ladies' chambers.[193]

A major realignment occurred in March 1522 when Henry and Wolsey deserted the French for an alliance with the Holy Roman Empire that was to be sealed by a marriage between Princess Mary and Charles V. The queen, who was the emperor's aunt, was enthusiastic about the match and took every opportunity to show Mary off to the Imperial representatives in London.[194] While the negotiations were proceeding, Wolsey threw a banquet for the ambassadors and king, followed by an allegorical pageant and masque. The female performers included the king's sister Mary, the countess of Devonshire, Anne Boleyn (recently returned from France), her sister Mary Carey, Jane Parker (George Boleyn's future wife), Mistress Brown (probably the Anne mentioned in the previous paragraph), and a Mistress Danet.[195] In June, Charles V himself arrived to complete negotiations for a treaty binding England to join him in a war against France.[196] Queen Katherine, Princess Mary, and their attendants greeted him warmly at Greenwich as he journeyed to London. Two days of tournaments, banquets, and disguisings followed. After supper on the first evening, the ladies, many almost certainly the queen's servants, danced for the emperor.[197]

Henry VIII's enthusiasm for tournaments and masques meant that he frequently staged them to divert himself and his friends even when there were no major diplomatic meetings, events in the royal family, or holidays to celebrate.[198] In November 1510, for example, he sponsored a two-day tournament at Richmond. He invited the Spanish ambassador and some visitors from the Imperial court to attend the banquet held at its conclusion and then to join him in the queen's chamber. There he and fifteen companions appeared in costume as mummers and "played" (i.e., gambled) with the queen and the foreigners.[199] A concert by some minstrels followed. Then the king, who had had time to change his costume, returned with five other disguised men and six disguised ladies to dance. After the performance, the queen removed the men's, but not apparently the ladies', masks. The sequence of events, in which the disguising was separated entirely from the tournament held earlier in the day, became the model for masques at Henry VIII's court. From then on they were independent productions and were usually performed after supper to entertain the king and his guests.[200]

Festivities of this sort frequently began or ended in the queen's chamber.[201] During the Christmas revels at Greenwich in 1514, for instance, four masked lords and ladies who had staged a mummery retired to Katherine of Aragon's chamber after their performance to dance "a great season." When they had finished and taken off their visors, the queen "heartily thanked the king's grace for her goodly pastime, and kissed him."[202] On Candlemas Eve, 1520, shortly after Katherine and the king returned together from evensong, a trumpet announced the arrival of four gentlemen dressed in blue damask bordered with gold and a richly dressed lady seated in a wagon. She read a challenge in which the four gentlemen undertook "for the love of their ladies" to answer all comers at a tilt to be held at a time appointed by the king.[203] Two years later, Henry and some of his favorites staged a masque in Katherine's chamber during the Christmas holidays.[204]

Wherever they were held, disguisings and the general dancing that followed involved the younger women who were living in the queen's household. In 1510, for example, the female disguisers included the king's sister Mary, who lived at court before her marriage to Louis XII; Margaret Bryan; and Mistress Knyvett. Three young women who belonged to Katherine's household, Margaret Bryan (now married to Henry Guildford), Elizabeth Carew, and Elizabeth Blount, were active maskers and dancers throughout the 1514–1515 Christmas season.[205] Carew and her husband performed in a play at court the following Candlemas.[206] In 1527, the French ambassadors reported that Henry VIII had danced with Anne Boleyn, then a Maid-of-Honor, in the queen's chamber at Greenwich.[207]

Because the performers in disguisings spent considerable amounts of time in rehearsing their semidramatic roles and dances and planning their costumes, the emergence of the masque as Henry VIII's favorite indoor activity vastly increased the potential benefits of residence in the royal household for the Maids-of-Honor and other young women living there. Those who participated interacted informally with the king and his closest friends on a regular basis. A postscript in a letter from Charles Brandon to Henry VIII in 1514 reveals the kind of friendship that was probably common between the women and the king's favorites but is rarely recorded in surviving documents. Brandon asked the king to remember him "to all my old fellows, both men and women; and I beseech your grace to tell Mistress Blount and Mistress Carew, the next time I shall write unto them or send them tokens, they shall either write to me or send me tokens again."[208]

The most enthusiastic dancers and maskers, Elizabeth Blount, Anne and Mary Boleyn, Elizabeth and Margaret Bryan, Mary Fiennes, and Anne Knyvett, to name the most prominent, gained substantially from the attention they attracted and their personal contact with Henry. They were the young women in the royal household who made the most illustrious court marriages. The king also often permitted them to keep the costumes and jewels they wore for their performances. In 1510, for example, he gave his sister and Mistresses Bryan and Knyvett the apparel they wore at the disguising at Richmond.[209] After the masque at Beaulieu in 1519, he rewarded the female performers with "many brooches and proper gifts."[210] Three years later, Henry presented the eight women who participated in the masque for the Imperial ambassadors with their costumes.[211] Given the luxury fabrics and jewels used for the clothes created for productions at court, these were extremely valuable gifts.

After 1530, the number of masques and revels at court declined precipitously. The aging of the king; the death of William Cornish, who had designed and produced most of the disguisings; the ruthless politics and bloodbaths that destroyed so many of the king's closest friends and drove others from court, all contributed to this change. Even lavish diplomatic festivities disappeared almost completely because of Henry's isolation following his divorce from Katherine of Aragon, marriage to Anne Boleyn, and break with Rome. Henry's visit to France with Anne Boleyn in 1532 is something of an exception, but even then the scale of activities did not compare with earlier court ceremonies.[212] According to the Venetian ambassador, twenty maids attended Anne.[213] In general, however, women at court were much more peripheral than they had been during Henry's youth and early middle age.

In the final years of the reign, Queen Katherine Parr occasionally entertained foreign ambassadors and visitors because Henry was ill and confined to the Privy Chamber. But none of the festivities she hosted compared to those mounted in the 1510s and 1520s. In 1543–1544, when the duke of Nájera visited England, the queen received him and his party with her brother William, recently created earl of Essex, and Henry, earl of Surrey. After Nájera's audience with the king, Katherine and her ladies entertained him and his entourage with dancing.[214] Two and a half years later, in August 1546, the Admiral of France arrived to formalize the last major peace treaty of the reign. The king signed and swore to the agreement in the chapel at Hampton Court but was too immobile and ill to join in the subsequent celebration, which included "rich masks every night with the Queen and ladies, with dancing." A contemporary list makes clear that the "ladies" were members of her household.[215]

The personal and familial connections that brought women to court to pursue careers in the royal household meant that their interest in politics centered on the pursuit of patronage for themselves, their kin, and their clients. In the 1530s, however, Henry VIII's break with Rome and divorce from Katherine of Aragon produced an unprecedented situation that propelled some of the women in the royal household into high politics (as historians have conventionally understood the term). The king's decisions and demands for obedience forced Katherine's servants and friends to choose between her and their allegiance to him, a decision that often created conflicts among their familial, dynastic, and religious loyalties. As we have seen, many members of her household moved from her service to that of her successors without leaving any discernible traces in the extant records of difficulty about their decisions. In contrast, a small group of the queen's long-term servants and friends—the king's sister, Mary, duchess of Suffolk (the French Queen); Elizabeth, duchess of Norfolk; Gertrude, marchioness of Exeter; and Margaret, countess of Salisbury, for example—openly opposed both the divorce and religious reform. Although there is no way of ascertaining the relative weight of personal, familial, and religious issues among their motives, their ties with the queen undoubtedly helped to determine their response.[216]

In some cases, loyalty to Katherine of Aragon produced open conflicts between her servants and their fathers or husbands, despite the overwhelming weight of traditional injunctions that women should submit to male authority in the family. These women had evidently developed a sufficient sense of autonomy to make independent choices when they faced the successive dynastic crises of the 1530s and 1540s. Unlike her husband, for example, the king's sister, Mary, duchess of Suffolk, avoided the court and refused to accompany her brother when he crossed the channel to introduce Anne Boleyn to Francis I.[217] Elizabeth, duchess of Norfolk, was driven from court for defending Katherine of Aragon at the very time her husband was actively pushing Henry's marriage to Anne Boleyn.[218] In contrast to her husband, who temporized, Anne, Lady Hussey, emerged as an outspoken opponent of the divorce and break with Rome. She was imprisoned in the Tower because she continued to address Henry's daughter Mary as princess after it became illegal to do so. After her release, she remained obdurate, refusing to take the Oath of Supremacy and openly supporting the Lincolnshire rebellion in 1536.[219] In that same year, the role of Jane, Lady Rochford, as a key witness against Anne and George Boleyn, her sister-in-law and husband, provided a dramatic example of the fracturing of aristocratic families under the pressure of dynastic and religious crisis. Although her motives for such vindictive behavior are obscure, one factor may well have been her prior relationship with Katherine of Aragon, whom she had served from at least the early 1520s.[220]

Women who came to court with Anne Boleyn and her successors escaped the personal and familial conflicts facing those loyal to Katherine of Aragon, but they were inevitably caught up in the king's successive matrimonial crises, which often had a politicizing effect on them. Their relationships with Henry's successive queens and their ties to families with vested interests in the break with Rome meant that they were far more likely than Katherine of Aragon's servants to support the king and move in the direction of religious reform. Mary, duchess of Richmond; Katherine, duchess of Suffolk; Anne Seymour, countess of Hertford; and Lady Joan Denny, all long-term members of the court, slowly emerged as advocates of reform in the 1540s.[221] By the end of the reign, they belonged to an openly Protestant faction in the royal household. The duchess of Suffolk was almost certainly evolving in this direction during her husband's lifetime since she was widely regarded as a staunch advocate of reform within months of his death in August 1545.[222] The conservative faction considered her dangerous enough to target, albeit unsuccessfully, in 1546 when Anne Askew, a radical sectary, was arrested and burned for heresy.[223]

Mary, duchess of Richmond, also openly adopted reforming views in this period, although her father, the third duke of Norfolk, was a prominent spokesman for the conservative faction on the Privy Council. Despite her relative youth, the duchess of Richmond was accustomed to acting independently. Only a few years earlier she had clashed with her father when she petitioned Henry VIII for her jointure herself after the death of her husband, the king's illegitimate son.[224] When disaster struck the Howards in the closing weeks of Henry's reign, however, the duchess's independence and initiative proved to be her family's most reliable resource. In the wake of the execution of her brother, the earl of Surrey; her father's arrest; and Henry VIII's death, the reformers who controlled Edward VI's council assigned her custody of Surrey's children.[225] Norfolk, who had once resented his daughter's unwillingness to leave her affairs in his hands, now benefited from her strong character. Despite their religious differences, she remained loyal to him and aggressively petitioned the council on his behalf. Hostile observers noted the "diligence" of her suits and worried that she would secure his release from the Tower. Although she ultimately failed and he remained in captivity until Mary ascended the throne in 1553, she gained regular access to him and significant improvements in the conditions of his imprisonment.[226] When Norfolk died in 1554, he rewarded her devotion and competence with a bequest of £500 "as well in consideration that she is my daughter as that also she hath been at great cost and charges in making suit for my deliverance out of my imprisonment; also in bringing up of my said son of Surrey's children."[227]

The duchess of Richmond's success in negotiating—or perhaps ignoring—the potential conflict between her loyalty to her father and her new religious views demonstrates the tensions between the significance of family in shaping aristocratic women's identity and priorities and the effect of service at court on their determination to act independently of the male heads of their families. At court, as in the great household, the family simultaneously subordinated and empowered its female members. On one hand, women arrived at court as the (presumably) obedient daughters or wives of patriarchal noblemen and knights and worked there on behalf of the families and dense kin networks that helped them to obtain their positions in the first place. In this respect, the aristocratic family continued to shape the behavior of its most visible female members. On the other hand, women who held offices in the royal household enjoyed unique opportunities for developing new, nonfamilial loyalties and ambitions. Their experience at court added new dimensions to their identities as daughters and wives and endowed some of them with a new sense of their own agency. One result was that a few of the queen's ladies chose to follow their own consciences rather than their fathers or husbands when they had to respond to the unprecedented dynastic and religious issues posed by Henry VIII's successive marriages and break with Rome.

While careers at court expanded women's opportunities to advance the interests of their familes and to define their own interests more independently, they in turn played a central role in changing the court as it evolved into the visual and performative center of the Yorkist and early Tudor monarchy. In an age when the courtly ideal was inextricably connected with the culture of romance and chivalry, the court required the presence of accomplished, richly dressed, aristocratic women to participate in royal celebrations and rituals. Without them, the tournaments, processions, masques, and banquets essential to the conduct of diplomacy and the spectacle of kingship could not have taken place. In addition, behind the scenes, the queen's ladies and maids performed the routine tasks necessary for the female side of the household to operate efficiently and acted on behalf of themselves, their families, and their friends in the endless pursuit of the king's favor and patronage. To the extent that the court contributed to the reestablishment and expansion of effective government and functioned as a major point of contact between the king and his subjects, aristocratic women played an essential part in the most important political achievement of the Yorkist and early Tudor periods.

CONCLUSION

*L*ADY LETTICE TRESHAM, with whom this book began, and Mary, duchess of Richmond, with whom it ended, both contributed to the survival and long-term prosperity of their families. Through marriage, they entered lifetime careers that gave them considerable power, even authority, over their families, servants, and local regions; opened politics to them; and, within limits, allowed them to shape their destinies. Although they dedicated themselves to securing the prosperity of their families, they were both independent and competent enough to outmaneuver male relatives—in one case a stepson, in another a father—who threatened their financial security. Despite these broad similarities, however, the details of their lives were quite different. Lady Tresham had three husbands, gave birth at least eight times, and launched two sons on successful political careers. The duchess of Richmond married only once, was widowed by the time she was 20, never had children, and emerged as one of the most influential women at the late Henrician and Edwardian courts. During these years, she was an effective advocate of religious reform and the ultimate resource of her natal family, the Howards, when disaster overtook them in 1546.

The differences between Lady Tresham's and the duchess of Richmond's lives remind us that although marriage opened careers as wives, mothers, and widows to aristocratic Yorkist and early Tudor women, biological chance and their own choices created enormous variety in their individual experiences. In addition, women from families connected to the court could add careers in the royal household to their careers in the family. If giving birth to the next generation was one of their primary functions, and the vast majority of wives did become mothers, childless women like the duchess of Richmond were able nonetheless to forge important roles for themselves at court or in their families and neighborhoods.

Behind this variety lay the complicated, evolving structure of the many families that provided the context of aristocratic women's lives. Beginning with their natal families, they accumulated families as they married and re-married and also became members, albeit more peripheral ones, of the families into which their children married. This multiplicity was one source of the flexibility that enabled them to protect their interests, to fulfill their responsibilities, and to exercise some control over their lives. Within these families, they gained additional flexibility from the different levels of obligation and emotional intensity attached to their interaction with their spouses, children, parents, siblings and siblings' children, close marital relatives, and more distant natal and marital kin. The size and complexity of their households and the frequent absence of their spouses further increased their power and opportunities to act with relative independence.

Because their families and households were centers of wealth and power, virtually everything aristocratic women did had political, as well as personal and domestic, significance. One of their most important functions was to cultivate their husbands' patrons and clients. In this area, their ability to facilitate mutually supportive relations between their natal and marital kin was particularly important. Wives from families connected to the reigning dynasty by blood or service operated on the still larger stage of the court and could have an even greater impact on their husbands' and children's careers. Widowhood and remarriage accentuated these patterns.

If, from this perspective, the family provided the foundation of aristocratic women's careers, it also functioned as the primary source of their dependence. Daughters relied on their fathers (or their substitutes) to accumulate their large cash dowries, to arrange their marriages, and to negotiate marriage contracts that provided them with adequate jointures. After their weddings, they depended on their husbands to protect their jointures, to support their activities as wives and mothers, and to leave them the legal and financial resources necessary to raise their children and maintain their standard of living in the likely event they were widowed. In addition, their status as *femes covert* meant that they had little leverage when their marriages failed, and that without their spouses' assistance they could do little to protect their inheritances or jointures against outside challenges. Finally, as widows, the complexity of their relationships with their marital families often involved them in prolonged legal battles to protect themselves and their children.

In practice, the aristocratic family's function as an oppressive institution was balanced much of the time by the benefits its female members gained from their class position. The daughters and wives of noblemen and knights experienced their identity as women through the prism of class. As wives, mothers, and widows, they commanded the service of enormous numbers of people, enjoyed an extravagant standard of living, and received the deference expected in a hierarchical society that regarded gentility and nobility as inherent qualities. In the round of their daily activities, their wealth, broad responsibilites, power, and careers in the family and at court were far more evident than the threats they faced from neglectful fathers and brothers, abusive and incompetent spouses, or grasping sons and stepsons. The advantages they gained from their class postion were as important as the disabilities of gender in shaping their experience and subjective identities.

With all its benefits, aristocratic women's privileged status did carry a major disadvantage: it subjected them to a restrictive, class-specific form of the arranged marriage. Their dependence on their families for the large dowries they needed to marry endogamously supported a system that enabled their fathers and brothers to exploit their matches to promote the men's interests and minimized their voice in the choice of their husbands. These marriage practices perpetuated the aristocracy's near monopoly of wealth, high social status, and political power by ensuring that most of its members would marry each other. The arranged marriage encapsulated the way in which gender and class converged to shape women's experience and subjectivity.

The familial, marital, and class structures and customs that shaped aristocratic women's lives functioned in a legal environment created in the first instance by the common law, which rigorously subordinated them to their husbands through the doctrine of coverture and restricted their ownership of land through the practice of primogeniture and the use of male entails. However, although these legal arrangements played a major role in subordinating aristocratic women as a group, in practice they often clashed with the material and emotional interests of individual families and men. Not surprisingly, therefore, aristocratic men and their lawyers developed a series of devices for circumventing these laws and procedures when they failed to serve their interests. Most obvious was the legal standing granted remarried wives who were executing their previous husbands' wills, although it was logically incompatible with their status as *femes covert*. Premarital agreements also limited the meaning of coverture by protecting women's separate property rights despite the fictive merging of their legal personalities with their husbands'. At the same time, enfeoffments, common recoveries, fines, and wills enabled knights and noblemen to leave land to their daughters and wives, secure in the knowledge that Chancery would uphold their arrangements. The legal system was, in short, far more flexible and multidimensional in its treatment of women than the unmodified doctrines of the common law would suggest.

The political system was equally bifurcated in its effect on aristocratic women. On one hand, men monopolized formal political institutions at every level of government. On the other hand, patronage-clientage networks that stretched from the aristocracy's great households to the court determined how these institutions actually operated. Because the crown was involved in every aspect of their lives, aristocratic women were just as active as aristocratic men in cultivating and exploiting these networks. Although they did not make laws or determine policies, they often affected the way in which laws and policies were implemented in particular instances. They also occupied an important place at court, the center of political influence and power.

Within this web of internally inconsistent institutions and practices, the particular relationships of individual aristocratic women and men shaped the way in which women experienced their subordinate position. On the most obvious level, women's personalities and the quality of their emotional interaction with their mates had a powerful effect on the degree to which their spouses took advantage of their prerogatives. Equally important was the fact that individual men had divergent interests in their female kin, depending on whether they were their daughters, mothers, stepmothers, sisters, spouses, or aunts. Furthermore, aristocratic men were likely to be dependent on women, particularly their widowed mothers and wives, at various points in their lives. This dependency complicated their relations with their female kin and influenced the way in which they used the power and authority at their disposal. Understanding the impact of patriarchal institutions and practices on aristocratic women, therefore, requires understanding their impact on aristocratic men as well.

Taken together, the internal and external contradictions of these personal relationships and patriarchal institutions produced the space in which aristocratic Yorkist and early Tudor women forged the careers that have formed the main subject of this book. Operating in an institutional and cultural context not of their own making, they took advantage of these contradictions to create lives as different as those of Lady Lettice Tresham and Mary, duchess of Richmond. They and their peers were simultaneously the subjects of their own lives and the subjects of male authority.[1] It is this double subjectivity— and indeed the double subjectivity of all women living in patriarchal societies—that challenges historians of women who seek to recover and articulate the balance between oppression and agency that best captures the experience of the particular groups of women they are studying. It is only writing this history in all its complexity and specificity that will enable us finally to understand the meaning of patriarchy in the past and its remarkable durability into the present.

GLOSSARY

Acrased, craysed diseased; mentally affected.

Advowson right of presentation to a religious office or living; patronage of an ecclesiastical office or religious house.

Agnus figure of a lamb, bearing a cross or a flag.

Antiphoner book of passages or verses sung or recited responsively by a choir.

Attainder conviction for treason or felony by Parliament that entailed forfeiture of the condemned person's real and personal property, corruption of his blood so he could neither inherit nor transmit property, and general extinction of all his civil rights.

Billament a decorative border, often made of gold and studded with jewels.

Bouche of court traditional allowance of bread and wine, fuel and candles for the chambers of people residing at court.

Buckram/bokeram kind of coarse linen cloth.

Camlet/chamlet Eastern luxury fabric of camel's hair and silk; in the sixteenth century, angora and silk, linen, or cotton.

Chaced of plate; ornamented with embossed work; engraved in relief.

Chantry an endowment for a term of years or in perpetuity to fund masses for the soul of the donor and anyone else specified; donors usually specified where they wanted the prayers to be said and often paid for the construction of new altars or chapels to be used specifically for their prayers.

Chattels movable or personal property.

Clareregalls see *regals*.

Clavichords musical instrument with keys and strings; in developed form, like a square pianoforte.

Counterpane outer covering of a bed, more or less ornamental; coverlet or quilt.

Coverture the common-law doctrine that a husband covered his wife's legal identity during their marriage; thus she had none of the legal rights normally allowed to all men or to never-married women or widows.

Cramp rings Gold rings made from the king's Good Friday offering; they were blessed at a special ceremony, during which the king rubbed them between his hands to impart to them the virtue of the oil used to consecrate him at his coronation; believed to be a remedy for any kind of cramp or convulsion and for epilepsy (*Lisle Letters*, 2: pp. 265–66).

Creppins/crepyns white linen caps worn under the French hood.

Dame title of respect given to knights' widows.

Demiceint a woman's girdle whose front part is of gold or silver and back part of silk.

Disparage to marry beneath one's rank; parents feared that daughters would marry clandestinely for love and disparage themselves, or that the crown might disparage heiresses who became royal wards; also an issue when the crown had the right to marry the widows of its feudal tenants.

Dower provision for widows under the common law; widows were entitled to the use (usufruct) of one-third of their husband's land; after their death, it passed to their husbands' heirs.

Dowry property given by the bride's family to her husband or father-in-law on her marriage, usually in the form of cash paid in installments over a period of years; the bride had no legal rights to her dowry; also called her marriage portion.

Enfeoffment see definition of *use* below.

Entail estate limited to a person and the heirs of his or her body or to certain classes of the heirs of his or her body; also called a fee tail or an estate in tail. As a verb, to settle property on a person in fee tail. The most common entail was a male tail, which limited inheritance to one's male descendants.

Equity authority to correct injustice caused by literal application of the law by applying the law of reason and conscience.

Estate degree, quantity, nature, and extent of a person's rights in his or her real property.

Execute in legal terminology, to validate an act by performing the formalities required by the law.

Freehold/land held in fee also known as fee simple, the estate in real property that includes the right of alienation and inheritance, without restriction on particular heirs; after the owner's death, it would descend according to the rules of primogeniture unless they had been altered by entail or will (after the Statute of Wills, 1542); land conveyed to feoffees is no longer held in fee.

Frontlet an ornament or band worn on the forehead.

Fustians sheets of coarse linen.

Garnish of pewter set of vessels of that metal for table use; twelve platters, dishes, and saucers.

Girdle narrow cord, band, or chain that followed the waistline; often of silver or gold or decorated with jewels; used to support items such as a purse or small prayerbooks with precious covers.

Gossip one who has contracted spiritual affinity with another by acting as a sponsor at baptism; familiar acquaintance, friend, chum; formerly applied to both sexes.

Heiress at law the female heir under the common law according to the rules of primogeniture.

Inquisition Post Mortem inquest held on the death of any tenant of the king to discover the land he or she held in fee, who his heir was, and what rights (e.g., wardship or escheat) were due to the king. Land held in enfeoffment, which was used to create jointures, was not subject to these rights.

Jointure land granted in joint tenancy to a husband and wife at the time of their marriage; the survivor continued to hold the land until his or her death; the husband received the income during the marriage; although the jointure supported the couple, its primary purpose was to provide for the wife in the event she was widowed. A woman continued to receive her jointure if she remarried.

Kirtle a woman's gown; a bodice and skirt; after 1545, the skirt alone.

Lawn fine linen.

Mark a unit of account that equaled two-thirds of a pound sterling; used very frequently in contracts and wills in the Yorkist and early Tudor period; 100 marks = £66 13s. 4d.; 300 marks = £200; 500 marks = £333 6s. 8d.; 1,000 marks = £666 13s. 4d.

Obit office, usually a mass, on behalf of the soul of a deceased person on anniversary of his or her death.

Ouche clasp, buckle, or brooch for holding together two sides of a garment.

Pantelette loose drawers with a frill at the bottom.

Paraphernalia the necessities and personal ornaments appropriate to women's degree.

Partlet an article of clothing worn around the neck and upper part of the chest; originally a neckerchief of linen or the like.

Placard article of dress, sometimes richly embroidered; worn by men and women in fifteenth and sixteenth centuries beneath an open gown or coat.

Pounced of plate; ornamented, embossed, or chased by way of decoration.

Primer (1) prayer book or devotional manual for the laity in England before the Reformation and for some time afterward; (2) elementary school book for teaching children to read. One cannot separate its use in these two senses in the fifteenth and sixteenth centuries.

Psalter Book of psalms; particular version of the book of psalms; a selection from, or particular portion of, the book of psalms; a copy of, or volume containing, the psalms, especially arranged for devotional or liturgical use.

Rebec medieval musical instrument with strings played with a bow; early form of fiddle.

Regals small portable organ.

Sackbut musical instrument; bass trumpet with a slide like that of a trombone for altering pitch.

Sarcenet silk.

Sperver/sparver complete set of hangings for a four-poster bed.

Stomacher ornamental covering for the chest, often covered with jewels, and worn by women under the lacing of the bodice.

Traverse curtain or screen.

Use an early form of the trust; the owner of the land conveyed legal title to (i.e., enfeoffed) persons known as feoffees for specific purposes designated in the deed of conveyance. The use separated legal ownership from receipt of the profit or benefit of the land. The common law did not recognize the use and therefore did not protect its beneficiaries if the feoffees violated the terms of the enfeoffment. Chancery recognized and enforced the use as a matter of equity. The spread of the use in the fifteenth century thus led to a massive shift of litigation about real property from the common-law courts to Chancery. The use permitted landowners to devise their land by will at their deaths, which was not possible under the common law. The trust developed out of the entail during the Elizabethan period.

Wardship   right of a feudal lord to custody of minor heirs (girls under 14; boys under 21). The lord also had the right to arrange his wards' marriages and to collect the profits of their lands during their minorities. In the case of boys, only the inheriting son became a ward; in the case of girls, because they inherited as co-heirs, they all became wards at the same time. In practice, since virtually all knights and nobles held at least some land as tenants-in-chief of the crown, almost all aristocratic minor heirs became the king's wards. The major exception occurred when all of the landowner's property was enfeoffed (see chapter 1 on enfeoffment). The crown often sold its rights for profit.

ABBREVIATIONS

Add'l Ms.	Additional Manuscript, British Library
BIHR	Bulletin of the Institute of Historical Research
BL	British Library
C	Chancery, PRO
C1	Early Chancery Cases, PRO
CCR	Calendar of Close Rolls
CPR	Calendar of Patent Rolls
CSP	Calendar of State Papers
CUL	Cambridge University Library
d	dorsal
d.	died
DNB	Dictionary of National Biography
E	Exchequer, PRO
Ed	Edward
EETS	Early English Text Society
EHR	English Historical Review
ERO	Essex Country Record Office
f.	folio
Folger	Folger Shakespeare Library, Washington, D.C.
fn.	footnote
GEC	George E. Cokayne et al., Complete Peerage
HampRO	Hampshire Record Office
HEH	Henry E. Huntington Library
Hen	Henry
HMC	Historical Manuscripts Commission
HMSO	Her Majesty's Stationary Office
HoL	House of Lords

HRO	Hertfordshire Record Office
HS	Harleian Society Publication
IHR	Institute for Historical Research, University of London
InqPM	Calendar of Inquisitions Post Mortem
L&P	Letters and Papers, Foreign and Domestic of the Reign of Henry VIII
LRO	Leicester Record Office
LincAO	Lincoln Archives Office
m.	membrane
Mss.	manuscripts
n.	note
n.d.	no date
n.p.	no publisher
NRA	National Register of Archives
NRO	Norfolk Record Office
n.s.	new series
OED	Oxford English Dictionary, 1971, Compact Edition
o.s.	old series
PCC	Prerogative Court of Canterbury
PRO	Public Record Office
Prob	Probate Records, PRO
Pt.	part
Reprt	reprint
Req	Court of Requests, PRO
RHS	Royal Historical Society, London
Rich	Richard
s.	shilling
SP	State Papers
SP1	State Papers of Henry VIII, PRO
SRO	Stafford Record Office
Stac	Star Chamber Records, PRO
STC	Short Title Catalogue
SuffRO	West Suffolk Record Office at Bury St. Edmunds
TE	*Testamenta Eboracensia*
TV	*Testamenta Vetusta*
v	verso
VCH	Victoria County History
WRO	Warwickshire Record Office

NOTES

Introduction

1. L&P, 14 (1):387 (1539); Bindoff, *Commons*, 1:527–29, on Sir Francis Bryan; on Lady Bryan, see chapter 9; to avoid confusion I refer to Lady Lettice Peniston Knollys Lee Tresham as Lady Tresham throughout this discussion.

2. Bindoff, *Commons*, 2:479, 505; Prob11/20/16 (1520); 14 (2):appendix 3 (1539).

3. Bindoff, *Commons*, 2:505.

4. Prob11/27/27 (1537); L&P, 14 (2):appendix 53.

5. C1/847/7 (1539–1544).

6. L&P, 14 (1):387 (1539).

7. SP1/143, f. 177 (1539).

8. SP1/151, f. 255 (1539).

9. L&P, 14 (2):appendix 3 (1539).

10. Bindoff, *Commons*, 3:482.

11. Prob11/40/28 (1557; probated June 1558).

12. Bindoff, *Commons*, 2:505.

13. Her two daughters by Knollys may have died relatively young since there is no record of their marrying, nor did their mother mention them in her will.

14. Bindoff, *Commons*, 2:479–81.

15. Ibid., 2:479–81.

16. Prob11/40/28 (1557); as the son of a second wife, Benet was not his father's heir; Bindoff, *Commons*, 2:479–81.

17. E.g., OED, 1:117; *Webster's*, 274.

18. E.g., *Letters and Papers of the Verney Family*, 25, Sir Ralph Verney (1478); *Wills from Doctors' Common*, 10, Dame Mabel Parr (1529); Prob11/34/33, Sir Edward Wotton (1551); Prob11/29/12, Dame Constance Culpepper (1541).

19. E.g., OED, 2:1427; *Webster's*, 1437.

20. For other historians who define the aristocracy in this way, see Guy, *Tudor England*, 46–48; Carpenter, *Locality and Polity*, 35–36; Acheson, *Gentry Community*, 159; McFarlane, *Nobility of Later Medieval England*, 6–8.

21. Cornwall, *Wealth and Society*, 142–44; for the numbers of noblemen and knights in a population that grew from 2 to 3 million between 1450 and 1550, see McFarlane, *Nobility of Later Medieval England*, 176; Guy, *Tudor England*, 32, 46–48; J. P. Cooper, "Social Distribution of Land and Men," 20–21.

22. Cornwall, *Wealth and Society*, 144; Guy, *Tudor England*, 46; Miller, *Henry VIII and the English Nobility*, 12.

23. Condon, "Ruling Elites in the Reign of Henry VII"; Guy, *Tudor England*, 44–50.

24. Bindoff, *Commons*, 2:194, 262, 363.

25. Ibid., 1:578–81.

26. Condon, "From Caitiff to Patriae," 138–39; Bindoff, *Commons*, 3:42–46, 92–96.

27. Starkey, "Age of the Household," 225–90; Mertes, *English Noble Household*.

28. For a different view, see Hanawalt, "Lady Honor Lisle's Networks," esp. 208–9.

29. C. Jordan, *Renaissance Feminism*, chap. 1, esp. 15–16; Rigby, *English Society*, 278–80.

30. Kandiyoti, "Islam and Patriarchy," 27, 34; Kandiyoti, "Bargaining with Patriarchy," 274, 279–81.

31. Girouard, *Life in the English Country House*, 54–56; Harris, *Edward Stafford*, 87–88; for inventories listing "my lady's chamber," see PRO, E154/2/36, Sir Edward Darrell (c. 1550); Prob2/199, Sir Thomas Lovell (1524); BL, Add'l Charters #74,187, Sir Gilbert Talbot (1517).

32. Klapisch-Zuber, *Women, Family and Ritual*, "'Cruel Mother,'" 118.

33. Koditschek, "Gendering of the British Working Class," 351; see also Rigby, *English Society*, 243.

34. Koditschek, "Gendering of the British Working Class," 351.

35. Ibid., *336*, 351–52; Bennett, "Feminism and History," 259–67.

36. Guy, *Tudor England*, 46–48; Carpenter, *Locality and Polity*, 35–36; Acheson, *Gentry Community*, 159; McFarlane, *Nobility of Later Medieval England*, 6–8.

37. On noblewomen before 1450, see Ward, *English Noblewomen* and *Women of the English Nobility*; Rosenthal, *Patriarchy and Families of Privilege*; and Rosenthal's articles cited in the bibiliography.

38. Starkey, "Age of the Household," 226; Mertes, *English Noble Household*, 8–9; Stone, *Crisis of the Aristocracy*, 15–17; Stone, *Family, Sex, and Marriage*, 85–91.

39. Harris, "New Look at the Reformation," 92–105.

40. In political history, a revisionist chronology that sharply reduces the significance of 1485 was first proposed by G. R. Elton almost fifty years ago and has won widespread acceptance; *Tudor Revolution*, introduction. Also Chrimes, *Lancastrians, Yorkists and Henry VII*; Lander, *Conflict and Stability*, chap. 7; Slavin, *Precarious Balance*, 49, 81, 85–86, 91; and Wolffe, *Crown Lands*; the most recent standard survey, Guy, *Tudor England*, chap. 1, endorses this view.

41. Haigh, *English Reformations*; Duffy, *Stripping of the Altars*; Scarisbrick, *Reformation and the English People*.

42. Bennett, "'History That Stands Still,'" 269–84; "Medieval Women, Modern Women," 147–75; "Theoretical Issues," 73–94.

43. See Rosenthal, "Other Victims," 213–30, 215–16, for statistics; K. B. McFarlane's (in "Wars of the Roses," 243–45, 257–59) argument that few noble families were *permanently* extinguished by the wars has been widely accepted, but he also recognized their large casualties in battle.

44. Harris, "View from My Lady's Chamber," 223–25.

45. The slow, fitful contraction of aristocratic women's political power went on for centuries. See Schwoerer, *Lady Rachel Russell*; Schwoerer, "Women and the Glorious Revolution," 208–13, 217–18; Poovey, "Covered but Not Bound," chap. 3; Jalland, *Women, Marriage and Politics*, pt. 3. See Vickery, *Gentleman's Daughter*, 1–12, for a critique of the idea that separate public and private spheres transformed the lives of genteel women in the eighteenth and early nineteenth centuries.

46. See Bennett, *Ale, Beer, and Brewsters*, chap. 8, for a different view of the relationship of experience and status.

47. McNamara and Wemple, "Sanctity and Power"; Wemple, *Women in Frankish Society*; Herlihy, "Land, Family and Women," 110–13; Herlihy, "Did Women Have a Renaissance?" 12–16.

48. McFarlane, "Wars of the Roses"; Lander, "Wars of the Roses," esp. 61–63, 66.

49. Neuschel, "Noblewomen and War," 124–44.

50. E.g., Joan Kelly, "Did Women Have a Renaissance?," 138–63; Howell, *Women, Production, and Patriarchy*, 174–83; Weisner, *Working Women*, 1–10; Roper, *Holy Households*, 1–5; Hanley, "Engendering the State"; Stone, *Family, Sex and Marriage*, chap. 5, 3–9.

51. For a recent overview of these issues, see Weisner, *Women and Gender*, 288–311.

52. Stretton, *Women Waging Law*; Erickson, *Women and Property*; see Hardwick, *Practice of Patriarchy*, for a similar approach by a French historian.

53. Burns, *Bodytalk*, 246.

54. The major exceptions are articles based on the printed collections of Lisle, Paston, Plumpton, and Stonor letters; see bibliography.

55. Roelker, "Role of Noblewomen," 168–95; Warnicke, *Women of the English Renaissance and Reformation*; King, "Patronage and Piety," 43–46; Hibbard, "Role of a Queen Consort," 394–414; Willen, "Godly Women," 561–80; Ward, *English Noblewomen*; Sánchez, *Empress, Queen, and Nun*.

56. Hicks, *Richard III and His Rivals*, chaps. 4–6, 9; Jones and Underwood, *King's Mother*; Ives, *Anne Boleyn*.

57. Klapisch-Zuber, *Women, Family, and Ritual*, 117–31, quote 118; 213–46, esp. 216; Hanley, "Engendering the State," 6–15.

58. Rosenthal, *Patriarchy and Families of Privilege*; Chojnacki, *Women and Men in Renaissance Venice*; Kettering, "Patronage Power," 817–41; Neuschel, "Noble Households" and "Noblewomen and War," 124–44.

Chapter 1

1. The obvious exception to this generalization, the debate about queenship, was a phenomenon of the second half of the sixteenth century. Furthermore, although opponents of female rulers attacked women's political capacity on traditional misogynist grounds, the defenders rested their case on Mary's and Elizabeth's special status as Henry VIII's heirs rather than on a broad defense of women's capabilities or character. E.g., see Aylmer, *Harborow for Faithfull and Trewe Subjectes*, B2; Sir Thomas Smith, *English Commonwealth*, 19.

2. These figures are based on genealogical information about 1,086 couples who had at least 2,473 daughters. Within this group, information indicates what happened to 2,209 of them. Of those who didn't marry, 4 percent died young or unmarried and 2 percent became nuns. Harris, "New Look at the Reformation," 92–93, has different

absolute figures because I collected additional information since it was published. But the percentages remained the same. For a different view, see Stone, *Family, Sex and Marriage,* 38–46.

3. Hajnal, "European Marriage Patterns," 101, first defined the European marriage pattern; Hajnal did not think it prevailed in the period covered in this monograph and especially noted statistics about the aristocracy in arguing that point (113–20, 134). Alan Macfarlane, *Marriage and Love in England,* 46–48, has argued forcefully that the northern European marriage pattern prevailed in England by the late medieval period, but he explicitly noted that it did not apply to the landed aristocracy.

4. Although the term *will* was used generically to describe bequests of real and personal property, strictly speaking the bequest of personal goods was called a testament and fell under the jurisdiction of the ecclesiastical courts.

5. If a live child were born during the marriage and the wife predeceased her husband, the husband had the right to use of his wife's inheritance until his death, a privilege known as the courtesy of England. When he died, her property descended to her heir(s), whether it was the child of their marriage or not.

6. Holdsworth, *History of English Law,* 3:542–44; Lawrence, *Laws Affecting the Property of Married Women,* 168–69.

7. Maud, Lady Conyers (1460), Lady Dorothy Howard (1530), Lady Katherine Gordon (1537), Dame Margery Chamberlain (1557), Anne, Lady Powis (1557), and Dame Lettice Tresham (1557).

8. 32 Henry VIII, c. 1 (Statute of Wills); 34 and 35 Henry VIII, c. 5 (1542), *Statutes of the Realm,* 3:744–46, 903–04. The exclusion appeared explicitly in the latter bill, which was passed to clarify the act of 1540.

9. Holdsworth, *History of English Law,* 3:543–44.

10. Baker, *English Legal History,* 396.

11. BL, Caligula, B. I, f. 135 (orig. 127).

12. Baker, *English Legal History,* 395. In a rare case of this kind, involving an aristocratic woman, Agnes Hungerford, widow of Sir Edward, was hanged at Tyburn in 1523 for murdering her first husband. GEC, 6:625 n. a.

13. Holdsworth, *History of English Law,* 5:216–17, 310–13.

14. The common law enforced a premarital contract only if the wife survived her husband into widowhood. Ibid., 5:311.

15. Ibid., 4: 428–29; Lawrence, *Property of Married Women,* 170; Baker and Milsom, *Sources of English Legal History,* 98–100.

16. In the case of *Mary Sankey alias Walgrave v. Golding,* 1581; Lawrence, *Property of Married Women,* 125; Maria Cioni, *Women and the Law,* 171–72.

17. *Rotuli Parliamentorum,* 6:284–85, 311–12; OED, I:151.

18. I have found five examples of such settlements. In addition, a rent roll of Humphrey, first duke of Buckingham, assigned an annuity to his wife. Markland, "Rent Roll of Humphrey Duke of Buckingham," 273.

19. Smyth, *Berkeley Manuscripts,* 2:142.

20. CUL, Hengrave Hall ms. 90, document marked 72, 4 Nov. 1548.

21. For another example, see Minet, "Capells at Rayne," 262; for a similar point, see Erickson, *Women and Property,* 104.

22. Prob11/6/35 (1478); Prob11/34/33 (1551). Sir Edward Wotton bound himself to leave his wife, the widow of an alderman of London, £400.

23. Prob11/33/18, Boughton (1549); Prob11/27/27, Clerk (1539); see also Prob11/25/32, Sir Robert Drury (1531), and Prob11/23/13, Sir Richard Fitzlewis (1527).

24. Prob11/29/11 (1542).

25. Prob11/37/29 (1555); altogether 62 of 523 wills of men who predeceased their wives contain provisions of this kind.

26. When land descended to collateral heirs in the absence of legitimate children, it passed undivided to brothers and then nephews in birth order and in equal shares to sisters and then nieces.

27. Spring, *Law, Land and Family*, 10–11.

28. The statute De Donis (1285), which applied to land held by feudal tenure and subject to the common law, permitted an entail to become perpetual. The male entail therefore kept land in the hands of men as long as it was biologically possible.

29. There is no statistical evidence about how widely spread the use of the entail, and specifically the male entail, was; Spring, *Law, Land and Family*, 28.

30. Simpson, *History of the Land Law*, 121–29; it was in force by 1472.

31. Baker, *English Legal History*, 235–36. From Henry VIII's reign, fines could also be used for this purpose; Simpson, *History of the Land Law*, 129.

32. SP1/244, f. 223, Shelton family (1544); Wake, *Brudenells of Dean*, 69–83; see Ellis, *Tudor Frontiers and Noble Power*, 85, for a case involving a granddaughter.

33. SP1/244, f. 229; Wake, *Brudenells of Dean*, 69–83.

34. Ives, "Genesis of the Statute of Uses," 686 and n. 2; Baker, *English Legal History*, 213; aristocratic landowners occasionally noted in their wills that all of their land was in feoffment; e.g., WRO, Throckmorton Papers, CR 1998, Box 73, #2, Sir Robert Throckmorton, 1518.

35. They either directed the feoffees about devising the land after they died or ordered them to transfer it to executors named in their wills who would do so.

36. Roughly speaking, the use was analogous to the modern trust: feoffees to trustees. A. W. B. Simpson, *History of the Land Law*, 174–75, believed that the main reasons for putting land in feoffment were to acquire the power to commit fraud (barring the widow's common dower would fall under this category), to devise it by will, to avoid feudal dues, and to facilitate the creation of land settlements.

37. The figure on peers is based on information in GEC; knights, on information in Bindoff, *Commons*.

38. Technically the widow received a life estate in the property; after her death, it passed to her husband's heirs, who were often the offspring of their marriage.

39. Marriage settlements established jointures for women as far back as the early fourteenth century. Holmes, *Estates of the Higher Nobility*, chap. 2.

40. Men received this income both before and after they came into their inheritances if they were heirs. In second marriages, the jointure often passed to the heir(s) of the groom by his first wife. Some marriage contracts contained elaborate provisions about the descent of the jointure land in the event that the groom had no legitimate children at the time of his death.

41. Baker, *English Legal History*, 229–30. Janet Loengard has suggested in conversations with me that barring women's common-law dower rights was one of the main reasons that men enfeoffed their land; see also Simpson, *History of the Land Law*, 174–75. Bean, *Decline of English Feudalism*, 136, disagrees with this view.

42. SP1/18, f. 165 (1519).

43. Prob11/25/17 (1532).

44. LRO, Throckmorton Papers, CR1998, Box 72, #4. The contract specifically stated that if the bride were widowed after the death of her father-in-law, she was "to be at her free liberty to claim dower." If she were widowed during his lifetime, a jointure was provided. There is no indication of the reason for this unusual provision.

45. There were fourteen cases about the failure of the groom's family to establish her jointure; two about infringements on the jointure during the marriage; forty-four about the widow's inability to take possession of the jointure after her husband died, usually because his executors, feoffees, or heirs would not enfeoff the land to her use; and thirty-nine about her inability to retain possession of her jointure or prevent trespasses on it after it was enfeoffed to her use. In twenty-six cases, the records described a feoffment that created a jointure without using that terminology. These are only a fraction of the cases involving widows' property.

46. Specifically, 103 confirmed or established jointures for the widows, 21 confirmed or established feoffments without calling them by that name, and 26 left land to the widow for her life in recompense of her jointure.

47. These were the people who most frequently arranged aristocratic marriages and negotiated the settlements accompanying them. The bride's portion was paid directly to the groom when he was an adult who was negotiating his own marriage. Otherwise it went to his father or his father's substitute. Given these realities, describing the portion as the wife's property, as Erickson does in "Common Law versus Common Practice," 28, hardly seems justified. Spring, *Law, Land and Family*, 175–77, is incorrect in asserting that aristocratic marriages were not arranged in the sixteenth century or that they conformed to the pattern of relatively late marriage ages.

48. Add'l Ms. 24,965, f. 173 (30 July 1523). See also *Lisle Letters*, 3:793 (1536), and CUL, Hengrave Ms. 88, 1, #140.

49. E.g., HEH, Hastings Collection, HAP Box 3, folder 19 (1536); CCR, Hen VII, I: 945 (1495).

50. SP1/26, f. 184 (1522).

51. Add'l Ms. 24,965, f. 200d (17 Dec. 1523).

52. Staves, *Married Women's Separate Property*, 29–30; Bean, *Decline of English Feudalism*, 287n.; Bonfield, *Marriage Settlements*, 3–6.

53. Five of fifty-two marriage settlements used in this study are explicit on this point: CCR, Hen VII, I: 945, marriage of Elizabeth, daughter of Thomas, first marquis of Dorset to Sir John Arundell, 1495; HEH, Hastings Collection, HAP O/S Box (25), marriage of Anne, daughter of Edward, Lord Hastings, to Thomas Stanley, second earl of Derby, 1505; HAP Box 7, folder 1, marriage of Catherine Pole, daughter of Henry, Lord Montague, to Francis Hastings, second earl of Huntingdon, 1531; Add'l Ms. 34,679, f. 2, marriage of Mary, daughter of Thomas Nevill of Holt, to William Timpyn, 1501; WRO, Throckmorton Papers, CR 1998, Box 72 #4, marriage of Anne, daughter of Sir George Throckmorton, to John Digby, 1548. Fifty-seven wills that provided jointures also explicitly barred the widow's right to claim dower or were in full recompense of her dower or of her jointure and dower.

54. E.g., Spring, *Law, Land and Family*, 47–58, quote on 47; Staves, *Married Women's Separate Property*, 29–30.

55. Bonfield, *Marriage Settlements*, 9–10. The marriage contracts used in this study support Bonfield.

56. Bean, one of the few historians primarily concerned with the period before the

Statute of Uses, takes issue with this conclusion in *Decline of English Feudalism*, 136, 287n. But his analysis ignores the central problem posed by enfeoffments to the dower rights of widows: the situation of women whose husbands' estates were enfeoffed before they married.

57. In recent decades scholars have produced an enormous literature on this hegemonic ideology; e.g., see Fletcher, *Gender, Sex and Subordination*, pt. 1; Mendelson and Crawford, *Women in Early Modern England*, chap. 1; Klapisch-Zuber, *History of Women*, chaps. 1–2; Rogers, *Troublesome Helpmate*; C. Jordan, *Renaissance Feminism*.

58. Vives, *Institutione Christianae Feminae*, xvii–xix; there were eight printed editions between 1529 and 1592, STC, 2:429.

59. C. Jordan, *Renaissance Feminism*, passim.

60. *Lisle Letters*, 4:980; SP1/215, f. 34.

61. C. Jordan, *Renaissance Feminism*, 35, 137.

62. SP1/115, f. 197.

63. BL, Cotton Ms., appendix L, f. 79.

64. BL, Cleopatra E. IV, f. 94 (orig. 82).

65. SP1/72, f. 55, and SP1/89, f. 154, marchioness of Dorset (1532 and 1535); SP1/96, f. 93, Lady Jane Guildford (n.d.); SP1/104, f. 187, and SP1/87, f. 131, Lady Mary Guildford (1533 and 1536).

66. William Thomas, "Treatise on Government," in Strype, *Ecclesiastical Memorials*, 2 (1):162 for date of publication; 2(2), appendix S, 375, for quote.

67. Vives, *Institutione Christianae Feminae*, p. b iii, verso.

68. Harrington, *Commendations of Matrimony*.

69. Prob11/31/3, Champernon (1545); PRO, Req2/6/173 (n.d. but after 1521, when her first husband died).

70. Prob11/42A/24 (1558).

Chapter 2

1. Vives, *Institutione Christianae Feminae*, bk. 1, chap. 11; quote from chap. 7, p. G4; OED, 1:362–63.

2. Prob11/27/27 (1537).

3. *Lisle Letters*, 4:887 (151–52; 1537). For similar views, see LRO, 26D53/1947 (1485), John Shirley, esq.; Prob11/20/16 (1520), Robert Knollys, esq.; Prob11/27/27 (1537), Sir Robert Lee.

4. *Privy Purse Expenses of the Princess Mary*, xli.

5. Robinson, *Original Letters Relative to the English Reformation*, 52:3.

6. See Pollock, "'Teach Her to Live Under Obedience,'" esp. 231–35, 237–38, for a superb discussion of this paradox that is based primarily on seventeenth-century evidence.

7. Prob11/11/7 (1496).

8. Prob11/40/2 (1556). Also *Somerset Medieval Wills (1383–1500)*, 192–93, Sir Robert Hungerford (1459); Prob11/24/5, Sir Robert Clere (1529).

9. *Household Books of John Howard*, xiii–xiv.

10. Ibid., pt. 2, 48–51, 98, 184–87, 199–206, 216, 317, 356–61, 383, 410, 417–50, 453–62.

11. Ibid., xiii; pt. 1, 555–56; pt. 2, 388, 399–400, 410, 417–45. Howard's first wife was Catherine, daughter of William, styled Lord Molyens. His second wife was Margaret

Chedworth, widow of John Norris, esq., and before that of Nicholas Wyfold, a grocer and mayor of London.

12. Harris, *Edward Stafford*, 47, 81–82; The indenture is SRO, D1721/1, f. 390. Buckingham had at least one son and two daughters at this time.

13. L&P, 3 (1):1285 (496).

14. *Privy Purse Expenses of Elizabeth of York*, xxv–xxvi, 33, 89; GEC, 4:330.

15. *Lisle Letters*, 5:1133 (85), 1201, 1269. Katherine, duchess of Suffolk, who gave birth on March 10 of the same year, was also at court in November.

16. BL, Vespasian, F. XIII, art. 198, f. 251; for the dating of the latter, see *Lisle Letters*, 5:1513a (4 Aug. 1539); L&P, 15:21 (1540); 14 (2):572 (1539); 16:380, f. 110 (1540); 21 (1), 969 (3; 1546); Denny, "Biography of Sir Anthony Denny," 197–216; Bindoff, *Commons*, 2:27–28.

17. GEC, 11:255.

18. *Lisle Letters*, 4:p. 106; 5:1495 (24 July 1539); see the will of her husband, Thomas, earl of Rutland (d. 1543), *North Country Wills, 1338–1558*, 134 (188–89).

19. Warnicke, *Rise and Fall of Anne Boleyn*, 116.

20. GEC, 11:254; HMC, *Rutland Papers*, 4:271.

21. HMC, *Rutland Papers*, 4:277–80.

22. *Lisle Letters*, 4:855a; 880 (144); 882; 887 (151), 889; 893 (160), 180–81.

23. Ibid., 5:1393 (448), 1395 (451), 1396a (453).

24. HMC, *Rutland Papers*, 4:289; *Lisle Letters*, 5:1495.

25. Vives, *Institutione Christianae Feminae*, bk. 2, chap. 11, pp. l ii verso to l iii verso.

26. Bullinger, *Christian State of Matrimony*, chap. 21, f. 92d.

27. The first example of *wet nurse* in the *Oxford English Dictionary* dates from 1620; OED, 2:332.

28. Emmison, *Tudor Secretary*, 125.

29. McLaren, *Reproductive Rituals*, 67–70.

30. These are all minimal figures since many children who died within hours or days of their birth and some girls were undoubtedly not recorded. I excluded women and couples with no children from my figures because I was interested in the effect of nursing on family size. The figures for women include children from all of their marriages.

31. Scofield, *Life and Reign of Edward IV*, 1:2–3.

32. MacGibbon, *Elizabeth Woodville*, 222–23.

33. Denny, "Pedigrees of Some East-Anglian Dennys," 19.

34. Collins, *Historical Collections*, 7–12.

35. Harris, *Edward Stafford*, 77.

36. HMC, *Rutland Papers*, 4:290–92.

37. Emmison, *Tudor Secretary*, 124–25, 152.

38. Jones and Underwood, *King's Mother*, genealogical tables beginning on xvii, 84–85, 114.

39. CCR, Henry VII, 2:243 (1503), to Gerald, earl of Kildare (d. 1534).

40. *Lisle Letters*, 3:13. Her mother, Sidney's daughter, died in 1542. DNB, 5:1150.

41. W. K. Jordan, *Edward VI*, 372; *Lisle Letters*, 3:13. Katherine Parr married Sir Thomas Seymour, Edward's uncle, shortly after Henry's death.

42. GEC, 6:374, 622 (married by 1480).

43. L&P, 3 (1):154 (5; 1519); Willoughby, *Continuation of the History of the Willougby Family*, 7–9.

44. C1/582/20, 20a (1515–29); C1/682/45 (1529–33).

45. *Plumpton Correspondence*, 6. Margaret was married to Roucliffe's son, John, and lived in his household.

46. *Household Books of John Howard*, pt. 1:218, 259, 261, 285, 286, 311, 312, 314, 318, 320, 394; for a general discussion of toys in the later Middle Ages, see Orme, "Culture of Children in Medieval England," 51–58.

47. Ibid., pt. 2:147.

48. Bridget, Lord Lisle's daughter by his first marriage, was 7 when he first went to Calais. *Lisle Letters*, 1:245; e.g., 3:536, 537 (92), 539; 540 (95); 5:1224 (219–20).

49. Pollock, "'Teach Her to Live Under Obedience,'" 236–37.

50. *North Country Wills*, 166 (229).

51. *Lisle Letters*, 4:862 (86), 906 (185); 5:1231, 1620 (730–31); 6:1653 (33); for other aristocratic women who cooked for Henry VIII, see *Privy Purse Expences of King Henry the Eighth*, 32, 50, 103, 184, 201, 205, 213.

52. Prob2/3.

53. *Stonor Letters and Papers*, 2:208 (1478).

54. SP1/50, ff. 96–97.

55. *Lisle Letters*, 2:399 (499–500); see also 5:1280 (299–300), 1541–42, on her medical skill.

56. Prob11/11/10, Dame Jane Dynham (1498); Prob11/39/5, Dame Elizabeth Spelman (1556); see also Sir John Paston's letter to his wife, Margery, in *Paston Letters and Papers*, 1:389; and Alice Crane's to Margaret Paston, 2:711.

57. C. H. Cooper, *Memoir of Margaret*, 5 and n.; *Clifford Letters*, p. 20; HMC, *Rutland Papers*, 4:277, 287; TV, George, Lord Darcy (1548), 2:725; Prob11/28/33, Sir Edward Chamberlain (1541).

58. Strickland, *Lives of the Queens of England*, 2:393–97; GEC, 2:421, n. e.

59. Prob11/28/6 (1540); see Add'l Ms. 28,174 f. 468, the will of Dame Dorothy Ferrers (1532), and Prob11/16/29, Dame Agnes Paston (1510), for evidence of aristocratic women's work on more ordinary fabrics.

60. Lady Marney had no daughters. Prob11/33/11 (1549).

61. Vives, *Institutione Christianae Feminae*, pp. C iii verso–D.

62. Prob11/21/35.

63. *Lisle Letters*, 3:583a, 587; see also E154/2/36 (1550), inventory of Sir Edward Darrell's goods; L&P, 16:1321 (1541), on Katherine Howard; *Testamenta Leodiensia*, 178, on Lady Jane Skargill (1547).

64. BL, Royal Ms. Appendix 58. She was probably Jane (née Halliwell), wife of Edmund, Lord Bray (d. 1539).

65. See McFarlane, "Education of the Nobility," 228–47; Moran, *Growth of English Schooling*, esp. 150–63, 196–211; Rosenthal, "Aristocratic Cultural Patronage," 522–48; and Bell, "Medieval Women Book Owners, 742–68, for convincing evidence for extending this claim back to the fourteenth and fifteenth centuries in the case of the aristocracy.

66. E.g., HMC, *Rutland Papers*, 4:296–97, 308.

67. E.g., *Stonor Letters and Papers*, Elizabeth Stonor, 2:168 (1476); *Lisle Letters*, I:xxxi, (pp. 330–31; 1532), Lady Anne Weston; SP1/128, f. 14 (1538), Mary, duchess of Richmond; Add'l Ms. 41,305 (1493–99) is the holograph account book of Dame Eleanor Townshend.

68. Orme, *From Childhood to Chivalry*, 159; *Paston Letters and Papers*, 1:p. xxxviii.

69. E.g., SP11/5, f. 76; SP11/6, f. 86 (1555), Gertrude Courteney, marchioness of Ex-

eter; SP1/97, f. 148 (1535), Katherine Howard Daubney, countess of Bridgewater; SP1/92, f. 76 (1538), Elizabeth Burgh, Lord Burgh's daughter-in-law; CUL, Hengrave Hall Ms. 88, vol. 3, no. 8 (1560), Elizabeth Cornwallis, daughter of Sir Thomas.

70. E.g., SP1/235, f. 167 (1527), Sir Giles Grevill; SP1/197, 146d (1535), Henry, Lord Daubney; CUL, Hengrave Hall Ms. 88, vol. 1, no. 165 (1561).

71. Brewer, preface to L&P, I:xciv, n. 1.

72. SP10/7, f. 1 (1549). For other holograph letters, see SP1/128, f. 14; SP1/131, f. 252; and SP1/135, f. 75. I have found no contemporary evidence about the duchess's education, but her letters, her role in the circle that produced the Devonshire Manuscript in the 1530s and 1540s, and her supervision of the education of the children of her brother, Henry Howard, earl of Surrey, after his execution establish her credentials as a cultivated and well-educated woman. King, "Patronage and Piety," 51; Southall, "Devonshire Manuscript Collection," 144–47. Retha Warnicke noted the tradition, probably accurate, that the dutchess was educated with her brother, in *Women of the English Renaissance and Reformation*, 38–40.

73. Howard, *Letters from the Original Manuscripts*, 525; on her education, see Ives, *Anne Boleyn*, 11, 33–35.

74. Hoffman, "Catherine Parr as a Woman of Letters, 352; Strype, *Ecclesiastical Memorials*, 2 (2):332; *Literary Remains of King Edward the Sixth*, 1:17 (16–17).

75. *Paston Letters and Papers*, lix, 362 (591).

76. L&P, 1:xciv, n. 1, preface.

77. Chevalier au Cynge, *Helyas, Knight of the Swan*; Harris, *Edward Stafford*, 35.

78. C24/29 (1553); each of them signed his deposition in this case. See DNB, 5:1150, on Sidney; 21:652–53, on Wingfield.

79. HMC, *Rutland Papers*, 4:296.

80. Kelso, *Doctrine of the English Gentleman*, 42; see Harrison, *Description of Elizabethan England*, 234, on the incompatibility of gentility and manual labor.

81. See Scragg, *History of English Spelling*, for an introduction to this subject.

82. Rosenthal's study of the wills of peers and their wives, 1350–1500, "Aristocratic Cultural Patronage," 535–36, shows that 48 percent of the women and 18 percent of the men bequeathed books.

83. These are minimal figures since the residue of a testator's goods may have contained books. The sample consists of 763 men's wills and 266 women's wills. Testators rarely mentioned the language in which law books were written, but I assume that they were not in English; they were always left by men to other men.

84. On Chaucer, see BL, Add'l Charters, 74, 187 (1517 inventory of husband's estate), Lady Etheldreda Talbot (d. 1505); Schwoerer, *Lady Rachel Russell*, 15, Jane, countess of Southampton (m. before 1533; d. 1574); Prob11/6/2, Dame Elizabeth Bruyn (1470); *Lincoln Diocese Documents*, 49, Sir Thomas Cumberworth, bequest of *Canterbury Tales* to niece, Dame Anne Constable (1451). On Froissart, see Margaret, countess of Richmond (1443–1509), in C. H. Cooper, *Memoir of Margaret*, 132; Ives, *Common Lawyers of Pre-Reformation England*, 427. On Lydgate, see C. H. Cooper, *Memoir of Margaret*, 132; *Paston Letters and Papers*, 1:352 (p. 575); Isabell and Anne Bourchier, Sir Thomas Bourchier's two wives, apparently owned or used a copy of Lydgate's *Life of Our Lady*, which had love lyrics on the pastedown where their names appeared, Boffey, *English Courtly Love Lyrics*, 122, n. 29. On Gower, see Prob2/3 (1465), Dame Elizabeth Lewkenor; and C. H. Cooper, *Memoir of Margaret*, 133 (Lady Margaret bequeathed her copy to a woman). On Merlin, see Meale, "Manuscripts and Early Audience," 97–105.

On Boccaccio, see C. H. Cooper, *Memoir of Margaret*, 132; ProbII/24/4, Dame Anne Danvers (1531); and TE 4:57 (116), Dame Margery Salvan (1496).

85. Lambley, *Teaching and Cultivation of French*, 61–85; Dowling, *Humanism in the Age of Henry VIII*, 198.

86. CSP, Spanish, I:203, p. 156.

87. *Plumpton Correspondence*, 6.

88. *Household Accounts of John Howard*, xxxix (1455), xl (1467).

89. Lambley, *Teaching and Cultivation of French*, 75.

90. BL, Add'l Ms., 24,965, f. 200d.

91. Lambley, *Teaching and Cultivation of French*, 80, 83–91, 105; Dowling, *Humanism in the Age of Henry VIII*, 191–92, 204.

92. See Lambley, *Teaching and Cultivation of French*, 26–85, for a survey of this subject.

93. Ives, *Anne Boleyn*, chap. 1, esp. 23, 31–43; Ellis, *Original Letters Illustrative of English History*, 2nd series, 2:pp. 10–12; Gunn, *Charles Brandon*, 31, 57; L&P, 2 (1):529.

94. L&P, I (2): 5483, 5484 (3357 in 2nd ed.).

95. *Lisle Letters*, 3:574 (147), 587, pp. 133–36.

96. Fleming, "The Hauts and Their 'Circle,'" 90–91.

97. ProbII/17/2 (1480).

98. C. H. Cooper, *Memoir of Margaret*, 45.

99. Fisher, *Mornynge Remembraunce*, 1906 ed., 16.

100. STC 6894.5.

101. C. H. Cooper, *Memoir of Margaret*, 132, 134; Jones and Underwood, *King's Mother*, 274. For other women who owned or bequeathed French books, see Scofield, *Life and Reign of Edward IV*, 2:452 and n., Elizabeth Woodville and her daughters; Hicks, "Piety of Margaret," 23; TE, 45:75 (152), Anne, Lady Scrope (1498); SP1/135, f. 255d, Lady Jane Guildford (1537). For men bequeathing French books to women, see TE, 4:51, Sir Peter Ardern (1467) to his daughter, 102n.; ProbII/6/33 (1477), John Wenlock to Elizabeth, duchess of Norfolk; TE, 3:122 (299), Richard Scrope (1485) to Margaret, duchess of Norfolk.

102. Cavendish, *Thomas Wolsey*, 105–6.

103. *Literary Remains of King Edward the Sixth*, #48 (p. 49; from BL, Harleian 6986, pt. 12); DNB, 3:1218; Hoffman, "Catherine Parr as a Woman of Letters," 353.

104. Richmond's grandfather, the second duke of Norfolk, asked Alexander Barclay to write a French grammar at the time that Richmond and her brother lived at Hundson Hall, Hertfordshire, one of his main residences, for part of the year. Lambley, *Teaching and Cultivation of French*, 2:77. The title of the book is *Here begynneth the introductory to wryte and to pronounce frenche compyled by Alexander Barclay, compendiously at the command of the right hye excellent and mighty prince, Thomas duke of Northfolke* (1521; STC #1381). See DNB, 7:207, on Richmond; 10:23 on her brother, Henry, earl of Surrey. The Suffolks commissioned a manual for teaching French from their son's tutor, Pierre Valence; Lambley, *Teaching and Cultivation of French*, 2:80–81. Their mother was Henry VIII's sister, Mary, the French Queen; their father, Charles, duke of Suffolk. The book bore the title *Introductions in Frensche for Henry the Young Erle of Lyncoln (childe of greate esperaunce) sonne of the most noble and excellent princess Mary (by the grace of God, queen of France etc.)* (1528; STC #14125.5).

105. Margaret's mother, Anne Grey, and Lady Jane Grey's father, Henry, marquess

of Dorset and duke of Suffolk, were siblings. "Extracts from the Collections of Cassandra Willoughby," 406, 518.

106. Fisher, "Mornynge Remembraunce," 1846 ed., 293.

107. Pollock, " 'To Teach Her to Live in Obedience,' " 241–43; for contemporary statements about why women were excluded from studying Latin, see Hyrde, Preface to Margaret More Roper's translation of Erasmus's *Pecatio Dominca*, 97–104; Vives, *Institutione Christianae Feminae*, bk. 1, chap. 4, pp. Diii, E.

108. Fisher, "Mornynge Remembraunce," 293.

109. Moreton, *Townshends and Their World*, 144.

110. Prob11/19/18; C1/526/29; Dame Jane, coheir of Sir Miles Stapleton (d. 1466), first married Christopher Harcourt (d. 1474); their son, Simon, was her heir; her second husband was Sir John Huddleston (d. 1512); she accused their eldest son of cheating her.

111. Orme, *From Childhood to Chivalry*, 211–12.

112. Ibid., 213–14, dates the new aristocratic interest in Latin from the 1490s; the second duke of Norfolk (d. 1524) recorded on his tomb that he had attended Thetford Grammar School; significantly, his father was not yet a member of the nobility or closely connected to the court in his youth. Sixteenth-century examples include Sir Francis Bryan (Bindoff, *Commons*, 1:527). On the transformation of aristocratic education in the Tudor period, see Ferguson, *Indian Summer of English Chivalry*, esp. chap. 5; Hexter, "Education of the Aristocracy," 45–70; Stone, "Educational Revolution in England," 41–80.

113. Prob11/21/11.

114. Prob11/14/23, Sir Henry Heydon (1503); Prob11/20/24, Sir Richard Elyot (1520).

115. For full discussions of these women, see Warnicke, *Women of the English Renaissance and Reformation*, and Dowling, *Humanism in the Age of Henry VIII*, chap. 7.

116. TV, 2:639. *Somerset Medieval Wills* (1501–1530), 29 (1501); Sir John Wadham left his niece £20 toward her marriage "for her good service in times past."

117. *Lisle Letters*, 5:1379 (432).

118. A. Crawford, "Career of John Howard," 95–96. The countess was Sir John's first cousin; the countess's daughter was Lady Jane Norris, wife of Sir William.

119. TE, 4:57 (116 and n.); her niece was her sister Margery's daughter.

120. BL, Titus B. I, f. 162 (orig. 152), Elizabeth, wife of the third duke of Norfolk. The girls were her brother's daughters. See also Prob11/7/5, Sir Richard Roos (1482); Prob11/29/6, Sir David Owen (1529).

121. E.g., *Lisle Letters*, 3:574 (147), 579, 586. Madame de Riou made similar remarks about Anne, 3:570 (141), 577 (150).

122. Folger, X. d. 486, ff. 9d, 11, 21. Although the accounts refer to her as Lady Cavendish's sister, she was her mother's daughter by her second husband, Ralph Leche. Durant, *Bess of Hardwick*, 6–8, 16. This kind of arrangement was probably what Sir John Gaynsford had in mind in 1540 when he directed his executors to "put forth [his daughters] to service." He had thirteen daughters by six wives. Prob11/28/12 (1540).

123. *Lisle Letters*, 5:1396a, 453.

124. L. B. Smith, *Tudor Tragedy*, 50–67.

125. See Wall, "Love, Money," for a well-documented case from Shakespeare's lifetime.

126. SP1/15, f. 33 (1517).

127. *Lisle Letters*, I:xxxi (1532).

128. Probii/32/30, Sir Alexander Unton (1547); Probii/31/24, Sir Giles Strangeway (1546).

129. TE, 4:133 (237–38).

Chapter 3

1. This language casts doubt on Eileen Spring's criticism in *Law, Land and Family*, 177, of historians who refer to the marriage market and describe marriage as a business. Eric Acheson, *Gentry Community*, 159–73, has also objected to comparing marriage to "a commercial enterprise" or "purely business transaction." Contrary to his formulation—that external constraints were relatively unimportant in the formation of marriage (172–73)— the evidence indicates that they were of key, even paramount importance. That a small number of couples defied their parents or guardians entirely, usually at great cost to themselves, does not alter that reality. Keith Dockray's more persuasive account, "Why Did Fifteenth-Century English Gentry Marry?" 61–80, carefully assesses the shifting balance of material and emotional factors from one situation and one family to another. My reading of the evidence is similar to his, although I give somewhat more weight to parental control and material interests. Christine Carpenter, *Locality and Polity*, 114–15, describes the arrangement of marriage in terms of the marriage market and as a speculation in which dowry and jointure functioned as venture capital.

2. Add'l Ms. 24,965, f. 23 (1523); f. 103 (1524); SP1/78, f. 61 (1533); see also SP1/244, f. 232 (1544), Dorothy Josselin to her brother Sir John Gates.

3. *Lisle Letters*, 3:793 (1536).

4. CUL, Hengrave Hall Ms. 88, vol. 1, no. 140.

5. E.g., *Letters and Papers of the Verney Family*, 25, Sir Ralph Verney (1478); Probii/19/30 (1519), Sir Edmund Denny; Probii/29/23 (1543), Andrew, Lord Windsor.

6. Wyndham, *Family History*, 23; *Household Books of John Howard*, xv (1467); Probii/22/7, Fenys (1526).

7. E.g., SP1/26, f. 184; CCR, Hen VII, I:945 (1495). Suits in Chancery often rested on this understanding of the exchange. See, e.g., C1/40/144 (1467–70); C1/1187/5 (1547–52).

8. HEH, Hastings Collection, HAP Box 3, folder 19 (1536).

9. Add'l Ms. 24,965, f. 231.

10. E.g., *Plumpton Correspondence*, p. 9 of Dockray's unpaginated introduction (1446); ERO, D/DP F143 (1513); SP1/137, f. 43 (1532). Occasionally the marriage was (or was intended to be) consummated before the bride was 16; see e.g., BL, Add'l Charters, 73,901 (1468).

11. The five exceptions in sixteen cases involved an heiress who was her future father-in-law's ward, another whose prospective father-in-law had agreed to pay the heavy costs of suing her land out of livery, and three women who were marrying into families of higher rank than their own. HEH, Hastings Collection, HAP Box 3, folder 25 and oversize Box 5, folder 13. HMC, Hastings, 1:1281 (303–4; 1474); *Plumpton Correspondence*, xcix–c (1496); C1/281/74 (1496, 1497); WRO, Throckmorton Papers, CR 1998, Box 72, 8 (1558).

12. In ten of sixteen cases to be exact. See e.g., WRO, Throckmorton Papers, CR 1998, Box 72, #1 (1501); SP1/33, f. 149 (1525); Finch, *Wealth of Five Northamptonshire Families*, 141 (1539).

13. E.g., WRO, Throckmorton Papers, CR 1998, Box 72, #1 (1501); SP1/140, f. 64 (1538); Prob11/17/13 (1513); Sir Thomas Cheyney of Irthlingborough, Northants, bequeathed 1,000 marks to his only daughter in case he had a male heir before he died.

14. Add'l Ms. 24,965, f. 23 (1523); f. 103 (1524); for failed negotiations involving Elizabeth Paston, see *Paston Letters and Papers*, 1:18 (c. 1449), 19 (1450), 27 (c. 1454), 50 (1454), 2:493 (1454?).

15. *Paston Letters and Papers*, 1:226, 300, 304; according to Gairdner, negotiations began by February 1477, *Paston Letters*, 5:264n.

16. SP1/235, f. 167 (1527).

17. ERO, D/DP F294, John Tyrrell of Heron, esq., son of Sir Thomas; also see Collins, *Letters and Memorials of State*, 1:14, for Edward, Viscount Lisle (1492).

18. Fifty-four, or 7 percent, of 763 testators left dowries to their granddaughters; forty-three, or 6 percent, to their nieces; eighteen, or 2 percent, to their sisters; and seven, or 1 percent, to their step daughters.

19. Prob11/16/17 (Fenys); HEH, Hastings Collection, HAP oversize Box 5, folder 25.

20. These figures are based on the dowries of the daughters of 256 knights and 99 peers recorded in marriage contracts, wills, and Chancery cases. Dowries were set in marks or pounds sterling. Figures here are in marks because that was the unit used more frequently in marriage contracts. A mark equaled two-thirds of a pound, 13s. 4d. See glossary for other equivalents. J. P. Cooper, "Patterns of Inheritance and Settlement," 311, found a higher average in a smaller sample of 90, £201–£250 (300–75 marks).

21. This conclusion contrasts with my earlier published statement, Harris, "New Look at the Reformation," 97, that the period was characterized by dowry inflation, a contrast probably explained by the fact that I now have a larger sample of the dowries of both knights' and peers' daughters. My conclusions about the movement of dowry size are based on comparing figures for five periods of twenty years each, beginning in 1450.

22. E.g., *Some Oxfordshire Wills*, 42, Sir Edmund Rede (1487); *Bedfordshire Wills*, 53 (71), Sir John Mordaunt (1504); Prob11/23/24, Sir J. More (1526); Prob11/38/23, Sir Richard Cotton (1556).

23. *Letters and Papers of the Verney Family*, 25.

24. Prob11/19/30 (1519).

25. Prob11/31/10 (1536).

26. SP1/152, f. 45 (1539); Henry, third marquess of Dorset, jilted her to marry Frances, daughter of Henry VIII's sister Mary and Charles Brandon, duke of Suffolk (GEC, 4:421); the implication of her letter is that her dowry had been paid; on the dowry as premortem inheritance, see Hughes, "Brideprice to Dowry," 278–82, 287–88.

27. TV, 1:273 (1455), and C1/44/186 (416), Hoo; TE, 5:100 (122), Fairfax (1520).

28. Men's bequests to their younger sons in their wills may not be the only provision they made for them, although the bequests' language usually suggests that they were. Fathers also often left offspring of both sexes, married and unmarried, movable goods. These could be token or substantial gifts.

29. E.g., TE, 3:124 (304), Henry, earl of Northumberland (1485); Prob11/17/21, Sir Giles Brugge (1511); Prob11/38/12, Sir John Kingsmill (1556).

30. These testators provided equally for all their younger sons.

31. Prob11/27/19 (1538).

32. J. C. Cooper, "Patterns of Inheritance and Settlement," 212–19. Neither his examples nor my figures support Eileen Spring's contention in *Law, Land and Family*, 86,

that before the strict settlement "younger sons did at least as well as daughters, and would seem often to have done considerably better."

33. The material in this and the two following paragraphs first appeared in my article "New Look at the Reformation," 89–113.

34. 1535 was the year of the royal visitation that preceded the dissolution of religious houses in England. It might have alarmed some fathers enough to affect the way they provided for their daughters even before the government actually dissolved the poorest nunneries.

35. According to J. P. Cooper, "Inheritance and Settlement," 306, 308n. (d), the minimal dowry for the daughter of a nobleman who was entering a convent was £100 in the early sixteenth century, a tenth of the average marriage portion, which was between 1,000 marks and £1,000. Thomas West, Lord de la Warre, reduced his daughter Mary's portion from 500 to 100 marks if she became a nun (Prob11/22/2, 1504), while Sir Edmund Denny left his daughters the same portion whether they married or entered convents (Prob11/19/30, 1519). Sir Piers Newton left his daughter only 5 marks toward her profession as a nun (Prob11/21/3, 1524).

36. Prob11/46, Brandon (1475); Macnamara, Memorials of the Danvers Family, 271, Danvers (1515); Prob11/17/21, Bridges (1521); Prob11/13/7, Dorset (1501); daughters whose fate is unknown probably died young and dropped out of family genealogies and other records.

37. CCR, Hen VII, I:945.

38. HMC, 7:584.

39. I owe this point to Judith Bennett.

40. Collins, Letters and Memorials of State, 1:14.

41. BL, Add'l Ms. 42,764, f. 7 (formerly 12; 1524).

42. Smyth, Berkeley Manuscripts, 2:252.

43. B.L., Add'l Ms. 24,965, f. 173 (1523).

44. Add'l Ms. 24,965, f. 231d. Dacre's figure of 10 percent in the 1520s is the one Eileen Spring, Law, Land and Family, 50–51, presents as an all-time low in the era of the strict settlement.

45. The second most common ratios between dowry and jointure were 6:1 and 4:1; the median figure was 7.5:1.

46. Forty-eight of the eighty-two marriage contracts used in this project indicated the value of the jointure land; the rest simply listed the specific estates and pieces of land to be used for that purpose.

47. HampRO, 5M53 935 (1545); the contract expressed her dowry in pounds (£300); I converted it for purposes of comparison; this marriage did not take place.

48. HampRO, 5M53 281 (1545); this marriage did take place.

49. LincAO, Ancaster Ms. 1. 5/B/1/P.

50. HRO, D/E Fn T37; she was the daughter of Sir Richard and sister of Sir Nicholas; Bindoff, Commons, 1:575–76.

51. C1/490/33, Dame Elizabeth Clere vs. Sir Robert Clere (1527–29); L&P, 4 (2):3741.

52. Despite this reply, the Privy Council assigned the countess an annuity of 100 marks in 1543. L&P, 18 (1):982 (p. 547).

53. C1/405/29 (1515–29); Dorothy was the widow of John, son of Christopher Codrington.

54. C1/1187/5 (1547–52); she was the widow of Sir John Gostwick and wife of Francis Russell at the time of the suit; see also C1/185/49 (1487–1504), C1/348/38 (1504–15).

55. *Statutes of the Realm*, 3:694. Dorothy was married to Richard, heir of Walter Devereux, Lord Ferrers.

56. HEH, Hastings Collection, HAP Box 5, folder 7, Edward, Lord Hastings (1506); Prob11/31/40, Sir John Horsey (1546); *Miscellanea Genealogica and Heraldica*, NS, 2:16, Sir John Gresham (1552).

57. The remaining seven cases involved dowries left to women by persons other than their fathers.

58. The scattered evidence from sources other than court cases confirms the impression that most difficulties about the payment of dowries arose after the bride's father died. See, e.g., SP1/115, f. 186d (1537); HampRO, 19M61 1300 (1557).

59. Fourteen cases were about assuring women's jointures under their marriage contracts; two, about infringements on their jointures during their marriages; forty-four, about obtaining their jointures after their husbands died; and thirty-nine, about continued peaceful possession of their jointures during their widowhoods or subsequent marriages.

60. Prob11/5/23; Vernon had evidently used his wife's jointure for his daughter-in-law's jointure.

61. Prob11/33/25 (1545); see also Prob11/21/35, John, Lord Marney (1525); and TV:1 (p. 273), Thomas, Lord Hoo and Hastings (1455).

62. E.g., Prob11/4/21, Humphrey, duke of Buckingham (1460); the duke's feoffees had not yet assured his daughter-in-law's jointure when his son, Sir Henry Stafford, died in 1471 (Prob11/7/5); Prob11/22/29, Sir William Waldegrave (1526); Prob11/17/21, Sir William Courteney (1511).

63. There is no way of knowing if the complaints in these suits were justified since no decrees or arbitration awards exist.

64. I owe this point to Olga Valbuena.

65. C1/228/68 (1487–1504).

66. C1/656/22 (1529–33).

67. SP1/137, f. 43 (1537); L&P, XII (2):137, 1018, 1019; XIII (2):448. For an earlier example, see C1/228/68 (1487–1504).

68. Prob11/25/29 (1535).

69. Prob11/19/30, Sir Edmund Denny (1519); for earlier examples of this strategy, see HEH, Hastings Collections, HAP, Box 4, folder 12, William, Lord Hastings (1481); and Prob11/15/33, Sir Robert Tyrrell (1507).

70. TE, 4:63 (124; 1497).

71. Prob11/22/2, Lord de la Warre (1525); Collins, *Historical Collections*, Sir William Holles (1542), 59.

72. Prob11/11/23, Sir Robert Radcliffe.

73. Prob11/42A/37, Sir John Shelton (1558).

74. Prob11/22/13, Charles Somerset, earl of Worcester (1525); challenges to ownership were more likely to arise over purchased rather than inherited land.

75. Prob11/11/23, Sir Robert Radcliffe (1496).

76. Prob11/39/6, Sir Edward Montague (1556).

77. LRO, 26D53/1947, Shirley (1485); Prob11/27/27, Lee (1537).

78. Prob11/39/33.

79. *Lincoln Diocese Documents*, 70 (1455).

80. TE, 6:109 (127; 1541).

81. I have purposely excluded Henry VIII's marriages and the schemes to marry

Edward VI from this discussion because they are so well known and so exceptional. On the fifteenth century, see Lander, "Marriage and Politics," 94–126.

82. Folger, W. b. 268, f. 125, Annals of the Seymours, 1540–98 (c. 1830); Robinson, *Original Letters*, Parker Society, 53 (2; 1847), 265, n. 4.

83. GEC, 10:411.

84. SP1/88, f. 88 (1534); Musgrave did not take Norfolk's advice.

85. Lambeth Palace, Shrewsbury Papers, 3206, f. 407 (1561).

86. Collins, *Historical Collections*, 56.

87. Prob11/32/27 (1545).

88. Prob11/6/34.

89. Prob11/32/37 (1545).

90. Prob11/40/16 (1557); see also TV, 2:71, Sir John Cornwallis (1544) and William, Lord Windsor; TV, 2:754 (1558).

91. E.g., Prob11/29/17, John Nevill, Lord Latimer (1542); Prob11/31/10, Sir John Fulford (1536); Prob11/42A/24, Sir John Baker (1558).

92. *Paston Letters and Papers*, 1:226, 378; pp. 605, 606; 2:789–91. See Richmond, "Pastons Revisited," 25–36, and Haskell, "Paston Women on Marriage," 466–69, for the variety of ways in which the interests of young couples and their families were balanced in a particularly well-documented family.

93. "Willoughby Letters," 7; 6 (20–21).

94. Willoughby, *Continuation of the History of the Willoughby Family*, 9.

95. *Paston Letters and Papers*, 1:203, 332.

96. Ibid., 282–83.

97. Req2/10/157; Prob11/22/40.

98. *Lisle Letters*, 4:989, 998, 1001, 1010–11, pp. 361–62 (1537); Grenville (Prob11/33/25, 1545) bequeathed her a dowry of 100 marks, the same amount he gave his other married daughter; by then Lee had been knighted.

99. Vives, *Institutione Christianae Feminae*, p. R iv; Bullinger, *Christian State of Matimony*, STC #4046, chap. 5; Kelso, *Doctrine for the Lady of the Renaissance*, 92.

100. See chapter 1, 20–22.

101. *Plumpton Correspondence*, lxxi.

102. Prob11/17/13 (1514); GEC, vol. 12 (pt. 2):221.

103. TV, I:274.

104. Macnamara, *Memorials of the Danvers Family*, 272 (1515).

105. Prob11/33/25 (1545).

106. Prob11/32/12 (1547); see also Prob11/7/27, Sir Richard Harcourt (1486); Prob11/16/22, Sir Richard Croft (1509).

107. C1/27/153 (1463–65).

108. C1/312/98 (1504–15); Dorset had left her 1,000 marks if she married with the consent of his executors. Prob11/13/7 (1501).

109. SP10/10, f. 9 (1550).

110. Prob11/22/26 (1527).

111. Prob11/23/22 (1527).

112. CUL, Hengrave Hall Ms. 90, #42 (1561).

113. In three cases, the women may have been stepmothers to some or all of the unmarried daughters mentioned in their fathers' wills.

114. They selected their daughter's paternal uncles in twenty-five, or almost 10 per-

cent, of the cases; their maternal uncles in seven, or 3 percent; and their (i.e., the brides') brothers-in-law in six, or 2 percent.

Chapter 4

1. *The Book of the Knight of the Tower* was written in French, a language many members of the aristocracy knew. It was translated into English for the first time during the reign of Henry VI (xix, 35). Vives, *Institutione Christianae Feminae*, bk. 2, p. a verso.

2. E. g., William Harrington, *Commendations of Matrimony*, p. D ii verso; Harrington was a doctor of canon law.

3. Becon, *Preface*, 20.

4. For a similar view, see Rosenthal, "Aristocratic Marriage," 181–94.

5. Chojnacki, *Women and Men in Renaissance Venice*, 12.

6. A. Crawford, "Career of John Howard," 103; *Household Books of John Howard*, xiii, xv–xvi, xxxviii, I:582, 2:106, 152, 154.

7. CUL, Hengrave Hall Ms. 88, vol. 1, nos. 91 and 115.

8. Ibid., f. 115 (1558); green sickness was a form of anemia, especially associated with girls around the age of puberty. OED, 1:404.

9. CUL, Hengrave Hall Ms. 88, vol. 1, no. 83 (1559). Jane's mother may well have been correct since she died before November 1560; vol. 1, nos. 88 and 57. For another example, see HMC, *Rutland Mss*, 4:295, 302–3, 306, the first earl of Rutland's household accounts. The Rutlands' daughter Gertrude and her husband appear in the accounts as Lord and Lady Talbot. Their heir, styled Lord Roos, married the earl of Westmorland's daughter Margaret, and their daughter Anne, styled Lady Nevill and married to Westmorland's heir Henry, were also living at home. Although Anne's husband does not seem to be a member of the household, they must have cohabited at least occasionally since she had a child during the period she resided at Belvoir.

10. Halstead, *Succinct Genealogical Proofs of the House of Green*, 197.

11. NRO, Lestrange of Hunstanton, A42; see Oestmann, *Lordship and Community*, 13, for date of Sir Thomas's death.

12. *Plumpton Correspondence*, pp. cxxv–cxxvi; *Plumpton Letters and Papers*, 192, 221, 229–31, 252, appendix 2:78.

13. Harris, *Edward Stafford*, 56.

14. Bindoff, *Commons*, 2:522; NRO, Lestrange of Hunstanton, A42. For other examples, see CCR, Hen VII, 2:694 (1506); HEH, Hastings Collection, HAP Box 2, folder 28 (1448); *Willoughby Letters*, 30.

15. *Plumpton Letters and Papers*, 159, 193, 195.

16. BL, Vespasian, F. XIII, art. 136, f. 187; on his age, see GEC, 4:420.

17. Hoyle, "Letters of the Cliffords," 42, 60; GEC, 3:567–68.

18. Bindoff, *Commons*, 2:522; NRO, Lestrange of Hunstanton, A42; Oestmann, *Lordship and Community*, 13.

19. *Plumpton Correspondence*, pp. cxxv–cxxvi; *Plumpton Letters and Papers*, 192, 221, 229–31, 252, appendix 2:78.

20. BL, Add'l Ms. 27,447, f. 74 (1529); Prob11/23/27, Lovell (1522); GEC, 11:105–8; Bindoff, *Commons*, 2:548. The countess's father was Sir William Paston (d. 1554).

21. BL, Titus B1, XI, f. 362 (1523).

22. *Paston Letters and Papers*, 1:128 (1448).

23. GEC, 10:245; SP1/27, 147, 148, 150, 151, 152d; BL, Hargrave Ms. 249, f. 223 (orig. 226).

24. Harris, "Women and Politics," 259–81. For the fifteenth century, see *Paston Letters and Papers*, passim, and *Plumpton Letters and Papers*, passim.

25. *Stonor Letters and Papers*, 2:260.

26. On this aspect of Margaret Paston's life, see Haskell, "Paston Women on Marriage," 460–66.

27. BL, Add'l Ms. 41,139 and 41,305, Townshend accounts; Eleanor Townshend was the wife of Sir Roger (d. 1493); ERO, D/DP A16, Account Book of John Tyrrell, 1539–40.

28. ERO, D/DP A 16, Account Book of John Tyrrell, 1539–40; D/DP A11, ff. 3–107 (1554–55), passim, f. 3 for figure; ERO, D/DP F 294. Lady Petre was one of her first husband's coexecutors. She was probably receiving money on their daughter Catherine's behalf, as well as her dower or jointure.

29. BL, Caligula B. VI, f. 152 (orig. 135); also Caligula B. II, f. 188 (orig. 178), an earlier letter on Scotland.

30. SP1/82, f. 248.

31. BL, Caligula B. VII, f. 207. Similarly, Margaret Paston kept her husband apprised of local politics when he was in London; see e.g., *Paston Letters and Papers*, 1:177, 178.

32. SP1/84, f. 100. She was the daughter of George, fourth earl of Shrewsbury.

33. There is no evidence about how they acquired this knowledge.

34. *Plumpton Letters and Papers*, 168 (1502).

35. SP1/233, ff. 53–54; C1/405/20; C1/421/7–12.

36. SP1/244, f. 223; she was married to Sir John Shelton (d. 1558). For other women who represented their husbands in legal matters or displayed legal knowledge, see SP1/46, f. 15 (1527), Joyce, first wife of Lord Edmund Howard; *Paston Letters and Papers*, 1:177 (1464), 178 (1465), 353 (1472; p. 577), on Margaret Paston; 2:545 (1465), on Dame Alice Ogard; BL, Vespasian F. XIII, art. 175, f. 227, Anne, Lady Conyers (1538).

37. CCR, Edward IV (1468–76), 2:132 (Merston); HMC, *Hastings Mss.*, 1:291 (Hastings); SP46/1, f. 29 (Grevill); VCH, Wiltshire, 13:221.

38. LincAO, 3 Ancaster 8/1/3; she was a widow from 1545 to 1553 and almost certainly had a prenuptial agreement that gave her control of her property during her second marriage—hence the transactions she executed alone.

39. SP1/231, f. 171–72 (1510); Lady Lucy, wife of Sir Thomas, was the widow of George Catesby.

40. Oestmann, *Lordship and Community*, 16.

41. NRO, Lestrange of Hunstanton, A38; Blomefield, 10:114–15; at least nine lived long enough to marry. Oestmann, *Lordship and Community*, 15.

42. Oestmann, *Lordship and Community*, 13–15.

43. Guerney, "Household and Privy Purse Accounts," 416–30; 428–29 for her lying-in.

44. There are accounts for 1520, 1522, 1525, and 1526; see ibid., 428–89 and 449, 489 for births.

45. Ibid., 489–510, 544–45, passim. I assume that Lady Lestrange kept the accounts that refer to "my husband" (e.g. 502, 506, 510–53). She seems to have kept the entire accounts for 1530, 1532, and 1533.

46. Ibid., 522; Oestmann, *Lordship and Community*, 16.

47. Guerney, "Household and Privy Purse Accounts," 532–34, 535.

48. Ibid., 536–42, 545–46, 548–49.

49. Ibid., 549.

50. Ibid., 500, 544–45; Oestmann, *Lordship and Community*, 13–15, 20; Prob11/15/2, Sir Roger Lestrange (1505).

51. Guerney, "Household and Privy Purse Accounts," 543–44.

52. Ibid., 449.

53. Ibid., 523. As so often happened, a simple kin term—in this case, *uncle*—actually referred to a much more distant affinal tie.

54. Ibid., 425, 427–30; three nonaristocratic women also attended her lying-in.

55. Ibid., 483, 485.

56. Ibid., 484–85, 488.

57. Ibid., 482–83; Oestmann, *Lordship and Community*, 14, n. 5.

58. HMC, *Rutland Mss.*, 4:260, 275, 295; GEC, 11:255.

59. HMC, *Rutland Mss.*, 4:291.

60. Ives, *Anne Boleyn*, 198; HMC, *Rutland Mss.*, 4:271, 274; *Lisle Letters*, 1:350; GEC, 11:254.

61. The countess's role in events leading up to Anne Boleyn's marriage to Henry; a letter to her father, indicating that the queen was going to visit her at Endfield; and references to the countess's presence at court while Boleyn was queen strongly suggest that she belonged to Anne Boleyn's household; unfortunately no complete list of Boleyn's household survives. Ives, *Anne Boleyn*, 198; *Lisle Letters*, 4:855, 855a, 874; Green, *Letters of Royal and Illustrious Ladies*, 3:168–69.

62. HMC, *Rutland Mss.*, 4, passim; *Lisle Letters*, 4, 5, passim.

63. HMC, *Rutland Mss.*, 4:294; *Lisle Letters*, 4:880, 887, 5:1495; Murray and Bosanquet, *Manuscripts of William Dunche*, 15.

64. Bindoff, *Commons*, 1:667.

65. *Lisle Letters*, 1:350, 4:882; 5:1091, 1223, 1404.

66. BL, Add'l Ms. 6113, f. 199d; Wriothesley, *Chronicle of England*, 50.

67. *Lisle Letters*, 5:1396a.

68. HMC, *Rutland Mss.*, 4:314, 315, 318.

69. Ibid., 4:271, 275, 281, 288.

70. E.g., ibid., 268, 273–74, 276.

71. Ibid., 269–70.

72. Green, *Letters of Royal and Illustrious Ladies*, 3:168–69.

73. HMC, *Rutland Mss.*, 4:288.

74. Ibid., 4:337.

75. *North Country Wills*, 134 (188–89); Rutland was using the terms *dower* and *jointure* loosely, probably as synonyms; widows could not claim both after 1536.

76. On Margaret Donington Kitson Long Bourchier, countess of Bath, see Bindoff, *Commons*, 2:545–46; GEC, 2:17; the earl died in 1561. To avoid confusion, I refer to her as the countess of Bath throughout this discussion, although she would have been known as Lady Kitson and then as Lady Long during her first two marriages.

77. Prob11/29/30; CUL, Hengrave Hall Ms. 89 (3), f. 229; Ms. 91; SuffRO, 449/5/2.

78. On wardship, see the glossary; CUL, Hengrave Hall Ms. 90, no. 40.

79. L&P, 21 (1):969 (2), 1384 (696–97).

80. Prob11/31/18.

81. CUL, Hengrave Hall Ms. 90, document marked 72 (1548). The marriage took

place, but Frances's husband predeceased his father in 1556 at the age of 27. They had a son, who became his grandfather's heir. GEC, 2:17.

82. CUL, Hengrave Hall Ms. 88, vol. 3, nos. 35, 48, 75. Three of her Kitson daughters were already married.

83. Ibid., Ms. 90, document marked 72 (1548).

84. SuffRO, Kitson of Hengrave, 449/5/5 (1551); the earl fulfilled his obligations in his will. Prob11/44/12 (1561).

85. E.g., CUL, Hengrave Hall Ms. 88, 1:22, 37, 54; Ms. 91 (various items in wrapper marked "correspondence").

86. E.g., ibid., Ms. 88, vol. 1, nos. 21, 23, 31, 46, 48, 54, 84, 87.

87. E.g., ibid., Ms. 88, vol. 1, nos. 23, 37.

88. Ibid., nos. 40, 88.

89. Ibid., Ms. 91 (in wrapper marked "18 memoranda, acquittances" etc.).

90. Ibid., Ms. 88, no. 86; Prob11/44/12.

91. Prob11/31/3 (1545).

92. Prob11/42A/34 (1558).

93. Vives, *Institutione Christianae Feminae*, bk. 2, p. c verso.

94. SP1/115, f. 70 (1537).

95. Harrington, *Commendations of Matrimony*, p. D ii; Vives, *Institutione Christianae Feminae*, bk. 2, p. U iii verso.

96. BL, Caligula, D. VI., f. 246 (orig. 242).

97. SP1/10, f. 79; see also BL, Caligula, D. VI., f. 253 (orig. f. 249).

98. Le Grande, *Boke of Good Maners*, bk. 4, chaps. v–vi; Vives, *Institutione Christianae Feminae*, bk. 2, p. U iii verso.

99. These were the vows in the Sarum Use, the most widespread form of the service in pre-Reformation England; they were taken over unchanged in the Book of Common Prayer. *Annotated Book of Common Prayer*, 266.

100. Quoted in Thomason, *Thomas Wyatt*, 10.

101. *Stonor Letters and Papers*, 2:180; her letters are from the 1470s.

102. Ibid., 169; see also 172, 175, 176, 226.

103. CUL, Hengrave Hall Ms. 88, vol. 1, f. 23; the Baths' letters are from the 1550s.

104. Ibid., Ms. 91, letter dated 12 May.

105. CUL, Hengrave Hall Ms. 88, vol. 1, f. 48; see also 19, 22 and Ms. 91 (in wrapper that says 'correspondence' etc.), letter dated 3 April.

106. Ibid., no. 49; see also nos. 21, 134, 136.

107. SP1/199, f. 176 (1545).

108. Ibid., f. 209. For another husband who was mourning a recently deceased and beloved wife, see BL, Add'l Ms. 24,965, f. 57, Humphrey Coningsby (1523).

109. SP1/125, f. 106 (1537).

110. SP1/143, f. 177 (1539).

111. HMC, *Rutland Mss.*, 1:31. The earl died the day before Paston wrote; GEC, 11:255.

112. Prob11/5/28 (1469).

113. Prob11/39/28, Morison (1550); Prob11/11/17, Bedingfield (1496); *North Country Wills*, 49 (68), Welles (1499); Prob11/30/40, Willoughby (1544). There are slight variations in their language.

114. Based on information in GEC.

115. HMC, *Rutland Mss.*, 4:270, 272, 304, 311, 338.

116. Guerney, "Household and Privy Purse Accounts," 431, 435, 451, 512, 517, 550.

117. Ibid., 426–29.

118. E.g., PRO, C24/23 (2), C24/1.

119. See Harris, "Marriage Sixteenth-Century Style," 371–82, for this dramatic story; for allegations of extreme mistreatment of another wife, see BL, Titus B. 1, f. 398, complaint of Elizabeth, Lady Hungerford, against Walter, Lord Hungerford.

120. Prob11/18/18, Sir William Knyvett (1515).

121. LincAO, 2 Ancaster 3/B/6 (1534). For details, see Gunn, *Charles Brandon, Duke of Suffolk*, 130–31. Sir William Petre also intervened to protect his daughter from her incompetent spouse, John Gostwick; see Emmison, *Tudor Secretary*, 287n.; ERO, D/DP Z13/8, f. 11.

122. BL, Hargrave Ms. 249, f. 223 (orig. 226). Oxford was 21 in 1520.

123. SP1/27, 151–52d.

124. BL, Hargrave Ms. 249, f. 223 (orig. 226).

125. C1/66/399 (1475–80 or 1483–85); her second husband, John Welles, was a party to the suit.

126. C1/66/95 (1475–80 or 1483–85).

127. Prob11/23/13 (1527).

128. Prob11/23/6 (1529).

129. "Early Berkshire Wills," 51 (1509).

130. HEH, Hastings Collection, HAP, Box 10, folder 1, will of Francis Hastings, second earl of Huntington; HMC, *Hastings Mss.*, 1:1295a (313–14); GEC, 6:656. The earl's will was not proved until after his death in 1560. Sir William Vernon also compensated his wife for her jointure, which he had transferred to his heir and daughter-in-law; Prob11/5/23 (1467).

131. C1/656/22 (1529–33). For a father who was instituting a similar suit, see C1/252/20 (1501–2), Thomas, Lord de la Warre vs. John, Lord Clinton.

132. SP1/100, f. 110.

133. SP1/239, f. 239 (1535).

134. Anstruther, *Vaux of Harrowden*, 50–53; *Statutes of the Realm*, 3:27, Henry VIII, cap. 30 (579–80).

135. L&P, 10:744 (1536).

136. HampRO, 23M586 (1541); they married in 1513. For suits claiming that husbands failed to assure their wives' jointures, see C1/58/62 (1475–80 or 1483–85), C1/310/60 (1504–15), C1/610/2 (1514–29).

137. Prob11/33/25 (1545).

138. C1/526/28 (1515–29); Prob11/17/21, Sir John Huddleston (1511); the quotation is from Huddleston's will.

139. Prob11/19/18, Dame Jane Huddleston (1518).

140. Req2/14/53; Bindoff, *Commons*, 1:291. Margery also claimed that she had brought him £700 in ready money, 500 marks' worth of plate, a furnished house worth 200 marks, 1,000 marks in good debts due to her father, and a crown office worth 400 marks.

141. Prob11/42A/20 (1558). Apparently, he never settled a jointure on her. For the Privy Council's decisive action to force William Bulmer to support his wife, see *Acts of the Privy Council*, 1:48, 81, 98, 148, 151, and *Proceedings and Ordinances of the Privy Council*, 7:321–22.

142. Bindoff, *Commons*, 2:303–4, 634; House of Lords Record Office, Original Acts, Private Bills, 32 Henry VIII, # 66. Lady Harper was still alive in 1546 when Morison married Bridget, daughter of Sir John Hussey; Morison settled one of his estates on her and their children before his marriage. Other cases include C78/2/78 (1540) on Humphrey Tyrell and his wife, Jane, heir of Robert Ingleton (Bindoff, *Commons*, 2:193–94) and C1/1178/7 (1547) on Sir John Gascoigne of Cardington and his wife, Margaret, coheir of Sir Robert Skargill.

143. Stretton, *Women Waging Law in Elizabethan England*, 143–54, discusses this phenomenon in the Court of Requests, which heard cases from a broader group of the population.

144. Req2/14/53 (Acton); *Acts of the Privy Council*, 1:pp. 48, 148, 151 (Bulmer).

145. Brundage, *Law, Sex, and Christian Society*, 358–60, 385–87, 485–87.

146. Other evidence shows that nine additional men in this group had illegitimate children.

147. Dugdale, *Antiquities of Warwickshire*, 586b, for Catesby's will (1485).

148. Harris, *Edward Stafford*, 51. Anne's husband, George, Lord Hastings, was created earl of Huntingdon in 1529; GEC, 6:655. The document recording that Compton took the sacrament is undated.

149. SP1/49, f. 8. Another courtier, Sir Thomas Brandon, left real estate to a woman at court, Lady Jane Guildford, to whom he was not related; "Early Berkshire Wills," 51 (1509).

150. HEL, Hastings Collection, HA 5274 (1528); Hastings was created earl of Huntingdon in 1529.

151. Ibid., HAP Box 7, folder 16 (1534; probated 1544).

152. L&P, 18 (1), 981 (89); Thomason, *Thomas Wyatt*, 69–73.

153. Prob11/10/34, Henry, Lord Grey (1492); TE, 5:47 (55), Sir Ralph Bigod (1515); TE, 6:155 (193), Sir Richard Holland (1548); Prob11/33/10, Sir Anthony Brown (1547). Brown empowered his widow to arrange his bastard daughter's marriage.

154. *Paston Letter and Papers*, 1:230 (1482); Prob11/29/2 (1541). Culpepper refers to her as "my husband's daughter"; there is no record that he was married previously.

155. Prob11/20/19 (1514).

156. Harris, "Marriage Sixteenth-Century Style," passim.

157. SP1/117, f. 172 (1537). No evidence indicates whether this appeal was more successful.

158. SP1/92, f. 76; SP1/126, f. 144; L&P, 18 (pt. 1):66, cap. 40, and 67 (2); *House of Lords Journals*, 1:217; House of Lords Record Office, Original Acts, Private Bills, 34–35 Henry VIII, c. 32; Prob11/33/27 (1550). The act declared that she had "partly confessed" her guilt, which may indicate that Margaret was legitimate but that her sons were not.

159. BL, Vespasian, F. IX, f. 115–16. Since the records of the Court of Arches do not survive, evidence of this divorce is indirect. See *North Country Wills*, Sir Charles Brandon, 159 (216); Prob11/39/33, Henry, earl of Sussex (1555); GEC, 12 (1), 521, n. k. William, marquess of Northampton, secured a statute that bastardized his wife's children (they were quite clearly not his offspring) and deprived her of dower in his estates; however, he settled 500 marks a year on her, although she persisted in living "as she listed." SP1/175, f. 78; GEC, 9:669–72; S. E. James, "Tudor Divorce," 199–205.

160. *Lisle Letters*, 4:4–5; CPR, Edward IV, 1:539–40 (1466).

161. Bindoff, *Commons*, 3:352, 354.

162. SP1/121, f. 193.

163. SP46/2, f. 124.

164. GEC, 6:143. Powis had three or four illegitimate children by Jane Orwell, for whom he provided in his will. ProbII/34/17 (1541; probated 1551).

165. LincAO, 3 Ancaster 8/1/1.

166. On Hungerford, see BL, Cotton Ms., Titus B I, f. 398, Miller, *Henry VIII and the English Nobility*, 71; and GEC, 6:625–26, 7:16–18; on Norfolk, see Harris, "Marriage Sixteenth-Century Style."

Chapter 5

1. Oliva, *Convent and the Community*, 53–54, found that 11 percent of the nuns in the Norwich diocese in 1350–1450 were from the nobility or upper gentry; however, she included the daughters of esquires in the upper gentry, whereas my figures include only the daughters of peers and knights.

2. Of 266 female wills, only 4 were written by never-married women.

3. The best study of nuns in the period is Oliva, *Convent and the Community*; for aristocratic laywomen's attitude toward and relations with convents, see Harris, "New Look at the Reformation," 96, 98–109.

4. Harris, "New Look at the Reformation," 111–12.

5. CCR, Hen VII, 2:524.

6. ProbII/25/35 (1535); he left them generous dowries if they made that choice.

7. ProbII/28/25 (1541).

8. Hampton, "Ladies of the Minories," 200; GEC, 12 (1), 453 n. g.

9. Hampton, "Ladies of the Minories," 198; ProbII/14/21 (1504).

10. ProbII/25/29 (1535).

11. ProbII/28/30 (1540).

12. C1/1205/66 (1544).

13. ProbII/33/14, Lady Jane Corbet (d. 1550); C1/1205/63–66 and C24/24 on Sir Richard's will (d. 1524).

14. See WRO, Throckmorton Papers, CR 1998, Box 73, #2, Sir Robert Throckmorton (1518); ProbII/25/29, Sir Edward Ferrers (1535); ProbII/29/11, Sir Thomas Barnardiston (1542).

15. TE, 6:126 (1542).

16. ProbII/33/28 (1550); by "employing" the money he almost certainly meant lending it at interest.

17. *Somerset Medieval Wills (1501–1530)*, 241 (Zouche, 1525); ProbII/31/24 (Strangeways, 1546).

18. *Miscellanea Genealogica and Heraldica*, 4 (n.s., 2), 150, 431.

19. ProbII/56/43 (1574).

20. *Household Books of John Howard*, xiv; ProbII/5/19 (1465). Norris and Chedworth had a son and daughter of their own.

21. ProbII/21/3; C1/179/15; GEC, 4:78.

22. *Lisle Letters*, 3:pp. 38–40.

23. L&P, 4(2):3479, Green, *Letters of Royal and Illustrious Ladies*, 1:313–14. The letter was written between 1527, when Mary's mother, Dorothy Capell, daughter of Sir William, died, and 1529, when Wolsey fell from power. *Catalogue, Holbein and the Court of Henry VIII*, 79–80; Murray and Bosanquet, *Manuscripts of William Dunche*, 21; L&P,

17:283 (28). There is no evidence that Zouche served in the households of Henry's later wives; she may have died before he married again.

24. ProbII/32/35 (1549); C1/1194/67, 69, 70 (1547–52); C4/8/171; Wake, *Brudenells of Deane*, genealogy chart, inside back cover.

25. C1/1116/61 (1544–47).

26. ProbII/15/29 (1503).

27. *Plumpton Letters and Papers*, 216, 252.

28. C1/1105/66.

29. IHR, Thynne Papers, 48, f. 165 (microfilm).

30. ProbII/16/5 (1508); Lady Broughton was probably the widow of Sir Robert, Dorothy's second cousin.

31. ProbII/29/15 (1542).

32. ProbII/12/22 (1500).

33. *Somerset Medieval Wills, 1383–1500*, 16:373 for St. Loe's will; ProbII/21/11. Nicholas, Lord Vaux, also gave his daughters their dowries at age 15. For dowries to be paid to women at age 25, see ProbII/31/42, Sir John Smyth (1546); ProbII/35/15, Sir Francis Lovell (1551).

34. For age 18, see SP1/49, f. 8, Sir William Compton (1523); ProbII/27/9, Sir Andrew Luttrell (1538); BL, Harleian Ms. 3881, f. 31, Francis, earl of Huntingdon (1544); for age 21, see ProbII/20/16, Robert Knollys, esq. (1520); ProbII/33/10, Sir Anthony Brown (1547); ProbII/41/44, Sir Thomas Cave (1556). None of the mothers who left dowries to their daughters (16 in a sample of 266 wills) made provisions of this sort.

35. C1/1205/66.

36. ProbII/33/28 (1550).

37. ProbII/11/22 (1494); ProbII/16/5 (1508).

38. Moor, "Bygods, Earls of Norfolk," 194.

39. ProbII/12/22 (1500).

40. TE, 5:159 (p. 201).

41. See TE, 5:93 (116), Sir Henry Thwaite (1520); TE, 211 (297), Dame Margaret Zouche (1530); ProbII/31/3, Sir Philip Champernon (1545). Some of the single daughters appointed as their parents' coexecutors married subsequently.

42. *Household Books of John Howard*, II, 145, 155, 167, 190.

43. *Plumpton Letters and Papers*, appendix 2:78 (292).

44. C1/1205/66.

45. *Lisle Letters*, 3:511, 513, 519; pp. 33, 70.

46. *Miscellanea Genealogica and Heraldica*, 4 (or n.s. 2):431. The Prerogative Court of Canterbury set the will aside and declared that Elizabeth had died intestate.

47. ProbII/12/22 (1500).

48. ProbII/23/16 (1526); C1/933/8.

49. TE, 5:211 (297).

50. *Plumpton Correspondence*, cxxv, cxxvii.

51. ProbII/22/9 (1525).

52. ProbII/16/5 (probated 1508).

53. ProbII/35/33 (1552).

54. *Lincoln Wills*, 17, 25.

55. ProbII/56/43 (1574).

56. See Howell, "Fixing Movables," 3–45, for the meaning of this phenomenon.

57. Tilley, *Dictionary of Proverbs*, D19, F609, H374.

Chapter 6

1. This figure refers to the offspring of all of the marriages of 2,557 women. Since some women had children with only one of their husbands, the percentage of infertile couples is somewhat higher. Of 2,654 couples, 87 percent had children. T. H. Hollingsworth, "Demography of the British Peerage," table 36, p. 46, gives a similar figure, 86 percent, for couples in which the wives were peers' daughters born between 1550 and 1574.

2. Almost the same percentages of fertile couples had large families because most of the women with five or more children married only once or had offspring with only one of their husbands. All of the figures given here are minimal since some infants who were stillborn or died in infancy or childhood were not recorded.

3. This figure includes children from all of a woman's marriages, so the figures for individual couples are slightly different. The average number of children born to fertile couples was 4. Hollingsworth, "Demography of the British Peerage," table 19, p. 30, shows an almost identical mean figure, 4.33, for peers' daughters born between 1550 and 1574. The results of his study of the daughters of dukes were similar: the mean family size of the cohorts born between 1330 and 1479 and 1480 and 1679 was 4.6. Hollingsworth, "British Ducal Families," table 26, p. 370.

4. Bindoff, *Commons*, 3:42; SP1/199, f. 48 (1545).

5. For a similar point about the seventeenth-century elite, see Pollock, "Embarking on a Rough Passage," 39–41.

6. *Paston Letters and Papers*, 1:573.

7. *Stonor Letters and Papers*, 2:309 (141).

8. *Lisle Letters*, 4:864.

9. Ibid., 3:809.

10. Ibid., 2:246.

11. Gibson, "Saint Anne and the Religion of Childbed," 104–7.

12. Ibid., 98; TE, 4:75.

13. Bennet, "College of St. John," 298.

14. *Paston Letters and Papers*, I:125 (217).

15. *Lisle Letters*, 2: pp. 139, 163; 4:904; *Stonor Letters and Papers*, 2:310 (143); SP1/154, f. 22 (1539).

16. *Lisle Letters*, 2:201.

17. Ibid., 5:1393 (448), 1395 (451), 1396a (453).

18. HMC, *Rutland Mss.*, 4:289; *Lisle Letters*, 5:1404.

19. *Lisle Letters*, 4:880.

20. Ibid., 4:887 (152).

21. Ibid., 3:399 (1536); 4:912.

22. Haynes, *Collection of State Papers*, 62.

23. See Pollock, "Embarking on a Rough Passage," 41, 45–49, for a similar point about the seventeenth-century aristocracy.

24. *Stonor Letters and Papers*, 2:310 (1482).

25. E.g., *Lisle Letters*, 4:926, 935, 1008 (1537).

26. Ibid., 3:809 (571–72).

27. Ibid., 4:871, 872; 4:952, 979 (1537).

28. Ibid., 3:586a (1536). Evidently the power lay in the saint's girdle as an object rather than in the sanctity of a particular saint since the records of the dissolution

show four other saints whose girdles belonged to monasteries and were lent to women during their lyings-in. L&P, 10:139–40, 143. I owe this reference to P. Crawford, "Construction and Experience of Maternity," 31, n. 28.

29. *Visitation of Suffolke*, 1:48.

30. *Lisle Letters*, 3:579a (1535).

31. *Lisle Letters*, 3:616 (1537).

32. Ibid., 5:1133 (Mar. 1538), 1201 (Aug. 1538).

33. Schofield, "Did the Mothers Really Die?" 259–60, concluded that the risk of dying in any particular childbirth was 1 percent; since a woman who lived to the age of 45 was likely to be pregnant six or seven times, she had a 6 or 7 percent risk of dying in childbed. Although Schofield recognized that women would not have been aware of the statistical reality, he concluded that "in the distant past women will have known of others who died giving birth to a child; but they may also have considered it such a rare event that there was little risk that the tragedy would befall them" (260). His statistics cannot, of course, take account of the pain and permanent injury that childbirth entailed, which certainly figured in women's attitudes.

34. I have found Adrian Wilson's account of childbirth, "Ceremony of Childbirth," 68–107, particularly helpful in pulling together and interpreting the scattered bits of information in my sources; HMC, *Rutland Mss.*, 4:287; Emmison, *Tudor Secretary*, 124.

35. Wilson, "Ceremony of Childbirth," 73.

36. *A Collection of Ordinances and Regulations for . . . the Royal Household*, 125, from BL, Harleian Ms., 642, ff. 198–217.

37. L&P, 14 (2):782 (335).

38. *Lisle Letters*, 4:866, 867, 868a, 870, 870a, 870b, 871, 872 (1537).

39. Ibid., 867 (119), 868.

40. Ibid., 868a, 870a.

41. Ibid., 872.

42. One sixteenth-century source, BL, Egerton Ms. 985, f. 98, stated that a royal lying-in should begin four to six weeks before the expected delivery; quoted in Staniland, "Royal Entry into the World," 301n. Jane Seymour "took her chamber" on 16 September 1537, and gave birth to Prince Edward on 12 October. *Lisle Letters*, 4: p. 173. The scanty evidence in household accounts indicates that aristocratic women had far shorter confinements.

43. *A Collection of Ordinances and Regulations for . . . the Royal Household*, 125.

44. *Lisle Letters*, 3:610, 614.

45. Beer and Jack, *Letters of William, Lord Paget*, 122.

46. L&P, 3 (1):1285 (499–500).

47. HMC, *Rutland Mss.*, 4:295, 296, 302, 305. The young mother was Anne Manners Nevill, daughter of the first earl of Rutland and wife of Henry Nevill, the earl of Westmorland's heir (1540).

48. CUL, Hengrave Hall Ms. 88, vol. 1, no. 19.

49. Guerney, "Household and Privy Purse Accounts," 428–29; 448 for identification of Mr. Banyard; the aunt was Elizabeth, née Radcliffe, daughter of Sir Thomas's grandmother by her second husband, Sir Robert Radcliffe of Hunstanton; she was married to Sir Roger Woodhouse.

50. HMC, *Rutland Mss.*, 4:290–93, 296.

51. Ibid., 289, 290.

52. Stonor, *Letters and Papers*, 2:222 (61), 224 (64), 225 (66).

53. SP1/82, f. 248 (1534).

54. SP1/170, f. 22 (1542); see also C24/23 (pt. ii), m. 5, 8.

55. *Paston Letters and Papers*, I:357 (585).

56. Emmison, *Tudor Secretary*, 124.

57. The word *gossip* was a corruption of *god-sib* or *god-sibling* and referred to a spiritual affinity contracted by acting as a sponsor at a baptism. OED, I:310. BL, Titus B1, f. 348 (orig. 343).

58. SP1/130, f. 143 (1538).

59. *Privy Purse Expenses of King Henry the Eighth*, 5, 117, 145, 197.

60. L&P, 14 (2), 782 (333, 334, 338, 340); Mewtas was a gentleman of the Privy Chamber.

61. HMC, *Rutland Mss.*, 4:270, 272, 318. Master Harvey was probably Sir Nicholas, given the dates in the king's and earl's accounts and Rutland's close connection to the court.

62. Add'l Ms. 6113, f. 117b. The French Queen was Henry VIII's sister, Mary, widow of Louis XII of France.

63. Ibid.; Add'l Ms. 5751, pt. A, f. 282.

64. Harris, *Edward Stafford*, 57; BL, Add'l Ms. 33,412, f. 36, will of Sir Anthony Hungerford (1558); the duke was probably Edward's godfather.

65. Emmison, *Tudor Secretary*, 124.

66. Guerney, "Household and Privy Purse Accounts," 428–29.

67. E.g., *Lisle Letters*, 4:864 (112), the countess of Rutland's son was born in November or December 1536, she was churched 22 January 1537; 4:870a, Lady Beauchamp (Anne Seymour, later duchess of Somerset); 5: p. 86, the countess of Sussex's son was christened 22 March 1538, she was churched 18 April; HMC, *Rutland Mss.*, 4:291–92, the countess of Rutland's daughter Katherine was born in July 1539, and she was churched in August. See *Travels of Leo of Rozmital*, 46–47, for a description of Queen Elizabeth's churching; Wilson, "Ceremony of Childbirth," 88–93, for a description based primarily on seventeenth-century evidence.

68. *Sarum Missal in English*, 164–65.

69. *Annotated Book of Common Prayer*, 304–5; Cressy, "Purification, Thanksgiving, and the Churching of Women," 118; Coster, "Purity, Profanity, and Puritanism," 382. Coster emphasizes the persistent significance of churching as a purification ceremony and cites the continued wearing of the veil as evidence. According to Keith Thomas, *Religion and the Decline of Magic*, 38–39, the interpretation of churching as a purification ceremony survived in popular culture, although the actual Anglican service treated it as a thanksgiving for a safe delivery.

70. Coster, "Purity, Profanity, and Puritanism," 383.

71. Wilson, "Ceremony of Childbirth," 84.

72. Ibid., 85.

73. Ibid., 87–88.

74. *Paston Letters and Papers*, 1:371 (602).

75. David Cressy, "Purification, Thanksgiving, and the Churching of Women," 110–11, has expressed doubt about interpreting the lying-in as a "zone of sexual politics and gendered conflict . . . where women took initiatives and achieved victories." He agrees rather with Susan Wright that it "represented little more than an opportunity to meet and celebrate with their peers." Both on general grounds and in light of remarks like Norfolk's and Sadler's it seems impossible to me to read the undoubtedly complex and multiple cultural meanings of churching and lying-in without situating

them, as Davis and Wilson do, in the larger context of asymmetrical gender relations, whatever women thought consciously when they participated in them.

76. In *Family, Sex and Marriage*, 105, Lawrence Stone concluded that relations between aristocratic parents and children were "usually fairly remote," at least partly because high infant and child mortality rates "made it folly to invest too much emotional capital in such ephemeral beings." Revisionist historians such as Linda Pollock, *Forgotten Children;* Ralph Houlbrooke, *English Family*, chaps. 6–7; Keith Wrightson, *English Society, 1580–1680*, chap. 4, who have criticized Stone's model have drawn most of their evidence from the Elizabethan and Stuart periods. My evidence on Yorkist and early Tudor mothers supports their interpretation without denying the differences between the way in which they raised their children and late twentieth-century views of good mothering.

77. For examples, see Req2/4/3 (1540–42); C1/1159/1 (1544–47); C1/1194/67 (1547); SP11/6, f. 3 (1555).

78. Prob11/32/37 (1545).

79. HEH, Hastings Collection, HA 10334 (1555).

80. Center for Kentish Studies, U26/T161 (1541).

81. SP1/129, f. 19 (1538).

82. HoL, Original Bills, Private Bills, 34–35 Hen VIII, #40 (1542–43).

83. L&P, 4 (2), 4436 (1528).

84. SP1/49, f. 64 (1528); her husband was Sir John Russell, later earl of Bedford.

85. L&P, 4 (3):6072 (21), 5:318 (21).

86. SP1/100, f. 91d (1535).

87. SP1/114, f. 155 (1537). For another example, see SP60/3, f. 108 (1536).

88. Hall, *Union of Lancaster and York*, 519.

89. Strype, *Ecclesiastical Memorials*, 2 (2), document L (339).

90. SP10/13, f. 107 (1551).

91. *Stonor Letters and Papers*, 1:113 (117).

92. Strype, *Ecclesiastical Memorials*, 2 (1):491–92.

93. Smyth, *Berkeley Manuscripts*, 2:253.

94. SP1/159, f. 266 (1539).

95. SP1/82, f. 158.

96. SP1/128, f. 152; SP1/129, f. 19.

97. *Stonor Letters and Papers*, 2:168 (10).

98. Ibid., 2:169 (11).

99. Ibid., 2:172 (15).

100. CUL, Hengrave Hall Ms. 88, vol. 1, no. 35.

101. C1/918/17 (1533–44).

102. HEH, Hastings Collection, HAP Box 4, folder 29 (1489).

103. CUL, Hengrave Hall Ms. 88, vol. 1, no. 129 (n.d.).

104. *Lisle Letters*, 3:573, 575, 578, 584, 587, 592, 620, 622a, 623a, 1495, 1574.

105. Ibid., 3:615.

106. Prob11/7/25, Starkey (1486); *North Country Wills*, 166 (227–28), Molyneux (1552); also Prob11/31/28, Sir Richard Bulkeley (1544).

107. *Paston Letters and Papers*, 1:226 (1477).

108. HEH, Hastings Collection, HA 10339 (1557).

109. Ninety-eight, or 86 percent, of 114 male testators appointed their wives as guardians of their noninheriting, minor, unmarried children.

110. SP1/111, f. 35 (1536).

111. SP1/125, f. 106 (1537).

112. Prob11/27/11 (1534; probated 1537); Bindoff, *Commons,* 2:100–1.

113. Prob11/30/4 (1543); Lady Englefield had nine children; two sons and three daughters lived to marry.

114. WRO, Throckmorton Papers, CR 1998, Box 72 #8 (1555); North Country Wills, 68 (91); see also SP1/41, f. 151, and SP1/235, f. 167 (1527), on Lady Anne Rede's success in negotiating her only daughter's marriage to Sir Giles Grevill.

115. *Lisle Letters,* I:p. 245, 3:524, 4:861 (83–84).

116. Harris, *Edward Stafford,* 55.

117. SP1/78, f. 61 (1533).

118. C1/586/66 (1515–29). Richard was the heir of her first husband, George Catesby; he married Dorothy, daughter of Sir John Spencer. By the time of this suit, Lady Lucy was married to her third husband, Richard Verney.

119. Kitson married Jane Paulet c. 1556; she died, apparently of consumption, before 1560, when he married Elizabeth Cornwallis. CUL, Hengrave Hall Ms. 88, vol. 1, no. 57, 89, 91, 159.

120. Ibid., Ms. 90, document marked 72 (1548). Frances's husband predeceased his father; GEC, 2:17.

121. Catherine married Sir John Spencer; Dorothy, Sir Thomas Packington; and Anne, Sir William Spring. SRO, Kitson of Hengrave, 449/4/1, is Katherine's marriage contract. Her mother gave her a dowry of 1,000 marks and a yearly rent of £8 during her (i.e., her mother's) lifetime.

122. E.g., CUL, Hengrave Hall Ms. 88, nos. 140, 149, 150.

123. Ibid., Ms. 90, no. 42 (1561). Catherine Long married Edward Fisher of Warwickshire after her mother died; Bridget Bourchier, one of her daughters by the earl of Bath, married Sir Arthur Price. There is no indication of what happened to her other daughters.

124. C1/186/49 (1487–1505).

125. Gunn, *Charles Brandon,* 95–96, 132. For Lady Willoughby's role, see SP1/44, f. 144d–145 (1527); SP1/47, f. 38 (1528); STAC2/27/69 (1528); Req2/4/141; LincAO, Ancaster Ms. 1 5/B/1/D (1530).

126. C1/208/71–73 (1504–15).

127. Prob11/11/18 (c. 1498).

128. C1/1074/5–9 (1533–44). Her claim that her father-in-law, Sir Robert Tailboys, had bequeathed the unpaid part of her dowry to her daughter, his granddaughter, is not sustained by his will; Prob11/10/24.

129. Prob11/19/32 (1519).

130. Prob11/37/35 (1555 or 1556).

131. E.g., C1/804/16, Gaynsford (1533–44); SP1/156, Musgrave, f. 78 (1539).

132. Jeayes, *Charters and Muniments of the Gresley Family,* 475 (1525); "Star Chamber Proceedings," 15.

133. For the struggle to secure the Beaumont inheritance, see *Lisle Letters,* 4:pp. 1–10; see also the entries under Beaumont lands in the index, 6:p. 324.

134. CCR, Hen VII, 2:414, 471; Stafford was nineteen years younger than his wife.

135. SP1/26, f. 185–87 (1522); Cecily confirmed these arrangements when she was widowed for a second time in 1524. Green, *Letters of Royal and Illustrious Ladies,* 2:pp. 1–2; Prob11/23/22 (1527).

136. SP1/72, f. 46; SP1/135, f. 72; BL, Add'l Ms. 636, f. 118.

137. SP1/72, f. 46.

138. SP1/82, f. 158 (Feb. 1534).

139. Ibid.

140. SP1/129, f. 19 (1538).

141. Ibid.

142. BL, Vespasian, F. XIII, art. 136, f. 187 (n.d.). Predictably, the quarrels between Lady Margaret and her son continued; SP1/144, f. 62 (Mar. 1539).

143. Other examples include CCR, Ed IV, Ed V, Rich III, 1476–85, 748; Joan, widow of Edward, Lord Cobham (1479); C1/279/55 and C1/304/13, Elizabeth Barnardiston, widow of Sir Thomas (1505–14); C1/420/24; C1/1194/67–70; C4/8/171, Elizabeth Brudenell, widow of Sir Thomas (1547).

144. C1/27/501; C1/29, 354; GEC, 4:9.

145. C1/66/454 (1475–80 or 1483–85); her father died in 1448.

146. Prob11/26/19, Alice Kneveton Mynours (1539).

147. Holdsworth, *History of English Law,* 3:528.

148. E.g., CPR, Edward IV, 1461–67, 87, Elizabeth, widow of John Fitzwalter, first Lord Ratcliffe (d. 1461), purchased the wardship of his heir; L&P, 3 (1):854 (7), Sir John Marney purchased the wardships of his wife's two daughters by her first husband, Sir Roger Newhouse (1520); L&P, 13 (1), 1097, Sir William Musgrave and his wife, Elizabeth, held the wardship of her son by Thomas Tamworth (1538).

149. Brigden, "Letters of Richard Scuadmore," 24 (133–34; 1550).

150. GEC, 8:523 and n. c.

151. Smyth, *Berkeley Manuscripts,* 2:143.

152. Prob11/26/14 (1539).

153. Prob11/40/2 (1556).

154. Prob11/19/25, Thomas Dinham (1519); Prob11/23/11, Edward Grevill (1528); Dinham's widow, sole executor of his will, had eleven surviving children from their marriage.

155. Prob11/28/25 (1541).

156. Prob11/25/3, Thomas, Lord Berkeley (1532).

157. C1/202/49 (1504–11).

158. C1/859/6–8 (1537); HoL, Original Bills, Private Acts, 34–35 Hen VIII, #31. Anne Strelley's father died in 1501; she and her three sisters were their coheirs.

159. C1/494, f. 15 (1515–29).

160. BL, Vespasian F. XIII, art. 158, f. 210.

161. *Lisle Letters,* 1:p. 245, 2:p. 18.

162. E.g., ibid., 2:134 (62), 377 (471), 401 (505); 3:513 (45), 799a.

163. Ibid., 5:1275, 1293 (1538).

164. Ibid., 3:534, 535, 539, 540; 5:1226.

165. Ibid., 5:1224, 1283, 1291.

166. Ibid., 3:1116 (54), 1125, 1137, 1155, 1162.

167. Ibid., 3:pp. 36–39.

168. Ibid., 3:712.

169. Ibid., 2:172a (133), 326.

170. Ibid., 3:p. 37, and no. 523.

171. CUL, Hengrave Hall Ms. 88, vol. 3, nos. 35, 48, 75.

172. Ibid., vol. 1, nos. 63, 65 (1556).

173. Ibid., no. 135.

174. Ibid., no. 118.

175. Ibid., nos. 37, 120.

176. Collins, *English Baronage*, 1:13.

177. CCR, Hen VII, 1:646a (1492); GEC, 8:63; 12 (2):737.

178. *Sede Vacante Wills*, 136, n. 137; for other stepmothers appointed as their husbands' executors, see Probii/22/2, Thomas West, Lord de la Warre (1525); Probii/29/1, Elizabeth Audley (1541).

179. Probii/29/17 (1542).

180. Probii/31/6 (1545).

181. Probii/37/3 (1553).

182. Probii/29/18 (1542).

183. Probii/40/19, Lady Anne Grey (1557): they were the daughters of Sir Richard Clement, her second husband. BL, Add'l Ms. 33,412, f. 40, Dame Dorothy Hungerford (1559): her husband, Sir Anthony, had been married previously to Jane Darrell, daughter of Sir Edward. She noted that the goblet she was bequeathing to Jane was "from Mr. Darrell."

184. E.g., CCR, Ed IV, Ed V, Rich III, 1476–85, 474 (134), Katherine Lewkenor, widow of Sir Roger and stepson Thomas; Smyth, Berkeley *Manuscripts*, 2:82, Joan, widow of James, Lord Berkeley and stepson William, marquess of Berkeley; 229, Cecily, widow of Thomas, eighth Lord Berkeley, and stepson Thomas.

185. Wright, *Derbyshire Gentry*, 34.

186. Probii/11/26 (1494).

187. Probii/21/21 (1521).

188. Probii/33/25 (1548).

189. E.g., C1/193/2; C1/195/25; C1/294/9–12 (1504–15), John, Lord Clinton and Say v. Anne, widow of Richard, Lord Clinton, his father and now wife of Richard Willoughby; C1/126/66, Sir John Constable (1504–15) v. stepmother, Dame Elizabeth.

190. C78/1/39 (1545); see also SP1/42, ff. 153, 165, for Anne Rede's difficulties in settling her jointure with her stepson Leonard without going to court (1526).

191. C1/569/69 (1515–29).

192. BL, Vespasian F. XIII, f. 181 (orig. 99).

193. Probii/28/30 (1535).

194. SP1/119, 199d–203d.

195. Moreton, *Townshends and Their World*, 95–102.

Chapter 7

1. Rosenthal, *Patriarchy and Families of Privilege*, 182, found that 68 percent of the peers summoned between 1399 and 1500 left widows.

2. E.g., ibid., 197–98; Mcfarlane, "Beauchamps and Staffords," 64–66, 204–7; Stone, *Crisis of the Aristocracy*, 172–73; Spring, *Law, Land and Family*, chap. 2; Payling, *Political Society in Lancastrian England*, 56–57. With the exception of Spring, this literature is remarkable for its identification with the interests of the patrilineage, particularly the immediate heir, and its negative attitude toward widows.

3. Archer, "Rich Old Ladies," 15–35, quotations on 23, 25, 31. Her view changed by

the time she published her 1992 essay "'How ladies ought to manage,'" 149–81, esp. 165–66.

4. According to Joel Rosenthal, *Patriarchy and Families of Privilege*, 215, fifteenth-century noble widows survived their husbands for somewhat shorter periods—49.5 percent of the widows in a sample of ninety-one survived their husbands for more than ten years; 27.4 percent for more than twenty—but their longevity was still impressive.

5. Ibid., 185, for the opposite position.

6. Ibid., 197–200, for a similar point about fifteenth-century dowager peeresses.

7. Ann J. Kettle, "My Wife Shall Have It," 100–1, found even higher percentages of men who appointed their widows as their sole executors or coexecutors in the early fifteenth century, but her sample was different from mine because she drew it from a broader socioeconomic group. In a sample of 116 male testators with living wives between 1414 and 1443, 78 percent named them as their executors; between 1280 and 1500, 80 percent of the men with living wives in the Lincoln episcopal registers appointed them as their executors; in Bristol between 1381 and 1500, 82 percent of those whose names were entered in the Great Orphan Book did so.

8. Heirs and heiresses became wards of the crown; on wardship, see the glossary.

9. E.g., Prob11/6/15, John, Lord Berners (1478); Prob11/15/15, Sir Antony Brown (1505); Prob11/25/29, Sir Edward Ferrers (1535).

10. Prob11/10/22 (1489).

11. Prob11/8/29 (1485).

12. Macnamara, *Memorials of the Danvers*, 271 (1515).

13. Prob11/31/3, Sir Philip Champernon (1545).

14. E.g., SP1/231, f. 172 (1510), Anne Whittlebury, widow of Robert; LincAO, Ancaster Ms. 1, 11/C/1/C, Katherine, dowager duchess of Suffolk (1546); neither document explains why they did so.

15. Prob11/12/21 (1501).

16. Prob11/27/19 (1538).

17. *Collectanea Topographica and Genealogica*, 6:170.

18. The enfeoffment to use kept most aristocratic property out of the hands of the crown. Even after the passage of the Statutes of Uses (1536) and Wills (1540), the crown gained control of only one-third of the real property of minor heirs and heiresses.

19. These figures are based on eighty-three jointures; twenty-eight jointures are in the first group, thirty-three in the second, and twenty-two in the third.

20. Often their fathers-in-law were knighted but their husbands had not yet been.

21. Dyer, *Standards of Living*, 18, 31; Cornwall, *Wealth and Society*, 144.

22. Cornwall, *Wealth and Society*, 142–44.

23. Relevant information does not exist about the remaining two couples.

24. For references, see note 2 above.

25. Prob11/40/2 (1556), Sir George Giffard appears in both the group of forty-one and the group of nineteen.

26. Thomas Hussey challenged his father's bequest of land to this stepmother and her heirs; Prob11/31/116, Sir Robert Hussey (1545); and C24/18, no. 8 (1547); the deponents supported the widow. This claim is based on 189 legal cases connected to marriage settlements (dowry, dower, and jointures) in the Courts of Chancery, Star Chamber, and Requests c. 1450–1550.

27. See Archer, "'How ladies ought to manage,'" 165–66, on this point.

28. Information on where widows lived or died is hard to find. My data come from female wills and entries in GEC on 192 peers who died between 1450 and 1550 and had surviving spouses.

29. ProbII/42A/20; Sir Robert Acton, d. 1558, was a notable exception. He prohibited his estranged wife from claiming any of his houses in Worcester on pain of losing his other bequests to her.

30. E.g., ProbII/11/9, Sir Thomas Fitzwilliam the Younger (1494); ProbII/24/5, Sir Robert Clere (1529); ProbII/32/27, Sir Anthony Denny (1545).

31. Seventy-five percent of the population in Tudor England lived south and east of a line drawn from the Severn River to the Humber; Guy, *Tudor England*, 34. The Archdiocese of Canterbury included this entire area plus the West-Midland counties north of it.

32. Holdsworth, *History of English Law*, 3:550–58.

33. There is no way of estimating the value of the residue in most cases since the records of the Court of Arches, which made inventories of wills probated in the Archdiocese of Canterbury, burned in the Great Fire of London in 1666.

34. *Paston Letters and Papers*, 1:p. 24.

35. InqPM, Hen VII, 1:434, 436.

36. Ibid., 436, 437.

37. *Paston Letters and Papers*, 1:123.

38. ProbII/14/40.

39. Bindoff, *Commons*, I:651–52.

40. ProbII/24/5.

41. E40/12173; Alice was one of her husband's coexecutors.

42. Bonfield, *Marriage Settlements*, 6.

43. E.g., InqPM, Hen VII, 1:976, 1138, 1245.

44. Until the passage of the Statute of Uses in 1536, only land held by feoffees could be devised by will. The statute eliminated the will of land completely. In 1540, however, the Statute of Wills gave freeholders the right to bequeath their land by will, and landowners who held land from the crown by knight service (virtually the entire aristocracy) the right to devise two-thirds of it by will. The other third had to descend according to the common law and was subject to incidents of feudalism such as wardship. Baker, *English Legal History*, 212–19.

45. Uses and enfeoffments were not enforceable in the common-law courts (ibid., 212).

46. Ibid., 229; e.g., see CCR, Ed IV, 1461–68, 1:pp. 5, 108, 117; CCR, Hen VII, 2:284–86.

47. I have not used the records of the common-law courts, where cases involving dowers were heard, but I do not believe doing so would change this conclusion substantially because most of the aristocracy's land was enfeoffed by this period.

48. In many cases, the women's opponents were their husbands' executors or feoffees. It is impossible to determine if they were acting in their own interest or on behalf of unnamed members of their husbands' families. In other cases, it is impossible to figure out the women's relationship to their adversaries.

49. Tim Stretton, *Women Waging Law*, 169, made a similar observation in his study of a broader group of female suitors in the Elizabethan Court of Requests.

50. E.g., Jeayes, *Descriptive Catalogue of . . . Gresley Charters*, 475 (1525); Stac2/

34/32; C1/511/33–34; C1/513/18, 35–36; and C1/635/16–17, Lady Alice Gresley Savage v. George Gresley.

51. Prob11/27/5 (1536); the will gave Whethill's widow a great deal of discretion over his goods as long as she remained single.

52. *Lisle Letters*, 4: pp. 338–39.

53. SP1/118, f. 229 (Apr. 1537).

54. SP1/126, f. 86 (Nov. 1537).

55. SP1/126, ff. 89–102 (Nov. 1537).

56. SP1/133, f. 18 (June 1538).

57. SP1/142, f. 178.

58. C1/1186/24 (1547); Prob11/29/25 (1542). Her other coexecutor, her son Gilbert, died by 1545; *Lisle Letters*, 4:338. On St. John, see Bindoff, *Commons*, 3:254–55. For other suits between mothers and their eldest sons in which the heirs were angry because of provisions for a large number of their siblings, see Margaret Throckmorton, widow of Thomas, and her son Sir Robert, in WRO, Throckmorton Papers, CR 1998, Box 72, #5 (1474); and Elizabeth Brudenell, widow of Sir Thomas, and her son Edmund, in Prob11/32/35 (1549); C1/1194/67–70 (1547–51); and C4/8/171.

59. Stac 2/21/37; since allegations of violence were necessary to secure a hearing in the Star Chamber, their inclusion in complaints does not mean that the violence had actually occurred.

60. Stac 2/21/40; Stac2/24/337 (c.1529–30).

61. C1/641/38 (1529–30).

62. Stac2/21/40.

63. C1/208/71(1504–15).

64. C1/208/72 (1504–15).

65. Prob11/11/18 (1498). For other disputes between widows and their brothers-in-law, see C1/204/56, Anne Peyton Gaynsford v. Sir Robert Peyton; SP1/156, f. 169, Bindoff, *Commons*, 3:269, Denise Sandys v. William, Lord Sandys; Bindoff, *Commons*, 2:476–79, SP1/137, 114d, C1/1269/47–48, C24/17, and Prob11/28/8, Jane Knightley v. Edmund Knightley and Sir Valentine Knightley.

66. C1/300/50, 52–54, 56, 60–62; see also C1/551/46–47 and C4/27/83, Mary Orell v. Elizabeth Orell; C1/1232/66, 68, Joan Husee vs. Dame Joan Wadham.

67. For routine cases, see CCR, Ed IV, 1468–76, 2:1232; CCR, Hen VII, 1:244; CCR, Hen VII, 2:284–286.

68. GEC, 12 (2):552–53.

69. CCR, Hen VII, I:1192–93. Darcy was created Lord Darcy of Temple Hurst in 1529; GEC, 4:73–74.

70. L&P, 3 (2):2820 (1185–86).

71. BL, Vespasian, F. XIII, art. 177, f. 229 (n.d.); SP1/95, f. 47 (1535).

72. Ives, *Anne Boleyn*, 210–11.

73. BL, Vespasian, F. XIII, art. 177, f. 229.

74. SP1/105, f. 234; Smyth, *Berkeley Manuscripts*, 2:252. For another example in Henry VIII's reign, see E314/79, f. 136, and #10, portfolio 2, "Petitions of Sir Anthony Denny on Behalf of Robert Dacres."

75. A. Crawford, "Victims of Attainder," 15 (1989), 62; CPR, Ed IV, Ed V, Rich III, 1476–85, 337.

76. A. Crawford, "Victims of Attainder, 59–74; Hicks, "Last Days of the Countess of Oxford," 76–95; Rosenthal, "Other Victims," 221–22.

77. CPR, Ed IV, Ed V, Rich III, 1476–85, 94.

78. GEC, 12 (2): 393. The countess, widow of the "Kingmaker," was heir of her brother Henry Beauchamp, duke and earl of Warwick; Gloucester was the future Richard III.

79. Hicks, "Last Days of the Countess of Oxford," 76–86.

80. A. Crawford, "Victims of Attainder," 66; CPR, Ed IV, Ed V, Rich III, 1476–85, 254, 450. See CPR, Ed IV, 1461–67, 178, 181, 184, for earlier examples in Edward's reign.

81. GEC, 9:717; CPR, Ed IV, 1461–67, 42; A. Crawford, "Victims of Attainder," 62–63; CPR, Ed IV, Ed V, Rich III, 1476–85, 486.

82. BL, Harleian 433, f. 108d; HEH, Hastings Collection, HAP Box 4, folder 19.

83. Lander, "Attainder and Forfeiture," 143.

84. A. Crawford, "Victims of Attainder," 70–71; see also CPR, Hen VII, 1:47, 222–23; Campbell, Materials for the Reign of Henry VII, 2:550; GEC, 8:225.

85. A. Crawford, "Victims of Attainder," 66–69; Hicks, "Last Days of the Countess of Oxford," 76–95.

86. Chetwynd, "History of Pirehill Hundred," 48–49; Hicks, "Attainder, Resumption and Coercions," 68.

87. For a systematic discussion, see Lehmberg, "Parliamentary Attainder," 675–702.

88. Bindoff, Commons, 1:527–29; GEC, 2:153–54, 363.

89. L&P, 2 (2):1466, 1501; Hall, Union of Lancaster and York, 595; Bindoff, Commons, 1:575.

90. Bindoff, Commons, 1:575; L&P, 2 (1):1850 (1516); 2 (2), 2863 (1466).

91. Bindoff, Commons, 1:577; L&P, 14(1):37 (18). In 1535, he also granted her a free chapel with a little close; L&P, 8:239 (93).

92. SP1/156, f. 147.

93. SP1/144, f. 87. For joint grants to the Carews, see L&P, 2 (1), 1850, 2161; 3 (2), 2937, 3062 (5).

94. SP1/242, f. 224; L&P, 14(2), 403 (60).

95. L&P, 15:899.

96. L&P, 14 (2):113 (5).

97. BL, Add'l Ms. 29,606, f. 14; Bindoff, Commons, 1:577; L&P, 14:37 (18).

98. On Mary, Lady Dacre, see Proceedings and Ordinancess of the Privy Council, 7:207, and HoL, 33 Hen VIII, 1541, Original Acts, Private Bill #44; on Lady Anne Fortescue, see Bindoff, Commons, 3:63 and L&P, 17, 1012 (2).

99. CCR, Ed IV, Ed V, Rich III, 1476–85, 474 (135–36).

100. CCR, Hen VII, 1:1038.

101. Stonor Letters and Papers, 1:121 (124; Blount); C1/1112/26 (Clifford); Smyth, Berkeley Manuscripts, 2:82, 299.

102. NRA 0874, #83, p. 14 (stamped #024), and #315, p. 49 (stamped p. 59); LRO, 26D53/1947 (1485).

103. "Willoughby Letters," 40.

104. Harris, Edward Stafford, 49–50.

105. GEC, 2:137–38.

106. GEC, 2:137; Smyth, Berkeley Manuscripts, 2:254.

107. E317/79, nos. 758, 760 (Say); BL, Add'l Ms. 41,305 (Townshend); HRO, Cassiobury Papers 6454 (Salisbury); PRO, LR2/113 (Richmond); also HampRO, 5M53 955 (Wriotheseley).

108. Req2/3/306.

109. *Paston Letters and Papers*, 1:198 (1466).

110. Moreton, *Townshends and Their World*, 144.

111. SP1/41, f. 153.

112. SP1/45, f. 65.

113. SP1/41, f. 151.

114. HMC, *Rutland Mss.*, 1:12.

115. *Paston Letters and Papers*, 1:15, 16.

116. HEH, Hastings Collections, Deeds, HAD 2319–24 (1507–8); BL, Add'l Ms. 28,174, f. 457.

117. Stac2/29/126.

118. C1/1244/18; Richard, Lord Rich, to whom the bill was addressed, was chancellor only in 1547; on evidence about suits between widows and their tenants in the Elizabeth period, see Stretton, *Women Waging Law*, 118.

119. HMC, *Hastings Mss.*, 1:1100 (239).

120. C1/632/50; see also NRO, Phillipp Mss., Phi/546–48, for leases by Jane Knyvett, sole heir of John, second Lord Berners, and widow of Sir Edmund Kynvett (d. 1539).

121. HMC, Third Report, Appendix, 46.

122. TE, 2:284.

123. Prob11/8/15 (1487).

124. Prob11/30/4 (1542). There are dozens of other examples of bequests of agricultural animals, equipment, and grain.

125. E.g., Prob11/14/13, Elizabeth Biconyll (1504); Prob11/31/6, Elizabeth Payton (1515).

126. Smyth, *Berkeley Manuscripts*, 2:254.

127. Jeayes, *Charters and Muniments at Berkeley Castle*, 703 (209).

128. SP1/245, f. 58.

129. TV, I:279.

130. Moreton, *Townshends and Their World*, 164.

131. Prob11/39/5 (1556).

132. Nichols, *Unton Inventories*, xxvii. Again, there are dozens of other examples.

133. Jeayes, *Charters and Muniments at Berkeley Castle*, 605, 606.

134. Jones and Underwood, *King's Mother*, 80, 270, 276.

135. *Household Books of John Howard*, pt. 1, xx, xlvii, 171; for other examples, see *Plumpton Letters and Papers*, 18 (255); Bindoff, *Commons*, 2:522.

136. *Paston Letters and Papers*, 2:500.

137. SP1/68, f. 139 (1531).

138. *Plumpton Letters and Papers*, 248–51 (1548–52); TE, 6:203 (262).

139. Jones and Underwood, *King's Mother*, 107, 171, 276.

140. HMC, Seventh Report, 1:Appendix 600.

141. C. H. Cooper, *Memoir of Margaret*, 54, 55; Jones and Underwood, *King's Mother*, 105, 196, 279.

142. Jones and Underwood, *King's Mother*, 106, 124, 128–30, 268.

143. *Kingsford's Stonor Letters and Papers*, 125.

144. SP1/106, f. 149.

145. *Sede Vacante Wills*, p. 140 (Lisle); "Kedington and the Barnardiston Family," 179; HampRO, 5M53 937 (Wriotheseley).

146. Campell, *Materials for the Reign of Henry VII*, 2:284.

147. C1/135/13 (1487–1504).

148. Req2/3/195.

149. C1/1157/19 (1544–47); for similar conflicts in the Elizabethan period, see Stretton, *Women Waging Law*, 118–19.

150. Harris, *Edward Stafford*, 19; Rawcliffe, *Staffords, Earls of Stafford and Dukes of Buckingham*, 123.

151. Moreton, *Townshends and Their World*, 29, 131.

152. CCR, Hen VII, 1:88 (Suffolk, 1486); Add'l Ms. 28,174, f. 460 (Ferrers, 1526).

153. *Visitation of Norfolk*, ed. Dashwood, 1:396; Prob11/33/14 (1550); see also TE, 3:91, Dame Alice Nevill of Liversedge (1478).

154. Prob11/19/2, Margaret Capell (1522); Prob11/39/5, Elizabeth Spelman (1556).

155. Prob11/14/22 (1503).

156. Prob11/29/18 (Cotton, 1542); Prob11/36/11 (Denny, 1553); TE, 6:96 (106); Foster, *Pedigrees of the County Families of Yorkshire*, 2, pedigree of Constables of Flambrough etc.

157. Bindoff, *Commons*, 3:360–61; Add'l Ms. 25,079, f. 2, Susan Spencer, widow of Sir William, 1549; Prob11/40/32, Isabell Spencer, widow of Sir John, 1558.

158. Prob11/22/10, Dame Elizabeth Barnardiston (1526), widow of Sir Thomas (d. 1503); *Visitation of Suffolke*, 2:21–22, Dame Anne (1560), widow of Sir Thomas (d. 1542).

159. For widows from a broader social class who were acting as their husbands' executors, see Stretton, *Women Waging Law*, 110–16.

160. Prob11/12/11, Sir William Carew (1501); TE, 3:107 (270 and n.), Sir John Saville (1482). Saville was sole adminstrator of her husband's goods; Prob11/25/23, Sir Richard Knightley (1529); Prob11/23/11, Sir Thomas Barnardiston (1542).

161. Prob11/27/27, Coffin (1538); Prob11/32/31, Knyvett (1548).

162. E.g., Prob11/10/23, Sir William Calthorp (1494); Prob11/18/13, Sir William Capell (1515); Prob11/24/23, Sir Henry Guildford (1532); Prob11/41/44, Sir Thomas Cave (1556).

163. *Paston Letters and Papers*, 1:212 (359).

164. Ibid., 274 (458); see also 283, 1473.

165. Ibid., 371 (602).

166. Ibid., 311.

167. Ibid., 228, 311.

168. Prob11/30/45, Mountjoy (1545); Prob11/33/27 (1550).

169. Prob11/22/24, Sir John More (1526); Prob11/37/29, Sir Edward Green (1555); Prob11/40/19, Sir Thomas Hasting (1558).

170. Duffy, *Stripping of the Altars*; Haigh, *English Reformations*; Scarisbrick, *Reformation and the English People*.

171. E.g., Prob11/5/16, Sir John Burcester (1466); Prob11/14/21, Sir Guy Wolston (1504); Prob11/23/3, Sir Richard Brooke (1529); Prob11/43/36, Sir Thomas Giffard (1559).

172. Prob11/4/21 (1460).

173. *Bedfordshire Wills*, 32 (44–45).

174. Hicks, "Chantries, Obits and Almshouses," "Counting the Cost of War," "Piety and Lineage in the Wars of the Roses," and "Piety of Margaret."

175. Hicks, "Chantries, Obits and Almshouses," 87–89.

176. Probii/6/37, Leynham (1479); CPR, Ed IV, Ed V, Rich III, 3:260 (1482). Leynham was her husband's "principal" executor. Probii/7/21, Choke (1483), CPR, Ed IV, Ed V, Rich III, 3:457 (1484); Probii/18/9, Vernon (1519), Pevsner, *Shropshire*, 303.

177. Probii/20/12 (1520); Probii/21/20 (1524).

178. *Paston Letters and Papers*, 2:926.

179. C1/279/55 (1504–9).

180. L&P, 2 (2):3149.

181. Probii/22/10 (1526); "Kedington and the Barnardiston Family," 131n.

182. "Kedington and the Barnardiston Family," 131n.

183. C1/38/17 (1467–70 or 1471–73).

184. *Lisle Letters*, 1:489–90 (1533).

185. C1/903/48 (1533–44).

186. Probii/ 31/14 (1531).

187. E.g., TE, 4:33 (73), Thomas, Lord Scrope of Masham (1495); Probii/4/21, Humphrey, duke of Buckingham (1460).

188. Probii/24/33, Guildford (1532); Probii/31/35, Jenyns (1544).

189. E.g., Probii/19/4, Sir Thomas Bryan (1518); Probii/32/27, Sir Anthony Denny (1545). Testators may have left separate schedules without mentioning them.

190. Probii/12/20, Sir Henry Wentworth (1499); Probii/31/14, Sir Thomas Elyot (1531); Probii/30/45, Sir William Butts (1545).

191. Req2/7/81, f. 3; see C1/289/66, Dame Lucy Brown (1503–14) and C1/585/42, Katherine Brandon (1504–1529) for a similar defense.

192. E.g., C1/1051/4, Elizabeth Saville (1533–44); C4/9/60, Anne Knyvett (n.d.).

193. C4/9/94 (after 1550).

194. C1/45/132 (1471–73).

195. C78/5/47 (1549).

196. Probii/39/40.

197. Probii/27/27 (1538); see also Probii/32/31, Sir Anthony Knyvett (1548); Probii/32/38, Sir Roger Copley (1549).

198. SP1/87, f. 131 (1534).

199. SP/103, f. 204 (Apr. 1536).

200. SP1/104, f. 187 (1536). Lady Anne Conyers also sought Cromwell's help, BL, Vespasian, F. XIII, art. 175, f. 227, SP1/154, f. 38.

201. HEH, Hastings Collection, HAP Box 4, folder 12 (1481).

202. BL, Harleian Ms. 433, f. 108d. (1483).

203. HEH, Hastings Collection, HAP Box 4, folder 29.

204. GEC, 11:709 (Shrewsbury).

205. Bedingfield: CPR, Hen VII, 2:169 (1499). Parr: L&P, 3 (1):1121 (414; 1520); L&P, 4 (1), 2362 (26; 1526); L&P, 4 (3), 6751 (26; 1530); L&P, 4 (3):5508 (2;1529). Baynham: CPR, Ed VI, 2:p. 3 (1548).

206. Add'l Ms. 24,965, f. 23 (1523); f. 103 (1524); GEC, 2:423, n. e.

207. Probii/18/13 (1515).

208. Probii/40/16 (1557).

209. Bindoff, *Commons*, 1:701; 2:57–58, 60–61. The marriage of Elizabeth Drury and Robert Drury of Rougham took place; Muskett, *Suffolk Manorial Families*, 1:347.

210. HEH, Hastings Collection, HAP Box 4, folder 12 (1481); for other examples, see TV, 2:639, Sir Edward Knyvett (1528); and Probii/37/12, Thomas, Lord de la Warr (1554).

211. Collins, *Letters and Memorials*, 1:13, Lisle (1492); Prob11/23/4, Uvedale (1528); Prob11/39/24, Hussey (1554).

212. E.g., Prob11/11/7, Sir Edmund Bedingfield (1496); Prob11/19/4, Sir Thomas Bryan (1518); Prob11/27/5, Sir Richard Whethill (1538).

213. Prob11/15/15, Thomas Frowick (1505); Prob11/18/13, Elizabeth Frowick (1515).

214. TE, 6:126 (153), Constable (1542); for two other sole executors charged with paying their sisters-in-law's dowries, see *Somerset Medieval Wills (1383–1500)*, 193, Robert, Lord Hungerford (1459); TE, 5:29 (47), Sir John Gower (1513).

215. See Rosenthal, *Patriarchy and Families of Privilege*, 213, for a similar point about the whole fifteenth century.

216. E.g., CCR, Ed IV, 1461–68, 1:p. 5; 1468–76, 2:1232 (1475); CCR, Hen VII, 1:1, 951 (1497).

217. CPR, Ed IV, Ed V, Rich III, 1476–85, 3:141 (1479); CPR, Hen VII, 2:597 (1509); L&P, 3 (1), 405 (4; 1519).

218. CCR, Ed IV, 1461–68, 1:128 (1462).

219. CPR, Ed IV, 1461–67, 1:222 (1463); CCR, Ed IV, 1468–76, 2:22, 202, 1240; CPR, Hen VII, 2:365 (1504); L&P, 4 (3):6072 (23; 1529); SRO, D1721/1/1, f. 378d.

220. Ross, *Edward IV*, 93; GEC, 9:607.

221. GEC, 10:827; Jones and Underwood, *King's Mother*, 58–59.

222. GEC, 2:73.

223. SP1/46, f. 222 (1527); C1/610/2.

224. Green, *Letters of Royal and Illustrious Ladies*, 2:269–70.

225. SP1/141, f. 44 (Dec. 1537); SP1/142, f. 212 (Feb. 1538); on Sutton's economic plight, see Miller, *Henry VIII and the English Nobility*, 39.

226. C1/601/2 on Strickland; for other matches successfully brokered by the king or his servants, see Lambeth Palace, Shrewsbury Papers, 3192, f. 45 (ms. A, when the papers were at the College of Arms); and Bindoff, *Commons*, 1:667, Margaret, widow of Richard Vernon, to Sir William Coffin; L&P, 21 (2), 199 (28), and Bindoff, *Commons*, 1:574, Mary, Sir George Carew's widow to Sir Arthur Champernon; Req2/6/173, Alice, widow, of Sir Edward Belknapp to John Bruggs.

227. Green, *Letters of Royal and Illustrious Ladies*, 2:269–70.

228. SP1/128, f. 47 (Jan. 1538).

229. GEC, 2:137.

230. 3 Henry VII c. 2 (3), *Statutes of the Realm*, 2:512.

231. Cameron, "Complaint and Reform in Henry VII's Reign," 83–89; Ives, "'Agaynst Taking Away of Women,'" 25–30.

232. Ives, "'Agaynst Taking Away of Women,'" 26–28; Cameron, "Complaint and Reform in Henry VII's Reign," 83–89. In this same period, Thomas, Lord Dacre, abducted and married Elizabeth, heir of Sir Robert Greystock; GEC, 4:21, n. a; and Richard, earl of Kent, abducted Elizabeth Trussell; Bernard, "Fortunes of the Greys, Earls of Kent," 674.

233. See Ives, "'Agaynst Taking Away of Women,'" 30, for the number of times the law was cited. According to Ives, the common law was ineffective because of complicated procedures, perjured juries, and the legal ingenuity of defendants. For effective action, Margaret appealed directly to the king: "Executive justice was infinitely superior to the due process of the common law" (44).

234. BL, Titus B 1, f. 60; Stac2/22/227.

235. These figures come from data in Bindoff, *Commons*, and GEC. Many parlia-

mentary knights married widows at least once—132 in a sample of 356. Very often these women, their second or third wives, survived them, which accounts for the fact that so many of these widows married more than once over the course of their lives, although their remarriage rate after the parliamentary knights died was lower. Rosenthal, *Patriarchy and Families of Privilege*, 183, found high remarriage rates among fifteenth-century noblewomen: 41 percent and 68 percent if one includes women who were married previously. In comparison, 31 percent of 83 widows in early fifteenth-century Douai remarried (Howell, *Marriage Exchange*, 152). In fifteenth-century Florence, one-third of women widowed in their 20s remarried, as did one-tenth of those widowed at 30 or older (Crabb, "How Typical Was Alessandra Macinghi Strozzi?" 49).

236. Prob11/28/22 (1540).

237. Prob11/34/33 (1551).

238. Prob11/6/18 (1474); PRO, E516/4 (1468).

239. Richmond, *John Hopton*, 118.

240. CUL, Hengrave Hall Ms. 90, document marked 72 (1548).

241. GEC, 2:17.

242. In three of forty-three cases, they were marrying upward within the peerage.

243. Five of these women went to court alone; in the remaining 103 cases, their husbands were their codefendants or coplaintiffs.

244. In contrast, Tim Stretton, *Women Waging Law*, 140–42, concluded that securing their husbands' legal assistance was one of the main reasons for the remarriage of widows who were litigating in the Elizabethan Court of Requests, where almost all were of lower social status and more modest means.

245. Bindoff, *Commons*, 2:478–79; Prob11/28/8 (1538); SP1/137, 114d (1538); C1/1269/47–48; PRO, C24/17; for quotation, see SP1/242, f. 8 (1538).

246. Harris, "Power, Profit, and Passion," 64–67.

247. CUL, Hengrave Hall Ms. 88, vol. 1, no. 10.

248. SP1/141, f. 44.

249. Caligula, D. VI, f. 246d, 253; see Harris, "Power, Profit, and Passion," 59–88, for a complete account.

250. Howard, *Collection of Letters*, 525; on Stafford, knighted in 1545, after Mary died, see Bindoff, *Commons*, 3:364–66.

251. GEC, 12 (1):460 (Suffolk); 6:375 (Hastings, 1509); 1:252 (Maltravers, 1573–80); Rutton, *Family of Wentworth*, 194.

252. GEC, 4:421–22 (1554–57).

253. GEC, 2:17; CUL, Hengrave Hall Ms. 88, 1:122 (1557).

254. There are actually eighty-three men's wills because one women had two husbands and another had three.

255. Prob11/8/20.

256. Prob11/22/16 (1535).

257. CCR, Hen VII, 2:414 (1504); SP1/26, ff. 185–87 (1522).

258. Prob11/29/18 (1543); she had no sons by her second husband.

259. E40/12173 (1538).

260. Prob11/30/4 (1543); Prob11/27/11 (1534).

261. *Miscellanea Genealogica and Heraldica*, 9 (or 3rd ser., 1):168 (1558).

262. Prob11/27/29 (1538).

263. Nichols, *Unton Inventories*, xxv–xxvii (1536); Prob11/35/11.

264. Prob11/9/22 (1490); Prob11/10/10 (1494).

265. *North Country Wills*, 67 (88, 90), Sir Thomas Parr (1517); 68:91, Dame Maud Parr (1529). Her elder daughter, Katherine, was already married; the gift was to her younger daughter, Anne. Prob11/28/30, Sir Alexander Culpepper (1540); Prob11/29/12, Dame Constance Culpepper (1541).

266. Prob11/32/27 (1545); Prob11/36/11 (probated 1553).

267. CUL, Hengrave Hall, Ms. 90, #42, Ms. 92; Gage, *History and Antiquities of Suffolk*, 185–87.

268. Prob11/14/23 (1503); Prob11/16/28 (1510). By this time the Heydons' two other married daughters—Anne or Amy Lestrange, wife of Sir Roger, and Elizabeth, wife of Sir Walter Herbert—had died without children; Oestmann, *Lordship and Community*, 13. Herbert married the sister of the third duke of Buckingham as his second wife in 1500; Harris, *Edward Stafford*, 49. Dame Heydon's will also mentioned a deceased son, William.

269. *North Country Wills*, 68 (93).

270. *Some Oxfordshire Wills*, Sir Edmund (1489), 42–46; Katherine (1498), 58.

271. Prob11/19/9, Sir John Speke (1516); *Somerset Medieval Wills (1501–1530)*, 195–96, Dame Elizabeth Speke (1518); see also Prob11/27/5, Sir Roger Mynors (1534); Prob11/26/19, Dame Alice Kneveton, Lady Mynors (1539).

272. Prob11/29/10 (1540); Prob11/19/25, Dynham (1519); Prob11/23/11, Grevill (1528); *North Country Wills*, 96 (135–38), Fitzwilliam (1534).

273. Prob11/9/21, Sir Richard Hawte; Prob11/10/4, Dame Katherine Hawte (1493).

274. Prob11/29/12 (1541). Her third son by Culpepper, also named Thomas, was the Gentleman of the Privy Chamber executed for committing adultery with Queen Katherine Howard; L. B. Smith, *Tudor Tragedy*, 212–13.

275. Her husbands were Thomas Baldington, d. 1435; Sir John Fray, d. 1461; John, Lord Wenlock, d. 1474; and Sir John Say, d. 1478; her will is Prob11/6/34 (1478).

276. Prob11/6/34 (1478).

277. Prob11/7/6 (1482). Most likely, John Brown was the son of her sister Agnes, by her first husband, William Brown; Agnes subsequently married Sir Geoffrey Gates (d. 1478) and appears by this name in her mother's, Agnes Say's, will; *Visitation of Gloucestershire*, 65.

278. Scrope's only son died without children; he also had a daughter, Dorothy, who died unmarried.

279. TE, 3:122 (297; 1485).

280. GEC, 12 (1):453, n. g.; *Letters and Papers Richard III and Henry VII*, 283; L&P, 2:1446, 1450.

281. Prob11/21/3, Sir Thomas Wyndham (1522), Sir John's heir, mentioned the transaction in his will; Wyndham, *Family History, 1410–1688*, 26.

282. Prob11/15/1 (1505).

283. Of the daughters for whom we don't have wills, the last mention of Katherine is in her mother's 1505 will (Prob11/15/1); Anne, the nun, was still alive in 1515 (Prob11/18/6); Eleanor died by 1509 since her husband's son by his second wife was born c. 1510 (Wyndham, *Family History*, 53; Prob11/21/3); Frances, wife of Sir John St. Clere, and Jane, wife of Thomas Brews (Bruce) were living in 1546 (Prob11/32/33).

284. Foster, *Pedigrees of the County Families of Yorkshire*, 2, Scrope pedigree, no pagination. Elizabeth Pechey was the daughter of Robert Scrope, her father's brother; GEC, 12 (1):453; Hasted, *History of Kent*, 1:311.

285. Prob11/18/6 (1515).

286. Anderson, *DeVeres of Castle Hedingham*, 137.

287. ProbII/27/11.

288. ProbII/32/22 (1546); Bindoff, *Commons*, 2:443.

Chapter 8

1. Add'l Ms., 27,447, f. 74 (1529); ProbII/23/27, Lovell (probated 1528). The earl's first wife was Lovell's niece.

2. Green, *Letters of Royal and Illustrious Ladies*, 3: p. 169.

3. Ibid.; Add'l Ms., 27,447, f. 75 (1533).

4. HMC, *Rutland Mss.*, 1:31.

5. Add'l Ms., 27,447, f. 76; Green, *Letters of Royal and Illustrious Ladies*, 1: pp. 170–71.

6. C24/2; L&P, 13 (1):424, 586.

7. SP1/130, f. 122; SP1/141, f. 235 (1538).

8. Brigden, "Letters of Richard Scuadmore," 100 and n. 81; L&P, 18 (2):241 (60). Elizabeth's marriage to Hoby took place sometime before 1540; Bindoff, *Commons*, 2:366. Lady Hoby subsequently inherited Wreysbury from her father and was buried there; VCH, Buckinghamshire, 3:323.

9. Brigden, "Letters of Richard Scudamore," 7 (100).

10. The earl's difficult personality undoubtedly played some role in the situation since he was also estranged from his brothers.

11. BL, Caligula, B. 1, f. 135 (orig. f. 127).

12. Add'l Ms., 24,965, f. 106.

13. SP1/111, f. 78 (5 Nov. 1536).

14. BL, Egerton Ms. 2603, f. 22.

15. SP1/102, f. 203; SP1/111, f. 78; SP1/126, f. 24; SP1/128, f. 112; SP1/129, ff. 51, 226, 229; Lambeth Palace, Shrewsbury Papers, 3192, 3206, ff. 39, 55.

16. De Fonblanque, *Annals of the House of Percy*, 1:457.

17. Arundel Castle, T2, f. 13.

18. Lambeth Palace, Shrewsbury Papers, 695, f. 73; L&P, 18 (1):982 (547).

19. SP1/84, f. 100.

20. Ibid., f. 107; Lord Dacre was acquitted.

21. GEC, 2:287; Lambeth Palace, Shrewsbury Papers, 3206, f. 279; 696, f. 116. Lord Bray was released after a year in the Tower.

22. ProbII/7/27, Harcourt (1486); ProbII/21/22, Wotton (1523); ProbII/35/14, Sidney (1548). For larger, but less frequent legacies, see ProbII/10/23, Sir William Calthorp (1494); and ERO, D/DP Z13/8, Sir William Petre (1571).

23. ProbII/10/30 (1496).

24. TE, 5:76 (94; 1518).

25. ProbII/18/20.

26. ProbII/21/28 (1524).

27. ProbII/39/6 (1556).

28. ProbII/29/6, Owen (1529); Arundel Castle, T2, Shrewsbury (1537).

29. SP1/114, ff. 56–57 (Jan. 1537).

30. BL, Vespasian, F. XIII, art. 94, f. 144 (probably Jan. 1537). In fact, Norfolk wrote to Cromwell at least six times in the next few months: SP1/114/56–57; L&P, 12 (1):252, 336, 381, 469, 967.

31. SP1/128, f. 14 (Jan. 1538).

32. Green, *Letters of Royal and Illustrious Ladies*, 2:376–77 (6 Apr. 1538); see also L&P, 13 (1):741 (12 Apr. 1538).

33. Norfolk wrote a letter from London on May 13; a letter dated July 15 noted that the duchess was leaving the court the next or the following day. L&P, 13 (1):989, 1375.

34. L&P, 14 (1):651; p. 595.

35. Req2/10/157; Prob11/22/40 (1526).

36. Prob11/7/24 (1484); his father, Sir Robert, died in 1459.

37. C1/863/1 (1533–44); see also NRO, Lestrange of Hunstanton, AE 4, Sir Nicholas Lestrange (1547).

38. "Willoughby Letters," 2:2 (76); see also *Plumpton Correspondence*, 179.

39. SP1/117, f. 172.

40. Whether Sir Thomas returned to his wife permanently or not is unclear, but when he died, he left a considerable amount of land to his mistress and the son she had borne him. CSP, Spanish, 6 (1), 155; Thomason, *Sir Thomas Wyatt*, 19–20; L&P, 18 (1):981 (89).

41. Her marriage took place before her father died in 1513; GEC, 11:108, 444.

42. HampRO, 23M586.

43. *Clifford Letters*, 93–94 (1518); GEC, 3:566.

44. *Clifford Letters*, 34 (108); Hoyle, "Letters of the Cliffords," 49–52, 97–100 (98).

45. "Letters of the Cliffords," 49.

46. Harris, *Edward Stafford*, 50.

47. Ibid., 58–59.

48. Lambeth Palace, Shrewsbury Papers, 3205, f. 12; GEC, 11: 710–11. The letter is undated.

49. HMC, *Rutland Mss.*, 1:61 (1550s).

50. SP1/232, f. 94 (1518).

51. SP1/78, ff. 59–60; SP1/238, f. 194 (1533); Stac2/32/22 (1531); SP2/Folio. O, ff. 215–19; Stac2/26/266; Stac2/32/113 (n.d.).

52. Bindoff, *Commons*, 2:198–99, 455. Dorothy was the daughter of Sir Geoffrey Gates; her brother was married to Anthony Denny's sister Mary. See Shaw, *Knights of England*, 1:151, on Josselin's knighthood.

53. E314/79, 52 (or 136).

54. SP1/244, f. 13 (1542); see also SP1/243, f. 298, and SP1/244, f. 12.

55. SP1/243, f. 293 (1542); SP1/244, f. 234 (1544).

56. SP1/245, ff. 167, 169.

57. SP1/243, f. 298 (1542).

58. SP1/244, ff. 232, 233 (1544). Dorothy had at least seven children; six survived long enough to marry; *Visitations of Essex*, 13:225.

59. Arundel Castle, G1/5; 21 Hen VIII, c. 26, *Statutes of the Realm*, 3:317.

60. For a complete account, see Harris, "Marriage Sixteenth-Century Style," 371–82.

61. SP1/76, f. 39 (1533).

62. On their father's trial, see Harris, *Edward Stafford*, chap. 8; L&P, 5:70, 238 (1531); 6:585 (1533).

63. SP1/76, ff. 38–39 (1533).

64. BL, Cotton Ms. Titus B. I, ff. 383b (1537), 383c (1537), 383d (1539).

65. L&P, 12 (2):1332 (1537).

66. Prob11/42A/31 (1558).

67. Green, *Letters of Royal and Illustrious Ladies*, 3:p. 189.

68. *Paston Letters and Papers*, 2:813 (456); on Lovel, see GEC, 8:225.

69. James, *Kateryn Parr*, 15, 62.

70. PRO, C24/23 (pt. ii), mm. 8, 13.

71. HMC, *Rutland Mss.*, 1:56.

72. CUL, Hengrave Hall Ms. 88, vol. 1, no. 119.

73. Prob11/6/34, Say (1478); Prob11/19/2, Capell (1516).

74. CUL, Hengrave Hall Ms. 88, vol. I, no. 8.

75. Ibid., no. 157.

76. GEC, 4:73–74; *Plumpton Correspondence*, 160 (196) and genealogy facing viii–ix.

77. C1/405/29 (1517–29).

78. TV, 1:359 (1480); InqPM, Hen VII, 1:905, 906 (1494); GEC, 7:480, on Latimer; SP1/141, f. 212 (1538); L&P, 12 (1):1263; GEC, 4:481, and n. f on Dorset; Prob11/33/14 (1544); C1/1205/66 and C24/24, on Corbet.

79. SP1/156, f. 147 (1539).

80. SP1/139, f. 97 (1538).

81. L&P, 16:1320, 1321, 1385, 1440.

82. Thirteen left dowries to their daughters' daughters, eight to their sons' daughters, and three to the daughters of both; thirty-eight bequeathed cash or movable goods to their daughters' daughters, twenty-two to the daughters of their sons, and eight to the daughters of both.

83. BL, Titus B., XI, f. 362, Elizabeth, countess of Kildare, 1523; SP1/26, f. 184, Lady Cecily Dudley, 1522.

84. C1/1080/61 (1540); Req2/4/3; Prob11/32/4; *Letters and Papers of the Verney Family*, 49.

85. Lambeth Palace, Shrewsbury Papers, 695, f. 89.

86. *Clifford Letters*, 44.

87. *Lisle Letters*, 1:xxviii, xxxvi; see also 1:80 (5); 2:277, 5:1095.

88. Ibid., 1:xxix, 80, 277.

89. Ibid., 4:971.

90. *Plumpton Correspondence*, 132.

91. Green, *Letters of Royal and Illustrious Ladies*, 3:169–70; HMC, *Rutland Mss.*, 4:296, 315.

92. *Miscellanea Genealogica and Heraldica*, NS, 2:431; Longleat House, Thynne Papers, vol. 48, f. 165 (microfilm at IHR).

93. SP1/232, f. 94 (1518).

94. HMC, *Rutland Mss.*, 1:56.

95. E.g., Prob11/6/5, Lady Anne Vere (1472); Moor, "Bygods," 195, Katherine Bigod (1506); Prob11/33/11, Bridget, Lady Marney (1549).

96. Prob11/30/21 (1541).

97. Prob11/33/11, Bridget, Lady Marney (1549); Prob11/14/22, Hussey (1503); Prob11/5/31, Nevill (1470).

98. 21 Hen VIII, c. 26, *Statutes of the Realm*, 3:317; the fourth earl of Westmorland and the fifth Lord Bergavenny.

99. Lambeth Palace, Shrewsbury Papers, #3205, f. 10 (Dec. 22).

100. Green, *Letters of Royal and Illustrious Ladies*, 3:272 (Dec. 29); GEC, 3:567, 4:22. Neither date indicates the year.

101. *Lisle Letters*, 2:450, 4:1014.

102. Ibid., 1:32 (510–511).

103. Add'l Mss., 25,460, f. 93 (temp. Ed VI).

104. SP1/141, ff. 44, 212 (1538). Dudley's suit failed.

105. CPR, Ed VI, 1550–53, 4:237.

106. Robinson, *Original Letters*, 52:165 (340–41); Bindoff, *Commons*, 3:332.

107. *Paston Letters and Papers*, 1:122 (1467).

108. SP1/134, f. 288; L&P, 1 (1):1978 (1511).

109. *Lisle Letters*, 1:xxxviii (1533), p. 342; 2: pp. 164–67, 170–71; 201, 202, 202a (1534), 312, 429 (1535); 4:825 (1535), 904 (1537).

110. Ibid., 2:pp. 359–60, 4:848, 849 (1536); for examples of his activity, see 2:482 (1535), 4:847 (1536), 5:1380 (1539).

111. Ibid., 2:269b (1534).

112. Ibid., 3:749 (1536), 5:1335.

113. Ibid., 2:224 (n.d.); 5:1530 (p. 640; 1539).

114. Ibid., 2:346–47 (1535), pp. 428–29; 3:p. 282.

115. Ibid., 3:p. 537, 812 (1536).

116. Ibid., 4:p.338; 2:428; 5:1087 (1538).

117. Ibid., 4:pp. 361–62, 998, 1000, 1001 (1537).

118. Ibid., 4:1010, 1012 (1537).

119. Ibid., 5:1486 (1539).

120. E.g., Prob11/7/6, Margaret Leynham (1482); Prob11/14/38, Jane Talbot (1505); *North Country Wills*, 77, Katherine Babington (1537).

121. TV, 1:p. 277 (1455).

122. Prob11/29/12 (1541); her brother was Sir Ralph Chamberlain.

123. Prob11/20/19 (1514). Lucy was the daughter of her sister Lucy Brown and her second husband, Sir Anthony. Her sister had a son by her first husband, Sir William Fitzwilliam, and another by Brown. Bindoff, *Commons*, 1:518, 2:142.

124. Prob11/42A/1 (1558); *Statutes of the Realm*, 3:412–13, 23 Hen VIII, c. 32; *Visitation of Northampton*, 103; Bindoff, *Commons*, 2:476, states incorrectly that Ursula Knightley had six daughters.

125. E.g., Prob11/7/6, Margaret Leynham (1476); Pilkington, *History of the Pilkington Family*, 264, Dame Joan Pilkington (1498); Prob11/17/2, Sibill Danvers (1511).

126. Prob11/16/16, Elizabeth Tailbois Greystock (1505).

127. Prob11/26/28 (1582). Mary and Martha were daughters of Sir Edmund Denny; Martha was married to Sir Wymond Carew; her eldest son was Thomas. Bindoff, *Commons*, 1:581, 2:198.

128. Prob11/37/15 (1554); see also Prob11/22/29, Sir William Waldegrave (1526); Prob11/25/3, Thomas, Lord Berkeley (1532).

129. Guerney, "Extracts from the Household and Privy Purse Accounts," 517.

130. Prob11/8/15 (1487).

131. *Somerset Medieval Wills (1531–1558)*, p. 87; Sir John Berkeley, her son by her first husband, Sir Richard, was one of her overseers; his wife was one of her executors.

132. Prob11/10/4, Katherine Hawte; TE, 4:75 (152), Anne, Lady Scrope (1498).

133. *Household Books of John Howard*, 1:introduction, xv.

134. Horrox and Hammond, *British Library Harleian Manuscript 433*, 2:131; GEC, 9:220, 12 (1), 450.

135. GEC, 12 (2), 534; she died there in 1555.

136. Emmison, *Tudor Secretary*, 33.

137. SP1/154, f. 172.

138. SP1/157, f. 72.

139. HEH, EL 11,064.

140. Prob11/34/29, Dame Constance Ferrers (1551); Prob11/37/35, Dame Ursula Hynde (1557).

141. Prob11/10/12, Sapcote (1483); Prob11/28/6, Waldegrave (1540).

142. Prob11/19/32, Bourchier (1519); Prob11/29/25, Whethill (1542).

143. Prob11/19/2 (1516).

144. *Paston Letters and Papers*, 1:145, 150.

145. Ibid., 85.

146. Ibid., 92, 93.

147. HMC, *Rutland Mss.*, 4:268.

148. Ibid., 269, 270, 274, 277.

149. Ibid., 273, 276.

150. Harris, "Women and Politics," 263–64. The duchess's husband received the wardship of Margaret's brother, Thomas, Sir Henry's heir. CPR, Ed VI, 4:11 (1550).

151. Prob11/14/41 (1505).

152. Prob11/15/15 (1505, codicil 1506).

153. Prob11/18/13 (1515).

154. Prob11/26/28 (1582).

155. Prob11/14/38 (1505). Her husband was Sir Humphrey Talbot.

156. Prob11/20/25 (1521). He was the son of her husband's sister.

157. SP1/90, f. 153 (1535).

158. See K. Robertson, "Tracing Women's Connections," 149–64, for an extended female network from the late Elizabethan-Stuart period; like Margaret Paston's network, many of the connections were through Raleigh's mother.

159. *Paston Letters and Papers*, 1:156 (Nov. 1460), 2:657 (1460–67); see also 2:485 (79), 607 (328n.).

160. Richmond, *Paston Family*, 149; the younger Sir William died in 1495.

161. *Paston Letters and Papers*, 1:pp. lxii–xiii, 206, 220 (371).

162. Ibid., 417, 418.

163. Richmond, *Paston Family*, 168n. 4; *Paston Letters and Papers*, 1:25 (p. 37), 54 (Fastolf calls John Paston cousin in his will, p. 88).

164. E.g., *Paston Letters and Papers*, 1:133 (1449), 320 (1462), p. 630.

165. Ibid., 1:18, 2:446 (1449).

166. Ibid., 1:146 (250).

167. Richmond, *Paston Family*, 183, n. 82; 188 (1464).

168. *Paston Letters and Papers*, 1:206 (1470).

169. Ibid., 1:95 (1474), 209 (1471), 221–23 (1475).

170. E.g., ibid., 2:500, 594, 600 (before 1459–60).

171. Ibid., 597 (before 1459).

172. Ibid., 594 (before 1459).

173. Ibid., 1:630.

174. Ibid., 108–9 (1479).

175. HMC, *Rutland Mss.*, 4:188; Seaton, *Sir Richard Roos*, 40–41.

176. Mary Roos's sister Elizabeth seems to have died unmarried.

177. TV, 1:284 (1457). I have not been able to figure out their precise relationship.

178. *Lisle Letters*, 3:6 (1538).

179. SP1/106, f. 149 (1536).

180. Add'l Ms., 24,965, f. 103.

181. SP1/83, f. 39.

182. Bindoff, *Commons*, 3:2–3.

183. SP10/10, f. 8 (Apr. 1550); f. 60, 72 (Sept.); f. 83 (Oct.). On Cecil, see Bindoff, *Commons*, 1:605–6.

184. SP10/11, f. 9 (Nov.).

185. Arundel Castle, G1/5; 21 Hen VIII, c. 26, *Statutes of the Realm*, 3:317.

186. Add'l Ms., 46,457, f. 56.

187. Prob11/29/10 (1540); Finch, *Wealth of Five Northamptonshire Families*, 102; see also Add'l Ms., 33,412, f. 40, Dame Dorothy Hungerford (1559); Prob11/33/11, Bridget, Lady Marney (1549).

188. Guerney, "Extracts from the Household and Privy Purse Accounts," 425, 428–29, 436, 448, 452–54, 467n., 484–85, 488–89, 494, 527–28, 537, 539, 550.

189. HMC, *Rutland Mss.*, 4:296, 304, 335, 337.

190. Ibid., 290, 293–94; see also 313–14, 319.

191. HMC, *Rutland Mss.*, 4: 295, 302, 311.

192. Ibid., 292, 311; Bindoff, *Commons*, 1:562.

193. HMC, *Rutland Mss.*, 4:332, 335–36; Bindoff, *Commons*, 2:569–70.

194. CCR, Ed IV, Ed V, Rich III, 1476–85, 479 (139).

195. TE, 4:75 (149).

196. InqPM, Hen VII, 2:114 (75).

197. Edward IV gave her a primer that she eventually left to her highest-ranking godson, the earl of Suffolk. TE, 4:75 (152).

198. InqPM, Hen VII, 2:114 (75); TE, 4:75 (154; 1498); Blomefield, *Topographical History of the County of Norfolk*, 1:321.

199. *Household Books of John Howard*, xv, xx; Wyndham, *Family History*, 23, 26.

200. GEC, 11: 545–46; Bennet, "College of St. John Evangelist of Rushworth," 298.

201. InqPM, Hen VII, 2:193; GEC, 11:545–46.

202. InqPM, Hen VII, 2:114; *Visitation of Norfolk*, ed. Dashwood, 1:157; *Visitation of Norfolk*, ed. Rye, 28.

203. Morant, *History and Antiquities of Essex*, 396n.; *Visitations of Essex*, 1:45.

204. Scofield, *The Life and Reign of Edward IV*, 231–32.

205. Prob11/10/22, Sir Thomas Montgomery (1489). According to the will of Montgomery, her brother-in-law, she had life rights in the manors of Much Tey, Essex, and Charlton, Hampshire. Round, "Descent of Faulkbourne," 42–44; Morant, *History and Antiquities of Essex*, 2:205, 1:494.

206. *Paston Letters and Papers*, 1:383 (618); Carlin, "Holy Trinity Minories," 41. There is no evidence of her whereabouts between 1462 and 1479.

207. Virgoe, "Recovery of the Howards," 15; Davis, *Paston Letters and Papers*, I:354, 354a.

208. Carlin, "Holy Trinity Minories," 41.

209. Prob11/7/24 (1484); Prob11/8/20 (1489). Anne and Amy were interchangeable names in the period.

210. Parker, *History of Long Melford*, 57.

211. Prob11/11/22 (1494).

212. Parker, *History of Long Melford*, 44, lists seven; Weever, *Ancient Funeral Monuments*, 609, and Prob11/7/6, Dame Margaret Leynham (1482), name two others.

213. Prob11/10/22 (1489); Hampton, "Sir Thomas Montgomery," 154; VCH, Hampshire, 3:95, 105.

214. Prob11/11/23 (1489).

215. Hampton, "Ladies of the Minories," 197–98; Carlin, "Holy Trinity Minories," 16.

216. Prob11/14/38, Talbot (1505); Prob11/15/25, Norfolk (1506).

217. Prob11/29/12 (1541).

218. Durant, *Bess of Hardwick*, 21.

219. Talbot, "Letter of Sir William Sharington to Sir John Thynne," 51.

220. Prob11/18/2 (1513).

221. Prob11/22/9 (1525).

222. E152/2/42 (1544).

223. Prob11/37/34 (1554).

224. SP1/104, f. 117 (Blount); Add'l Ms., 25,460, f. 93 (Mountjoy); Bindoff, *Commons*, 1:695.

225. Waters, "William Lord Berkeley," 70–71; Smyth, *Berkeley Manuscripts*, 2:103; Cooke, "Great Berkeley Law-Suit," 305–13.

226. GEC, 12 (1), 447–50; *Paston Letters*, 1:212; Griffiths, *Henry VI*, 596–97.

227. *Paston Letters and Papers*, 1:36, 38; Griffiths, *Henry VI*, 587–88.

228. *Paston Letters*, 1:pp. 93–94.

229. GEC, 12 (1):446–48.

230. *Paston Letters*, 1:129, 132 (p. 232), 152; 2:460, 471–72; 691; Griffiths and Sherborne, *Reign of Henry VI*, 586; Wyndham, *Family History*, 4–10, 16–17.

231. *Paston Letters*, 2:609; *Calendar of Fine Rolls, Henry VI, 1452–61*, 19:289; CPR, *Edward IV and Henry VI*, 20:9.

232. *Paston Letters and Papers*, 1:168 (1462).

233. Ibid., 1:188.

234. Ibid., 1:p. xlv, 195–96; *Paston Letters*, 1:218–23, 226–27, 231–32, 245–46.

235. *Paston Letters and Papers*, 1:194.

236. Ibid., 2:911 (1469?).

237. Ibid., 2:752.

238. Ibid., 754.

239. Ibid., 2:764 (Nov. 1468–Sept. 1469).

240. Ibid., 1:201, 333 (544–45).

241. Ibid., 1:lix.

242. Ibid., 187.

243. Ibid., 324.

244. Ibid., 354a.

245. E.g., see ibid., 1:263, 338, 354, 334, for surrender.

246. Ibid., 366.

247. Ibid., 300; GEC, 9:609.

248. See Richmond, *Paston Family*, 172–97, for origins and development of the dispute; see *Paston Letters and Papers*, 1:108, 109, p. 191, on friendship with the duchess; 385, 387 for John III's position; 112 for William II's.

249. *Paston Letters*, 1:397, 112 (193).

250. Ibid., 417.

251. Ibid., 418.

252. Richmond, *Paston Family*, 201–2.

253. *Paston Letters and Papers*, 2:830. Heydon's daughter married Paston's heir, Richmond, *Paston Family*, 203.

254. Ibid., 835.

255. InqPM, Hen VII, 1:1228.

256. GEC, 2:137–38; her husband was Thomas, sixth Lord Berkeley.

257. Smyth, *Berkeley Manuscripts*, 2:266–68.

258. Stac2/4/221.

259. Smyth, *Berkeley Manuscripts*, 2: 268–69.

260. *Proceedings and Ordinances of the Privy Council*, 7:249–50 (1541); L&P, 16:1227, 1229.

261. Smyth, *Berkeley Manuscripts*, 2:252.

262. Ibid., 270; Ellis, *Original Letters*, Series 3, 3:142–44.

263. BL, Caligula B. VI, f. 152 (orig. 135); see also Caligula B II, f. 188 (orig. 178); Caligula B VII, f. 207; SP1/82, f. 248.

264. PRO, E36/122, f. 43.

265. SP1/115, f. 197.

266. SP1/118, f. 155.

Chapter 9

1. E.g., Starkey, *English Court*, 1–24, 71–118; Coleman and Starkey, *Revolution Reassessed*, "Court and Government," 29–58.

2. Gunn, "Courtiers of Henry VII," 35–36. The brief discussion of the court in his more recent survey of early Tudor government does not mention women at all; see Gunn, *Early Tudor Government*, 33–38.

3. E.g., Goff, *Woman of the Tudor Age*; Ives, *Anne Boleyn*; Jones and Underwood, *King's Mother*; King, "Patronage and Piety"; MacGibbon, *Elizabeth Woodville*; Mattingly, *Catherine of Aragon*.

4. Griffiths, "King's Court," esp. 11–17; Horrox, *Richard III*, 251–52.

5. Morgan, "King's Affinity," 1–4.

6. "Thus the only definition of the Court which makes sense in the sixteenth century is that it comprised all those who at any given time were within 'his grace's house'; and all those with a right to be there were courtiers." Elton, "Tudor Government," 45.

7. On the multiple political functions and character of the court, see ibid., 38–54; Griffiths, "King's Court," 11–32; Gunn, *Early Tudor Government*, 33–38; Horrox, *Richard III*, 250–264; Ives, *Faction in Tudor England*; Ives, "Henry VIII," 13–23; Loades, *Tudor Court*; Morgan, "King's Affinity," 1–25; Starkey, "Court, Council, and Nobility," 175–203; Starkey, *English Court*, chaps. 1–3; Starkey, "Representation Through Intimacy," 187–224.

8. On the growth of the crown's estates, see Wolffe, *Crown Lands*; Gunn, *Early Tudor Government*, 24–28, 113–21.

9. Gunn, *Early Tudor Government*, 34–38, 54–55; Horrox, *Richard III*, 250–64; Loades, *Tudor Court*, 133–47.

10. E.g., Kelly, "Did Women Have a Renaissance?" 138–63; Howell, *Women, Production, and Patriarchy*, 174–83; Weisner, *Working Women in Renaissance Germany*, 1–10;

Roper, *Holy Households*, 1–5; Hanley, "Engendering the State," 4–27; Stone, *Family, Sex and Marriage*, 3–9, chap. 5.

11. On the development of the disguising, see Kipling, *Triumph of Honor*, chap. 5; Anglo, "Evolution of the Early Tudor Disguising," 3–44; Anglo, *Spectacle Pageantry*, chap. 3. Both Anglo and Kipling treat productions that contemporaries variously described as disguisings, masques, and mummeries as comparable forms of entertainment. See, for example, the court calendar for 1509–28 in Anglo, *Great Tournament Roll of Westminster*, 138–46. For Burgundian-French influence on English court culture, see Ives, *Anne Boleyn*, chap. 1, and Paravinci, "Court of the Dukes of Burgundy," 94–96; on the influence of chivalric values and cultural forms, see Ferguson, *Indian Summer of English Chivalry*.

12. See e.g., *Receyt of the Ladie Katherine*, 55–57, on the first disguising at Prince Arthur's and Katherine of Aragon's wedding; Hall, *Union of Two Noble and Illustrious Families*, 526 (1512), 631 (1522), 723 (1527).

13. Anglo, *Spectacle Pageantry*, 99; BL, Cotton Ms., Julius, B. XII, f. 91; *Letters and Papers of Richard III and Henry VII*, "Creation of Henry Duke of York," 388–404.

14. Anglo, "William Cornish," 348–50.

15. Ibid., 350–53; Anglo, *Spectacle Pageantry*, 100–3; Kipling, *Triumph of Honor*, chap. 5; *Receyt of the Ladie Katherine*, 55–68, 74–76.

16. Cavendish, *Thomas Wolsey*, 105–6.

17. Anglo, *Spectacle Pageantry*, 246.

18. Thurley, *Royal Palaces*, 11–12, 16.

19. The regulations were probably written during 1471 and 1472. *Household of Edward IV*, 33, 92.

20. Contemporary accounts often do not distinguish between the queen's Presence and Privy Chambers but refer to them generically as the queen's chamber. In this chapter, I have tried to distinguish between them from the context and character of the event being described.

21. On the development of the Privy Chamber, see Starkey, *English Court*, 14–16, 82–118; Coleman and Starkey, *Revolution Reassessed*, "Court and Government," 29–58.

22. Thurley, *Royal Palaces*, 33 (Tower of London, c. 1540), Plans 7 and 8 (Hampton Court), 13 (Whitehall), 14 (Windsor); these plans are all c. 1547.

23. *Collection of Ordinances and Regulations*, 152–53, cap. 50. *Lisle Letters*, 4:887 (p. 151); Husee, the Lisles' man of business in London, also looked after their affairs at court.

24. *Lisle Letters*, 3:658.

25. Hall, *Union of Two Noble and Illustrious Families*, 513.

26. E.g., L&P, 1:82 (41), 14 (2):572 (202).

27. *Collection of Ordinances and Regulations*, 151.

28. Scofield, *Life and Reign of Edward IV*, 1:377. Edward IV allowed Elizabeth Woodville 100 servants and an annual allowance of £2,200 for her whole household. *Household of Edward IV*, 9, n. 3; 38, n. 5 & 6.

29. CPR, Edward IV and Richard III, 1476–1485, 241.

30. *Privy Purse Expenses of Elizabeth of York*, 99–100. The list does not indicate which women were Ladies-in-Waiting and which Maids-of-Honor.

31. Ibid., xxv–xxvi, 17, 32–33, 89, 99–100.

32. L&P, 1:82 (41). Eight other gentlewomen, listed as Gentlewomen of the Privy Chamber and chamberers, do not seem to have been from noble or knightly families.

33. These women, the queen's "Ladies Ordinary" (27) and the queen's maids (8), all participated in Henry VIII's funeral in 1547, PRO, LC2/2. Queen Katherine's household also included 85 men, for a total size of around 130, Hamilton, "Household of Queen Katherine Parr."

34. *Privy Purse Expenses of Elizabeth of York*, 99, 214; L&P, 1 (1):82 (38, 41).

35. On Norfolk, see BL, Cotton Ms., Titus, B. 1, f. 383a (in pencil, 388); on Parr, see HMC, *Rutland Mss.*, 1:22 (1514–15); L&P, 3 (1):491 (1519); PRO, E101/420/4 (1528); Martienssen, *Queen Katherine Parr*, 6–7.

36. Ives, *Anne Boleyn*, 336; *Lisle Letters*, 2:299, 299a, p. 332; 3:658; 4:863; L&P, 7:9 (2), 10:40, 799.

37. HMC, *Rutland Mss.*, 1:22; *Lisle Letters*, 2:p. 56–57; Murray and Bosanquet, *Manuscript of William Dunche*, 20, 30; SP1/241, f. 280 (1538); Howard, *Collection of Letters from Original Manuscripts*, 312; L&P, 14 (2):572 (201; 1539). She may have been in Mary's household as early as 1536 (L&P, 10:968), and she married Sir William Kingston by 1534.

38. Hall, *Union of Two Noble and Illustrious Families*, 631; L&P, 3 (2): p. 1559; GEC, 10:142.

39. *Lisle Letters*, 6: p. 277.

40. Horrox, *Richard III*, 264; Orme, *From Childhood to Chivalry*, 13; Campbell, *Materials for the Reign of Henry VII*, 2:349, 391.

41. Jones and Underwood, *King's Mother*, 165; *Privy Purse Expenses of Elizabeth of York*, 99; L&P, 2 (1):569.

42. GEC, 11:400; L&P, 1:82 (41), 3 (1):491.

43. *Lisle Letters*, 6:p. 277; see chap. 13, pt. 2, for Lord Lisle's fall.

44. *Lisle Letters*, 4:863.

45. Leland, *De Rebus Britannicus*, 4:204–6, 234, 236–37, 245, 253–54.

46. Katherine, countess of Devon from 1511, was disbursing money from the queen's privy purse in 1502–3, GEC, 4:330, note 31 above; on Stafford, see *Privy Purse Expenses of Elizabeth of York*, 41, 80, 99.

47. L&P, 1:82 (41); Ives, *Anne Boleyn*, 125.

48. L&P, 21 (1):969 (3).

49. GEC, 12 (2):216 and n. e.

50. Harris, "Women and Politics," 275; Bindoff, *Commons*, 2:263; 3:521; Jones and Underwood, *King's Mother*, 121–22, 165; Anstruther, *Vaux of Harrowden*, 10–11.

51. Sir Humphrey predeceased his father and therefore never held his title. Her grandfather was the queen's chamberlain; her grandmother was governess of Edward IV's daughters. Scofield, *Life and Reign of Edward IV*, 1:377; MacGibbon, *Elizabeth Woodville*, 68. This branch of the Bourchier family was distantly related to the queen through her sister Anne's marriage to Sir William Bourchier, heir of the first earl of Essex; the first Lord Berners was the earl's younger brother.

52. He was Chancellor of the Exchequer from 1516 to 1533 and Deputy Governor of Calais from 1520 to 1526 and 1531 to 1533. GEC, 2:153–54; DNB, 2:920–22; Miller, *Henry VIII and the English Nobility*, 171, 179–80.

53. Sandys was Lord Chamberlain of the royal household from 1526 to 1540. GEC, 11:441–43 and n. c; DNB, 17:784–85; Miller, *Henry VIII and the English Nobility*, 175.

54. Bindoff, *Commons*, 1:527.

55. L&P, 1 (1), 82 (41); 2 (1), 2736; Bindoff, *Commons*, 1:527; Jordan, *Edward VI*, 38.

56. Bindoff, *Commons*, 1:527, 575; 2:263. Margaret Bryan married Lady Jane Guildford's son, Henry; Elizabeth Bryan married Sir Nicholas Carew.

57. *Lisle Letters*, 4:896.

58. Ibid., 850 (2, p. 109), 876; despite this, Sir John Wallop apparently assisted Anne by approaching the king directly on her behalf (880).

59. Ibid., 4:850 (ii), 868a, 870, 874, 875, 880, 884, 887; see BL, Vespasian, F. XIII, art. 121, f. 172, for letters about the suit.

60. *Lisle Letters*, 4:863. Mistress Arundell was Lady Lisle's neice Mary; she married the earl of Sussex in January 1537 and appears thereafter in the correspondence as Lady Sussex.

61. Ibid., 4:870, 874, 880, 882, 887; BL, Vespasian, F. XIII, art. 121, f. 172.

62. *Lisle Letters*, 3:p. 367, 717 (409), 718 (410); 4:866, 870, 874.

63. Ibid., 4:874, 875, 887.

64. Ibid., 4:870.

65. Ibid., 4:878, 879, 879a, 881, 887.

66. Ibid., 4:878.

67. Ibid., 4:881.

68. Ibid., 4:883, 886, 887.

69. Ibid., 4:887.

70. Ibid.

71. Ibid., 4:867, 6:1653 (34); L&P, 19 (2):201 (1544).

72. *Lisle Letters*, 4:894 (162), 895.

73. *Travels of Leo of Rozmital*, 48 (1466).

74. Hall, *Union of Two Noble and Illustrious Families*.

75. Ibid., 490, 493, 604 (1520).

76. CSP, Venetian, 4:105 (59, 60).

77. Hall, *Union of Two Noble and Illustrious Families*, 793.

78. *Lisle Letters*, 6:1653 (34). On the importance of women's physical appearance at court, see 4:899 (172); see Ives, *Anne Boleyn*, 39, for a comment by Sir Richard Wingfield.

79. "Record of Bluemantle Pursuivant 1471–2," 385–87.

80. "Narrative of the Reception of Philip," 288–89.

81. Hall, *Union of Two Noble and Illustrious Families*, 703.

82. Warnicke, *Rise and Fall of Anne Boleyn*, 56–57; L&P, 10:1036.

83. L&P, 14 (2):572 (4; p. 202). The women were the duchess of Suffolk; Ladies Baynton, Dudley, Wingfield, Cheyney, Browne, Denny, and Heneage; and Mistress Parker. I have excluded three—the countess of Sussex, Lady Kingston, and Mistress Mewtas—because they held positions in the queen's household before they were married, and the countess of Rutland because she was a Lady-in-Waiting before her husband became Anne of Cleves's Lord Chamberlain.

84. L&P, 14 (2):574 (202); *Lisle Letters*, 6:1634 (8).

85. Leland, *De Rebus Britannicus*, 4:204–6, 245, 260; *Receyt of the Ladie Katherine*, 53.

86. King, "Patronage and Piety."

87. L&P, 14 (2):572 (4, p. 202); 15:21 (9).

88. L&P, 21 (1):969 (478–79); Bindoff, *Commons*, 2:470.

89. L&P, 17:258, f. 9; 19 (1):1036 (649).

90. The dates of the girls' marriages indicate that they were in Lady Bryan's care when she was in the queen's household.

91. L&P, 2 (2):pp. 1493, 1501; Giustinian, *Four Years at the Court of Henry VIII*, 2:225; Hall, *Union of Two Noble and Illustrious Families*, 595; Bindoff, *Commons*, 1:577, 2:263.

92. Bindoff, *Commons*, 1:578; L&P, 14:37 (18). In 1535, he also gave her a free chapel with a little close. L&P, 8:239 (93).

93. L&P, 1:82 (41); 2:3489; 3 (1):491, 528; 3 (2):2483 (1049); Martienssen, *Queen Katherine Parr*, 7, 31, 33, 35.

94. Ives, *Anne Boleyn*, 47–49. Anne returned in January and appeared in the masque in March. L&P, 3 (2):1994; Cavendish, "Life and Death of Cardinal Wolsey," 31; Warnicke, *Rise and Fall of Anne Boleyn*, 38, 55–56.

95. *Wills from Doctors' Common*, 19; *Lisle Letters*, 4:891 (157); Martienssen, *Queen Katherine Parr*, 38; L&P, 21 (1):969 (3).

96. GEC, 6:627, n. e; Ives, *Anne Boleyn*, 17–20.

97. GEC, 12 (1):602–3; L&P, 3 (2):2356 (18), 14–15, Henry VIII, c. 34, *Statutes of the Realm*, 3:280–81.

98. L&P, 4 (1):464 (196), 1264; 2002 (20); 2218 (12); 5:686 (306). The last grant was given jointly to William and Mary Carey.

99. *Lisle Letters*, 4:192–93; Green, *Poets and Princepleasers*, 19; L&P, 21 (1):148 (27, 28), 1165 (58); 21 (2), 475 (118).

100. *Lisle Letters*, 4:193.

101. *Household of Edward IV*, 93.

102. *Collection of Ordinances and Regulations*, 198–99.

103. *Lisle Letters*, 4:868a, pp. 156, 161, 192.

104. Ibid., 4:p. 123.

105. *Privy Purse Expenses of Elizabeth of York*, 99.

106. Childe-Pemberton, *Elizabeth Blount*, 52; L&P, 5:686 (309).

107. Starkey, *Henry VIII*, 101; *Lisle Letters*, 4:161.

108. *Lisle Letters*, 4:p. 191.

109. HMC, Sixth Report, appendix, 224. She was listed as a member of Elizabeth of York's household in 1502–3. *Privy Purse Accounts of Elizabeth of York*, 99, 214. The accounts of John Heron, Treasurer of the Chamber, strongly suggest she had joined it by 1495–96. PRO, E101/414/6, ff. 11d–12, 24, 36, 39, 47, 55d, 58, 64d.

110. *Lisle Letters*, 4:p. 198 (1510).

111. CPR, Ed IV, Ed V, Rich III, 1476–85, 241 (1481); Campbell, *Materials for the Reign of Henry VII*, 2:370.

112. L&P, 2 (2), 2946 (1517); L&P, 3 (1), 361 (1519).

113. See, e.g., L&P, 1 (1):381 (25); 3 (1):805, for wardships; and for land, L&P, 1 (2), 3226 (7); 2 (1):1155 (304–5); 15:1032 (1540). The first grant to Elizabeth Lisle was specifically made at the queen's request.

114. L&P, 16:1389. Lady Carew (née Norris) had been a maid in Anne Boleyn's and Jane Seymour's households and continued as a maid to Anne of Cleves. *Lisle Letters*, 4:pp. 191, 198; L&P, 7:9; 14(2):572 (4). She may also have belonged to Katherine Howard's household, although she is not named in L&P, 15:21.

115. Hamilton, *Household of Katherine Parr*, 169.

116. L&P, 19 (2), 688 (1544); PRO, E315/161, #201 (1543).

117. L&P, 18 (1), 981 (88).

118. CPR, Hen VII, 2:85; PRO, E101/422/15, f. 53. By 1540 Mary Roos was twice widowed, having married Hugh Denys and then Sir Giles Capell.

119. L&P, 1 (2), 5401, 3324 (1399); 5628; 2 (1), 569, 2736 (874); 15:1032; Anstruther, *Vaux of Harrowden*, 10.

120. L&P, 7 (1), 147 (4); she was probably the first marquess of Dorset's daughter.

121. See L&P, 17:283 (28); *Lisle Letters*, 4:p. 191, 1038; 6:p. 277, for Anne Basset's annuities between Henry VIII's marriages and after his death.

122. L&P, 2 (2):pp. 1443, 1449.

123. *Letters and Papers of the Verney Family*, 42–43. Weston was in Elizabeth of York's household in the previous reign. Verney's uncle (another Sir Ralph, d. 1528) was married to Eleanor Pole, a daughter of Margaret Beaufort's half-sister, Edith St. John, and served Henry VIII's parents and sisters. These connections show how interrelated the families that served the Tudors were and how the ties between them were perpetuated from one generation to another. L&P, 2 (1):1110 (293).

124. L&P, 1 (2), 2055 (131).

125. LincAO, Ancaster Ms. 1. 5/B/1/P.

126. HRO, D/E Fn T37; Bindoff, *Commons*, 1:575–76; see L&P, 3:854 (19) and 3214 (11), for grants to them.

127. Ives, *Anne Boleyn*, 210–11; Smyth, *Berkeley Manuscripts*, 2:252.

128. *Lisle Letters*, 4:870 (125), p. 171.

129. L&P, 3 (2):2356 (20, p. 998).

130. Parr was a member of Katherine of Aragon's household; L&P, 3 (1):491, 4 (1):1939 (865–66). Lane, Southampton, and Suffolk were members of Katherine Parr's household; L&P, 21 (1):969 (3). At the time, Southampton's husband had not received his earldom and she was Lady Wriotheseley. For the grants, see L&P, 3 (1):1121 (6); 4 (1):2362 (22), for Parr; HampRO, 5M53 198, for Southampton; L&P, 17:443 (13), for Lane; and 21 (1):963 (2), for Suffolk.

131. For the grants, see L&P, 1 (1), 867, for Weston; 2 (1), 696, and 2 (2), p. 1487, for Devon; 3 (1), 805, for Salisbury; 17, 1012 (7), for Edgecombe.

132. SP1/144, f. 87; SP1/156, f. 147; SP1/242, f. 224; L&P, 14 (2):113 (5).

133. *Lisle Letters*, 5:1620.

134. Ibid., 6:1653 (1540); see also 5:1513.

135. CSP, Spanish, 6 (1):230 (1542).

136. *Household of Edward IV*, 92.

137. L&P, 1:82 (41); 3 (1):491 (170), 528 (180–81); 15:21 (9).

138. *Lisle Letters*, 4:895.

139. *Collection of Ordinances and Regulations*, Eltham Ordinances,cap. 48, 152.

140. L&P, 1:82 (41); see also L&P, 14 (2):572, for male yeoman ushers in Anne of Cleve's household.

141. *Collection of Ordinances and Regulations*, Eltham Ordinances, 154–58.

142. E.g., *Lisle Letters*, 4:887 (151); BL, Cotton Mss., Titus B. 1, f. 383a.

143. *Collection of Ordinances and Regulations*, Eltham Ordinances, 156; this quote applies the description of the duties of the gentlemen of the king's Privy Chamber to the queen's servants.

144. E.g., Oxford University, Bodleian Library, Ashmole Ms., 1116, in Russell, *Field of Cloth of Gold*, 211, 214; CSP, Venetian, 4:59–60 (1527); Cavendish, "Life and Death of Cardinal Wolsey," 76; Hall, *Union of Two Noble and Illustrious Families*, 835–37 (1540); "Narrative of the Visit of the Duke de Nájera," 353–54.

145. E.g., 1 Hen VIII c. 14, *Statutes of the Realm*, 3:9; 6 Hen VIII c. 1 (1514–1515), ibid., 3:121–22; 7 Hen VIII c. 6, ibid., 3:179–82; 24 Hen VIII c. 13, ibid., 3:430–32. Women are specifically mentioned in the earliest of these statutes. The others do not mention them at all, but speak only of men.

146. *Stonor Letters and Papers*, 2:172 (14).

147. *Lisle Letters*, 4:903.

148. Ibid., 4:895 (17 Sept. 1537).

149. Ibid., 4:895, 896 (2 Oct. 1537).

150. Ibid., 4:900 (16 Oct. 1537), p. 174.

151. Ibid., 4:905, 908 (1; 19 Dec. 1537).

152. Ibid., 4:906, 908 (190; 14, 19 Dec. 1537).

153. Ibid., 4:906.

154. Ibid., 4:896 (2 Oct. 1537).

155. Ibid., 4:906. Before 1545, the word *kirtle* referred to a bodice and skirt; after 1545, to the skirt alone; Ashelford, *Visual History of Costume*, 143.

156. Jones and Underwood, *King's Mother*, 31.

157. *Privy Purse Expenses of Elizabeth of York*, 30.

158. C. H. Cooper, *Memoir of Margaret Countess of Richmond*, 5 and n. 3.

159. Ibid.

160. George Wyatt, cited in Ives, *Anne Boleyn*, 270.

161. HMC, *Rutland Mss.*, 4:276, 277, 287. According to the OED, a *plight* was a recognized length or piece of lawn.

162. L&P, 4(1):1906 (845; 1526); 5:686 (1532).

163. *Privy Purse Expenses of Princess Mary*, 96–97, 143. The OED defines *wrought* as decorated or ornamented, as with needlework; elaborate, embellished, embroidered.

164. "Record of Bluemantle Pursuivant," 386; *Collection of Ordinances and Regulations*, Eltham Ordinances, 156–57.

165. Gambling was often included in festivities at court; see e.g., Hall, *Union of Two Noble and Illustrious Families*, 513 (1510), 595 (1518); Giustinian, *Four Years at the Court of Henry VIII*, 2:225.

166. Jones and Underwood, *King's Mother*, 157.

167. *Privy Purse Expenses of Elizabeth of York*, 52.

168. Mattingly, *Catherine of Aragon*, 190.

169. *Receyt of the Ladie Katherine*, 7–8.

170. Ibid., 38; Thurley, *Tudor Palaces*, 78.

171. Ives, *Anne Boleyn*, 25.

172. "Record of Bluemantle Pursuivant," 386; "Narrative of the Reception of Philip," 288; CSP, Spanish, supp. 1513–43, 73–74.

173. Craig-Tudor, *Richard III*, 23; *Privy Purse Expenses of Elizabeth of York*, 44, 91; "Privy Purse Expenses of Henry VII," 96 (Lady Margaret Beaufort); L&P, 3 (2):p. 1533 (Katherine of Aragon); "Narrative of the Visit of the Duke de Nájera," 352 (Katherine Parr); Price, *Patrons and Musicians*, 2.

174. "Privy Purse Expenses of Henry VII," 116, 133; Leland, *De Rebus Britannicus*, 4:285.

175. "Narrative of the Reception of Philip," 289.

176. CSP, Spanish, supp., 1513–42, 74; Loades, *Mary Tudor*, 43.

177. Hall, *Union of Two Noble and Illustrious Families*, 703; Ives, *Anne Boleyn*, 36–37; Strickland, *Lives of the Queens of England*, 2:182; L&P, 10:1036.

178. L. B. Smith, *Tudor Tragedy*, 50.

179. *Lisle Letters*, 3:583a (1535), 3:587, 620.

180. Price, *Patrons and Musicians*, 14.

181. *Receyt of the Ladie Katherine*, xxiii, 67.

182. *Travels of Leo of Rozmital*, 47.

183. "Record of Bluemantle Pursuivant," 386–87; GEC, 12 (2):755.

184. Scofield, *Life and Reign of Edward IV*, 1:374, 419.

185. *Great Chronicle of London*, 251.

186. *Letters and Papers of Richard III and Henry VII*, "Creation of Henry Duke of York," 388–404, 395, 398, 400.

187. *Chronicle of Calais*, 4.

188. Hall, *Union of Two Noble and Illustrious Families*, 517–19; Anglo, *Great Tournament Roll*, 139. The five men included the earl of Devonshire as Bon Voloir, Sir Thomas Knyvett as Bon Espoir, and Sir Edward Nevill as Valiant Desire, characters they personified on the first day of the tournament. There is no way of identifying the other two male disguisers or the female performers.

189. Giustinian, *Four Years at the Court of Henry VIII*, 2:97.

190. L&P, 2 (2):3446; Lady Jane Guildford; Margaret, marchioness of Dorset; Elizabeth, countess of Surrey; Mary, Lady Willoughby; Lady Mabel Fitzwilliam; Lady Elizabeth Boleyn; Alice, Lady Mountjoy; and Lady Elizabeth Grey; *Privy Purse Expenses of Elizabeth of York*, 99; L&P, 1:82 (41), 3 (1):491 (1519). Mary Fiennes probably belonged to the household as one of the queen's maids or one of her ladies' maids since she was frequently mentioned in court records in this period; see e.g., L&P, 1 (2), 3357; Hall, *Union of Two Noble and Illustrious Families*, 594. There are no complete lists of the queen's household for this period.

191. Giustinian, *Four Years at the Court of Henry VIII*, 2:98.

192. Hall, *Union of Two Noble and Illustrious Families*, 594.

193. Ibid., 595. The queen's maids are difficult to identify since many lists of the queen's household refer to them collectively; see, e.g., L&P, 3 (1), 491 (170), 528 (180–81); 4 (1):1939. However, since Brown (Russell, *Field of Cloth of Gold*, 164, 170; probably the daughter of Sir Matthew; her mother was Sir Henry Guildford's half-sister); Carew, an unmarried sister of Sir Nicholas [Russell, *Field of Cloth of Gold*, 203; L&P, 3 (2):2305, p. 977]; Fiennes [L&P, 1 (2):3357, 2 (2):3446]; Wotton (Russell, *Field of Cloth of Gold*, 203); and Bruges frequently appear in court records, they probably lived there.

194. CSP, Spanish, supp. 1513–42, 71–74.

195. Hall, *Union of Two Noble and Illustrious Families*, 631; SP1/29, f. 224–33. Mary Tudor married the French king in 1514; after her return to England in 1515, she was usually called the French Queen in court records. I have not been able to identify Mistress Dannett, but she was almost certainly related to Gerald Dannett, a squire of the king's body. An eighth woman whose name was left blank in the revels accounts also participated in the disguising. The performance was Anne Boleyn's first recorded appearance at court. Ives, *Anne Boleyn*, 49.

196. Guy, *Tudor England*, 95.

197. Hall, *Union of Two Noble and Illustrious Families*, 635–37; CSP, Spanish, 2:734 (444–45). For a similar series of entertainments in 1527, see CSP, Venetian, 4:101, 105; Cavendish, "Life and Death of Cardinal Wolsey," 75–76; Hall, *Union of Two Noble and Illustrious Families*, 722–24.

198. Court calender in Anglo, *Great Tournament Roll*, 138–46.

199. It is clear from the costumes that here Hall was using the term *mummer* in its original sense as an entertainment in which silent, masked and/or costumed figures played mumchance for stakes. Welsford, *Court Masque*, 20, 29–31.

200. Anglo, *Great Tournament Roll*, 45–46, 51.

201. For examples besides those discussed in this paragraph, see Hall, *Union of Two*

Noble and Illustrious Families, 520 (1511), 580 (1515), 585 (1516), 597, 599 (1519); L&P, 3 (2), p. 1556 (1521).

202. Hall, *Union of Two Noble and Illustrious Families,* 580.

203. Ibid., 600–1; for a similar episode in 1524, see 688.

204. L&P, 3 (2), p. 1556.

205. L&P, 2 (2):pp. 1493,1501–2.

206. Ibid., p. 1466.

207. Warnicke, *Rise and Fall of Anne Boleyn,* 56.

208. BL, Cotton Ms., Caligula D. VI, f. 149 (25 Oct. 1514).

209. L&P, 2 (2):p. 1493; see also p. 1497 for Epiphany 1512; pp. 1500–1 for Epiphany 1514.

210. Hall, *Union of Two Noble and Illustrious Families,* 599.

211. L&P, 3 (2): p. 1559.

212. Hall, *Union of Two Noble and Illustrious Families,* 793; L&P, 5:1484 (624); Ives, *Anne Boleyn,* 196–201.

213. CSP, Venetian, 1527–33, 4:882 (361).

214. "Narrative of the Visit of the Duke de Nájera," 351–52.

215. Hall, *Union of Two Noble and Illustrious Families,* 867; Wriothesley, *Chronicle of England,* 173; L&P, 21 (1):1384 (696–97).

216. Harris, "Women and Politics," 276–78.

217. CSP, Venetian, 4:761, 802 (1532); Ives, *Anne Boleyn,* 206–7.

218. L&P, 5:70, 238 (1531); 6:585 (1533). Norfolk was Anne's uncle.

219. M. James, "Obedience and Dissent," 242; Dodds and Dodds, *Pilgrimage of Grace,* 1:26, 113, 131; GEC, 7:16–17.

220. Hall, *Union of Two Noble and Illustrious Families,* 631; L&P, 3 (2), p. 1559; Ives, *Anne Boleyn,* 377–82.

221. The duchess of Suffolk was Katherine Willoughby, who married Charles Brandon in 1533, shortly after his wife, Mary, Henry VIII's sister (the French Queen) died.

222. Gunn, *Charles Brandon,* 198–201. On the duchess as a supporter of reform, see King, "Patronage and Piety," 55–58.

223. Warnicke, *Women of the English Renaissance and Reformation,* 72.

224. BL, Cotton Ms., Vespasian, F. XIII, art. 94, f. 144; SP1/114, ff. 56–57; SP1/128, f. 14; SP1/131, f. 252; SP1/135, ff. 73, 75 (1537–38).

225. Warnicke, *Women of the English Renaissance and Reformation,* 101; DNB, 7:582; GEC, 9:622, n. b; Nott, *Works of Henry Howard,* cx.

226. Brigden, " Letters of Richard Scuadmore," 97, 102–4.

227. Prob11/37/14.

Conclusion

1. In this paragraph, I have paraphrased Walkowitz, *City of Dreadful Delight,* 9, and Burns, *Bodytalk,* 246.

BIBLIOGRAPHY

Manuscript Sources

Arundel Castle: Papers of Duke of Norfolk
British Library
   Additional Charters
   Additional Manuscripts
   Cotton Manuscripts
   Egerton Manuscripts
   Harleian Manuscripts
   Lansdowne Manuscripts
   Stowe Manuscripts
Cambridge University Library: Hengrave Hall Manuscripts
Center For Kentish Studies
Essex Country Record Office: Petre Papers
Folger Shakespeare Library
   Hatfield Manuscripts (microfilm)
   Losely Manuscripts (microfilm)
Hampshire Record Office
   Banker Mill Papers
   Kingsmill of Sydmonton
   Wriothesley Papers
Henry E. Huntington Library: Hastings Collection
Hertfordshire Record Office
Lambeth Palace: Shrewsbury Papers
Leicestershire Record Office: Papers of Earl Ferrers of Staunton Harold
Lincolnshire Archives Office: Ancaster Manuscripts
Longleat Manuscripts: Thynne Papers (microfilm at IHR, London)
Norfolk Record Office
   Jerningham Manuscripts
   Knyvett-Wilson Family Papers
   LeStrange of Hunstanton

Phillipps Manuscripts
Public Record Office
  Chancery
    Early Chancery Cases: Pleadings and Answers
    Town Depositions
  Court of Requests
  Exchequer
    Accounts, Miscellaneous Treasury of Receipt
    Court of Augmentations
    Inventories
    King's Remembrance, Various Accounts
  Prerogative Court of Canterbury Wills
  Star Chamber
  State Papers, Henry VIII, Edward VI, Mary I, Elizabeth I
Warwickshire Record Office
  Lucy of Charlecote
  Throckmorton Papers
West Suffolk Record Office: Kytson of Hengrave

Reference Works

Bindoff, S. T. *The Commons 1509–1558.* 3 vols. London: Secker & Warburg, 1982.

Clay, John William. *Dugdale's Visitation of Yorkshire.* 3 vols. Exeter: William Pollard, 1917.

———. *The Extinct and Dormant Peerages of the Northern Counties of England.* London: James Nisbet, 1913.

Cokayne, George E. et al. T*he Complete Peerage of England, Scotland, Ireland, Great Britain and the United Kingdom.* 13 vols. Gloucester: Alan Sutton, [1910–1959] 1987.

Collins, Arthur. *The English Baronage or an Historical Account of the Lives and Most Memorable Actions of Our Nobility.* . . .Vol. 1. London: Robert Gosling, 1727.

Compact Edition of the Oxford English Dictionary, Complete Text Reproduced Micrographically, 1971 ed. Oxford: Oxford University Press, 1971 (page numbers start at 1 for each letter).

Dictionary of National Biography. Ed. Sir Leslie Stephen and Sir Sidney Lee. 22 vols. London: Oxford University Press, [1855–1902] 1917.

Foster, Joseph. *Pedigrees of the County Families of Yorkshire.* 2 vols. London: W. Wilfred Head, 1874.

The Four Visitations of Berkshire. . . .Vol. 1. Ed. W. Harry Rylands. Harleian Society, 56 (1907).

Jeayes, I. H. *Descriptive Catalogue of the Charters and Muniments.* . . . *at Berkeley Castle.* Bristol, Conn. Jeffries & Sons, 1892.

———. *Descriptive Catalogue of the Charters and Muniments of the Gresley Family at Drakelow.* London: J. Clark, 1895.

Muskett, Joseph J. *Suffolk Manorial Families Being the County Visititions and Other Pedigrees.* Vol. 1. Exeter: William Pollard, 1900.

Pedigrees Made at the Visitation of Cheshire, 1613. . . . Ed. Sir George J. Armytage. Harleian Society, 59 (1909).

Pevsner, Sir Nikolaus. *Derbyshire, Buildings of England.* Rev. Elizabeth Williamson. New York: Penquin Books, 1978.
———. *Shropshire.* Harmondsworth, Eng.: Penquin Books, 1958.
Shaw, William A. *The Knights of England.* Vol. 1. London: Sherratt & Hughes, 1906.
A Short Title Catalogue of Books Printed in England, Scotland, and Ireland and of English Books Printed Abroad 1454–1640. Compiled by A. W. Pollard and G. R. Redgrave, with the help of G. F. Barwick and others. London: Bibliographical Society, 1946.
A Short Title Catalogue of Books Printed in England, Scotland, and Ireland and of English Books Printed Abroad 1475–1650. First compiled by A. W. Pollard and G. R. Redgrave; 2nd ed., rev. and enlarged, begun by W. A. Jackson and F. S. Ferguson, completed by Katharine F. Pantzer. 3 vols. London: Bibliographical Society, 1986.
Tilley, Morris Palmer. *A Dictionary of Proverbs in England in the Sixteenth and Seventeenth Centuries.* Ann Arbor: University of Michigan Press, 1950.
Victoria County History, Buckinghamshire. 4 vols. London: A. Constable, 1905–27.
Vistations of Essex. . . . 2 vols. Ed. Walter C. Metcalfe. Harleian Society, 13–14 (1878–79).
Visitation of Gloucestershire . . . 1623. Ed. Sir John Maclean and W. C. Heane. Harleian Society, 21 (1886).
The Visitation of Norfolk in the Year 1563, by William Harvey. 2 vols. Ed. G. H. Dashwood. Norwich: Miller & Leavins, 1878, 1895.
The Visitation of Norfolk in the Year 1563 . . . by William Harvey . . . Enlarged with . . . Many Other Descents. . . . Ed. Walter Rye. Harleian Society, 32 (1891).
Visitation of the County of Northampton in the Year 1681. Ed. Rev. Henry Isham. Harleian Society, 87 (1935).
The Visitation of Suffolke, Made by William Hervey, Clarenceux King of Arms, 1561. Ed. Joseph Jackson Howard. London: Golding & Lawrence, 1876.
Visitation of the Country of Warwick . . . 1619. Ed. William Camden. Harleian Society, 12 (1877).
Warner, G. F., and J. P. Gibson. *Catalogue of Western Manuscripts in the Old Royal and King's Collections in the British Museum.* 2 vols. London: For the Trustees, 1921.
Webster's New Twentieth Century Dictionary. Unabridged, 2nd ed. Ed. Jean L. McKechnie. New York: William Collins, 1980.
Wedgewood, Josiah. *History of Parliament, Biographies of the Commons House, 1439–1509.* London: HMSO, 1936.

Printed Sources

Acts of the Privy Council. Vols. 1–2. Ed. James Roche Dasent. London: HMSO, 1890.
Anglo, Sidney, ed. *The Great Tournament Roll of Westminster.* Oxford: Clarendon Press, 1968.
The Annotated Book of Common Prayer. Pt. ii. Ed. Rev. John Henry Blunt. London: Rivingtons, 1866.
"Arrival of King Edward IV." *Three Chronicles of the Reign of Edward IV.* Intro. Keith Dockray. Wolfeboro, N.H.: Alan Sutton, 1988.
Aylmer, John. *An Harborow for Faithfull and Trewe Subjectes.* London: n.p., 1559.

Becon, Thomas. Preface to Heinrich Bullinger, *The Christian State of Matrimony*. Trans. Miles Coverdale. London: J. Maylor for J. Gough, 1546. STC #4047.

Bedfordshire Wills Proved in the Prerogative Court of Canterbury, 1385–1548. Ed. Margaret McGregor. Bedfordshire Historical Record Society, 58 (1979).

Beer, Barrett L., and Sybil J. Jack, eds. *The Letters of William, Lord Paget of Beaudesert, 1547–63*. Camden Miscellany, vol. xxv, Camden Fourth Series, no. 13. London: RHS, 1974.

Bennet, Rev. Dr. "The College of S. John Evangelist of Rushworth." *Norfolk Archaeology*, 10 (1888), 277–380.

Bentley, Samuel. *Excerpta Historica, or Illustrations of English History*. London: Richard Bentley, 1831.

Blomefield, Francis. *An Essay Toward a Topograhical History of the County of Norfolk . . .* 2nd. ed., 11 vols. London: William Miller, 1805–10.

The Book of the Knight of the Tower. Trans. William Caxton, ed. M. Y. Offord. EETS, Supp. Series no. 2. New York: Oxford University Press, 1971.

Brigden, Susan, ed. "The Letters of Richard Scuadmore to Sir Philip Hoby, Sept. 1549–March 1555." *Camden Miscellany*, xxx, Camden Fourth Series, vol. 39, 67–148. London: Royal Historical Society, 1990.

Bullinger, Heinrich. *The Christian State of Matrimony*. Trans. Miles Coverdale. London: J. Maylor for J. Gough, 1543. STC #4046.

Calendar of Close Rolls, Edward IV, Edward V, Richard III, 1467–1485. London: HMSO, 1954.

Calendar of Close Rolls, Henry VII. 2 vols. London: HMSO, 1955, 1963.

Calendar of Patent Rolls, Edward IV, 1461–67. London: HMSO, 1897.

Calendar of Patent Rolls, Edward IV and Henry VI, 1467–77. London: HMSO, 1900.

Campbell, William, ed. *Materials for the Reign of Henry VII*. 2 vols. London: Longman, 1873, 1877.

Cavendish, George. "The Life and Death of Cardinal Wolsey." In *Two Early Tudor Lives*, ed. Richard S. Sylvester and Davis P. Harding. New Haven, Conn., and London: Yale University Press, 1962.

———. *The Negotiations of Thomas Wolsey, the Great Cardinal of England Containing His Life and Death*. London: William Sheares, 1641.

———. *Thomas Wolsey, Late Cardinal, His Life and Death*. Ed. Roger Lockeyer. London: Folio Press, 1973.

Chevalier au Cynge. *The History of Helyas, Knight of the Swan*. Trans. Robert Copland. London: Wynkin de Worde, 1512. Reprint, London: W. Pickering, 1827.

The Chorography of Norfolk: An Historical and Chorographicall Description of Norffolck. Ed. Christopher M. Hood, transcribed Mary A. Blyth. Norwich: Jarrold & Sons, 1938.

The Chorography of Suffolk. Ed. Diarmaid MacCulloch. Suffolk Records Society, vol. xix (1976).

The Chronicle of Calais in the Reigns of Henry VII and Henry VIII to 1540. Ed. John Gough Nichols. Camden Society, Old Series, vol. 35 (1846).

Clifford Letters of the Sixteenth Century. Ed. A. G. Dickens. Surtees Society, vol. 172 (1957).

Collectanea Topographica and Genealogica. 8 vols. Ed. John Gough Nichols. London: 1834–43.

A Collection of All the Wills . . . of the Kings & Queens of England. Ed. John Nichols. New York: AMS Press, [1750] 1969.

A Collection of Lancashire and Cheshire Wills. Ed. William F. Irvine. Lancashire and Cheshire Record Society, vol. 30 (1896).

A Collection of Ordinances and Regulations for the Government of the Royal Household, Made in Divers Reigns from King Edward III to King William and Mary. London: John Nichols for the Society of Antiquaries, 1790.

Croft, John, ed. Excerpta Antiqua: Or a Collection of Original Manuscripts. York: William Blanchard, 1797.

"Early Berkshire Wills." Ed. George F. Tudor Sherwood. The Berkshire, Buckinghamshire and Oxfordshire Archaelogical Journal, 1 (1895), 51–52, 89–90.

Ellis, Henry. Original Letters Illustrative of English History. Third Series. London: Harding & Lepard, 1824, 1827, 1846.

English Historical Literature in the Fifteenth Century. Ed. C. L. Kingsford. Oxford: Clarendon Press, 1913.

"Extracts from the Collections of Cassandra Willoughby." In HMC, Report on the Manuscripts of Lord Middleton. London: HMSO, 1911.

Extracts from the Records of the City of York. Ed. Robert Davies. London: n.p., 1843.

Fisher, John. A Mornynge Remembraunce, Had at the Moneth Minde of Her Noble Prynces Margarete, Countesse of Richmonde and Darbye. . . . London: Essex House Press, [1509] 1906.

———. "A Mornynge Remembraunce, Had at the Moneth Minde of Her Noble Prynces Margarete, Countesse of Richmonde and Darbye. . . ." In English Works of Bishop John Fisher. EETS, Early Series, 27, (1876), 289–310.

Foster, Joseph. Pedigrees of the County Families of Yorkshire, Vol. 1, West Riding; Vol. 2, North and East Riding. London: n.p., 1874.

Giustinian, Sebastian. Four Years at the Court of Henry VIII. 2 vols. Trans. Rawdon Brown. London: Smith, Elder, 1854.

The Great Chronicle of London. Ed. A. H. Thomas and I. D. Thornley. London: G. W. Jones, 1938.

Green, M. A. E. Wood. Letters of Royal and Illustrious Ladies of Great Britain. 3 vols. London: Colburn, 1846.

Guerney, Daniel. "Extracts from the Household and Privy Purse Accounts of the LeStranges of Hunstanton." Archaeologia 25 (1834), 411–569.

Hall, Edward. The Union of the Two Noble and Illustrious Families of Lancaster and York. London: J. Johnson, [1548] 1809.

Halstead, Robert. Succinct Genealogical Proofs of the House of Green. London: privately printed, 1685.

Harrington, William. Commendations of Matrimony. London: J. Scot, 1528.

Harrison, William. A Description of Elizabethan England. Harvard Classics, 5, 229–404. New York: P. F. Collier & Son, 1910.

Haynes, Samuel. A Collection of State Papers Relating to Affairs in the Reigns of King Henry VIII, King Edward VI, Queen Mary, and Queen Elizabeth from the Year 1542 to 1570 . . . Left by William Cecil, Lord Burghley. London: William Bowyer, 1740.

Historical Manuscripts Commissions. Report on the Manuscripts of the Duke of Rutland, Belvoir. Vols. 1, 4. London: HMSO, 1888, 1905.

———. Report on the Manuscripts of the Late Reginald Rawdon Hastings, Esq. of the Manor House, Ashby-de-la-Zouche. Vol. 1. Ed. Francis Bickely. London: HMSO, 1928.

"Historie of the Arrivall of Edward IV etc." In Three Chronicles of the Reign of Edward IV, ed. John Bruce, intro. Keith Dockray. Wolfeboro, N.H.: Alan Sutton, 1988.

Hood, Christobel M., ed. *The Chorography of Norfolk, An Historicall and Chorographicall Description of Norffolck*. Norwich: Jarrold & Sons, 1938.

Hope, Sir William H. St. John. "The Last Testament and Inventory of John de Vere, Thirteenth Earl of Oxford." *Archaeologia*, 66 (1915), 275–348.

Horrox, Rosemary, and P. W. Hammond. *British Library Harleian Manuscript 433*. Gloucester: Alan Sutton for Richard III Society, 1979.

The Household Books of John Howard, Duke of Norfolk, 1462–71, 1481–83. Ed. Anne Crawford. Wolfeboro Falls, N.H.: Alan Sutton, 1992.

The Household of Edward IV: The Black Book and the Ordinance of 1478. Ed. A. R. Myers. Manchester: Manchester University Press, 1959.

The Household of Queen Elizabeth Woodville, 1466–7. Ed. A. R. Myers. John Rylands Library, Bulletin 50 (1967–68), 207–35.

Howard, Leonard. *A Collection of Letters from the Original Manuscripts*. . . . London: privately printed, 1753.

Hoyle, R. W., ed. "Letters of the Cliffords, Lords Clifford and Earls of Cumberland, c. 1500–c. 1565." In *Camden Miscellany*, vol. xxxi. Camden Fourth Series, vol. 44 (1992).

Hyrde, Richard. Preface to Margaret More Roper's Translation of Erasmus *Precatio Dominica*. In *Erasumus of Rotterdam, A Quincentennial Symposium*. Ed. Richard L. De Molen, 87–104. New York: Twayne Publishers, 1969.

Journals of the House of Lords. vol. 1. London, HMSO, 1846.

"Kedington and the Barnardiston Family." *Proceedings of the Suffolk Institute of Archaeology*, 4 (1864–74), 121–82.

Ketley, Rev. Joseph. *The Two Liturgies, A.D. 1549 and A.D. 1552*. Cambridge: Cambridge University Press, 1844.

Kingsford's Stonor Letters and Papers 1290–1483. Ed. Christine Carpenter. Cambridge: Cambridge University Press, 1996.

Le Grande, Jacques. *The Boke of Good Maners*. London: Wynken de Worde, 1507.

Leland, John. *De Rebus Britannicus Collectaneorum*. Vol. 4. Ed. Thomas Hearne. London: Benjamin White, 1774.

Letters and Account of William Brereton [d. 1536] of Malpas. Ed. E. W. Ives. Lancashire and Cheshire Record Society, vol. 116, 1976.

Letters and Papers, Foreign and Domestic, of the Reign of Henry VIII. 2nd. ed., vol. 1 and addenda. Ed. J. S. Brewer, James Gairdner, and R. H. Brodie. London: HMSO, 1867–1910; 1929–32.

Letters and Papers Illustrative of the Reigns of Richard III and Henry VII. Ed. James Gairdner. 1861. Reprint, New York: AMS, 1980.

Letters and Papers of the Verney Family Down to the End of the Year 1639. Ed. John Bruce. Camden Society, Old Series, vol. 56 (1853).

Lincoln Diocese Documents 1450–1544. Ed. Andrew Clark. EETS, orig. series, vol. 149. London: Kegan, Paul, Trench, Trübner, 1914.

Lincoln Wills Registered in the District Probate Registry at Lincoln. Vol. 2 (1505–30). Ed. C. W. Foster. Lincoln Record Society, vol. 10 (1918).

The Lisle Letters. 6 vols. Ed. Muriel St. Clare Byrne. Chicago and London: Chicago University Press, 1981.

Literary Remains of King Edward the Sixth. Ed. John Gough Nichols. 1867. Reprint, New York: Burt Franklin, 1964.

Lodge, Edmund. *Illustrations of British History, Biography and Manners in the Reigns of Henry VIII, Edward VI, Mary, Elizabeth, and James I.* 3 vols. London: G. Nichol, 1791.

Miscellanea Genealogica and Heraldica. 19 vols. Ed. J. J. Howard. 1868–1908.

Murray, A. G. W., and Eustace F. Bosanquet. *The Manuscripts of William Dunche.* Exeter: n.p., 1914.

"A Narrative of the Reception of Philip King of Castile in England in 1506." In James Gairdner, *Memorials of King Henry the Seventh,* Rolls Series, no. 10. London: Longman, Brown, Green, Longmans & Roberts, 1858.

"Narrative of the Visit of the Duke de Nájera to England, in the Year 1543–4." *Archaeologia.* 23 (1831), 344–57.

North Country Wills, 1338–1558. Ed. J. W. Clay. Surtees Society, vol. 116 (1908).

The Paston Letters, A.D. 1422–1509. 6 vols. Ed. James Gairdner. New York: AMS, [1904] 1973.

The Paston Letters and Papers of the Fifteenth Century. 2 vols. Ed. Norman Davis. Oxford: Clarendon Press, 1971, 1976.

Phaire, Thomas. *The Boke of Chyldren.* 1545. Reprint, Edinburgh and London: E. & S Livingstone Ltd., 1957.

"Pleadings and Depositions in the Duchy Court of Lancashire." 2 vols. Ed. Henry Fishwick. *Lancashire and Cheshire Record Society,* vols. 32 and 35 (1896–97).

The Plumpton Correspondence. Ed. Thomas Stapleton, intro. by Keith Dockray. 1839. Reprint, Wolfeboro Falls, N.H.: Alan Sutton, 1990.

The Plumpton Letters and Papers. Ed. Joan Kirby. Camden Society, 5th series, vol. 8. Cambridge: University Press for Royal Historical Society, 1996.

Privy Purse Expenses of Elizabeth of York; Wardrobe Accounts of Edward the Fourth. Ed. Nicholas H. Nicolas. London: William Pickering, 1830.

"Privy Purse Expenses of Henry VII." In Samuel Bentley, *Excerpta Historica or Illustrations of English History.* London: Richard Bentley, 1831.

The Privy Purse Expences of King Henry the Eighth. Ed. Nicholas Harris Nicolas. London: William Pickering, 1827.

Privy Purse Expenses of the Princess Mary, Daughter of King Henry the Eighth, Afterwards Queen Mary. Ed. Frederick Madden. London: William Pickering, 1831.

Proceedings and Ordinances of the Privy Council of England, 1386–1542. 7 vols. Ed. N. H. Nicolas. London: n.p., 1834–37.

The Receyt of the Ladie Katherine. Ed. Gordon Kipling. EETS, no. 296. Oxford: Oxford University Press, 1990.

"Record of Bluemantle Pursuivant 1471–2." In *English Historical Literature in the Fifteenth Century,* ed. C. L. Kingsford, 385–86. Oxford: Clarendon Press, 1913.

The Reports of Sir John Spelman. Ed. J. H. Baker. Selden Society, vol. 93. London: Selden Society, 1977.

Robinson, Hastings. *Original Letters Relative to the English Reformation, Written During the Reigns of King Henry VIII, King Edward VI, and Queen Mary, Chiefly from the Archives in Zurich.* Parker Society, vols. 52–53 (1846–47).

Roesslin, Eucharius. *The Birth of Mankind; Otherwise Named The Woman's Book, Set forth in English by Thomas Raynold Physician.* 1540. Reprint, London: n.p. 1626.

Rotuli Parliamentorum. Vol 6. Ed. J. Strachey et al. London: n.p., 1777.

Rutland Papers, Original Documents. Ed. William Jerdan. Camden Society, Old Series, vol. 21 (1892).

The Sarum Missal in English. 2 vols. Trans. Frederick E. Warren. Alcuin Club Edition. Milwaukee and London: A. R. Mowbray; Young Churchman, 1913.

Sede Vacante Wills: A Calendar of Wills Proved Before the Commissary of the Prior and Chapter of Christ Church, Canterbury. . . . Ed. C. Eveleigh Woodruff. Kent Archaeological Society, Records Branch, Kent Records, vol. 3 (1914).

Select Cases in the Council of Henry VII. Ed. C. G. Bayne and William Huse Dunham, Jr. Selden Society, vol. 75. London: B. Quaritch, 1958.

Smyth, John. *The Berkeley Manuscript: The Lives of the Berkeleys, 1066–1618.* Ed. Sir John Maclean. Gloucester: John Bellows, 1883.

Some Oxfordshire Wills Proved in the Prerogative Court of Canterbury, 1393–1510. Ed. J. R. H. Weaver and A. Beardwood. Oxfordshire Record Society, vol. 39 (1958).

Somerset Medieval Wills 1383–1500. Ed. F. W. Weaver. Somerset Record Society, 16 (1902).

Somerset Medieval Wills 1501–1530. 2nd series. Ed. F. W. Weaver. Somerset Record Society, vol. 19 (1903).

Somerset Medieval Wills 1531–1558. 2nd series. Ed. F. W. Weaver. Somerset Record Society, vol. 21 (1905).

Some Surrey Wills in the Prerogative Court of Canterbury. Ed. Hilda J. Hooper. Surrey Archaeological Collections, vols. 51 and 52 (1949, 1950–51).

"Star Chamber Proceedings, Henry VIII and Edward VI." In *Collections for a History of Staffordshire.* William Salt Archaeological Society, n.s., vol. 15 (1912), 1–207.

Statutes of the Realm, Vols. 2, 3. London: G. Eyre and A. Strahan, 1816–1817.

The Stonor Letters and Papers, 1290–1483. Ed. Charles L. Kingsford. Camden Society, 3rd series, vols. 29 and 30 (1919).

Testamenta Eboracensia, A Selection of Wills from the Registry at York. Vols. III–VI. Ed. J. Raine and J. W. Clay. Surtees Society, vol. 45 (1864), vol. 53 (1868), vol. 79 (1884), vol. 106 (1902).

Testamenta Leodiensia, Wills of Leeds, Pontefract, Wakefield, Otley and District, 1539–1553. Ed. George Denison Lumb. Thoresby Society, Record Series, vol. 19 (1913).

The Travels of Leo of Rozmital. Trans. and ed. M. Letts. Hakluyt Society, 2nd series, vol. 108 (1957).

Trevelyan Papers. Pt. 1. Ed. J. Payne Collier. Camden Society, Old Series, vol. 67 (1857).

Tytler, Patrick Fraser. *England Under the Reigns of Edward VI and Mary . . . Illustrated in a Series of Original Letters Never Before Printed.* London: Richard Bentley, 1839.

Vives, Juan Luis. *De Institutione Christianae Feminae.* 1523. Trans. Richard Hyrde as *A Very Fruitful and Pleasant Book Called the Instruction of a Christian Woman.* 1529. In Diane Bornstein, *Distaves and Dames, Renaissance Treatises for and about Women.* New York: Scholars' Facsimiles and Reprints, 1978.

Weever, John. *Ancient Funeral Monuments.* London: Thomas Hardy, 1631.

"Willoughby Letters of the First Half of the Sixteenth Century." Ed. Mary A. Welch. *Nottinghamshire Miscellany,* no. 4. Thoroton Society Record Series, vol. 24 (1967), 13–74.

Wills and Inventories from the Registry of the Archdeaconry of Richmond. Ed. James Raine, Jr. Surtees Society, vol. 26 (1853).

Wills from Doctors' Common. Ed. John Gough Nicols and John Bruce. Camden Society, vol. 83 (1862).

Wriothesley, Charles. *A Chronicle of England During the Reign of the Tudors, AD 1485–1559.* Camden Society, n.s., vol. 11 (1875).

bibliography

Secondary Sources

Acheson, Eric. *A Gentry Community: Leicestershire in the Fifteenth Century, c. 1422–c. 1485.* Cambridge: Cambridge University Press, 1992.

Anderson, Verily. *The DeVeres of Castle Hedingham.* Lavenham, Eng.: Terrance Dalton, 1993.

Anglo, Sydney. "The Court Festivals of Henry VII." *Bulletin of the John Rylands Library,* 44 (1960–61), 12–45.

———. "The Evolution of the Early Tudor Disguising, Pageant, and Mask." *Renaissance Drama,* n.s., vol. 2 (1986).

———. *Spectacle Pageantry and Early Tudor Policy.* Oxford: Clarendon Press, 1969.

———. "William Cornish in a Play, Pageants, Prison, and Politics." *Review of English Studies,* n.s., 10 (1959), 347–60.

Anglo, Sydney, ed. *Chivalry in the Renaissance.* Woodbridge, Eng.: Boydell Press, 1990.

Anstruther, Godfrey. *Vaux of Harrowden.* Newport, Wales: R. H. Johns, 1953.

Archer, Rowena E. " 'How ladies . . . who live on their manors ought to manage their households and estates': Women as Landholders and Administrators in the Later Middle Ages." In *Woman Is a Worthy Wight: Women in English Society c. 1200–1500,* ed. P. J. P. Goldberg, 149–81. Wolfeboro, N.H.: Alan Sutton, 1992.

———. "Rich Old Ladies: The Problem of Late Medieval Dowagers." In *Property and Politics, Essays in Later Medieval English History,* ed. A. J. Pollard, 15–35. New York: St. Martin's Press, 1984.

Archer, Rowena E., and B. E. Ferme. "Testamentary Procedure with Special Reference to the Executrix." In *Medieval Women in Southern England.* Medieval Studies, vol. 15. Reading: University of Reading, 1989.

Ashelford, Jane. *A Visual History of Costume: The Sixteenth Century.* London: B. T. Batsford, 1983.

Baker, J. H. *An Introduction to English Legal History.* 2nd ed. London: Butterworth, 1979.

Baker, John H., and S. F. C. Milsom. *Sources of English Legal History: Private Law to 1750.* London: Butterworth, 1986.

Barron, Caroline M., and Anne F. Sutton. *Medieval London Widows, 1300–1500.* London & Rio Grande, Ohio: Hambledon Press, 1994.

Bayne, Diane Valeri. "The Instruction of a Christian Woman: Richard Hyrde and the Thomas More Circle." *Moreana,* 12 (1975), 5–15.

Bean, J. M. W. *The Decline of English Feudalism, 1250–1540.* New York: Barnes & Noble, 1968.

Bell, Susan Groag. "Medieval Women Book Owners: Arbiters of Lay Piety and Ambassadors of Culture." *Signs,* 7 (1982), 742–68.

Bennet, Rev. Dr. "The College of S. John Evangelist of Rushworth, Norfolk." *Norfolk Archaelogy,* 10 (1888), 277–380.

Bennett, Judith M. *Ale, Beer, and Brewsters in England.* Oxford and New York: Oxford University Press, 1996.

———. "Feminism and History." *Gender and History,* 1 (1989), 259–67.

———. " 'History That Stands Still,' Women's Work in the European Past (a Review Essay)." *Feminist Studies,* 14 (1988), 269–84.

———. "Medieval Women, Modern Women: Across the Great Divide." In *Culture and History 1350–1660: Essays on English Communities, Identities and Writing,* ed. David Aers, 147–75. London: Wayne State University Press, 1992.

————. "Theoretical Issues: Confronting Continuity." *Journal of Women's History*, 9 (1997), 73–94.

Bernard, G. W. "The Fortunes of the Greys, Earls of Kent, in the Early Sixteenth Century." *The Historical Journal*, 25 (1982), 671–85.

————. *The Power of the Early Tudor Nobility: A Study of the Fourth and Fifth Earls of Shrewsbury.* Sussex and Totowa, N.J.: Harvester Press and Barnes & Noble, 1985.

Berry, Boyd. "The First English Pediatricians and Tudor Attitudes Toward Childhood." *Journal of the History of Ideas*, 35 (1974), 561–77.

Boffey, Julia. *Manuscripts of English Courtly Love Lyrics in the Later Middle Ages.* Dover, N.H.: D. S. Brewer, 1985.

Bonfield, Lloyd. *Marriage Settlements, 1601–1740.* Cambridge: Cambridge University Press, 1983.

Brown, O. F. *The Tyrells of England.* Chichester, Eng.: Phillimore, 1982.

Brucker, Gene A. "Monasteries, Friaries, and Nunneries in Quattrocento Florence." In *Christianity and the Renaissance: Image and Religious Imagination in the Quattrocento*, ed. Timothy Verdon and John Henderson, 41–62. Syracuse, N.Y.: Syracuse University Press, 1990.

Brundage, James A. *Law, Sex, and Christian Society in Medieval Europe.* Chicago: University of Chicago, 1987.

Burns, E. Jane. *Bodytalk: When Women Speak in Old French Literature.* Philadelphia: University of Pennsylvania Press, 1993.

"The Calthorps of Burnham." *Norfolk Archaelogy*, 9 (1884), 1.

Calvi, Giulia. "Reconstructing the Family: Widowhood and Remarriage in Tuscany in the Early Modern Period." In Trevor Dean and K. J. P. Lowe, *Marriage in Italy 1300–1650*, 275–96. Cambridge: Cambridge University Press, 1998.

Cameron, A. "Complaint and Reform in Henry VII's Reign: The Origins of the Statute of 3 Henry VII, c. 2?" *BIHR*, 51 (1978), 83–89.

Carlin, Martha. "Holy Trinity Minories: Abbey of St. Clare, 1293/4–1539." In *St. Botolph Aldgate Gazetteer, Historical Gazetteer of London before the Great Fire*, ed. Derek Keene. London: Centre for Metropolitan History London, 1987. Typescript available at IHR.

Carpenter, Christine. *Locality and Polity: A Study of Warwickshire Landed Society, 1401–1499.* Cambridge: Cambridge University Press, 1992.

Catalogue, Holbein and the Court of Henry VIII. The Queen's Gallery, Buckingham Palace. London: n.p., 1978–79.

Chambers, E. K. *Sir Thomas Wyatt and Some Collected Studies.* New York: Russell & Russell, 1965.

Charlton, Kenneth. "'Not publike onely but also private and domesticall'; Mothers and Familial Education in Pre-industrial England." *History of Education*, 17 (1988), 1–20.

Chetwynd, Walter. "History of Pirehill Hundred." *Collections for a History of Staffordshire.* The William Salt Archaeological Society, n.s., vol. 12 (1909).

Childe-Pemberton, William S. *Elizabeth Blount and Henry the Eighth with Some Account of Their Surroundings.* London: E. Nash, 1913.

Chojnacki, Stanley. *Women and Men in Renaissance Venice.* Baltimore: Johns Hopkins University Press, 2000.

Chrimes, S. B. *Lancastrians, Yorkists and Henry VII.* London: St. Martin's Press, 1964.

Cioni, Maria. *Women and the Law in Elizabethan England with Particular Reference to the Court of Chancery.* New York and London: Garland, 1985.

Coleman, Christopher, and David Starkey, eds. *Revolution Reassessed, Revisions in the History of Tudor Government and Administration.* Oxford: Clarendon Press, 1986.

Collins, Arthur. *Historical Collections of the Noble Families of Cavendish, Holles, Vere, Harley, and Ogle.* London: E. Withers, 1752.

Collins, Arthur, ed. *Letters and Memorials of State: The Sydney Letters.* 2 vols. London: T. Osborne, 1746.

Condon, Margaret. "From Caitiff and Villain to Pater Patriae: Reynold Bray and the Profits of Office." In *Profit, Piety and the Professions in Later Medieval England*, ed. Michael A. Hicks, 137–59. Wolfeboro, N.H.: Alan Sutton, 1990.

———. "Ruling Elites in the Reign of Henry VII." In *Patronage, Pedigree, and Power in Later Medieval England*, ed. Charles Ross, 109–42. Totowa, N.J.: Rowman & Littlefield, 1979.

Cooke, James Herbert. "The Great Berkeley Law-Suit of the 15th and 16th Centuries. A Chapter of Gloucestershire History." *Transactions of the Bristol and Gloucestershire Archaeological Society*, 3 (1878–79), 305–24.

Cooper, Charles Henry. *Memoir of Margaret Countess of Richmond and Derby.* Ed. John E. M. Mayor. Cambridge: Cambridge University Press, 1874.

Cooper, J. P. "Patterns of Inheritance and Settlement by Great Landowners from the Fifteenth to the Eighteenth Centuries." In *Family and Inheritance: Rural Society in Western Europe, 1200–1800*, ed. Jack Goody, Joan Thirsk, and E. P. Thompson, 192–337. Cambridge: Cambridge University Press, 1976.

———. "The Social Distribution of Land and Men." In *Land, Men and Beliefs, Studies in Early-Modern History*, ed. G. E. Aylmer and J. S. Morrill, 17–42. London: Hambledon Press, 1983.

Cooper, William D. "The Families of Braose of Chesworth and Hoo." *Sussex Archaeological Collections*, 8 (1856), 97–131.

Copinger, W. A. *The Manors of Suffolk.* 6 vols. Manchester: Taylor, Garnett, & Evans, 1907.

Cornwall, J. C. K. *Wealth and Society in Early Sixteenth Century England.* London: Routledge & Kegan Paul, 1988.

Coronation of Elizabeth Woodville. Ed. George Smith. London: Ellis, 1935.

Coster, William. "Purity, Profanity, and Puritanism: The Churching of Women, 1500–1700." *Studies in Church History*, 27 (1990), 377–87.

Crabb, Ann Morton. "How Typical Was Alessandra Macinghi Strozzi of Fifteenth-Century Florentine Widows?" In *Upon My Husband's Death: Widows in the Literature and Histories of Medieval Europe*, ed. Louise Mirrer, 47–68. Ann Arbor: University of Michigan, 1992.

Craig-Tudor, Pamela. *Richard III.* Totowa, N.J.: Rowman & Littlefield, 1977.

Crawford, Anne. "The Career of John Howard, Duke of Norfolk, 1420–1485." M. Phil. thesis, University of London, 1975.

———. "Victims of Attainder: The Howard and DeVere Women in the Late Fifteenth Century." In *Medieval Women in Southern England.* Reading Medieval Studies, 15 (1989), 59–74.

Crawford, Patricia. "The Construction and Experience of Maternity in Seventeenth-Century England." In *Women as Mothers in Pre-Industrial England, Essays in*

Memory of Dorothy McLaren, ed. Valerie Fildes, 3–38. London and New York: Routledge, 1990.

Cressey, David. *Birth, Marriage and Death, Ritual, Religion, and the Life-Cycle in Tudor and Stuart England*. Oxford and New York: Oxford University Press, 1997.

———. "Purification, Thanksgiving, and the Churching of Women in Post-Reformation England." *Past and Present*, no. 141 (Nov. 1993), 107–46.

Davies, Kathleen M. "Continuity and Change in Literary Advice on Marriage." In *Marriage and Society: Studies in the Social History of Marriage*, ed. R. B. Outhwaite, 58–80. New York: St. Martin's Press, 1981.

Dean, Trevor. "The Courts." *The Journal of Modern History, The Origins of the State in Italy, 1300–1600*, 67, supp. (Dec. 1995), 136–51.

Dean, Trevor, and K. J. P. Lowe. *Marriage in Italy 1300–1650*. Cambridge: Cambridge University Press, 1998.

De Fonblanque, Edward Barrington. *Annals of the House of Percy*. Vol. I. London: R. Clay & Sons, 1887.

DeMolen, Richard L., ed. *Erasmus of Rotterdam, A Quincentennial Symposium*. New York: Twayne Publishers, 1969.

Denny, Rev. H. L. L. "A Biography of the Right Honorable Sir Anthony Denny, P.C., M.P." *East Hertfordshire Archaeological Society Transactions*, 3, no. 2 (1905), 197–216.

———. "Pedigrees of Some East-Anglian Dennys." *Genealogist*, n.s., 38 (1922), 19.

Dockray, Keith. "Why Did Fifteenth-Century English Gentry Marry?: The Pastons, Plumptons and Stonors Reconsidered." In *Gentry and Lesser Nobility in Late Medieval England*, ed. Michael Jones, 61–80. New York: St. Martin's Press, 1986.

Dodds, M. H., and Ruth Dodds. *The Pilgrimage of Grace 1536–1537 and the Exeter Conspiracy*. 2 vols. Cambridge: Cambridge University Press, 1915.

Dowling, Maria. *Humanism in the Age of Henry VIII*. London; Dover, N.H.; and Sydney: Croom Helm, 1986.

Duffy, Eamon. *The Stripping of the Altars, Traditional Religion in England 1400–1580*. New Haven, Conn.: Yale University Press, 1992.

Dugdale, William. *The Antiquities of Warwickshire*. London: Thomas Warren, 1651.

Durant, David N. *Bess of Hardwick: Portrait of an Elizabethan Dynast*. London: Weidenfield & Nicolson, 1977.

Dyer, Christopher. *Standards of Living in the Later Middle Ages, Social Change in England c. 1200–1500*. Cambridge: Cambridge University Press, 1989.

Elias, Norbert. *The Court Society*. Trans. Edmund Jephcott. New York: Pantheon Books, [1969] 1983.

Ellis, Steven G. *Tudor Frontiers and Noble Power: The Making of the British State*. Oxford: Clarendon Press, 1995.

Elton, G. R. "Tudor Government: The Points of Contact. III. The Court." In *Studies in Tudor and Stuart Politics and Government, Vol. 3, Papers and Reviews 1973–1981*, 38–57. Cambridge: Cambridge University Press, 1983.

———. *Tudor Revolution in Government*. Cambridge: Cambridge University Press, 1953.

Emmison, F. G. *Tudor Secretary, Sir William Petre at Court and Home*. 2nd ed. Chichester: Phillmore, 1970.

Erickson, Amy L. "Common Law versus Common Practice: The Use of Marriage Settlements in Early Modern England." *Economic History Review*, 2nd ser., 43 (1990), 21–39.

————. *Women and Property in Early Modern England*. London and New York: Routledge, 1993.

Esdaile, Katharine A. *English Church Monuments 1510–1840*. New York: Oxford University Press, 1947.

Evergates, Theodore, ed. *Aristocratic Women in Medieval France*. Philadelphia: University of Pennsylvania Press, 1999.

Ferguson, Arthur. *The Indian Summer of English Chivalry, Studies in the Decline and Transformation of Chivalric Idealism*. Durham, N.C.: Duke University Press, 1960.

Finch, Mary E. *The Wealth of Five Northamptonshire Families 1540–1640*. Oxford: University Press for the Northamptonshire Record Office, 1956.

Fleming, P. W. "The Hautes and Their 'Circle': Culture and the English Gentry." In *England in the Fifteenth Century*, ed. Daniel Williams. Proceedings of the 1986 Harlaxton Symposium, 85–102. Wolfeboro, N.H.: Boydell Press, 1987.

Fletcher, Anthony. *Gender, Sex and Subordination in England 1500–1800*. New Haven, Conn., and London: Yale University Press, 1995.

Foxwell, A. K. *A Study of Sir Thomas Wyatt's Poems*. New York: Russell & Russell, 1964.

Friedman, John B. *Northern English Books, Owners, and Makers in the Late Middle Ages*. Syracuse, N.Y.: Syracuse University Press, 1995.

Frye, Susan. *Elizabeth I: The Competition for Representation*. New York and Oxford: Oxford University Press, 1993.

Gage, John. *History and Antiquities of Suffolk: Thingoe Hundred*. London: S. Bentley, 1838.

Gibson, Gail McMurray. "Saint Anne and the Religion of Childbed: Some East Anglian Texts and Talismans." In *Interpreting Cultural Symbols: Saint Anne in Late Medieval Society*, ed. Kathleen Ashley and Pamela Sheingorn, 94–110. Athens: Unversity of Georgia, 1990.

Girouard, Mark. *Life in the English Country House*. New Haven, Conn., and London: Yale University Press, 1978.

Goff, Lady Cecilie. *A Woman of the Tudor Age*. London: John Murray, 1930.

Goffin, R. J. R. *The Testamentary Executor in England and Elsewhere*. Buffalo: William S. Hein, [1901] 1981.

Green, Richard Firth. *Poets and Princepleasers: Literature and the English Court in the Middle Ages*. London and Buffalo: University of Toronto Press, 1980.

Griffin, Ralph. "An Inscription in Little Chart Church." *Archaeologia Cantiana*, 36 (1923), 131–42.

Griffiths, Ralph A. "The Crown and the Royal Family in Later Medieval England." In *Kings & Nobles in the Later Middle Ages, A Tribute to Charles Ross*, ed. Ralph A. Griffiths and James Sherborne, 15–26. New York: St. Martin's Press, 1986.

————. "The King's Court during the Wars of the Roses." In *King and Country, England and Wales in the Fifteenth Century*, 11–32. London and Rio Grande: Hambledon Press, 1991.

————. *The Reign of Henry VI*. Berkeley and Los Angeles: University of California, 1981.

Gunn, S. J. *Charles Brandon, Duke of Suffolk*. Oxford and New York: Basil Blackwell, 1988.

————. "The Courtiers of Henry VII." *English Historical Review*, 108, no. 426 (1993), 23–49.

————. *Early Tudor Government, 1458–1558*. New York: St. Martin's Press, 1995.

Guy, John A. "The Development of Equitable Jurisdictions, 1450–1550." In *Law, Litigants and the Legal Profession*. Papers presented to the Fourth British Legal History Conference at the University of Birmingham, 10–13 July 1979. Royal Historical Society Studies in History Series No. 36. Ed. E. W. Ives and A. H. Manchester. London: RHS; Atlantic Highlands, New Jersey: Humanities Press, 1983.

———. *Tudor England*. Oxford and New York: Oxford University Press, 1988.

Haigh, Christopher. *English Reformations: Religion, Politics, and Society under the Tudors*. Oxford: Clarendon Press, 1993.

Hajnal, J. "European Marriage Patterns in Perspective." In *Population in History, Essays in Historical Demography*, ed. D. V. Glass and D. E. C. Eversley, 101–43. Chicago: Aldine, 1965.

Halstead, Robert (pseud. Henry Mordaunt, Earl of Peterborough). *Succinct Genealogy of the House of Drayton*. London: privately printed, [1685] 1896.

Hamilton, Dakota. "Household of Queen Katherine Parr." Ph.D. thesis, Somerville College, Oxford, 1992.

Hampton, W. E. "The Ladies of the Minories." In *Richard III: Crown and People*, ed. J. Petre, 195–202. Gloucester: Alan Sutton, 1985.

———. *Memorials of the Wars of the Roses: A Biographical Guide*. Upminster, Eng.: For Richard III Society, 1979.

———. "Sir Thomas Montgomery." In *Richard III: Crown and People*, ed. J. Petre, 149–55. Gloucester: Alan Sutton, 1985.

Hanawalt, Barbara A. "Lady Honor Lisle's Networks of Influence." In *Women and Power in the Middle Ages*, ed. Mary Erler and Maryanne Kowaleski, 188–212. Athens: University of Georgia Press, 1988.

Hanley, Sarah. "Engendering the State: Family Formation and State Building in Early Modern France." *French Historical Studies*, 16 (1989), 4–27.

Harding, Alan. *Law Making and Law Makers in British History*. London: RHS, 1980.

Hardwick, Julie. *The Practice of Patriarchy: Gender and the Politics of Authority in Early Modern France*. University Park: Pennsylvania State University Press, 1998.

Harris, Barbara J. *Edward Stafford, Third Duke of Buckingham, 1478–1521*. Stanford, Calif.: Stanford University Press, 1986.

———. "Marriage Sixteenth-Century Style: Elizabeth Stafford and the Third Duke of Norfolk." *Journal of Social History*, 15 (1982), 371–82.

———. "A New Look at the Reformation: Aristocratic Women and Nunneries, 1450–1540." *Journal of British Studies*, 32 (1993), 89–113.

———. "Power, Profit, and Passion: Mary Tudor, Charles Brandon, and the Arranged Marriage in Early Tudor England." *Feminist Studies*, 15 (1989), 59–88.

———. "Property, Power, and Personal Relations: Elite Mothers and Sons in Yorkist and Early Tudor England." *Signs*, 15 (1990), 606–32.

———. "The View from My Lady's Chamber: New Perspective on the Early Tudor Monarchy." *Huntington Library Quarterly*, 60 (1999), 215–47.

———. "Women and Politics in Early Tudor England." *The Historical Journal*, 33 (1990), 259–81.

Harris, Barbara J., and JoAnn K. McNamara, eds. *Women and the Structure of Society*. Durham, N.C.: Duke University Press, 1984.

Haskell, Ann S. "The Paston Women on Marriage in Fifteenth-Century England." *Viator*, 4 (1973), 459–71.

Hasted, Edward. *The History of Kent*. 4 vols. Canterbury: W. Bristow, 1778–99.

Helmholz, R. H. *Marriage Litigation in Medieval England.* Cambridge and New York: Cambridge University Press, 1974.

Herlihy, David. "Did Women Have a Renaissance? A Reconsideration." *Medievalia et Humanistica,* n.s., 13 (1985), 1–22.

———. "Land, Family and Women in Continental Europe, 701–1200," *Traditio,* 18 (1962), 89–120.

Hexter, J. H. "The Education of the Aristocracy in the Renaissance." In *Reappraisals in History: New Views on History and Society in Early Modern Europe,* 45–70. New York: Harper Torchbooks, 1963.

Hibbard, Caroline M. "The Role of a Queen Consort: The Household and Court of Henrietta Maria, 1625–42." In *Princes, Patronage, and the Nobility: The Court at the Beginning of the Modern Age, c. 1450–1650,* ed. Ronald C. Asch and Adolf M. Birke, 394–414. London: Oxford University Press, 1991.

Hicks, Michael. "Attainder, Resumption and Coercions, 1461–1529." In *Richard III and His Rivals: Magnates and Their Motives in the Wars of the Roses,* 61–77. Rio Grande, Ohio: Hambledon Press, 1991.

———. "The Changing Roll of the Wydevilles in Yorkist Politics to 1483." In *Patronage, Pedigree and Power in Later Medieval England,* ed. Charles Ross, 60–86. Totowa, N.J.: Rowman & Littlefield, 1979.

———. "Chantries, Obits and Almshouses: The Hungerford Foundations, 1325–1478." In *Richard III and His Rivals: Magnates and Their Motives in the Wars of the Roses,* 79–98. Rio Grande, Ohio: Hambledon Press, 1991.

———. "Counting the Cost of War: The Moleyns Ransom and the Hungerford Land-Sales, 1453–87." In *Richard III and His Rivals: Magnates and Their Motives in the Wars of the Roses,* 185–208. Rio Grande, Ohio: Hambledon Press, 1991.

———. "The Last Days of the Countess of Oxford." *EHR,* 103 (1988), 76–95.

———. "Piety and Lineage in the Wars of the Roses: The Hungerford Experience." In *Richard III and His Rivals: Magnates and Their Motives in the Wars of the Roses,* 165–84. Rio Grande, Ohio: Hambledon Press, 1991.

———. "The Piety of Margaret, Lady Hungerford." *Journal of Ecclesiastical History,* 38 (1987), 19–38.

———. *Richard III and His Rivals: Magnates and Their Motives in the Wars of the Roses.* Rio Grande, Ohio: Hambledon Press, 1991.

Hoffman, C. Fenno, Jr. "Catherine Parr as a Woman of Letters." *Huntington Library Quarterly,* 23 (1960), 349–67.

Holdsworth, W. S. *A History of English Law.* 3rd ed., vols. 3–5. Boston: Methuen, 1923–24.

Hollingsworth, T. H. "A Demographic Study of the British Ducal Families." In *Population in History, Essays in Historical Demography,* ed. D. V. Glass and D. E. C. Eversley, 354–78. Chicago: Aldine, [1957] 1965.

———. "Demography of the British Peerage." *Supplement to Population Studies,* vol. 18 (1964).

Holmes, G. A. *The Estates of the Higher Nobility in Fourteenth-Century England.* Cambridge: Cambridge University Press, 1957.

Horrox, Rosemary. *Richard III: A Study in Service.* Cambridge and New York: Cambridge University Press, 1989.

Houlbrooke, Ralph. *Death, Religion, and the Family in England, 1480–1750.* Oxford: Clarendon Press, 1998.

————. *The English Family 1450–1700*. London and New York: Longman, 1984.

Howell, Martha C. "Fixing Movables: Gifts by Testament in Late Medieval Douai." *Past and Present*, no. 150 (1996), 3–45.

————. *The Marriage Exchange: Property, Social Place, and Gender in Cities of the Low Countries, 1300–1500*. Chicago: University of Chicago Press, 1998.

————. *Women, Production, and Patriarchy in Late Medieval Cities*. Chicago: University of Chicago Press, 1986.

Hughes, Diane. "From Brideprice to Dowry in Mediterranean Europe." *Journal of Family History*, 3 (1978), 262–96.

Ives, E. W. " 'Agaynst Taking Away of Women': The Inception and Operation of the Abduction Act of 1487." In *Wealth and Power in Tudor England, Essays Presented to S. T. Bindoff*, ed. E. W. Ives, R. J. Knecht, and J. J. Scarisbrick, 21–44. London: Atholone Press, 1978.

————. *Anne Boleyn*. Oxford and New York: Basil Blackwell, 1986.

————. *The Common Lawyers of Pre-Reformation England. Thomas Kebell: A Case Study*. Cambridge and New York: Cambridge University Press, 1983.

————. *Faction in Tudor England*. London: Historical Association, 1979.

————. "Genesis of the Statute of Uses." *English Historical Review*, 82 (1967), 673–97.

————. "Henry VIII: The Political Perspective." In *The Reign of Henry VIII, Politics, Policy and Piety*, ed. Diarmaid MacCulloch. New York: St. Martin's Press, 1995.

Jalland, Pat. *Women, Marriage and Politics 1860–1914*. Oxford: Oxford University Press, 1988.

James, Mervyn. "Obedience and Dissent in Henrician England: The Lincolnshire Rebellion, 1536." In *Society, Politics and Culture: Studies in Early Modern England*, 188–269. Cambridge: Cambridge University Press, 1986.

James, Susan E. *Kateryn Parr, The Making of a Queen*. Brookfield, Vt.: Ashgate, 1999.

————. "A Tudor Divorce: The Marital History of William Parr, Marquess of Northampton." *Transactions of the Cumberland and Westmorland Antiquarian and Archaeological Society*, n.s., 90 (1990), 199–205.

Jewel, Helen N. " 'The Bringing Up of Children in Good Learning and Manners': A Survey of Secular Educational Provision in the North of England, c. 1350–1550." *Northern History*, 18 (1982), 1–25.

Jones, Michael K., and Malcolm G. Underwood. *The King's Mother: Lady Margaret Beaufort, Countess of Richmond and Derby*. Cambridge: Cambridge University Press, 1992.

Jordan, Constance. *Renaissance Feminism, Literary Texts and Political Models*. Ithaca, N.Y.: Cornell University Press, 1990.

Jordan, W. K. *Edward VI: The Young King. The Protectorship of the Duke of Somerset*. Cambridge, Mass.: The Belknap Press of Harvard University Press, 1968.

Kalas, Robert J. "The Noble Widow's Place in the Patriarchal Household: The Life and Career of Jeanne de Gontault." *Sixteenth Century Journal*, 24 (1993), 519–39.

Kandiyoti, Denise. "Bargaining with Patriarchy." *Gender and Society*, 2 (1988), 274–90.

————. "Islam and Patriarchy: A Comparative Perspective." In *Women in Middle Eastern History: Shifting Boundaries in Sex and Gender*, ed. Nikki R. Keddie and Beth Baron, 23–42. New Haven, Conn.: Yale University Press, 1991.

Kaufman, Gloria. "Juan Luis Vives on the Education of Women." *Signs*, 3 (1978), 891–96.

"Kedington and the Barnardiston Family." *Proceedings of the Suffolk Institute of Archaeology*, 4 (1864–74), 124–82.

Kelly, Joan. "Did Women Have a Renaissance?" In *Becoming Visible: Women in European History*, ed. Renate Bridenthal and Claudia Koonz, 138–63. Boston: Houghton Mifflin, 1977.

Kelso, Ruth. *Doctrine for the Lady of the Renaissance*. Urbana: University of Illinois Press, 1956.

———. *The Doctrine of the English Gentleman in the Sixteenth Century*. Gloucester, Mass.: Peter Smith, [1929] 1964.

Kettering, Sharon. "The Patronage Power of Early Modern French Noblewomen." *The Historical Journal*, 32 (1989), 817–41.

Kettle, Ann J. " 'My Wife Shall Have It': Marriage and Property in the Wills and Testaments of Later Medieval England." In *Marriage and Property*, ed. Elizabeth M. Craik, 89–103. Aberdeen: Aberdeen University Press, 1984.

King, John N. "Patronage and Piety: The Influence of Catherine Parr." In Margaret P. Hannay, *Silent but for the Word: Tudor Women as Patrons, Translators, and Writers of Religious Works*, 43–60. Kent, Ohio: Kent State University Press, 1985.

Kipling, Gordon. "Henry VII and the Origins of Tudor Patronage." In *Patronage in the Renaissance*, ed. Guy Fitch Lytle and Stephen Orgel, 117–64. Princeton, N.J.: Princeton University Press, 1982.

———. *The Triumph of Honor: Burgundian Origins of the Elizabethan Renaissance*. The Hague: Leiden University Press, 1977.

Klapisch-Zuber, Christiane. *Women, Family and Ritual in Renaissance Italy*. Chicago: University of Chicago Press, 1985.

Klapisch-Zuber, Christiane, ed. *A History of Women: Silences of the Middle Ages*. Cambridge, Mass.: Harvard Belknap Press, 1992.

Koditschek, Theodore. "The Gendering of the British Working Class." *Gender and History*, 9 (1997), 333–63.

Krieder, Alan. *English Chantries: The Road to Dissolution*. Cambridge, Mass.: Harvard University Press, 1979.

Lambley, Kathleen. *The Teaching and Cultivation of the French Language in England During the Tudor and Stuart Times*. Manchester: University Press, 1920.

Lander, J. R. "Attainder and Forfeiture, 1453–1509." In *Crown and Nobility 1450–1509*, 127–58. London: Edward Arnold, 1976.

———. *Conflict and Stability in Fifteenth Century England*. London: Hutchinson University Library, 1969.

———. "Marriage and Politics in the Fifteenth Century." In *Crown and Nobility 1450–1509*, 94–126. London: Edward Arnold, 1976.

———. "The Wars of the Roses." In *Crown and Nobility 1450–1509*, 57–73. London: Edward Arnold, 1976.

Lawrence, Basil Edwin. *The History of the Laws Affecting the Property of Married Women in England*. Littleton, Col.: F. B. Rothmang [1884] 1986.

Lehmberg, Stanford E. "Parliamentary Attainder in the Reign of Henry VIII." *Historical Journal*, 18 (1975), 675–702.

Leveson-Gower, G. "Notices of the Family of Uvedale of Titsey, Surrey, and Wickham, Hants." *Surrey Archaeological Collections*, 3 (1865), 63–192.

Loades, David. *Mary Tudor: A Life*. Oxford and Cambridge, Mass.: Basil Blackwell, 1989.

————. *The Tudor Court.* Totowa, N.J.: Barnes & Noble Books, 1987.

Loengard, Janet Senderowitz. " 'Legal History and the Medieval Englishwoman' Revisited: Some New Directions." In *Medieval Women and the Sources of Medieval History,* ed. Joel T. Rosenthal, 210–37. Athens: University of Georgia Press, 1990.

Lubkin, Gregory. *A Renaissance Court: Milan Under Galeazzo Maria Sforza.* Berkeley and Los Angeles: University of California Press, 1994.

MacCulloch, Diarmaid. *Suffolk and the Tudors: Politics and Religion in an English County, 1500–1600.* Oxford: Clarendon Press, 1986.

Macfarlane, Alan. *Marriage and Love in England: Modes of Reproduction 1300–1840.* Oxford and New York: Basil Blackwell, 1986.

MacGibbon, David. *Elizabeth Woodville 1437–1492: Her Life and Times.* London: Arthur Barker, 1938.

Maclean, Sir John. "A Short Account of the Families of Carew and Cary." *The Herald and Genealogist,* 7 (1893), 19–26.

Macnamara, F. N. *Memorials of the Danvers Family of Dauntsey and Culworth.* London: Hardy & Page, 1895.

Mann, J. G. "English Church Monuments, 1536–1625." *Walpole Society,* 21 (1932–33), 1–22.

Markland, James. "Some Remarks on the Rent Roll of Humphrey Duke of Buckingham, 1447–48." *Archaeological Journal,* 8 (1851), 259–81.

Marks, Richard. "The Howard Tombs at Thetford and Framlingham: New Discoveries." *Archaeological Journal,* 141 (1984), 255–57.

Martienssen, Anthony. *Queen Katherine Parr.* London: Secker & Warburg, 1973.

Mate, Mavis E. *Daughters, Wives and Widows After the Black Death: Women in Sussex, 1350–1535.* Suffolk and Rochester, N.Y.: Boydell Press, 1998.

Mattingly, Garrett. *Catherine of Aragon.* London: Jonathan Cape, 1963.

McFarlane, K. B. "The Beauchamps and the Staffords." In *Nobility of Later Medieval England,* 187–213. Oxford: Oxford University Press, 1973.

————. "The Education of the Nobility in Later Medieval England." In *The Nobility of Later Medieval England,* 228–47. Oxford: Oxford University Press, 1973.

————. *The Nobility of Later Medieval England.* Oxford: Clarendon Press, 1973.

————. "The Wars of the Roses." In *England in the Fifteenth Century,* 231–61. London: Hambledon Press, 1981.

McLaren, Angus. *Reproductive Rituals: The Perception of Fertility in England from the Sixteenth to the Nineteenth Century.* New York: Methuen, 1984.

McNamara, JoAnn, and Suzanne F. Wemple. "Sanctity and Power: The Dual Pursuit of Medieval Women." In *Becoming Visible: Women in European History,* ed. Renate Bridenthal and Claudia Koonz, 90–118. Boston: Houghton Mifflin, 1977.

Meale, Carole M. "The Manuscripts and Early Audience of the Middle English *Prose Merlin.*" In *The Changing Face of Arthurian Romance: Essays on Arthurian Prose Romances in Memory of Cedric E. Pickford,* ed. Alison Adams, Armel H. Diverres, Karen Stern, and Kenneth Varty, 92–111. Wolfeboro, N.H.: Boydell Press, 1986.

Mendelson, Sara, and Patricia Crawford. *Women in Early Modern England 1550–1710.* Oxford: Clarendon Press, 1998.

Mertes, Kate. *The English Noble Household, 1200–1600.* Oxford and New York: Basil Blackwell, 1988.

Metzger, Franz. "The Last Phase of the Medieval Chancery." In *Law-Making and Law-Makers in British History,* 79–89. Papers presented to the Edinburgh Legal History Conference, 1977. RHS Studies in History Series, no. 22. Ed. Alan Harding. London: RHS, 1980.

Michalove, Sharon D. "Equal in Opportunity? The Education of Aristocratic Women 1450–1550." In *Women's Education in Early Modern Europe: A History, 1500–1800*, ed. Barbara Whitehead, 47–74. New York and London: Garland, 1999.

Miller, Helen. *Henry VIII and the English Nobility*. Oxford: Basil Blackwell, 1986.

Minet, William. "The Capells at Rayne 1486–1622." *Essex Archaeological Society*, n.s., 9 (1906), 243–72.

Mirrer, Louise, ed. *Upon My Husband's Death: Widows in the Literature and Histories of Medieval Europe*. Ann Arbor: University of Michigan, 1992.

Miscellanea Genealogica et Heraldica, vols. 1–15, ed. J. J. Howard; 16–19, ed. W. Bruce Bannerman (1868–1902).

Moor, Rev. Charles. "The Bygods, Earls of Norfolk: Bygod of Settrington etc." *Yorkshire Archaeological Journal*, 32 (1936), 172–213.

Moran, Jo Ann Hoeppner. *The Growth of English Schooling 1340–1548: Learning, Literacy and Laicization in Pre-Reformation York Diocese*. Princeton, N.J.: Princeton University Press, 1985.

Morant, Philip. *History and Antiquities of Essex*. London: T. Osborne, 1768.

Moreton, C. E. *The Townshends and Their World: Gentry, Law, and Land in Norfolk c. 1450–1551*. Oxford: Clarendon Press, 1992.

Morgan, D. A. L. "The King's Affinity in the Polity of Yorkist England." *Transactions of the Royal Historical Society*, 5th ser., 23 (1973).

Neuschel, Kristin B. "Noble Households in the Sixteenth Century: Material Settings and Human Communities." *French Historical Studies*, 15 (1988), 595–622.

———. "Noblewomen and War in Sixteenth-Century France." In *Changing Identities in Early Modern France: Essays in Memory of Nancy Lyman Roelker*, ed. Michael Wolfe, 124–44. Durham, N.C.: Duke University Press, 1997.

Nott, George Frederick. *The Works of Henry Howard, Earl of Surrey and of Sir Thomas Wyatt the Elder*. London: T. Bensley for Longman, Hurst, Rees, Orme, & Brown, 1815–16.

Nichols, John Gough, ed. *The Unton Inventories Relating to Wadley and Faringdon, co. Berkshire . . . with a Memoir of the Family of Unton*. London: For Berkshire Ashmolean Society, 1841.

Nolte, Cordula. "Gendering Princely Dynasties: Some Notes on Family Structure, Social Networks, and Communication at the Court of the Margraves of Brandenburg-Ansbach around 1500." Pauline Stafford and Anneke B. Mulder-Bakker, eds. *Gender and History, Special Issue: Gendering the Middle Ages*, 12 (2000), 704–21.

Oestmann, Cord. *Lordship and Community: The Lestrange Family and the Village of Hunstanton, Norfolk, in the First Half of the Sixteenth Century*. Woodbridge, Eng.: Boydell Press, 1994.

Oliva, Marilyn. *The Convent and the Community in Late Medieval England*. Woodbridge, Eng.: Boydell Press, 1998.

Orme, Nicholas. *From Childhood to Chivalry: The Education of the English Kings and Aristocracy 1066–1530*. London and New York: Methuen, 1984.

———. "The Culture of Children in Medieval England." *Past and Present*, No. 148 (1995), 48–88.

Paravinci, Werner. "The Court of the Dukes of Burgundy: A Model for Europe?" In

Princes, Patronage, and the Nobility: The Court at the Beginning of the Modern Age c. 1450–1650, ed. Ronald G. Asch and Adolf M. Birke, 69–102. Oxford: Oxford University Press and the German Historical Institute London, 1991.

Parker, Sir William. *The History of Long Melford*. London: Wyman & Sons, 1873.

Payling, S. J. *Political Society in Lancastrian England: The Greater Gentry of Nottinghamshire*. Oxford: Clarendon Press, 1991.

Payling, Simon. "The Politics of Family: Late Medieval Marriage Contracts." In *The McFarlane Legacy: Studies in Late Medieval Politics and Society*, ed. R. H. Britnell and A. J. Pollard, 21–47. New York: St. Martin's Press, 1995.

Petre, J., ed. *Richard III: Crown and People*. Gloucester: Alan Sutton, 1985.

Pilkington, Lieut.-Col. John. *History of the Pilkington Family of Lancashire, 1066–1600*. Liverpool: privately printed, 1912.

Pollock, Linda. "Embarking on a Rough Passage: The Experience of Pregnancy in Early-Modern Society." *Women as Mothers in Pre-Industrial England: Essays in Memory of Dorothy McLaren*, ed. Valerie Fildes, 39–67. London and New York: Routledge, 1990.

———. *Forgotten Children: Parent-Child Relations from 1500 to 1900*. New York: Cambridge University Press, 1983.

———. " 'Teach Her to Live Under Obedience': The Making of Women in the Upper Ranks of Early Modern England." *Continuity and Change*, 4 (1989), 231–58.

Poovey, Mary. "Covered but Not Bound: Caroline Norton and the 1857 Matrimonial Causes Act." In *Uneven Developments: The Ideological Work of Gender in Mid-Victorian England*, chap. 3. Chicago: University of Chicago Press, 1988.

Price, David. *Patrons and Musicians of the English Renaissance*. London and New York: Cambridge University Press, 1981.

Prouty, C. T. *George Gascoigne, Elizabethan Courtier, Soldier and Poet*. New York: Columbia University Press, 1942.

Rawcliffe, Carole. *The Staffords, Earls of Stafford and Dukes of Buckingham, 1394–1521*. Cambridge: Cambridge University Press, 1978.

Rich, Adrienne. "Compulsory Heterosexuality and Lesbian Existence." *Signs*, 5 (1980), 631–60.

Richardson, Walter C. *Mary Tudor, The White Queen*. Seattle: University of Washington Press, 1970.

Richmond, Colin. *John Hopton, A Fifteenth Century Gentleman*. Cambridge: Cambridge University Press, 1981.

———. *The Paston Family in the Fifteenth Century: The First Phase*. Cambridge: Cambridge University Press, 1990.

———. "The Pastons Revisited." *Bulletin of the Institute of Historical Research*, 58 (1985), 25–36.

Rigby, S. H. *English Society in the Later Middle Ages: Class, Status and Gender*. New York: St. Martin's Press, 1995.

———. "Gendering the Black Death: Women in Later Medieval England." *Gender and History*, 12 (2000), 745–54.

Robertson, Karen. "Tracing Women's Connections from a Letter by Elizabeth Raleigh." In *Maids and Mistresses, Cousins and Queens: Women's Alliance in Early Modern England*, ed. Susan Frye and Karen Robertson, 149–64. New York and Oxford: Oxford University Press, 1999.

Robertson, Mary L. "Thomas Cromwell's Servants: The Ministerial Household in

Early Tudor Government." Ph.D. diss., University of California, Los Angeles, 1975.

Roelker, Nancy L. "The Role of Noblewomen in the French Reformation." *Archive for Reformation History*, 63 (1972), 168–95.

Rogers, Katherine M. *The Troublesome Helpmate: A History of Misogyny in Literature.* Seattle: Washington University Press, 1966.

Roper, Lyndal. *The Holy Household: Women and Morals in Reformation Augsburg.* Oxford: Clarendon Press, 1989.

Rosenthal, Joel T. "Aristocratic Cultural Patronage and Book Bequests, 1350–1550." *Bulletin of the John Rylands University Library of Manchester*, 64 (1982), 522–48.

———. "Aristocratic Marriage and the English Peerage, 1350–1500: Social Institution and Personal Bond." *Journal of Medieval History*, 10 (1984), 181–94.

———. "Aristocratic Widows in Fifteenth Century England." In *Women and the Structure of Society*, ed. Barbara J. Harris and JoAnn K. McNamara, 36–47. Durham, N.C.: Duke University Press, 1984.

———. "Fifteenth-Century Widows and Widowhood: Bereavement, Reintegration, and Life Choices." In *Wife and Widow in Medieval England*, ed. Sue Sheridan Walker, 33–58. Ann Arbor: University of Michigan Press, 1993.

———. "Other Victims: Peeresses as War Widows, 1450–1500." *History*, 72, no. 235 (1987), 213–30.

———. *Patriarchy and Families of Privilege in Fifteenth-Century England.* Philadelphia: University of Pennsylvania Press, 1991.

Roskell, J. R. *The Commons and Their Speakers in English Parliaments 1376–1523.* New York: Barnes & Noble, 1965.

Ross, Charles. *Edward IV.* Berkeley and Los Angeles: University of California Press, 1974.

Round, J. H. "The Descent of Faulkbourne." Essex Archaeological Society, *Transactions*, n.s., 15 (1921), 35–59.

Rowney, Ian. "Arbitration in Gentry Disputes of the Late Middle Ages." *History*, 67, no. 221 (1982), 367–76.

Russell, Jocelyne G. *The Field of Cloth of Gold: Men and Manners in 1520.* New York: Barnes & Noble, 1969.

Rutton, William Loftie. *Three Branches of the Family of Wentworth.* London: Mitchell & Hughes, 1891.

Sánchez, Magdalena S. *The Empress, the Queen, and the Nun: Women and Power at the Court of Philip III of Spain.* Baltimore: Johns Hopkins University Press, 1998.

Scarisbrick, J. J. *The Reformation and the English People.* Oxford and New York: Basil Blackwell, 1984.

Schofield, Roger. "Did the Mothers Really Die? Three Centuries of Maternal Mortality in 'The World We Have Lost.'" In *The World We Have Gained: Histories of Population and Social Structure*, ed. Lloyd Bonfield, Richard M. Smith, and Keith Wrightson, 321–60. London: Basil Blackwell, 1986.

Schwoerer, Lois. *Lady Rachel Russell, "One of the Best of Women."* Baltimore: Johns Hopkins University Press, 1988.

———. "Women and the Glorious Revolution." *Albion*, 18 (1986), 195–218.

Scofield, Cora. *The Life and Reign of Edward the IV.* 2 vols. London: Frank Cass, [1923] 1967.

Scragg, D. G. *A History of English Spelling.* New York: Barnes & Noble, 1974.

Seaton, Ethel. *Sir Richard Roos c.1410–1482, Lancastrian Poet*. London: Rupert Hart-Davis, 1961.

Sheehan, Michael M. *The Will in Medieval England, From the Conversion of the Anglo Saxons to the End of the Thirteenth Century*. Pontifical Institute of Medieval Studies, Studies and Texts 6. Toronto: Pontifical Institute of Medieval Studies, 1963.

Simpson, A. W. B. *An Introduction to the History of the Land Law*. Oxford: Oxford University Press, 1961.

Slavin, A. J. *The Precarious Balance: English Government and Society, 1450–1640*. New York: Knopf, 1973.

Smith, Lacey Baldwin. *A Tudor Tragedy: The Life and Times of Catherine Howard*. London: Jonathan Cape, 1961.

Smith, R. B. *Land and Politics in the England of Henry VIII. The West Riding of Yorkshire: 1530–46*. Oxford: Clarendon Press, 1970.

Smith, Sir Thomas. *On the English Commonwealth*. Menston, Eng.: Scolar Press, [1583, facsimile ed.] 1970.

Smyth, John. *The Berkeley Manuscripts: Lives of the Berkeleys*. 2 vols. Ed. Sir John Maclean. Gloucester: J. Bellows, 1883.

Southall, Raymond. *The Courtly Maker*. New York: Barnes & Noble, 1964.

———. "The Devonshire Manuscript Collection of Early Tudor Poetry, 1532–41." *Review of English Studies*, n.s., 15 (1964), 142–50.

Spring, Eileen. *Law, Land and Family: Aristocratic Inheritance in England, 1300 to 1800*. Chapel Hill and London: University of North Carolina, 1993.

Staniland, Kay. "Royal Entry into the World." In *England in the Fifteenth Century*. Proceedings of the 1986 Harlaxton Symposium, 297–313. Ed. Daniel Williams. Wolfeboro, N.H.: Boydell Press, 1987.

Starkey, David. "The Age of the Household: Politics, Society, and the Arts c. 1350–1550." In *The Context of English Literature: The Later Middle Ages*, ed. Stephen Medcalf, 226–89. London: Holmes & Meier, 1981.

———. "Court, Council, and Nobility in Tudor England." In *Princes, Patronage, and the Nobility: The Court at the Beginning of the Modern Age c. 1450–1650*, ed. Ronald G. Asch and Adolf M. Birke, 175–203. London: Oxford University Press and the German Historical Institute London, 1991.

———. *The English Court from the Wars of the Roses to the Civil War*. London and New York: Longman, 1987.

———. *Henry VIII: A European Court in England*. London: Collins & Brown, 1991.

———. "Ightham Mote: Politics and Architecture in Early Tudor England." *Archaeologia*, 107 (1982), 153–61.

———. *The Reign of Henry VIII: Personalities and Politics*. London: George Philip, 1985.

———. "Representation Through Intimacy." In *Symbols and Sentiment: Cross Cultural Studies in Symbolism*, ed. Ioan Lewis, 187–224. New York: Academic Press, 1977.

Staves, Susan. *Married Women's Separate Property in England, 1660–1833*. Cambridge, Mass.: Harvard University Press, 1990.

Stevens, John. *Music and Poetry in the Early Tudor Court*. London: Methuen, 1961.

Stone, Lawrence. *The Crisis of the Aristocracy 1558–1641*. Oxford: Clarendon Press, 1965.

———. "The Educational Revolution in England, 1560–1640." *Past and Present*, no. 28 (1964), 41–80.

———. *The Family, Sex and Marriage in England 1500–1800*. London: Weidenfeld & Nicolson, 1977.

Stretton, Tim. *Women Waging Law in Elizabethan England*. Cambridge: Cambridge University Press, 1998.

Strickland, Agnes. *Lives of the Queens of England*. London: George Bell & Sons, 1890.

Strype, John. *Annals of the Reformation and Establishment of Religion . . . During Queen Elizabeth's Reign*. 4 vols. Oxford: Clarendon Press, 1824.

———. *Ecclesiastical Memorials, Relating Chiefly to Religion, and the Reformation of It . . . Under King Henry VIII, King Edward VI, and Queen Mary I. . . .* 3 vols. Oxford: Clarendon Press, 1822.

Talbot, C. H. "On a Letter of Sir William Sharington to Sir John Thynne." *Wiltshire Archaeological and Natural History Magazine,"* 26 (1892), 50–51.

Thomas, Keith. *Religion and the Decline of Magic*. New York: Scribner, 1971.

Thomason, Patricia. *Sir Thomas Wyatt and His Background*. Stanford, Calif.: Stanford University Press, 1965.

Thurley, Simon. *The Royal Palaces of Tudor England*. New Haven, Conn.: Yale University Press, 1993.

Todd, Margot. "Humanists, Puritans and the Spiritualization of the Household." *Church History*, 49 (1980), 18–33.

Tucker, Melvin. *The Life of Thomas Howard, Earl of Surrey and Second Duke of Norfolk, 1443–1524*. The Hague, London, and Paris: Mouton, 1964.

Vickery, Amanda. *The Gentleman's Daughter: Women's Lives in Georgian England*. New Haven, Conn.: Yale University Press, 1998.

Virgoe, Roger. "The Recovery of the Howards in East Anglia, 1485–1529." In *Wealth and Power in Tudor England: Essays Presented to S. T. Bindoff*, ed. E. W. Ives, R. J. Knecht, and J. J. Scarisbrick, 1–20. London: Athlone Press, 1978.

Von Arx, Walter. "The Churching of Women After Childbirth: History and Significance." In *Liturgy and Human Passage*, ed. David Power and Luis Maldonado, 63–71. New York: Seabury Press, 1979.

Wake, Joan. *The Brudenells of Deane*. London: Cassell, 1953.

Walker, Sue Sheridan. *Wife and Widow in Medieval England*. Ann Arbor: University of Michigan, 1993.

Walkowitz, Judith R. *City of Dreadful Delight: Narratives of Sexual Danger in Late-Victorian London*. Chicago: University of Chicago Press, 1992.

Wall, Alison. "For Love, Money, or Politics? A Clandestine Marriage and the Elizabethan Court of Arches." *Historical Journal* (1995), 511–33.

Ward, Jennifer C. *English Noblewomen in the Later Middle Ages*. London and New York: Longman, 1992.

Ward, Jennifer C., trans. and ed. *Women of the English Nobility and Gentry 1066–1500*. New York: Manchester University Press, distributed by St. Martin's Press, 1995.

Warnicke, Retha. *The Rise and Fall of Anne Boleyn*. New York and London: Cambridge University Press, 1989.

———. *Women of the English Renaissance and Reformation*. Westport, Conn.: Greenwood Press, 1983.

Waters, Gwen. "William Lord Berkeley." *Richard III: Crown and People*, ed. J. Petre, 69–78. Gloucester: Alan Sutton, 1985.

Wayne, Valerie. "Some Sad Sentence: Vives' Instruction of a Christian Woman." In *Silent but for the Word*, ed. Margaret Hannay, 15–25. Kent, Ohio: Kent State University Press, 1985.

Weisner, Merry. *Women and Gender in Early Modern England*, 2nd ed. New York: Cambridge University Press, 2000.

———. *Working Women in Renaissance Germany*. New Brunswick, N.J.: Rutgers University Press, 1986.

Welsford, Enid. *The Court Masque: A Study in the Relationship between Poetry and the Revels*. Cambridge: Cambridge University Press, 1927.

Wemple, Suzanne Fonay. *Women in Frankish Society: Marriage and the Cloister 500 to 900*. Philadelphia: University of Pennsylvania Press, 1981.

Westcott, Margaret. "Katherine Courtenay, Countess of Devon, 1479–1527." *Tudor and Stuart Devon: The Common Estate and Government, Essays Presented to Joyce Youings*, ed. Todd Gray, Margery Rose, and Audrey Erskine, 13–38. Exeter: University of Exeter Press, 1992.

Willen, Diane. "Godly Women in Early Modern England: Puritanism and Gender." *The Journal of Ecclesiastical History*, 43 (1992), 561–80.

Willoughby, Cassandra. *The Continuation of the History of the Willoughby Family, being vol. II of the Manuscript*, ed. A. C. Wood. Eton, Windsor: Shakespeare Head Press, 1958.

Wilson, Adrian. "The Ceremony of Childbirth and Its Interpretation." In *Women as Mothers in Pre-Industrial England: Essays in Memory of Dorothy McLaren*, ed. Valerie Fildes, 39–67. London and New York: Routledge, 1990.

Wingfield, Lieut.-Col. John M. *Some Records of the Wingfield Family*. London: John Murray, 1925.

Wolffe, B. P. *The Crown Lands, 1461–1536*. New York: Barnes and Noble, 1970.

Wright, Susan M. *Derbyshire Gentry in the Fifteenth Century*. Derbyshire Record Society, 8 (1983).

Wrightson, Keith. *English Society, 1580–1680*. New Brunswick, N.J.: Rutgers University Press, 1982.

Wyndham, H. A. *A Family History, 1410–1688. Vol. 1, The Wyndhams of Norfolk, Somerset, Sussex*. London: Oxford University Press, 1939.

Yost, John K. "The Value of Married Life for the Social Order in the Early English Renaissance." *Societas*, 6 (1976), 25–39.

Young, Alan. *Tudor and Jacobean Tournaments*. Dobbs Ferry, N.Y.: Sheridan House, 1987.

INDEX

Note: With a few exceptions that conform to contemporary usage, women are listed by their last married name; where necessary to avoid confusion, their maiden name is in parentheses, earlier married names and/or husbands' names follow. Titles "Dame," "Lady," and "Sir" have been indicated for purposes of identification, but they do not affect alphabetization. Page numbers in italics indicate illustrations.